THE HANDS-OFF INVESTOR

THE HANDS-OFF INVESTOR

An *Insider's* Guide *to* Investing *in* Passive
REAL ESTATE SYNDICATIONS

BRIAN BURKE

BiggerPockets®
PUBLISHING
Denver, Colorado

Praise for the Series

THE HANDS-OFF INVESTOR

"For far too long, many of us, including myself, have evaluated sponsors by making a small investment to 'test them out.' No matter how small that investment, it's not going to be less than the cost of this book and a couple of hours of time. . . . I highly recommend this if you are looking to learn the right questions to ask to make better investment decisions and become a better steward of your own capital."

—Mark Abdou, Securities Attorney, Libertas Law Group

"This book was extraordinarily well done—clearly written, well organized, and appropriately detailed. . . . [It's] a good reminder that 'passive' investing in real estate also requires lots of time and experience."

—Chris Demetra, Passive Investor

"I wish this book had been around 10 years ago when I started syndicating. It would have saved me a lot of struggle! Brian is the type of person who you wish you could have lunch with once a week to 'pick his brain.' . . . But since there are too many of us who want his time and precious advice, the next best option is having access to the wealth of knowledge he packs into this book. It will no doubt help thousands of passive investors make better and more informed decisions on where to invest their hard-earned money."

**—Kathy Fettke, Co-CEO of Real Wealth Network
and host of *The Real Wealth Show***

"The content [is] very understandable, yet Brian's knowledge is encyclopedic enough to be used as a text in an undergraduate real estate course, or a training course for commercial real estate analysts or lending officers. Wow!"

—Steve Darby, MBA, Passive Investor

"I am glad and appreciative that Brian took the time to write this book for the passive investor community, as it has been needed for many years. I look forward to recommending this book to fellow passive investors, as I have no doubt that most, if not all, passive investors will benefit from reading this book."

—Jeremy Roll, President of Roll Investment Group

"*The Hands-Off Investor* is a must-read for anyone considering [to invest] or actively investing in syndicated real estate or sponsor-led investment offerings. . . . If you are going to invest your hard-earned money in passive real estate investments, then you owe it to yourself to invest two hours of your time digesting this book—the ROI will most likely be better than any real estate deal you allocate to. Most investors learn what is taught in this book he hard way . . . through getting burned, frustrated, taken advantage of, or ignored after their money is taken."

—Richard C. Wilson, CEO and
Founder of Family Office Club

"[This book] is full of insights from an industry insider's perspective, and digs deep into showing how the sausage is made. . . . Well-organized, clearly written, and comprehensive—but like peeling an onion, with each layer providing more granularity and technical details that keep the reader engaged."

—Joe Fang, Passive Investor

The Hands-Off Investor: An Insider's Guide to Investing in Passive Real Estate Syndications
By Brian Burke
Published by BiggerPockets Publishing, LLC, Denver, CO
Copyright © 2020 by Brian Burke. All Rights Reserved.

Publisher's Cataloging-in-Publication
Names: Burke, Brian, 1969-, author.
Title: The Hands-off investor : an insider's guide to investing in passive real estate syndications / Brian Burke.
Description: Denver, CO: BiggerPockets Publishing, 2020.
Identifiers: LCCN: 2020930357 | ISBN: 9781947200272 (pbk.) | 9781947200296 (ebook)
Subjects: LCSH Real estate investment. | Real estate investment--Syndication. | Real estate limited partnerships. | Real estate business. | Personal finance. | BISAC BUSINESS & ECONOMICS / Real Estate / General | BUSINESS & ECONOMICS / Investments & Securities / General | BUSINESS & ECONOMICS / Personal Finance / Investing
Classification: LCC HD1382.5 .B83 2020 | DDC 332.63/247--dc23

Published in the United States of America
Printed in the on recycled paper
10 9 8 7 6 5 4 3 2 1

Dedication

To everyone who ever invested with me, without you, I would never have had the experience and knowledge to write this book. And to everyone who didn't invest with me, your reasons can be the greatest lessons and the biggest motivators.

TABLE OF CONTENTS

INTRODUCTION

Anyone who has watched late-night television infomercials has seen the endless stream of real estate investment tycoons purporting to teach how to invest in real estate with no money down. They say, "Use OPM," which stands for "other people's money." But what if *you* are one of those "other people"? You have money and you want to invest in real estate, but you don't want to chase properties, tenants, and termites. Or even if you did, you don't have the time. The good news is that you can invest in real estate completely passively, and this method is becoming increasingly popular.

A real estate syndication is a structure or relationship between a company, called a "sponsor," and multiple investors who pool their money to invest in real estate. The investors are passive, and the sponsor oversees buying, operating, and ultimately selling the property. That company and its key principals are also responsible for many other things, such as accounting, tax returns, and making distributions to the investors. In essence, you invest your money and a real estate expert does all the work.

The bad news is there are countless people out there who would love to take your investment dollars, and many of them are unqualified or unprepared for the responsibility, or simply handle the job poorly. There's an old saying about these deals: "At the beginning, the investors have all the money and the sponsor has all the knowledge. At the end, they switch places."

It's easy to see why the syndication industry has earned this reputation. The field is largely unregulated, with no minimum qualifications, no real oversight, and lots of newbies. But if done properly, investing in real estate private offerings can be a safe way to invest and diversify your portfolio.

Oddly, despite the existence of countless books that teach how to buy real estate with other people's money, there haven't been any comprehensive guides for the "other people" that teach how to invest in these opportunities—until now. If you've picked up this book, you're preparing to learn how to become the "other person" the right way, and help preserve your wealth and grow your income faster.

My goal is not to teach you how to actively acquire real estate—there's a seemingly endless supply of books on that topic, and you can find many of them on BiggerPockets.com. Instead, my goal is to teach you how to *evaluate* both the real estate you'll be investing in and the sponsors you'll be investing with. In order to properly evaluate a passive investment, you need to know some fundamentals of real estate investing and analysis, just as a building inspector needs to have a fundamental knowledge of construction techniques. With this knowledge, you can properly evaluate opportunities and make an educated judgment as to whether they are viable.

I often see investors choose an investment opportunity because it promises the highest returns, the lowest fees, the highest profit split, or a large capital investment by the offering's sponsor. These are all numerical quantities that you can easily measure, and they are just like icebergs: You see the very tips of them and think you're seeing what's important. But you might be unaware of the enormous mass under the surface, and that's where the danger lies. Making wise investment choices involves investigating under the surface, revealing the entire iceberg, and taking a measurement that matters. This book will show you how.

Tales of Struggle and Wealth

I wish there were no need for this book. In a perfect world, only the highest-skilled real estate investors would be charged with the responsibility of being good stewards of other people's money, and those folks would make perfect decisions and operate with the highest level of integrity. The investments would be well thought out, with realistic expectations and fair compensation for the sponsor.

But we don't live in a perfect world. Many years ago, a friend of mine, a career journeywoman grocery clerk, had saved up some money and invested in a fourplex. Over a couple of decades this property appreciated tremendously in value and created a very sizable amount of equity. If she'd played her cards right, she would have been set for life when she retired. Instead, she ultimately sold the property and then invested her entire life savings in a real estate private offering that was investing in a senior housing project. She didn't do much due diligence on the sponsor, nor would she have even known what to ask if she had. It turns out the sponsor was a crook. The investments were mismanaged, funds were misappropriated, and the entire scheme went down in a huge ball of flames. My friend lost her entire life savings, never to recover a penny. Now in her seventies, she is driving for a rideshare service just to put food on the table. The sponsor is in prison.

For every story like that, there are many more stories of people hitting the jackpot, doubling or even tripling their money in a relatively short time. But this isn't roulette, where the ball lands on either black or red. Most of the time, these investments simply provide a decent income stream and/or capital growth. Your goal is to ask the right questions, invest with the right sponsors, invest in the right real estate, and, to the extent you can, diversify among various sponsors, locations, and property types so that you eliminate any single point of failure.

Some Background

I've been investing in real estate for more than, 30 years. I'm the founder and, for the last 20 years, CEO of a real estate syndication sponsor firm. This business has given me the privilege of buying more than 700 properties, including thousands of apartment units worth more than half a billion dollars, and I've raised $100 million-plus from individual investors.

At first, I wondered if I was really the right person to write this book. Shouldn't it be written by someone who does nothing but invest in syndications as an investor? However, the more I thought about it, the more I realized that I am exactly the right person. As an experienced real estate investor who has survived multiple market cycles, I'm intimately familiar with the fundamentals of investing in real estate. As an insider in the syndication industry, I know the secrets that sponsors don't want you to know. I'll share this knowledge, and these secrets, with you.

I have the opportunity to see a lot of deals that sponsors are peddling to investors. Many of these deals are excellent, but some leave me feeling like I'm watching a herd of cattle being led to slaughter. Many of the deals I've seen, as well as stories like that of my friend who lost it all, are part of what has motivated me to write this book. If I can prevent just one investor from making a devastating decision, this project will have been worthwhile.

How to Use This Book

This book is divided into five sections. Section 1 gives you the lay of the land, so you have a foundation of knowledge for the topics that follow. Section 2 is about evaluating real estate sponsors. It is no accident that this section comes before talking about real estate. The success or failure of any investment is heavily influenced by the quality and character of the sponsor you invest with. Before you seriously consider investing in any real estate syndication, you must first be confident that you are partnering with the right team.

Section 3 dives deep into evaluating real estate. You'll learn about various strategies, markets, and demographics, along with tons of information on reading operating statements and understanding various measurements for your investment returns. This is a good section to bookmark and annotate, because after you've read this book and turn your attention toward evaluating investment opportunities, you'll want to use section 3 as a reference guide.

Section 4 teaches you how to evaluate the various types of syndications you'll see. Different sponsors structure their syndications differently, and even the same sponsor will often structure their next syndication differently from their last.

The order of these sections is like peeling the layers of an onion—first get comfortable with the sponsor, then get comfortable with the real estate, and, finally, get comfortable with the syndication offering itself. In the real world, you should approach all your investment decisions in the same way.

Finally, section 5 will explain the investing process: how to interpret documents, the process and procedures for making an investment, and what to expect during the investment period, as well as after the property is sold and the investment has concluded.

If the book seems slanted toward multifamily apartment investments, that's because apartment buildings make up a large slice of the landscape of passive real estate offerings, and it's the asset class that my world is absorbed in. However, most of the concepts in this book apply equally to investments in any of the various real estate asset classes.

I'll often say, "Ask the sponsor this" or "Ask the sponsor that." You really shouldn't have to ask the sponsor all these questions—experienced sponsors anticipate the needs of prospective investors and include the answers to common questions in their various marketing documents and corporate biographies. Hopefully you'll get most of the answers you need by studying these documents, but if there are unanswered questions, asking the sponsor by phone or email is free game. The details are important!

SECTION 1
INVESTING IN SYNDICATIONS

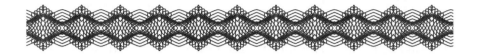

CHAPTER 1

THE HANDS-OFF WAY TO REAL ESTATE

I know a lot of investors who have experience investing in stocks. I know which ones they are because when they first start investing in my real estate offerings they call every few days asking, "How are things going?" I laugh to myself because I know exactly what is going on in their minds—"Am I rich or poor today?"

For about a year I tried my hand at trading commodities futures contracts. I was working the evening shift and would get off work around 2 a.m. I would get up every morning around 4:30, call my broker and place my trade, then go back to bed. I'd wake up a few hours later and check on how I'd done. Some days were amazing, others were a disaster. After doubling my account over a few weeks, I lost it all over a few days. That was the end of my commodities trading "career."

This is exactly why I love real estate: I don't have to wake up every morning and wonder whether I'm rich or poor. Real estate just moves too slowly to require a daily health checkup. If you study markets properly, buy the right properties at the right price, and operate them correctly, you can achieve consistent and somewhat predictable results. This doesn't mean that things always go your way, but if stocks and commodities turn like a fighter jet, real estate turns like a battleship.

This is part of the reason that the old-school 60/40 stock/bond portfolio is dead. Modern portfolio theory emphasizes portfolio diversification, maximizing risk-return profiles, and flattening spikes in portfolio volatility. Real estate adds a non-correlated asset class to your investment portfolio to help you achieve all those things.

Diversification

If you agree that diversification is a good reason to add real estate to your portfolio, I have even more good news. Real estate offers diversification not only from stocks, bonds, and commodities but from other real estate as well.

You can buy different types of properties. You can buy properties in different cities and even different states. But doesn't that add a lot of risk? Haven't you always heard that you should only buy property that you can drive to in less than an hour? What if you know absolutely nothing about apartment buildings or industrial sites? How can real estate that you know nothing about be a positive addition to your portfolio? What if you don't want to deal with tenants, toilets, and trash? Or you don't have the time to spend countless hours searching for properties? Or you just prefer not to spend your time that way? Those are just a few of the many challenges that investing in real estate presents. But they can all be solved, and I'll explain how before you finish this section of the book.

How much of your investment portfolio should you dedicate to real estate? Diversifying into real estate isn't diversification at all if you allocate all your capital to real estate or if you allocate all your real estate capital to one single investment. Consider limiting your real estate exposure to 20 percent of your net worth if you are conservative or 50 percent if you are more aggressive. You should also consider spreading your risk by dividing your real estate allocation over several different investments. Perhaps you limit any one investment to no more than 20 percent of your total real estate allocation. The bottom line is that the right answer for you is a personal decision and may depend on a lot of factors, so do what feels right but don't go all in too fast. No opportunity will be the last one you'll ever see!

Benefits of Real Estate

Real estate offers a lot of benefits besides diversification.
- **It's less correlated to the public markets.** This simply means that if

stocks go down, real estate doesn't automatically follow, unlike stocks or mutual funds that are tied to stock indexes.

- **You can use leverage.** Basically, you can use debt to amplify gains. By way of a simple example, if you purchase a property and borrow 75 percent of the property's cost, and the property value goes up 25 percent, you've doubled your money.

- **Real estate is resistant to inflation.** In an inflationary environment rents tend to go up. Increasing rents mean increased income. Expenses go up too, so don't be fooled into thinking it's a one-way street, but it's very likely that rents will go up more than the higher expenses will offset. Inflation can also cause home prices to appreciate. Increasing home prices can put homeownership out of reach, forcing more people into the rental pool. Increasing demand from renters puts upward pressure on rents.

- **Real estate is a hard asset.** There will always be some value in the land and buildings. While stocks can go to zero, real estate does not.

- **Real estate tends to appreciate.** If you are looking to grow your capital (and who isn't?), you're in luck with real estate. But you don't have to rely just on the market to increase its value. You can make repairs and upgrades, improve management, and reduce expenses to force the income and value higher. Try doing that with stocks! The concept of "forced appreciation" is one of the most important elements of investing in real estate.

- **Real estate can keep Uncle Sam at bay.** Even though real estate tends to appreciate in value, tax laws recognize that buildings and improvements on real estate don't last forever. The law allows real estate owners to depreciate the structures and improvements over specific periods of time. This means that it's possible, and perhaps even likely, that you can receive positive cash flow while recognizing a tax loss.

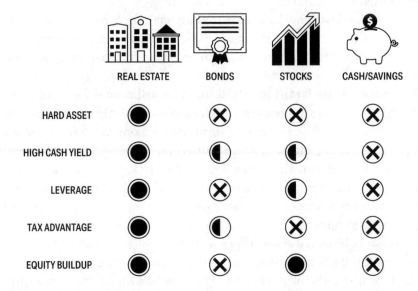
Advantages in Investing in Real Estate

	REAL ESTATE	BONDS	STOCKS	CASH/SAVINGS
HARD ASSET	●	⊗	⊗	⊗
HIGH CASH YIELD	●	◑	◑	⊗
LEVERAGE	●	⊗	◑	⊗
TAX ADVANTAGE	●	◑	⊗	⊗
EQUITY BUILDUP	●	⊗	●	⊗

Disadvantages of Real Estate

With all these factors in mind, it's easy to see why real estate is such a desirable investment. So why isn't everyone investing in it? The main reason is that owning real estate can be a pain. It's not like a stock that you buy in your brokerage account and forget about for a few weeks, a few years, or a few decades.

My great-grandmother worked as a live-in housekeeper for a well-off family back in the early 1900s. Her boss once told her that she should buy stocks in oil companies and utilities, so she bought a few shares. She put the share certificates in a safe-deposit box, and after she passed away, the certificates went to my grandmother and then to my mother. None of them did one single thing with those share certificates. They were never even taken out of the safe-deposit box. But the dividend checks came like clockwork, and the value of the shares went up. Try doing that with real estate! If my great-grandmother had bought a property that was then completely ignored for three generations, it would have been abandoned, overrun by transients, cited for code violations, and eventually demolished by the city. The city would then lien the property for the cleanup costs and foreclose on the property taxes—not quite the happy ending anybody is looking for.

Real estate is also somewhat cyclical. You probably saw the huge rout that took place in the mid-2000s. Deep depressions are rare, possibly even once-in-a-lifetime events, but real estate is not immune from ups and downs, and you might have to weather a storm or two. Many people don't know how to "read" the market or just don't want to. Professional real estate investors who are active in the market not only study the related economics consistently, they are also buying and selling and renting continuously, which gives instant, up-to-the-minute feedback on the market. Casual investors are often intimidated by the market and choose to avoid investing in real estate altogether.

Real estate is also expensive. If you want to own real estate but don't want to be involved in the day-to-day drudgery that comes with it, you can hire a property manager. The quality of management increases as the size of the property increases. Generally speaking, the management system overseeing a $30 million apartment complex is going to be more sophisticated than the one overseeing a $30,000 single-family home. Not everyone can afford to go out and buy a $30 million apartment complex, so they either buy smaller properties, even though they might struggle with management challenges, or skip real estate investing entirely.

Fortunately, there is a better way, one where you can have it all: the ability to own very large assets without having to invest millions of dollars or deal with any of the hassles of owning property. This book is dedicated to teaching you how to do just that.

What Is a Syndication?

A syndication, as mentioned in the introduction, is the structure or relationship between a sponsor and multiple investors who pool their money to fund a real estate acquisition or other venture. Investing in a real estate syndication means investing passively, alongside multiple other passive investors, with one person or company in charge of buying, operating, and ultimately selling the property. That person or company is also responsible for many other things, such as accounting, tax returns, and making distributions to the investors. In essence, you invest your money, and a real estate expert does all the work.

Syndications are often referred to as "passive real estate offerings," "private offerings," "private placements," and, incorrectly, "crowdfunding deals" (which are just syndications advertised online). In this book

I'll use the terms "private offerings" and "syndications" interchangeably.

I suppose it's obvious that a *syndicator* would be someone who arranges a syndication. You will often see a syndicator referred to as a *sponsor,* and in some cases, an *operator* or *operating partner,* or even as a *GP* or *general partner,* which is a carryover from the days when limited partnerships were the preferred entity structure for private offerings. In this book I'll refer to this role as the *sponsor* or the *syndicator,* and sometimes as the *operator.*

Syndicators have a variety of motivations for sponsoring a syndication. Some don't have money of their own to invest in real estate, so they use investors' money instead. Others are leveraging their own money with money from others, which boosts the yield on the sponsor's capital. And others have built a brand as a financial services business to serve their clients' needs for alternative investments, just as a bank or financial advisory business serves its clients' needs for conventional investments.

Merriam-Webster's online dictionary has another definition for a syndicate, "a loose association of racketeers in control of organized crime."[1] As a syndicator myself, I think this is pretty funny. But investors in private offerings might see this definition as far less humorous and even a bit scary (rightfully so).

Stories abound about unscrupulous investment sponsors absconding with the money and disappearing, and, sadly, I've seen this firsthand on several occasions. No, I don't mean that I've seen a guy boarding a plane to Jamaica with a briefcase full of money, but I've had opportunities to acquire properties where the investment sponsor fled with the money, leaving the investors holding the bag. Eventually these guys get a whole new wardrobe of orange jumpsuits with a serial number, but that's no comfort to the investors who will never see their cash again.

Before I got into this business, I was in law enforcement. I've seen the trauma that crime brings to victims, and it infuriates me to see people take advantage of others. Not only do these crooks victimize investors, they also victimize honest investment sponsors who must now explain to prospective investors why they aren't crooks.

When I was dramatically expanding my business shortly after the great financial collapse, it seemed like every conversation with a new investor eventually turned to Bernie Madoff, and how was my business

---

1 www.merriam-webster.com/dictionary/syndicate?src=search-dict-hed

different from his, and how would the investor know that I wouldn't do what Madoff did. What can you say to that? "I won't steal your money" isn't going to cut it. I don't know how other syndicators got past these concerns, but my law enforcement background served me well. Once I told investors about it, the discussion could move on to other things. There are a lot of very honest sponsors in this business who don't come from a law enforcement background, and I'm sure each has the task of convincing investors they are honest. It's a constant fight, and investors are right to be careful, because at the end of the day, the moral character of the sponsor can be the most critical variable—and the most difficult to measure.

The potential remains for investment sponsors to throw morals out the window, of course, but more common than fraud and theft is incompetence: sponsors who get in over their heads, take improper risks, have insufficient analytical tools, or don't manage assets properly. Any of these can result in getting into a bad deal or totally screwing up a perfectly good one.

This underscores the importance of properly screening the investment sponsors you will entrust with your valued capital. Many people who invest in syndications don't know what questions to ask, how to recognize a properly underwritten acquisition, or how to properly compare one opportunity to another. Hopefully this book will help fix that.

I've also seen many syndications that are underwritten extremely poorly or have a really bad business plan. I observe these offerings getting filled with capital from investors who probably don't know any better, and I fear the outcome. As I mentioned in the introduction, if I can help just one investor avoid a mistake that changes their life, writing this book will have been worthwhile.

Why Invest in Syndications?

Real estate is a low-barrier-to-entry investment. If you have the down payment and can get the financing, you can buy real estate. So why would anyone invest in a syndication instead of just buying property directly? Let's run through the most common reasons.

Tenants, toilets, and trash. Yes, dealing with tenants can be challenging and time-consuming, and everyone has heard landlord horror stories of 2 a.m. clogged toilet calls or rogue tenants that trash the place.

There are ways to mitigate these annoyances, but many people stay away from real estate because of these issues alone.

Time. If you have the cash to invest in real estate, you probably earned it by doing something you're really good at, and whatever that is probably takes up a lot of your time. Or maybe you have enough wealth that you don't need to work. Instead, you choose to spend your time traveling, golfing, sailing—whatever makes you happy. Trekking around looking at real estate isn't how you would choose to spend your time, or perhaps you have no extra time to do it even if you wanted to. Let's not forget that looking at property is only the beginning. Getting financing takes time. Managing properties, or managing your property manager, takes time. Refinancing, reading management reports, responding to maintenance decisions, filing insurance claims, selling the property—all these things take time.

Lack of local investments. My office is based in the San Francisco Bay Area, and a lot of my investors are in Silicon Valley, where a starter home can easily cost more than $1 million. I talk to a lot of investors who say, "I have $200,000 available for a real estate investment, but that isn't enough for a 25 percent down payment plus closing costs where I live." That's true, and it doesn't even address the fact that the returns on a $1 million rental home likely don't make a lot of sense. Another option is to look for properties two to three hours away, where the numbers are more favorable, but many people in this situation don't have the time to hunt for and manage such properties.

Expensive markets aren't the only ones presenting problems. What if you live in a stagnant market, where homes are cheap but don't appreciate much? If houses in your area sell for $50,000 and you have that same $200,000 for a real estate investment, you'll have to buy several houses, increasing the management burden, which, if you lack time, could be an issue. You could buy a larger property, such as a small apartment complex, but you'd be doing so in a stagnant market, remember? Perhaps that's not the best choice, especially if you could invest in a syndication that gives economy of scale on a larger property located in an emerging or strong market.

Diversification. This is one of the most common motivations I hear from investors in private offerings. There are a couple of subcategories of diversification that syndications can help you accomplish. Portfolio diversification means that you are just looking to add real estate to your investment portfolio, and are doing it through syndications in large part due to one or more of the reasons listed above. Geographic and asset class diversification are major reasons for investing in syndications, since you can invest smaller amounts of money in several assets in different areas and in different property types, versus investing a large sum in one single property that you own directly. Sponsor diversification means that you can invest with several different sponsors, which helps to mitigate sponsor risk by not over-allocating to any one group.

Liability. Let's face it, wealthy people are targets for lawsuits. If you have substantial assets, making money is less important to you than not losing what you have. Let's say the resident manager at your twenty-unit property is on her way to the office supply store to buy envelopes for the late notices and runs over a kid in the crosswalk. The grieving family is going to sue you, and your insurance company will defend you until they call one day and say that you forgot to purchase non-owned auto coverage, so this loss isn't covered by your policy. You're on your own. The multimillion-dollar judgment that comes next wipes you out—or at the very least, it hurts *a lot*.

That's a risk you don't incur when investing in stocks, bonds, and mutual funds. Likewise, your investments in syndications don't present this same risk profile. Your risk is generally limited to the amount that you invested in the offering. If you invested $250,000 in an offering, in the above scenario, even with a multimillion-dollar judgment, you can only lose up to $250,000.

Cash. This one cuts both ways. Some people don't have enough money, others have too much. "Not enough money" could mean a variety of things, such as simply not having enough to invest in your specific market (like the one with million-dollar starter homes). Or perhaps you have enough to invest in a single-family home, duplex, fourplex, or even a fifty-unit apartment building, but you don't want to invest in a small property. You want the economy of scale offered by a 200-unit apartment complex, but you don't have enough money (or experience) to buy one on your own. You can invest in a syndicated 200-unit apartment building alongside other investors and reap the rewards of scale without having to come up with all the money yourself.

Ultra-high-net-worth investors absolutely must have larger scale. Imagine buying tens of thousands of homes! There are some investors who won't write checks for less than $20 million. In many cases they invest with operating partners so they don't have to get into the real estate business themselves. Then there are the folks in between, people who have a few million to allocate to real estate but don't want to invest in one or two properties. They would rather spread their money around to various markets, in a variety of property types, with multiple sponsors. This gives them ultimate diversification.

Lack of desire. Some people just don't want to be in the real estate business. They have the money, they have the time, they have local investment options available to them, but they would rather just invest in a syndication and move on. They have no desire to travel around hunting for properties to buy, nor to be involved in the day-to-day operation or management of property.

Can't find a deal. I talk to a lot of people who have spent countless hours searching for property and come up empty-handed. They get outbid, the brokers don't return their phone calls, they don't hear about the good deals, or maybe they don't really know how to properly underwrite an income property. They give up on the do-it-yourself route and opt to invest in a sponsor's syndicated offering instead.

Syndications Solve These Problems

The good news is that if any of the above obstacles (or other reasons that aren't on this list) apply to you, syndicated real estate offerings can provide a path for you to invest in real estate. Syndications can solve other problems as well. One is what I call the "professional advantage."

Let's say your roof leaks. You are somewhat handy, so you go up on the roof and put some caulking around a vent pipe. Problem solved, right? Several days later, it rains again and the roof is still leaking. You go back up and replace a few shingles. Next rain, more leaks, more trips to the roof, more trips to the hardware store, more trial and error, and you just can't fix it. You finally call a roofer. In fifteen minutes, the roofer spots the problem and fixes it with parts he carries in his truck. No more leak.

Sometimes the professional just outperforms the weekend warrior. Such is the case with real estate. After the great financial collapse, I was buying more than 100 foreclosed homes per year in the Bay Area at extreme discounts to market value, in some cases for prices that the homes had sold for in the 1980s. At the same time, amateur would-be home flippers were making offers and coming up dry. One of the most common questions I was asked was, "How come I don't get good deals like that?" The answer is pretty simple: I do this for a living. I had a team of people looking at nearly a thousand houses per week, and we were bidding on dozens of properties per week. There is just no way the casual investor who looks at one bank-owned property and submits an offer on it is going to strike oil. It takes persistence, consistency, elbow grease, and systems.

Such is the case in the world of commercial real estate. Brokers want to sell to buyers they know, buyers they are sure will perform. The casual investor is at an immediate disadvantage. The only way the one-off investor beats the pro is if their offer is so egregiously high that the seller would be a fool to ignore it.

Investors often fear that they are giving something up by investing in a syndication versus buying property directly because sponsors earn their living by charging fees and splitting the profits. If you buy properties on your own, you save those fees and splits, or so the theory goes. But if you aren't a professional investor, you're passing up dollars to chase dimes. A great real estate sponsor can get better deals than the casual investor, buy larger deals than many casual investors, and operate the property and execute the business plan better than an inexperienced investor. All those advantages squeeze more juice from the fruit, so it's certainly possible that a good syndicator can produce a net return to the investor (after splits and fees) that is equivalent to, and possibly even more than, the amount the casual investor would achieve on their own through direct real estate ownership. Plus, that all happens while you are spending your time and energy on other things that you actually want to spend time doing. That's the beauty of financial freedom.

Leverage

Investing in syndications comes down to one word: leverage. In real estate we think of leverage as debt, which amplifies return on the invested capital. But in the context of syndications, leverage takes on a whole different meaning.

Leverage in this sense means the passive investor can:
- Leverage the sponsor's **knowledge** to find the right investment and implement the right strategy, in the right place, at the right time
- Leverage the sponsor's **experience**, contacts, and systems to source deals that they couldn't source on their own

- Leverage the sponsor's access to **deal flow** located by their full-time staff who are dedicated to finding investment opportunities
- Leverage the sponsor's **financial strength** to obtain the best financing terms
- Leverage the sponsor's **team** to professionally manage the asset
- Leverage the sponsor's **market research** and skill to execute the business plan by making decisions that maximize return and minimize downside
- Leverage the sponsor's **time** to find the right properties and execute a complicated business plan so the investor can do other things
- Leverage the sponsor's **network** to find the right properties, the right financing, and the right insurance; form the right legal structure; and handle construction and remodeling
- Leverage the **capital** of other investors so that, as a group, the investors can invest in deals larger than they could or would invest in on their own

I frequently say that the primary job of a syndication sponsor is to add value. By that, I don't mean they add value to the real estate (although they should be doing that too). I mean that they should add value to the relationship, to their client, the passive investor. Sure, you can invest in real estate without an operating partner. But if syndicators add value and help you accomplish your goals, they satisfy a need for you. Every sponsor should aim to add value at every phase of the investment process, and every passive investor should be seeking sponsors who do just that.

Are Syndications Suitable for You?

People invest in syndications for a variety of reasons. They're a great tool for solving a lot of problems or creating a better path to add real estate to your portfolio, but they aren't for everyone. Suitability is an important and often overlooked factor in the syndication world.

Stories abound of the blind leading the blind as inexperienced and undercapitalized sponsors accept capital from uninformed investors. The most frequent example is the first-time sponsor who raises money from his pals at the country club or his inner circle of family and friends. The investors go in on the deal because they know and trust the sponsor, not because of the sponsor's track record of success or their own extensive knowledge of real estate and ability to recognize a great deal.

This happens all the time, sometimes with great results for all. However, sometimes the inexperienced sponsor fails to execute, or the market turns and the sponsor doesn't know what to do, or the sponsor's lack of underwriting experience starts the deal off destined for disaster due to improper assumptions or simple formula errors in a home-built spreadsheet. My point here isn't to pick on the inexperienced sponsor. In fact, this is really the only way a first-timer gets a deal done—using family and friends to fund their freshman year at the school of hard knocks. I was there once too, along with every other newly minted real estate entrepreneur. My point is that it's very likely that such investments aren't suitable for the investors, either because the sponsor isn't experienced enough to stack the deck in the investors' favor, or because "friends and family" investors probably can't afford to lose their capital without an impact to their financial well-being or lifestyle.

An unsuitable investor is bad for the sponsor: If the deal goes awry, the sponsor could have some explaining to do for admitting an investor who didn't understand the risks. It's also bad for the investor because they might not have understood the risks they were taking.

Accredited Investors

One common litmus test for suitability is the concept of the accredited investor (See appendix). There is no class, test, or certification for becoming accredited, so the term is a bit misleading. An accredited investor is someone who meets the definition set forth in the securities code.

At the time of this writing, anyone whose individual net worth, or joint net worth with that person's spouse, exceeds $1 million (excluding the value of their primary residence) automatically qualifies as an accredited investor.[2]

Another yardstick is income. Any person who had an individual income in excess of $200,000 in each of the two most recent years, or joint income with that person's spouse in excess of $300,000 in each of those years, and has a reasonable expectation of reaching the same income level in the current year qualifies as an accredited investor regardless of net worth.

While the above two tests are the most common, they are not the only

---

2 Rule 501 of Regulation D at www.sec.gov

tests of accreditation. The other definitions are somewhat obscure and apply to business entities, trusts, and IRAs, among others. A complete list appears in appendix A at the end of this book.

Being an accredited versus a non-accredited investor has a few important distinctions. Most important, being accredited opens the door to invest in certain syndications that non-accredited investors cannot. In chapter 2 I'll introduce different types of syndications and highlight which ones are restricted to accredited investors.

Other Suitability Factors

Many investors and sponsors alike think that the accredited investor test is the only suitability factor. Many also believe, incorrectly, that you must be an accredited investor to invest in syndicated offerings. Luckily, this is simply not true! Many syndications qualify for non-accredited investors to invest in them.

Suitability comes down to a variety of factors far beyond the investor's net worth and income. Most important, are you familiar enough with real estate investments and syndications to properly evaluate the opportunity and understand the risks? After reading this book, I hope that the answer to this is yes!

Is your capital a match for the business plan? In other words, you don't want to invest short-term capital in long-term projects. Conversely, investing long-term capital in short-term projects might not be the best idea, either.

Are you borrowing money to invest in a syndicated offering? This might sound strange at first glance, but I see it happen frequently. Just as people leverage their real estate to buy other real estate, they frequently do cash-out refinances or equity lines of credit on appreciated real estate, and invest that cash in syndicated offerings. If you thoroughly understand the additional risk you are taking, are comfortable with that risk, and have ample reserves, perhaps this is fine for you. But be careful! If you are using borrowed money, investing it in an offering that doesn't produce a higher level of cash flow than the debt service on the borrowed money can not only affect the risk profile, it can affect your livelihood. You could be forced to divert some of your other income to service this debt. Perhaps this is all part of your plan, but think it through very carefully. Lack of cash flow to service your investment debt could be a factor in a deep value-add project, a ground-up development offering, or a vacant or mostly vacant commercial building. Borrowed capital might not be suitable for those types of offerings.

Do you live off the cash flow of your investments? If you do, a ground-up development deal might not be suitable for you. You might be better suited to a stabilized property that is throwing off good cash flow from day one, or even a debt fund that produces steady periodic income with less exposure to risk, albeit without much upside.

If you are a growth-oriented investor focused on growing a base of risk capital, the same stabilized property or debt fund that's a good fit for a retiree is probably not the most suitable for you. You might be better suited to the ground-up development or heavy value-add property that produces less (or no) cash flow but has more upside potential, as long as the higher risk doesn't bother you.

Then there are the in-betweens, which are likely the most common offerings out there—medium value-add properties where resident profile improvements, management changes, and light to moderate physical upgrades will increase the property's cash flow over time and grow the value of the investment in tandem with that growth of income. These are suitable for most investors if they understand the risks, and the cash flow and overall return satisfy their goals.

Limited Liquidity and Risk Tolerance

Most real estate investments have a lack of liquidity, meaning you can't get your money back whenever you want it. Investing in a project with a business plan to purchase a home, fix it up, and immediately resell it has a fairly high liquidity component because the home is likely to be owned for a relatively short period, such as a few months. But purchasing a stabilized, cash-flowing multifamily property could have a five- or even a ten-year business plan—or a five-year plan that turns into ten if the market isn't cooperating at the time of the intended sale. In either event, your capital could be tied up in that property for the entire hold period with no way to get any of it out, except for selling your ownership interest to someone else. But unlike conventional stocks, there is no secondary market for you to sell your interests. They are very difficult if not impossible to sell, unless you have a friend or family member who wants it, or perhaps a well-capitalized sponsor who would buy you out. My point is that if you might need your capital in a short period of time, a longer-term business plan is unsuitable for you.

There is also the issue of your risk tolerance versus the risk profile of the investment. If you are risk-averse, a ground-up development deal might not be suitable for you, despite your overall goal of capital growth and your lack of need for current cash flow.

Wrapping Up

Investment sponsors should be taking the time to get to know you and set up a phone call with you. During that call, they should ask about your goals and objectives, your risk tolerance, and your priorities as they relate to cash flow and capital growth. Are you employed, retired, or independently wealthy?

I've heard sponsors say, "It's not my job to decide for my investors. This is their decision." While there is some truth to that, it *is* the sponsor's job to root out unsuitable investors in their offerings to the extent possible. Making an unsuitable investment is bad for the investor, but it is also bad for the sponsor. Having an investor who needs to get out of a deal is a big problem, and one that can't always be solved. Any business suffers if it has unhappy customers, and syndication sponsors are no different.

In addition to learning about you during the introductory phone call, the sponsor should clearly explain what it is they do, without a lot of jargon. They should take the time to answer every question you have. If they don't have the answer, they shouldn't make it up; they should research it and get back to you promptly.

The objective of this conversation is to establish a relationship with you and to learn which offerings might or might not be suitable for you. Be leery of sponsors who don't seem to care if you are a suitable investor. This likely means they don't care if their other investors are suitable either. That might not seem like your problem, but it is if unsuitable investors are investing in the same offering with you. Their problems can turn into your problems when the going gets tough.

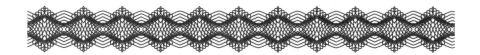

CHAPTER 2

SPONSORS AND OFFERINGS

The question comes in through email, private message, or on the BiggerPockets forums: How do I find a deal to invest in? For anyone asking this question, the good news is I will cover that later in this chapter. The bad news is it's the wrong question to be asking.

More Important: Property or Sponsor?

Which is more important: the property or the sponsor? This question is akin to asking if it's the horse or the jockey, the plane or the pilot, the racecar or the driver. Accomplishing any objective requires collaboration between the person making the attempt and the vehicle they are using to attempt it.

Let's not forget, however, that there is also a third element—the environment in which the attempt is being made. Just as a pilot cannot control the weather and a racecar driver cannot control the track, the syndication sponsor can't control the market. Yet the weather, track, and market will affect performance and outcomes.

Anyone who follows NASCAR knows that there are a few teams that win consistently, while other teams can struggle for their entire careers and never win a race. The chassis of the cars, the engines, the shape of the body—these things are highly regulated by the sanctioning body with tolerances down to the fractions of an inch. One could argue that the cars are all the same, but they are not. Some teams know exactly how to tune the car to perform at specific tracks, and some drivers know exactly how to enter a corner to get the most speed coming out.

The same applies to making sound real estate investments. It's important to evaluate the real estate, and it's important to understand the market. But it's critical to have the right team calling the shots.

A Story of Inexperience and Mismanagement

Never was the importance of the right team more apparent to me than in the case of a multifamily property I once analyzed. My team was looking at a 150-unit property in one of the strongest metro markets in the country. The property was built in 1995 and well located. From all external appearances it should have been a nice, stable value-add acquisition. One of the steps I take when contemplating an acquisition is to have a roundtable discussion with my acquisitions team. To prepare for that discussion I first review the numbers in our acquisition model, which includes a side-by-side comparison of the property's historical income. In one column we have the annual income for the last twelve months, and in another column we have the income for the last three months, which we annualize so we have an apples-to-apples comparison.

It took me about five seconds to see a real problem here. To see for yourself, here are the numbers in our model:

	BROKER PROFORMA		LAST 12 MONTHS		LAST 3 MONTHS	
Rental Revenue						
Gross Potential Rent	$2,102,000		$2,017,226		$2,017,864	
Loss to Lease	$10,510	0.50%	$179,393	8.89%	$112,112	5.56%
Vacancy Loss	$104,575	4.98%	$289,054	14.33%	$373,333	18.50%
One-Time Concessions	$10,457	0.50%	$21,546	1.07%	$27,369	1.36%
Recurring Rent Concessions		0.00%	$6,957	0.34%	$27,184	1.35%
Bad Debt Loss	$31,372	1.49%	$98,377	4.88%	$51,532	2.55%
Non-revenue Units	$14,640	0.70%	$3,261	0.16%	$4,440	0.22%
Net Rental Inc. / Econ. Vac.	$1,930,446	8.17%	$1,418,638	29.67%	$1,421,894	29.54%

What were the warning signs? No, not the broker's proforma (*pro-forma* is just a fancy word for *estimate*); we just ignore those for the most part. The warning signs were the 14 percent vacancy, which had increased to 18.5 percent over the last three months, and the nearly 5 percent in bad debt losses. Plus, the leases were below their goal line by nearly 9 percent (evidenced by the 8.89 percent loss to lease number). We'll dive deeper into what these numbers are and what they mean in chapter 7, but suffice it to say that these are extremely high for a newer property in good condition in a good market. What could be so wrong?

My comment in our roundtable discussion was that there must be a mistake somewhere. Normally I'd blame this on a really bad operator, but there was no way this operator was a total idiot. This property was being sold as part of a portfolio of more than a dozen other properties totaling around 2,000 units. Surely anyone who has acquired 2,000 units must know what they are doing.

Our next step was to talk with the broker and get more of the backstory on the deal. Lo and behold, the talk with the broker got interesting quickly. The first question I asked was, "What's up with this owner?" The answer was very telling. The seller bought his first multifamily property three years ago. Somehow he convinced a lot of investors, and even one or more institutional partners, that he really knew what he was doing, because in the three years that followed, he bought 25 more properties. We are talking thousands of units, and hundreds of millions of dollars.

After only two years of experience, this operator decided to form his own management company and self-manage the entire portfolio. It took only a year to blow the whole thing up. The guy at the top wasn't experienced at all and was just figuring it out on his own, and he wasn't figuring it out very well. There was consistent turnover at the management company, with several leaders in just the first year, each lasting only a few months before quitting. The property-level staff had constant turnover. The whole portfolio quickly spun into a disaster.

This operator was trying to upgrade the properties that they bought, but they weren't paying their vendors. As a result, they couldn't renovate units because the vendors didn't want to work for them. This property got a new assistant manager who was trying really hard despite the lack of leadership from above. When she took over, she found 300 unpaid invoices stuffed in a file. When I asked why the bad debt losses were so high, I heard one of the most incredible stories I've heard in all the years I've been buying real estate: The residents had gotten into the habit of not paying rent, and when management called their eviction company to get help with evictions, they were refused assistance because the owners hadn't paid the invoices to the eviction company!

This is one of the best examples of the great horse versus jockey debate. There was nothing wrong with the real estate or the market. Everything was wrong with the sponsor. The investors in those deals stand to lose their entire investment unless the market bails them out. There is little time left for that to happen, as the sponsor's institutional partner is forcing the sale of the entire portfolio. They know that they need to bail out and cut their losses before the sponsor can completely drive the assets into the ground and lose them all to foreclosure.

A Story of Fraud

Another good example is a 900-unit apartment complex I was offered the opportunity to purchase. As it turned out, the onetime owners had amassed a portfolio of more than 7,000 units in a short period of time. A lot of the properties were financed with very high-leverage debt. Somehow the leader of the sponsorship group had managed to abscond with all the renovation money, and the portfolio went down the tubes. Many of the properties were uninhabitable, and others had major physical problems and low occupancy.

The sponsor was in the wind, so there was no captain left on the ship. He went overboard and sailed off on the only remaining lifeboat, never to be found again. Ultimately the entire portfolio fell into receivership and was auctioned off except for a few properties that didn't sell, and the lenders were stuck with them. One of them was this 900-unit property. Vacancy was high but none of the units were move-in ready. The office needed a complete remodel, the grounds were barren, the swimming pool was closed. Basically, the place was a total mess and someone (the investors and the lender) lost millions.

The Property or the Sponsor? The Answer

The lesson here is that a good sponsor can use their depth of knowledge and experience to finagle the best outcome in the face of adverse circumstances. Perhaps they can also leverage other strengths, such as more negotiating power with lenders, a better ability to raise additional needed capital, or the availability of a broader range of creative financing vehicles. However, just as easily as a good sponsor can save the day, a bad sponsor can destroy a perfectly good real estate deal. While it is important to evaluate the deal, it is equally if not more important to evaluate the sponsor. At the beginning of this chapter I said that "How do I find a deal to invest in?" is the wrong question to ask. The right question is "How do I find a good sponsor to invest with?"

Types of Offerings

This book isn't intended to be a primer in securities law for two reasons: First, I'm not a lawyer, and any book trying to teach law should probably be written by a lawyer. Second, an in-depth discussion of securities law is dry, boring, and simply unnecessary to accomplish the educational objective of this book.

Still, we need to cover a few basics so that you'll know why syndication investments are so hard to find and why it sometimes seems like they're part of an underground investment society that only insiders know about. Plus, if you are not an accredited investor, there are some offerings you aren't eligible to invest in, and you'll need to know which those are.

Syndication Investments Are Securities, Like Stocks

A security is a tradable financial asset, like a stock, for example. In the simplest sense, a security is any investment interest where the investor isn't the one in control. The true definition is much more technical (and boring), but suffice it to say that any time someone receives investment money from investors and the investors are passive participants in the venture, the transaction involves the sale of a security. Any claim by the syndicator to the contrary is most likely untrue. Let's face it: This is what syndications are all about! You are a passive investor, and the sponsor is in control. This doesn't present a problem; it just means there are rules that the sponsor needs to follow.

The Securities Act of 1933 was established in response to the stock market collapse of 1929. The goals of the act were to ensure more transparency in the sale of securities, and to establish laws against misrepresentation and fraud in the securities markets. The act tackled the need for better disclosure by requiring companies to register with the government, specifically the newly created Securities and Exchange Commission (known as the SEC), prior to selling securities.

Registering Syndications Is Impractical

The end goal of the Securities Act was to require that investors receive specific financial information regarding securities offered for public sale. But the registration process is cumbersome, time-consuming, and expensive. Those three things might be inconvenient when taking a maturing company public, but they are prohibitive when a venture is acquiring a piece of real estate by raising smaller amounts of money from just a limited pool of investors.

Legislators recognized this when they created the Securities Act, and they addressed the problem by offering specific exemptions from the registration requirement. Why is it necessary for the syndicator to want an exemption? Why not just register the security? A typical real estate acquisition takes one to three months on average from the time the offer is accepted until the time escrow closes. Registering the syndication as a public offering would take longer than it would for the escrow to close, so the timing just doesn't work. Throw on top of that the cost of registration, which could run from the tens of thousands into the millions of dollars to prepare and file. All but the largest real estate transactions cannot support that level of transactional cost. Exemption from the registration requirement becomes a must.

The exemptions are defined in a body of law known as Regulation D. You will often hear real estate syndications referred to as "Reg D offerings." This is just a nickname that refers to the regulation granting exemptions from registration. Reg D is also known as a "safe harbor," which is a provision that affords the sponsor some protection from liability or penalty under specific situations or if certain conditions are met. There are several different registration exemptions in the regulations, but only two are commonly seen in the real estate syndication world: Rule 506(b) and Rule 506(c) of Reg D. Which of these two exemptions the sponsor chooses to use will affect who can invest in the offering and how the sponsor is allowed (or not) to spread the word. Let's explore the two, and see how and why.

506(b) Exemption

Rule 506(b) has been around a long time and for many years was almost always the exemption used by real estate syndicators. This rule allows the syndicator to raise an unlimited amount of money from an unlimited number of accredited investors as long as the syndicator *does not advertise* for those investors with a general solicitation, such as a public advertisement, article, or notice, whether in a newspaper or magazine, or on the internet, or even during a seminar or meeting whose attendees have been invited by a general solicitation.

Investments can also be accepted from up to thirty-five non-accredited investors, but the sponsor will need to provide much more information than if the investment was limited to accredited investors. The reasoning is that non-accredited investors may be less sophisticated about investment concepts than accredited investors, so the SEC has added additional requirements, such as providing information similar to (but not as much as) what would be in a registration statement for a registered public offering.

If you are not an accredited investor, you can invest in a 506(b) offering if the sponsor will allow it. You should also have sufficient knowledge and experience in financial and business matters to evaluate the merits and risks of the investment that you intend to make. Keep in mind that some sponsors who use rule 506(b) do not allow non-accredited investors to invest in some or all of their offerings, but some do. All you have to do is ask the sponsor whether they'll allow you in.

Advertising that does not offer the opportunity to purchase a security is typically not a general solicitation. For example, a company offering syndications may have a website and give information about the business and the industry without mentioning any offerings or projections, and that may not be a general solicitation. This is why you might see companies advertise themselves in ways that don't make it clear that they are syndication sponsors, and why they don't advertise their investment offerings.

Pre-existing Relationships

If sponsors of 506(b) offerings cannot advertise, how can they prove that you didn't find out about the investment opportunity through an advertisement? After the adoption of Regulation D, the SEC made clear that the existence of a "pre-existing substantive relationship" was enough to establish that the investor was not attracted through a general solicitation. Many people believe that a pre-existing relationship is required, but it is not. It is one way, but not the only way, to demonstrate that the investor was not introduced by a general solicitation. A "substantive" relationship means that the syndicator has sufficient information to evaluate the person's status as an accredited or sophisticated investor. There is no minimum length of time this relationship must exist, nor any specific parameters on how many times the two parties must have interacted. This leaves what is and isn't a "substantive" relationship somewhat opaque.

A common way to begin developing this relationship is through a personal meeting or phone call where the syndicator asks questions about the investor's goals and objectives, income, net worth, financial background, risk awareness, and so on. For this reason, don't be surprised if sponsors want to have a phone call or meeting with you before they begin showing you investment opportunities. This is also another reason why I'm preaching in this book to find sponsors first, investment opportunities second. Even though a pre-existing relationship is not required, it is still the most common (and probably the easiest) way for sponsors to show that you didn't invest in their syndication as a result of an advertisement.

506(c) Exemption

In 2012, Congress passed the Jumpstart Our Business Startups Act (JOBS Act). One of the directives of the act was for the SEC to remove the prohibition on advertising some securities offerings in order to make it easier for a company to find investors and raise capital. To fulfill this directive, a new rule was added to Regulation D, and it was numbered 506(c). Under this rule, syndicators are allowed to widely advertise their offerings. But if they do, all investors admitted to the offering must be accredited investors. If you are not an accredited investor, you can't invest in a 506(c) offering, and there are no exceptions. To ensure compliance, the sponsor is required to take reasonable steps to verify that you are accredited. They can't just take your word for it.

This means you'll have to jump through some hoops to prove that you are an accredited investor. One way sponsors can verify you is for you to supply proof to the syndicator that you are accredited, such as a tax return or W-2 to verify that you meet the income requirement, along with a written statement indicating that your income will likely continue in the current year. Another method is for you to supply a balance sheet backed by a bank or brokerage statement to show that you meet the net worth requirement. You can also supply a letter written by your attorney, certified public accountant, SEC-registered investment advisor, or registered broker-dealer certifying that you are accredited, and that they have knowledge of such facts as necessary to make that statement.

The verification process can be cumbersome, so this new body of law has spawned a cottage industry of third-party validation services. These firms handle the verification process for the sponsor so they don't have to do it themselves. Nevertheless, some syndicators either don't like the verification process or don't like to subject their investors to it, so they choose to use 506(b) instead of 506(c) and forgo the benefits of advertising their offerings. If they already have a broad base of investors, this decision is easier because they don't need to advertise anyway.

Online Crowdfunding

The JOBS Act and Rule 506(c) exemption have led to a second cottage industry—the crowdfunding portal. These are online portals where investors can shop from a menu of available investment offerings. People sometimes are confused by crowdfunding portals, thinking that crowdfunding is a type of offering or syndication. However, crowdfunding is simply a different way of marketing the same syndicated offerings that have always been in the marketplace but were selling privately without the use of advertising.

"Crowdfunding" itself has become somewhat of a generic term used to describe just about any pooled offering found online. But there are vast differences in the various offerings in the marketplace.

Crowdfunding portals use four tools to structure their offerings. Some use a Regulation A+ exemption, which allows them to raise a limited amount of money from both accredited and non-accredited investors. Because of the size limitations and specific limits on how much investors are allowed to invest (a small percentage of their net worth), this is one of the lesser-used structures.

Some portals use a non-traded REIT. This is a Real Estate Investment Trust, somewhat like the ones found in the conventional investment world, but they are not traded on the conventional markets. Instead, they are funded directly in an investor-to-REIT investment transaction. REITs offer the advantage of allowing an unlimited number of non-accredited investors to invest in them. These REITs in turn invest in joint ventures with real estate operators or as preferred equity (which is somewhat like debt and somewhat like equity), or they simply make secured loans to real estate owners.

Rule 506(c) is widely used because it allows advertising, so it's an obvious shoe-in for an online advertising platform, which is essentially what crowdfunding is.

Rule 506(b) is also widely used, which may seem counterintuitive given that the exemption specifically prohibits advertising. But portals often work around the rule by allowing only existing customers to invest in their 506(b) offerings. The strategy is basically to acquire the customers with advertising 506(c) offerings. Then after establishing a relationship with the investors, they can open up the path for those investors to participate in future 506(b) offerings.

Two Types of Crowdfunding

There are essentially two ways that crowdfunding portals utilize the 506(b) and (c) exemptions. The first is for investors to invest in a syndication that is sponsored by the portal. The portal in turn invests in an operator's syndication, either as the only investor, alongside other investors, or as preferred equity or debt. In this instance, you are an investor with the portal, not with the operator (sponsor). You have no direct relationship with the operator, and the operator likely doesn't know that you are indirectly an investor in their offering. Your reporting and distributions will come from the crowdfunding portal, and the crowdfunding portal is likely scraping off some fees and splitting the profits with you (after the operator has already split the profits with the portal, so you are getting only a split of the split). They might also be charging the sponsor some fees, which the sponsor is sure to pass on to the deal, which means you are paying those fees as well, albeit indirectly.

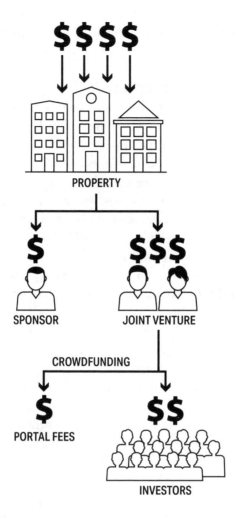

PROPERTY

SPONSOR · JOINT VENTURE

CROWDFUNDING

PORTAL FEES · INVESTORS

The other strategy used by some portals is to act as more of a matchmaker or marketing platform. In this instance, the portal lists offerings from sponsors, and if you wish to invest in the offering, the portal connects you with the sponsor and you invest in their offering directly. Your distributions and reporting will come from the sponsor (operator), and you will have the chance to build a relationship with them. These portals typically charge fees to the sponsor for making the connection and might have ongoing monthly, quarterly, or annual fees charged to the sponsor as long as the investment is outstanding. Not unlike the previous scenario, the sponsors are most certainly passing those fees to the venture, meaning that you are paying for it, indirectly. But in this case, you would not typically be splitting the profits with both the crowdfunding portal and the sponsor; you would only be splitting with the sponsor.

Is Crowdfunding a Game Changer or Not?

Crowdfunding portals were once seen as game changers, shaking up the way capital has been raised by sponsors for decades. But so far that prediction hasn't come true. The model got off to a slow start because sponsors and investors alike have long been used to this being a relationship business. Taking it online removes the personal touch, and that has proved to be an obstacle in many cases. As a result, the portals have had more success in placing debt, somewhat like hard money loans, and preferred equity, which is somewhat of a hybrid of debt and equity. They've had some success in placing smaller slugs of common equity but have only recently gained momentum in raising large placements.

Due in part to these challenges, and in part to a lot of competition in the space, several portals have gone out of business. Even some of the once well-regarded dominating platforms are no longer in existence. This has left some investors wondering what would happen to their investments and who would be there to oversee them.

There will likely be new players, some further consolidation, and even more attrition as this industry matures. The good news is that some portals do a pretty good job. And for some investors these portals add value because they bring offerings to their attention that the investor would otherwise have been unaware of. The even better news is that you don't need crowdfunding portals to successfully invest in private offerings. You can invest directly with sponsors and avoid portal fees if you know how to find sponsors on your own. It's been done that way for decades, and that will likely never change.

Finding Syndication Sponsors

The prohibition against general solicitation for offerings using the 506(b) exemption leaves a lot of would-be investors in the dark, asking the question, "Where do I find these deals?" Many investors are left feeling like an invitation to an exclusive club is eluding them. On the flip side, if the sponsors can't advertise, building investor interest is a challenge at the beginning.

By far the best way to find great syndicators is to get recommendations from friends and colleagues who are already investing. This is easy for people who have lots of friends investing in passive real estate opportunities. But it can be impossible for others who just don't have those resources. Fortunately, there are many ways to find great syndicators; it just takes a bit of time and effort. This list, although not exhaustive, includes most of the best ways to find quality firms to invest with.

Conferences. Experienced syndication sponsors are considered experts in the real estate field, and are often invited to various investment conferences to speak in keynote presentations and on expert panels. This is a great way to hear their thoughts on markets, strategy, and a host of other topics. Sometimes the speakers have trade show booths where you can speak directly with them, or they are available before or after their speaking session. Some conferences will publish a list of their speakers and/or attendees so you don't even have to attend: You could simply reach out to them directly after researching their firms online. Search for "real estate investment conferences" and "family office conferences."

Buyer lists. Large commercial real estate brokers love to promote themselves by listing the properties they've sold over the last month, quarter, year, or even longer. Often these transaction reports will say who the buyer was. Let's say you've studied various metropolitan areas and have concluded that there are four areas with very favorable market conditions for buying the type of commercial property you are interested in investing in. Search online for the largest commercial real estate brokers in those areas, visit their websites, and look for data on their closed sales. If you can't find it, you might be able to get them to send it to you if you email or call them. Check those lists to see who has bought properties similar to those that interest you, then visit the companies' websites and research them. You'll likely find that many of these buyers are syndication sponsors.

Meetups. Similar to conferences but usually on a much smaller scale, meetups are typically organized by other investors who invite guests to speak to their group. Syndicators are often sought out to be those speakers. Search online for "real estate meetups" and check their websites for upcoming speakers.

Networking events. These can range from local real estate clubs all the way up to multifamily-specific events such as the National Multi Housing Council's annual meeting. You'll likely find the most experienced syndicators at larger events and newer, smaller syndicators at local clubs.

Real estate websites. Sites such as BiggerPockets.com have many syndicators who participate in online question-and-answer forums. Read what they are posting to sort out who is experienced and who is not.

Podcasts. There are dozens of real estate podcasts out there. Go to your favorite podcast app and search for "real estate," "multifamily," or "syndication"; you should find many podcasts that talk about these subjects. Many of the podcast hosts are syndicators themselves, as are many of the guests, so you can learn a ton about the various players.

Blogs. Syndicators write blogs for their own websites as well as for sites such as www.BiggerPockets.com, www. Entrepreneur.com, www. Forbes.com, and more. Reading what they have to say gives you a window into the mind of the syndicator. After a while you'll develop a knack for figuring out who really knows what they're talking about and who is just full of it.

Company websites. Nearly all experienced syndication sponsors have a website. Searching for terms such as "real estate investment firms," "real estate syndicators," "real estate private equity," and such should reveal the websites of many syndication sponsors.

News articles. Active syndicators are frequently quoted in news articles or have entire articles written about them in trade and mainstream publications. Many will issue press releases when they close on acquisitions, which result in articles in publications like *Multi Housing News*, *GlobeSt*, and *Multifamily Biz*, as well as a variety of business journals. Watch for the companies' and their spokespeople's names, then search those names online to find out more about the firm.

Online crowdfunding. Discussed in more detail earlier in this chapter, these portals provide a service for some investors by giving access to passive deal flow that they might not otherwise find. However, it often comes at a cost, because crowdfunding portals are businesses and have to receive revenue in order to survive. This might be worth it to you if the site introduces you to deal flow that you wouldn't have found on your own.

If you use the tips in this book to find quality sponsors on your own and do proper due diligence on them, you can save an entire layer of cost by investing directly with those carefully selected sponsors versus investing through online crowdfunding portals.

Broker-dealers. Some syndications are sold by licensed salespeople known as "broker-dealers." Stockbrokers are broker-dealers, but most stockbrokers don't sell real estate syndication interests. However, some do, and some even specialize in syndication. The downside to purchasing through a broker-dealer is that the commission adds fee load to the investment, which can be a drag on returns. Nonetheless, for investors who don't have the time to seek out opportunities using the methods outlined in this chapter, buying through a broker-dealer might make a lot of sense.

Registered Investment Advisors. Otherwise known as RIAs, these professionals are licensed to give investment advice to investors. Although most RIAs focus on retail investments such as stocks, bonds, and mutual funds, some RIAs will seek out alternatives and make recommendations to invest in.

Advertisements. If you are an accredited investor, you can invest in syndications that advertise. Syndications formed using the 506(b) exemption cannot advertise, so they are harder to find. You'd have to use all the methods above to locate those opportunities. But syndications using the 506(c) exemption can advertise as long as the sponsor allows only verified accredited investors to invest in the offering. This limitation causes many sponsors to avoid using the 506(c) exemption, but some do use it and you can find their offerings if you spot their ads.

SECTION II
EVALUATING SPONSORS

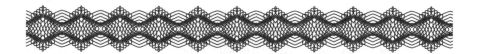

CHAPTER 3

THE PEOPLE

Although I often hear people ask how to find syndication deals, so far I've discussed only ways to find sponsors. That is not an oversight! Investors frequently approach this industry backward, by searching for *deals to invest in* when they should be looking for *sponsors to invest with*.

If you invest with a good sponsor, you shouldn't have to look for deals because good sponsors tend to bring good deals. While searching for a good sponsor might make the investment process harder in the beginning, it actually makes it easier over the long term. Once you find quality sponsors to invest with, you can then narrow your research to simply vetting the opportunities they present to you. Approach this like a marathon, not a sprint.

First impressions matter. When you initially contact a sponsor, how do they respond? Do they simply offer to put you on their mailing list, or do they not respond at all? The best sponsors begin every relationship by being as interested about you as you are about them. The ideal response to a new inquiry is for the firm to set up an introductory phone call, where they can learn about your goals and objectives, tolerance for risk, and suitability for investing in private placements. If they skip this step, I'd consider that a red flag. Sponsors should make every effort to make sure that their investors are investing in deals that are suitable for them. Plus, this is the start of that "pre-existing relationship" we discussed earlier. For accredited investors investing in advertised 506(c) offerings, a pre-existing relationship isn't necessary, but having a relationship with the sponsors you invest with is still a good idea, whether or not it's required.

Look for firms that are professional, with a consistent message, an online presence, and a brand. You want to invest with firms that have skin in the game, and no skin is more vulnerable than a brand because it takes years to earn trust but only seconds to destroy it. In a business that relies heavily on word-of-mouth and referrals, a firm's track record is extremely meaningful. Investing with groups that don't have a brand and reputation to protect is scary.

The introductory phone call isn't just an opportunity for the syndicator to learn about you (but be sure they do). It's also an opportunity for you to learn about the syndicator. Interview them! This section will tell you how.

During the initial conversation, you'll want to find a sponsor who is confident but humble and even carries a healthy dose of fear. Sponsors who seem too excited about real estate, the market, or the opportunity are scary. While it's good to be excited and confident, syndicators who run from hype to hype should make you worried. Real estate carries risk, and downside potential is real. Too many sponsors ignore those risks at their own peril and to the detriment of their investors. Don't take the ride with them no matter how great they make it sound.

Ask about where they invest and why. Do their markets make sense and align with your beliefs? Do they even know why they are investing where they are? Have they conducted research into those markets, or are they just winging it? What type of research do they do?

What is their typical acquisition profile? If all their experience consists of, for example, buying 50- to 75-unit properties in Denver for $5 million to $10 million, be suspicious if the deal they are currently offering is 500 units in Seattle for $75 million. You want to invest in offerings that align with the sponsor's experience. There's no need to accompany them on a test flight.

For bonus points, visit the sponsor's office. I'm amazed at how many people invest extremely large sums of money with my company without ever coming to our office. However, those investors who do visit turn out to be the most active, investing repeatedly, in larger amounts, and giving more referrals to other investors than most clients who have not visited. We've had investors travel from as far as India, Australia, Thailand, the UK, Singapore, and Israel just to stop by for a couple of hours.

Visiting a sponsor's office might be time-consuming and expensive, and with today's technology it might not even seem necessary. But there is no substitute for a personal connection, and touching and feeling the core of the firm by seeing the operation for yourself.

The Team

Investing in syndications is a great way for the individual investor to invest in real estate without the hassle of real estate ownership. But syndicating the deals is anything but an individual venture. It requires an entire team. The smallest of shops have a team, even if that simply means that they have developed a network of outside consultants. One person simply can't run the business entirely on their own.

Understanding the composition of a syndicator's team, both internal and external, is important because not all syndicators are created equal. Some have every angle covered by a core group of highly experienced executives while others have assembled a loose-knit compilation of "partners" and "advisors," who may or may not have a true stake in the outcome.

Quite frankly, there is no element of this business that has a greater impact on the outcome than the team. So much so, in fact, that the rest of this section is dedicated to various aspects of making a thorough evaluation of the team that you are considering partnering with.

Structure

How is the company structured? Is it a company at all? Yes, there are individual syndicators out there. I'm sure some are very successful; they just never found the need to create a cohesive team and a brand. But the most active groups know that having a solid management team, as well as a brand, is vitally important for long-term success.

You'll also find syndicators that operate with various joint venture partners or a "student army" consisting of beginners that the syndicator "mentors." They partner with whoever brings the next deal or whoever brings them investors. Each deal might have a variety of different players in the game. There is a lack of focus as a team, and no individual has a stake in the global outcome.

Roles and Responsibilities

The various team members should have defined roles and responsibilities. It's not unusual for team members to take on more than one role or responsibility, but there should be some order to the chaos so that things don't slip through the cracks.

Examples of roles are acquisitions, due diligence, equity and debt structuring, entity and transaction legal, insurance, accounting, asset management, property management, investor relations, investor reporting, and tax matters. In your conversations with sponsors, try to find out how they have delegated their roles and who is responsible for the various areas. Confirm that their plan is well thought out and well designed. Watch out for groups that haven't defined the roles yet, or don't even seem to be aware of the various roles and tasks that will be expected of them. That's a clear sign of lack of experience.

Debt Guarantors

The sponsor is required to provide their lender certain types of guarantees. I'll cover the various types of debt and guarantees in more detail in a later chapter, but no matter what type of loan the partnership is using, there will be some sort of guarantee required by the lender.

The lender will want to know that there is some enforceability to the guarantees, so they underwrite the sponsor to determine if they have the strength to make the guarantees worth something. Typical requirements are for the sponsor to prove that they have some cash in the bank, some net worth, and relevant experience in the type, size, and location of the property being acquired. How much cash and how much net worth varies from lender to lender.

For example, some lenders require the sponsor to have a net worth equal to the loan amount and liquidity of six months of payments on the loan. Other lenders might require a net worth of 50 percent of the loan amount and liquidity of 10 percent of the loan amount. While the amounts of each vary, one thing is fairly common, and that is meeting the threshold is typically cumulative. In other words, if there are three principals of the sponsor firm, the combined net worth and liquidity of all the partners can be counted.

A good question to ask as you interview sponsors is who is providing the loan guarantee. Oftentimes newer sponsors have little to no liquidity and net worth of their own, so they "hire out" the loan guarantor. That means the sponsor might provide a split of the sponsor fees or a piece of the profit split to a wealthy person who is willing to sign on as a loan guarantor in exchange for compensation. This can be concerning on a couple of levels.

First, if the sponsor hasn't had the success to build up their own capital and net worth, that doesn't provide much assurance that they have the experience to oversee the investment you are about to make with them. Certainly there are exceptions, so if the sponsor lacks their own ability to guarantee the loan you should dig deeper to understand why, and then decide if you are comfortable enough with the answer before investing.

Second, if the sponsor's principals aren't personally signing on the loan guarantees (and have the balance sheet to back it up), they really have no skin in the game. The threat of a lender coming down on them hard if they commit fraud, steal the capital improvement money, fail to pay the property taxes, or declare bankruptcy helps keep the sponsor on the straight and narrow. Shifting that risk to someone else gets the sponsor off the hook way too easily. That increases the risk profile of the investment, and you have to decide if that risk is within your tolerance limit.

If you are investing in a syndication, you have done well enough for yourself to build up the net worth and liquidity to allow you to make the investment. It makes sense that you would want to invest with people who have also done well for themselves and have something to lose if they screw up. Weak sponsors aren't good enough for the lenders to trust them, so it's quite likely that you shouldn't trust them either.

Tenure

How long has the team been together? The mere fact that a team was recently assembled doesn't mean that the investment is in peril, but it does add an additional layer of risk. New partnerships frequently fail, and you don't want to be caught up in a partnership dispute or left hanging if the partners don't get along and go their separate ways.

It's a good idea to ask about the length of the partnership and what plans they have in place should one or more partners break off. Who would be in charge of the assets? Who would fill the role of the departing partner? What would happen to your investment?

This is a significant concern. I've seen crowdfunding portals go out of business and had investors ask what happens to their investment in deals with the portal. It can be a real mess. But that mess would be so much worse if it was the operator that went out of business.

Character

The moral character of the sponsor and their principals is perhaps the most critical element in the success of any venture, especially if the going gets tough. Unfortunately, determining their character in advance is difficult. It's not as if you can ask them if they have good character. Of course they'll say yes, and the ones with the worst character would make every effort to be the most convincing. How many times have you heard the story of the innocent person being taken advantage of by someone they said seemed like a really nice, honest guy?

Still, figuring out their character is worth every bit of effort you put into it. How do you learn about the character of the sponsor? The best way I know of is to ask about a deal gone bad: their worst deal, one that failed to meet projections or presented an unusual challenge. You are *not* hoping to hear that this has never happened to them. Any investor that hasn't had a deal go sideways just hasn't been in the business long enough or done enough deals yet.

Instead of looking for perfection, what you are looking for is how they handled the situation. A person's real character isn't on display when everything is going according to plan; it's revealed when the going gets tough. If they brush you off on this topic, that's a big red flag.

Also ask about any criminal history. Sponsors are required to disclose felony convictions and misdemeanor convictions involving financial crimes, fraud, and securities violations. However, just because they are required to do so doesn't mean they will. People with a track record of breaking one law might be more inclined to break other laws, such as the ones requiring them to disclose that they broke laws!

You could order a background check on the sponsor from a private investigating firm or an online background-checking website, but this can get costly and is not at all common, although I know people who have done it. You might consider it if the answers you are getting don't convince you. Then again, if you don't like the answers, you should probably move on and look for other sponsors.

Another common method of learning about a sponsor's background is to do an online search on the company and the individuals. However, this might produce mixed results. Anyone can post pretty much anything online about whomever they wish, so you could turn up some inaccurate information or even information pertaining to unrelated individuals with similar or identical names. Plus, often these comments are without context. Consider the source, as they say.

Key Person Risk

Let's say that you invest in a syndication led by a one-person syndication shop, where the lone principal fills every role that we talked about earlier. After you make your investment, they suddenly die of a heart attack. Now what?

This is what is known as "key person risk." It is the risk you take when the success of the venture relies on just one person. It can also describe a less-extreme scenario, for example, when there are two principals but only one really knows what's going on. The second person is either not as involved or is unable to fill the shoes of the other partner.

Asking about key person risk is fair game. I've lost count of the number of times I've answered the "What happens if you get hit by a bus" question. I'm not sure why it's always a bus, but apparently that's the biggest risk to any businessperson's life. My advice to businesspeople everywhere is to look both ways before crossing the street.

I took in my first investor capital when I was in my twenties, and by the time I was 31, I had a living trust, a corporate structure, and a complete succession plan. I didn't know any other 31-year-olds who had this in place, but it was necessary because I had other people's money at stake. Be sure that your syndication sponsors have thought this through.

Having multiple experienced team members isn't good just for checking off the "experience" box—it's also good protection against buses. If a member of the sponsor team forgets to look both ways before crossing the street, the other team members can absorb the departed principal's role and keep the business plan moving.

Outside Consultants

A strong syndication team might also include a host of outside consultants. Examples are law firms, accounting firms, and property management firms. Some sponsors have brought these functions in-house by creating their own management companies to oversee property management functions, and employing lawyers to be in-house counsel or accountants to be chief financial officers and tax preparers. Other sponsors use independent firms for some or all of these functions.

In my opinion there are advantages to having third-party legal and accounting, as you can get the best talent at the lowest cost. Lawyers aren't cheap, and employing a great lawyer as in-house full-time counsel can be risky and expensive for a group that doesn't have the transaction volume to support it. Accounting tends to be a high-workload function around tax time and less so the rest of the year, so having an outside firm allows sponsors to leverage the resources of the firm without bulking up on staff.

Several years back, I was in a meeting with a large institutional investor, and one of the early questions they asked was, "Who is your law firm?" It might seem like a strange question, but I've actually been asked many times. There are a couple of reasons for this. One is that securities law is a small world. Some investors know a lot of securities lawyers, so they ask who you use to see if they know them. Other investors may have established a level of trust with some firms because they know those firms would work only with good clients.

Most important, you want to be sure that a sponsor has these resources in place. If they don't, you should think twice before investing. You might be surprised how many would-be syndicators have yet to establish relationships with their legal and accounting consultants. A lot of efficiencies are gained as these relationships mature, and you'll be the beneficiary of that. But if the group you are investing with is doing their first deal with their legal team, that legal bill will be a lot higher as the two parties get used to working together.

Investor Relations

Smaller and newer sponsors might have a single person performing virtually every function, all the way from sourcing real estate to underwriting, conducting due diligence, asset management, and, yes, investor relations. Larger shops tend to have a person or even an entire team dedicated solely to investor relations.

One approach isn't necessarily better than the other. A sponsor doing one deal per year doesn't need a lot of human resources, nor can they afford them. On the flip side, having a large team creates larger overhead, which means that the firm has to transact with some degree of regularity in order to keep the lights on.

As you study each sponsor, note whether they have someone dedicated to investor relations and what other roles that person might be fulfilling. If the firm seems to be doing any reasonable amount of volume, you'll want to see that they have someone dedicated to investor relations. Otherwise, investor communication could suffer and you could be left behind wondering what's going on or even who to ask.

In my view, the person overseeing investor relations is the glue that binds the sponsor-investor relationship. This person should be savvy enough in financial matters to answer your questions about the investment, the company, the real estate itself, the specific market, the general real estate and financial markets, and how they all relate to one another.

Oftentimes the person dedicated to investor relations isn't deep in the weeds of the acquisitions and operations side of the business, so they might not know every detail about the real estate or the business plan. They might not be familiar with every aspect of operations, such as the current occupancy of a specific property, either. But they *should* know where to find the information or who in the organization to ask, and respond to you with an answer in a reasonable period of time. If your questions go unanswered or you are ignored, that's a red flag. Remember that this person will be at their best *before* you invest. After you invest, their performance isn't likely to get better.

An introductory phone call allows the sponsor to get to know you, but it is also an opportunity for you to get to know them: to get your questions answered, gain assurance that you will be a valued investor, and learn whether the sponsor will treat your money as if it were their own (or even better). The sponsor should take their time, not rush you, and answer all your questions, making sure you understand everything. Any questions they can't answer right away should be answered either in a follow-up call or by email after the call concludes.

Part of this process is an evaluation of the sponsor's investor relations practices. Will they take care of you after you've invested? Will they answer your questions or concerns in a timely manner? All too often sponsors spend an enormous amount of time trying to attract investors and raise capital, and then neglect them. But quality sponsors know that open communication builds long-term relationships.

References

One way to learn about the sponsor's responsiveness after the investment is to talk to some of their other investors. If you were referred to a sponsor by a friend, this step might not be as important since your friend is probably the best reference you can get.

It's fair to ask the sponsor for references, current and even former investors whom you can chat with to learn more about how the sponsor performs and communicates. You could ask for references during the introductory call, but it's best to wait until later.

Instead, get through the first phone call. Review and digest any marketing materials, then make a follow-up call to get any remaining questions answered. Once you are fairly sure you want to invest with this sponsor, ask for references as a final step. This will not only save the firm's current investors a lot of time on the phone, it will increase the chances that the firm will actually provide the references. They might not agree to it too early in the relationship so as to avoid wasting their investors' time talking to prospects who are simply kicking tires.

When you contact a reference, here are some questions you should ask:

- How is the sponsor's reporting?
- How have investments performed against projections?
- How well does the sponsor communicate?
- Do you get your K-1 (tax information reporting document) in a timely manner?
- Have you ever had to file an extension on your tax return because you were waiting for the K-1?
- Has the sponsor failed to deliver on any promises?
- How does the sponsor handle unforeseen problems?
- Are you satisfied with the way the sponsor handles difficulties?
- Does the sponsor deliver just the good news, or do they share the bad news too?

Remember that these references will be selected by the sponsor. It's unlikely that they will put you in touch with anyone they know is dissatisfied. The reference might be their brother, best friend, mother, or who knows what. References are great, but they aren't the gold standard for judging the quality of a sponsor. If they were, this entire section of the book dedicated to selecting sponsors would be a heck of a lot shorter. Consider this portion of the evaluation as just one of the many steps in making an educated selection.

Experience Matters!

Lately, it seems like everybody is a syndicator: first-time real estate investors, newbies, people with little experience—they're everywhere. New syndicators aren't likely to have a brand or a track record. Does that mean you shouldn't invest with them?

Think of it this way: You are preparing to board a flight and you hand your boarding pass to the gate agent. The agent scans your boarding pass, the green light flashes, and the scanner beeps. Before you leave the counter, the gate agent says, "Just so you know, due to staffing shortages both pilots on today's flight are student pilots." Are you going to get on that plane? I'll put my money on no.

When I was in high school, my first career aspiration was to be an airline pilot, so I got a job bagging groceries and used my paycheck each week to pay for one flying lesson after school. The ink was barely dry on my driver's license by the time I got my pilot license. I then went on to complete ground school and pass all the written tests for an airline pilot license before I figured out that I didn't have the money to do the rest of the flight training. I moved on to figure out a different career path, and the rest is history.

Flying a two-seat single-engine airplane on a clear, sunny day isn't difficult. With about ten hours of instruction, my 16-year-old self was able to fly the plane all alone. After about sixty hours of flight training and solo practice, I completed all the flight training modules and passed a flight test with an examiner appointed by the federal government. Passing that test earned me a private pilot certificate. With that license I could fly anywhere I wanted and carry passengers. But I could fly only in clear weather, and I couldn't carry passengers for hire. Those activities would require more advanced training and more flight tests.

Eventually I earned my instrument rating. This was extremely difficult because for more than fifty hours I wore a device that restricted my ability to see out the window of the plane. All I could see were the instruments on the panel. The objective was to learn to fly and navigate only by reference to instruments so that I could fly in the clouds.

What does all this have to do with syndications? Nothing and everything! Just like a teenager with minimal training flying on a sunny day, a new real estate syndication sponsor can most likely navigate a real estate investment when everything is going well. Buying at the bottom of a market cycle, for example, can make even the worst real estate operators look brilliant when the market rises enough to cover their mistakes and deliver a profit for their investors.

As market cycles begin to mature, storm clouds form on the horizon, and you'd better be sure that the pilot of your syndication has the advanced training and skill to navigate those storms. Sponsors in over their heads will just fly you to the scene of the crash.

It's up to you to check a sponsor's qualifications and experience. Let's identify a few ways to do that. While you're at it, remember that real estate acquisition isn't the only skill you need to evaluate; you also need to investigate a sponsor's management and operational skills. The management team will be responsible for executing the longest portion of the business plan, so it's very important to understand their operational experience just as well as, if not even better than, you understand their acquisition experience.

Time. How long have the principals been investing in real estate and, more specifically, in the type of real estate being contemplated for syndication? How long have the management team members been managing similar properties?

Units. How many properties has the team acquired? If they are in the multifamily business, how many units have they acquired? How many do they currently own? If they are in the commercial property business, how many square feet or how many hotel rooms, self-storage units, etc., do they own? How many units has the management team managed, and are those properties similar to the ones being acquired by this sponsor?

Market. How long has the sponsor been in the geographical market? How many units have they owned and managed in that market?

Cycle experience. Has the sponsor survived previous adverse market cycles? How did things work out for them? How did they handle the situation? As of the time of this writing, it's been more than a decade since we last experienced a major down cycle, so any sponsor that has been in business for less than ten years has seen only an up market. They might think that markets only go up, or lack respect for what happens when they go down. They almost certainly don't know how to handle the storms. Key giveaways are sponsors who say things like, "Real estate always appreciates," "Rents only go up," and "People always need a place to live." Such statements show a lack of respect for adverse market cycles.

Syndication experience. How long have they been doing syndications? How many have they done? How much money have they raised? How have their previous deals performed? How have they performed as compared to projections? Why did underperforming deals underperform, what did they learn from that, and what did they change in response?

Assets under management. Known in the business as AUM, assets under management is usually expressed in dollars, and could be the value of the real estate a sponsor owns or the amount of investor capital they manage. Be sure to understand which it is if you ask about the firm's AUM.

Full cycles. How many investments have gone full-cycle (bought, managed, and sold)? How did those perform relative to their original projections? Be sure to compare actual performance against the performance the sponsor projected when the deal was marketed to investors, not a subsequently modified projection. Many newer sponsors haven't gone full-cycle with any of their acquisitions yet. Everyone has to start somewhere, and it's just part of their growth path, so there's nothing wrong with that. But should you invest your money with them? Maybe, maybe not. It depends on your tolerance for risk and your level of trust. No airline passenger would ever board a plane that hadn't proved in the real world that it can both take off *and* land. The only people allowed on untested aircraft are test pilots. Investing with an untested syndicator makes you a test pilot. There's nothing wrong with that as long as you're aware that's what you are signing up for and willing to accept the extra risk. Just don't confuse being a test pilot with being a fare-paying passenger flying on a fully tested plane.

Current portfolio. What does the sponsor's current portfolio look like? How many units do they have and where? What types of real estate make up their portfolio?

Historical portfolio. Have they made similar investments in the past? How many and where? How similar are the properties in their portfolio to the property they are buying now?

Focus. Do they specialize in one specific strategy, location, or product type? It's okay to mix these up to some extent, but too much variety can lead to distraction. For example, some groups might focus on value-add multifamily in several locations across the country. Others might focus only on one particular city but might do multifamily, retail, and self-storage, and are absolute experts in that local market. Those combinations aren't particularly worrisome. However, a small group that is both buying existing and building new multifamily, office, hotels, and industrial property in fifteen different states is cause for concern.

Capital calls. A capital call is when a syndicator asks their investors for more money after they have made their investment. You should ask your sponsors if they've ever had to make a capital call and why. Try to decipher if it was because the sponsor simply failed to raise enough money to begin with (a very common occurrence with inexperienced sponsors, and something that happens more often than it should with experienced sponsors that don't plan well) or if there was a market-based reason that was beyond the sponsor's control. You might also ask what the sponsor tried to do to remedy the situation prior to asking for more money from their investors.

Similarly, sometimes a sponsor has to raise more money from new investors, diluting the existing investors' stake, instead of making a capital call. The key here is to understand the circumstances so you can determine if this became necessary due to poor planning, inexperience, or reasons beyond the sponsor's control.

Relationships

While there are lots of reasons why investors invest in syndications, one I often hear is that they want to buy real estate directly but just can't compete in the marketplace against other buyers. It's a great reason, actually, and runs deeper than just not finding a property that meets their needs.

Buying larger properties, whether multifamily, office, industrial, retail, or any other type of specialty property, is a relationship business. Sellers want buyers who will close, and they'll be asking their broker to give an opinion on the strength of the buyer.

Brokers want to avoid the embarrassment of flaky buyers, false promises, and, worst of all, having deals fall apart. They like to transact with people they know or people who are known by people they know. If they are going to vouch for the buyer, they want to have some history to back that up. This is a leading reason why casual individual investors find themselves unable to compete in the marketplace. What do you gain, as a passive investor, if you partner with a syndication sponsor that doesn't have relationships in the market? Nothing.

Ask the sponsors you are interviewing how they source their acquisitions. They should be casting a wide net in the areas where they have an operational footprint. They should be looking at every marketed property and making offers—not because they expect to buy them all, but because they will be the first one in line if the high bidder backs out. They should also have a healthy pipeline of off-market acquisitions that are brought to them by brokers who have confidence that they are the best buyer.

Bonus points go to the sponsor groups that have relationships with other owners. Perhaps the group has a team member who had a previous job with a large owner, or was a broker in the past, or even a lender. Any position where they developed a contact list of other owners who will take their call qualifies. This could lead to principal-to-principal transactions that never hit the market.

Off-Market Acquisitions

Off-market deals are often mischaracterized as somehow better deals than marketed properties. While there are rare cases where this is true, to a much larger extent it just isn't so, especially in the multifamily space. The multifamily real estate market is remarkably efficient, with sophisticated buyers and sellers who know the drill.

The only way a seller will sell a property without exposing it to the market is if a buyer is willing to hit the seller's bogey. While this price might be slightly less than they might achieve if they had multiple bidders, it's not likely to be shockingly different.

Where off-market does offer an advantage is in the buying process, which can be better for the buyer. They might have a better chance of getting a longer escrow, smaller deposits, flexibility on the closing date, or other minor advantages because they aren't competing against a slew of other buyers.

Perhaps the biggest advantage to the buyer is the ability to maximize their hit rate. In marketed transactions it's not at all uncommon for disciplined buyers to look at 100 or more properties for every one they acquire, mostly because other buyers outbid them. But the hit rate on off-market deals can be much more favorable, perhaps as good as ten or twenty peeks for every buy. By the way, if the sponsor's hit rate is much higher than one for a hundred, there's a good chance they lack the discipline needed to be in the game for the long haul. They are most likely offering too much.

Debt Relationships

No discussion of relationships would be complete without discussing debt. Sponsors need to have relationships with lenders to get their purchases financed. It's fair game to ask how the sponsors source their debt and to inquire about their lending relationships.

If they are in the multifamily business, sponsors should have relationships not only with loan originators but with the government-sponsored enterprises (GSEs). The GSEs, known as Freddie Mac and Fannie Mae, finance more multifamily properties than anyone. You would think that the GSEs would be faceless organizations with no idea who their borrowers are. In fact, they are quite aware, and tend to favor borrowers that are already customers of theirs and have a track record with them. They also tend to disfavor making loans to inexperienced sponsors, so having GSE relationships should score points on your evaluation scale.

The quality of the sponsor's relationships is a by-product of the sponsor's reputation. For brokers, lenders, and sellers, reputation means a lot. Judging the sponsor's reputation isn't always easy, but if they have a lot of quality relationships, that's usually a good sign.

Capacity to Execute

As you begin looking at investment options from sponsors, there is still a bit more due diligence to perform that is somewhat deal-specific. Let's consider a few questions to ask yourself and ask the sponsor as you look at their offerings.

How likely is it that they'll be able to raise the money? A sponsor's track record of raising capital is a separate issue from their operational track record. Simply because they were successful raising money for a value-add multifamily deal just last month doesn't mean they can raise double that amount for the hotel deal they are doing now. Is this the largest raise they've ever done? Is this a large raise coming right off the heels of another large raise, indicating that their well might be running dry? Is this venture in line with their previous strategies? All these things can affect their ability to complete the current raise.

Who is putting up the deposits? To get to the closing table, a lot of money must change hands. Earnest money deposits must be held in escrow. Lenders require good-faith deposits to ensure that they don't get stuck with costs if the borrower bails out and goes with another lender. Due diligence inspections either need to be paid up front or lenders may require that the cost of these third-party reports be placed on deposit, so they don't get stuck with the costs if the purchase doesn't close. Lenders might also require up-front application fees. All these costs have to be paid before money is raised from the investors. So, who is paying them?

Sponsors can fund these costs themselves or they can borrow the money. It might be coming from you, the investor. Sometimes they'll have a "lead partner" who is an investor that gets some type of compensation for contributing the up-front money. There are even companies that specialize in providing gap funding for deposits for a fee. It's helpful to know where the money is coming from.

What happens if the sponsor can't raise the money or if they can't close the deal? What will they do if they raise only half the money and can't raise the other half? Do they have someone willing to contribute the difference so that the deal closes, and can they continue raising money until that lender is repaid? Can the sponsor delay the closing to allow more time to raise the rest of the capital, or will they have to cancel the deal?

If the sponsor has to cancel the deal, what happens to the money already raised? Do the investors get it back, or would it be held by the sponsor for the next offering? Or would the sponsor use it to pay for the cost of the failed deal?

Is there any risk of loss of any or all of your investment if the sponsor can't complete the fundraising? Who absorbs the costs that were paid for due diligence and other unrecoverable expenses?

Seek answers to all these questions so that you're aware of all the risks you are signing up for.

CHAPTER 4

THE PROCESS

Certainly the people in a syndication shop are important, but these operations require more than just people and networks. They require processes, including marketing, financial analysis, market research, due diligence, investor reporting, and property management, to name a few. Let's explore each of these.

At some point, either before or after your conversation with a sponsor, you should be provided some marketing materials. They could come in a variety of formats, either printed or, more commonly, electronic, such as PDFs. A good starting point is a corporate slide deck. This deck should talk about the sponsor firm itself and, most important, what makes them different from everybody else. You should find information about their experience, track record, strategy, target markets, strategic advantage, case studies, biographies of the principals, and, yes, what their "process" is and how it works.

Track Record

One key element to focus on when evaluating a sponsor is their track record. This could take many different forms, and the content could vary a lot depending on the firm's history. For a group that has fixed and flipped homes, the track record should show before-and-after pictures and some statistics like purchase price, sale price, renovation cost, other expenses, and profit, along with the amount of cash invested and the length of time from purchase to sale.

For firms in the commercial real estate field, a track record goes beyond before-and-after pictures, and raw purchase and sale price data. More important is the return generated. There are three primary measurements for return:

- Cash-on-cash return
- Internal rate of return
- Equity multiple

I'll cover each of these in more detail in chapter 9, focusing on evaluating investment performance. For now, suffice it to say that this is a complex topic, and you can't always compare different sponsors with the same yardstick.

For example, if a firm does lots of projects that require heavy renovation and are held for relatively short periods of time, judging them by the cash-on-cash return they generated isn't a fair comparison because most heavy renovations produce a limited amount of cash flow in the early period of the investment. Just because a sponsor has a track record full of low-cash-flow projects doesn't by itself mean that the sponsor is a bad operator. The data should be evaluated with some context.

On the other hand, an operator that purchases stabilized downtown luxury apartments might have a track record with a lot of low overall rates of return. When comparing them to an operator buying older apartment complexes in rough neighborhoods that are generating very high returns, you might think that the operator with the history of higher returns is a better operator if you grade by returns alone. But older properties in rough neighborhoods come with a much higher risk profile than downtown luxury properties, so the difference in return makes sense.

The key here is to apply context as you study each firm's track record. Easier said than done, to be sure, so this analysis is a bit subjective. However, what is not as subjective is the quantity of properties in their history, and how long they've been in the business and in any specific sector of the business.

Another thing to look for in a track record is full-cycle deals. These are deals that are completed, having gone from purchase to renovation to operation to sale. The investors have been paid, and the returns have been tallied. Such examples are much more meaningful than examples showing projected returns and expected exit dates. This doesn't mean that projections don't belong in the track record—they absolutely do, but often they might be the only deals in their history, and there are no full-cycle offerings to show proven performance. That's more concerning. The sponsor would be learning how to be a seller on your dime. Even more important, until they have successfully full-cycled, they are truly untested.

Another consideration is to look at the timing of the properties in their history. If they acquired property before a deep recession and sold it after the recession, a low rate of return or even a break-even might be an excellent outcome. During such times some sponsors lose properties to foreclosure or sell at a partial or even total loss. A positive outcome in the face of adversity shows strength and an ability to navigate challenges. These deals are truly far more meaningful than any string of high-returning investments in the midst of an up cycle. No one really learns much or demonstrates what they're made of when everything beyond their control is running perfectly.

Even some degree of failure in a sponsor's history can be a positive. Some sponsors suffered deeply in the great financial collapse of 2008. Their track records would look horrendous if you saw only what was on their books during that time. More telling is whether they learned anything from the experience. Some people completely change their game and apply everything they learned to avoid ever experiencing such pain again, while others are just destined to always be the one to buy at the top. Figuring out which of these describes the sponsor you are talking to is a bit of a challenge. If they speak as if everything is always rainbows and unicorns, that might be a red flag. However, if they sound more like Chicken Little, discussing their plans on how to prepare for the sky to fall, that might be a better sign.

Website

The sponsor should have a website that explains what they do and gives some background on the firm. Still, the information you find on their website might be somewhat limited. Thanks to the securities laws, many sponsors can't discuss their offerings on their websites, and have to be careful about posting too much about their investment returns. To get around this, they might talk about their assets under management, number of units, time in business, and so on, but not much more.

Websites are great for case studies because they allow the company to show multiple pictures of assets or even post a video, which can be more effective than printed slide decks. Some firms are even abandoning the printed or PDF slide deck entirely, using a "video slide deck" instead, which is simply a "live" version of similar content in a multimedia format.

Sample Offering Documents

Sponsors might also provide you with sample offering documents from a previous closed offering. It's a great idea to familiarize yourself with these offering documents, which typically consist of a sales package, private placement memorandum (PPM), subscription agreement, and operating agreement. You might have to request sample offering documents, since they might not be provided otherwise.

Keep in mind that the returns projected in previous offerings likely don't represent returns you should expect in future offerings, either because of timing (older offerings might have been initiated earlier in a market cycle) or structure (the fees and profit splits can vary from one offering to another). Nevertheless, the projected return isn't what you're looking for. Instead, you are looking for clues to their underwriting style, which we'll dive into in depth in later chapters, and the general quality and thoroughness of their materials. Do their documents provide enough detail for you to make an educated decision, or are details kept vague or hidden, or do they appear intentionally confusing?

Summary

You want to partner with a firm that presents itself professionally, because that approach should pervade every aspect of their business. If their written materials are littered with grammatical and spelling errors, you can only imagine how such a lack of attention to detail will find its way into everything they do. These written materials are meant for the eyes of prospective clients who haven't yet invested. If ever there was a time for a firm to put its best foot forward, this would be it. If they fail here, they fail everywhere.

Going one step deeper, look for consistency in the way their information is presented. Does the slide deck contradict their website? Do they have a consistent color theme and branding? A professional logo? Is the content easy to understand? Is it written in a conversational style, or is it loaded with jargon and big words? Look for sponsors that offer professional marketing materials containing relevant information that assists you in making your decision, not those with sloppy materials that look like they were thrown together in a hurry with little thought.

Financial Analysis

Back to the flight analogies: It's been a long trip from one side of the country to the other—storms along the mountains, some spots of heavy rain, but finally you're almost home. You are comfortably buckled into your seat and ready for landing. You feel the plane slowing down and then a light touch followed by smooth brakes. You think to yourself, "This is a great pilot!"—never mind the skill required to navigate storms and find the way from one side of the country to the other. Nope. You grade the skill of the pilot entirely on the landing. We've all done it. But even the best pilots have bad landings, and the worst ones get lucky occasionally and grease it on.

Why should it be any different when evaluating an investment partner? You could judge their skill based solely on one factor, such as their website, shiny brochure, great podcast, or the number of units in their portfolio. But grading a sponsor on the obvious stuff is about as useful as grading a pilot only on the landing. Of course, grading on a multitude of factors is hard; I get that. It's much easier to grade based solely on one thing. If you are going to grade the quality of a sponsor on only one thing, that should be the quality of their financial analysis, or what we in the business call "underwriting." But what is underwriting?

Underwriting is financial modeling that should accomplish three objectives. First is to decide at what price a contemplated acquisition makes sense. Second is to make performance projections to show the income, expenses, and cash flow a property is expected to produce, and determine the cost of capital improvements and financing. Third, proper underwriting should reveal how much debt can be obtained and how much equity capital is needed, and calculate various performance indicators.

If that sounds like a lot, it is. Underwriting is the foundation upon which every investment is built and is the source of many mistakes that can adversely affect outcome. At the very least, flawed underwriting can raise improper expectations among investors.

Every sponsor you talk to will say the same thing about underwriting: "We underwrite conservatively." But what does that mean? And do they really? And would an inexperienced sponsor even know if they were being conservative? Underwriting should be methodical and factual, not emotional. How do you know if it is? Look for clues in the way the sponsor talks about the deal. If they talk about how great the property is and how excited they are to get this deal, that's probably normal. But if they go too far overboard in gushing about the deal, that could be a clue that they have become emotionally attached to it. Becoming emotionally attached can cause sponsors to tweak the numbers to make the deal work. I call this "underwriting the performance to the price." Instead, sponsors should be underwriting the price to the performance.

What that means is that factual and reasonable numbers go into the underwriting model (which is a spreadsheet or series of spreadsheets), along with conservative assumptions. From that information the sponsor should be able to determine what price they can pay for the property and deliver the performance that their investors are seeking. Underwriting the performance to the price, on the other hand, means that the sponsor has been told what price they must pay in order to get the deal, and then alters the assumptions in their model until they are able to show the performance their investors want. However, they'll ultimately have a hard time delivering that performance if the assumptions are too aggressive. Real estate already has a favorable risk-return profile; there is no need to stretch. If a deal doesn't work, sponsors should move on to the next one. But they don't always do so.

As sponsors underwrite, they should be placing a priority on capital preservation. In other words, their top priority should be to *not lose your money*! This means that they need a healthy margin between the property's expected performance and the ability to service the debt and expenses. Paying too high a price or miscalculating the projected income can cause the investment to plummet underwater.

Here are some common weaknesses in underwriting to look out for. Later I'll go into detail on each of these weaknesses, so if some of these terms are not familiar to you, they will be soon.

- Improper economic vacancy assumptions
- Aggressive year-one gross receipts projections (that is, immediately jumping the income to new rents with no phase-in, which is simply impossible)

- Underestimated expense assumptions
- Improper use of cap rates and/or incorrect exit cap rate assumptions
- Failure to properly account for property tax reassessment post-sale (in states that do this)
- Basing exit prices on capitalized value of the income without accounting for the subsequent owner's property tax reassessment
- Failure to account for all of the costs incurred in putting together this type of deal and purchasing real estate of this size
- Failure to raise enough money to pay the down payment, closing costs, finance costs, syndication costs, and immediate capital improvements, and still have enough money left over for capital reserves
- Incorrect calculations of income, cash flow, cash-on-cash return, and internal rate of return, and/or a clear lack of understanding of those calculations and how to use them
- Lack of waterfall calculations (chapter 16 is dedicated to this)
- Internal rates of return and cash-on-cash returns that are inflated because the sponsor isn't raising enough money

Due Diligence Procedures

You've already learned the importance of doing due diligence on sponsors, and in a later chapter we are going to talk about performing due diligence on offerings that you are considering for investment. But what about the sponsor's practices of performing due diligence on their acquisitions? You wouldn't be wrong if you said that the sponsors are responsible for performing this function. Still, you should discuss their practices and learn what they do and how they do it.

One of my early multifamily acquisitions was a distressed 60-unit property in Texas. I was trying to figure out how the property had landed in such condition, given that it was located in a strong market and it seemed to me that the rents should certainly provide adequate income to keep the owner out of trouble. Yet the property was in foreclosure. How could that be?

I learned one of the reasons: The owner had looked inside only a few units when he made his purchase offer, and he never went back to dig any deeper. Of course, the units the seller showed him were in good condition, and he simply assumed that they all were.

After closing escrow, he discovered that there were several down units, and some of those units required tens of thousands of dollars to bring them back to rentable condition. Perhaps he could have sued the seller for non-disclosure, but in the world of commercial real estate it's up to each buyer to conduct thorough due diligence and discover the property's deficiencies. And finding units that aren't in rentable condition is grade-school stuff.

In this case, the buyer didn't have enough money to bring all the units back online. So he prioritized, doing a lot of work around the property and bringing the easiest units back online over time. However, this stripped him of cash, and the income from the property suffered because of the unrentable units. Then the city code enforcement officials came down on him for the substandard condition of the property. The walls were closing in on him from two different directions until ultimately he defaulted on his loan.

The solution to his problem was actually very simple. Most purchase contracts are written with a "due diligence contingency period." This is a period of time, usually twenty-one to forty-five days, when the buyer has the opportunity to inspect every aspect of the property. What this aspiring owner should have done to ensure the condition of the units was to physically inspect every unit during this contingency period. Yes, every unit! If deficiencies are found, the buyer can ask the seller for a credit against the purchase price or a purchase price reduction, or request that the seller repair the deficiencies. But after the closing is too late.

This is why it's so important to understand the due diligence process that your sponsors perform when acquiring properties that will be included in their future investment offerings. Ask them about their procedures. Here are the things they should be looking at.

Interior inspection. The sponsor should be walking every unit. This doesn't have to be a proctology exam—just a quick walk-through is enough. They should be able to complete each walk-through in under five minutes per unit. Most operators send teams out to do unit walks and have enough staff to walk all units in less than one day, even for large properties. Sometimes larger properties, such as those over three hundred units, are covered over two days. Teams should be looking for down units and grading the general condition of the units, including the finishes, cabinetry, counters, appliances, and fixtures.

Lease file audit. The sponsor should also complete a lease file audit.

The auditor should compare the data on the rent roll (lease start and end dates, move-in dates, rent amount, concessions, security deposits, extra charges such as pet fees) to the actual written leases. They should also note where each resident is employed, whether they receive any rental assistance, the amount of their income, and if they were properly screened for credit and criminal history.

Maintenance record audit. The sponsor should audit the maintenance records. This review can reveal hidden defects or recurring problems in addition to how well the staff is responding to residents' maintenance requests. Failure to address maintenance items in a timely manner is a clue to mismanagement, and might also indicate whether keeping the existing staff makes sense.

Staff interview. The sponsor should interview the staff. This is not an employment interview, although it can serve as one to some extent, but an opportunity to learn more about the property and the market. It's likely that no one, including the owner, knows more about the property and the competition than the people who work there every day.

Component and systems inspections. The sponsor should inspect the structural components of the building, such as the siding, decks, and roofs, as well as the mechanical systems, such has heating, air conditioning, and boilers. They should also inspect the common areas, such as the landscaping, pool, clubhouse, maintenance shop, and parking lot, looking for defects and estimating the costs to remedy them.

Multiple property visits. The sponsor should visit the property at multiple times of the day, including at night. Is the parking lot full of cars and people hanging around all day during working hours? Are there crowded, loud parties at night?

Crime inquiry. Many sponsors do a crime study, which could range from data searches to visits to the police department and speaking with beat officers. This inquiry can vary widely depending on the level of cooperation from local law enforcement and whether they report their data to any of the commercial crime data websites.

Third-party reports. The sponsor's lender should be arranging for third-party inspection reports. These reports include a zoning study, environmental inspection, property condition report, and appraisal. The willingness of the lenders to share these reports with the sponsor varies from one lender to another. Some will release the entire report while others will only release relevant excerpts. In either case, the reports should uncover issues with the property that might not be readily visible during the sponsor's cursory inspection.

Investor Reporting

When you make your investment, you'll probably do so with some objectives in mind. Perhaps it's income, so you have certain cash-on-cash yield expectations. Or perhaps it's growth, so you have expectations for price inflation and an overall internal rate of return (IRR) or annualized return.

Along the journey you'll want to have some idea whether your expectations are being met. Is the plan on track? Are there challenges along the way? When reporting is done properly, that's how you'll find all this information.

Reporting for your stock investments comes every few seconds; you can just watch the ticker and see how you are doing. But what about your syndicated real estate investments? There is no ticker; instead, you are at the mercy of the sponsor to show you the numbers and tell you how things are going.

That seems easy enough, right? Not so fast. Just as every real estate transaction is unique, every sponsor is unique and has their own style of reporting. There is no universal standard. If the sponsor's reporting is inaccurate or incomplete, the measurement of performance becomes difficult and sometimes impossible.

Ask for Samples

If you are the type of person who would rather not watch, then perhaps reporting isn't important to you. But if you want to know how things are going, reporting more than matters: It's critical. Your first line of defense begins long before you decide to make your investment. During your due diligence examination of your new potential syndication partner, you should ask questions about their reporting. In fact, you should go a step further and ask for a sample report from another active offering. The objective isn't really to judge how well their other investment is performing, because they are unlikely to send you a report from an underperforming investment. Instead, the objective is to see what their reports look like. What data do they provide? How do they talk about the progress of the business plan? And most important, how complete and useful are the reports? You will likely receive a report after you make your investment, so you want to make sure the report will give you what you need.

Reporting Quality

Poor-quality quarterly reporting is one of the top complaints I hear from investors in syndications. I hear all sorts of stories about lack of content, meaningless or useless data, and no description about whether the investment is tracking according to plan or is suffering.

You might wonder how sponsors who are responsible for millions of dollars of other people's money could fail at reporting. The answer is quite simple: Most sponsors were real estate investors first and money managers second. Maybe they never really grasped the money manager concept; instead, they remain real estate investors first, second, and last. Investor relations, accounting, and reporting simply weren't part of the real estate investor's skill set, nor their focus. Some just never get good at it. In talking with people who invest with multiple sponsors, I've found that inadequate reporting is one of the most vexing problems with investing in syndicated real estate offerings.

What to Look for in an Investor Report

Now that you've asked the sponsor for some sample reports, let's examine what to look for. First, the reports should be clear, concise, and informative. The overall takeaway after reviewing the reports is that you should know whether things are going according to plan. If they aren't, you should know what the sponsor is doing about it. You should have some idea whether the next quarter's performance is expected to be materially different.

Reports should be frequent—quarterly is the industry standard. The production of the reports shouldn't take more than forty-five days from the close of the calendar quarter. The reports should contain a brief and informative narrative describing things that matter. A narrative full of "We replaced four air conditioners this quarter" or other non-relevant operational anecdotes doesn't tell you how the investment is performing. Instead, it just highlights that the sponsor is focused only on the real estate and is oblivious to the investors' concerns.

The narrative should describe relevant points, for example, "Occupancy increased to the highest level in three quarters and net operating income rose $10,000 over the previous quarter." You want to see that the sponsor is willing to deliver the bad news, not just the good. If occupancy is falling and delinquencies are rising, the sponsor shouldn't be telling investors that everything is going according to plan. If performance has been suffering for so long that distributions to investors stop, this shouldn't be a complete surprise. Investors should have known that things were sliding because the sponsor should have been telling them.

Performance Comparisons

The reports should show the amount of your contributed capital and any distributions that were made during the period, along with inception-to-date contributions and distributions. Most important, there should be some reference to actual versus expected performance.

Operators and property managers revise their expectations each year by creating annual budgets. Watch out for comparisons between actual performance and annual budgets. The trick here is that they can revise down the expected income in the budget, then report performance that is exceeding expectations because it is above the budget.

But you didn't see this budget when you made your investment. You couldn't have, because it hadn't been created yet, although you did see the sponsor's original projections. You made your investment decision based on those projections. Your performance reports should be showing you how the investment is performing relative to the data that you used to make your investment decision—the sponsor's original projection.

Transparency

Reports should be transparent. In other words, the information you are looking for should be easy to find—not hidden. In addition to the narrative and the performance comparison, reports should typically include a balance sheet and income statement. If the investment is a fund that will own several properties, you should be able to see property-level data, not just fund-level data. Grouping all properties together can hide poorly performing properties. Unfortunately, not all fund sponsors show you property-level detail, and some have so many properties that you'll see only the highlights, so be sure to ask ahead of time.

Reports should be easy to access. Many sponsors have online portals, where your reports are delivered to you via email instantly, and you also have the ability to log in and view all your historical reports. The best portals allow you to see all your investments with the sponsor, archive all your reports, and drill down to each investment, and view all your contributions and distributions. In some cases they will show the total amount of capital invested by all investors and show your ownership percentage. They might even have some details about the property itself and the debt on the property. These portals are fantastic tools for reporting transparency.

Audited Financials

Some investors like to see audited financials. These are financial reports such as a balance sheet and income statement that have been audited by an outside accounting firm. This is common with publicly traded companies and REITS. However, most syndication sponsors do not have their financials audited. Financial audits can cost many thousands of dollars and are cost-prohibitive for small real estate syndications, so you are unlikely to see them from most sponsors. Having confidence in their accounting practices is critical. Ask questions about their accounting methods, such as who is performing this function and what accounting experience they possess, and ask specifically about their accounting experience in real estate operations.

Tax Reporting

Sponsors are not only responsible for producing quarterly reports that serve as progress updates. They are also responsible for completing the partnership's income tax return, and then providing the proper tax forms to investors. Unfortunately, they don't always do this as fast as you'd like.

Most syndication investments are structured as limited liability companies (LLCs) or limited partnerships (LPs). The income resulting from LLCs and LPs flows through the entity and is taxed to each partner and investor, and is ultimately reported on the investor's individual tax return. This means that in order for you to complete your tax return, you must first know the income derived from your investment in the syndication. This isn't as simple as getting a 1099 by the end of January, as is the case with an investment in a money market account.

First, the sponsor must complete the partnership's tax return. As with any tax return, there are a lot of forms attached. One of those forms is the Schedule K-1, or just K-1, which is an IRS form used for reporting each partner's income from pass-through entities. There is one Schedule K-1 for each investor in the partnership. Because this is a schedule to the partnership's tax return, the entire partnership's tax return must be completed before a K-1 can be issued. Sponsors must scramble to get partnership returns completed, which can be a challenge, especially with complex corporate and operational structures. Once their return is complete, the sponsors of your syndication investments will be sending you your K-1, which provides your tax preparer all the information necessary for them to complete your personal tax return.

Unlike bank 1099s, there is no legal deadline for sending K-1s to investors. But there is a practical deadline: Partnership tax returns must be filed by March 15, and because K-1s are part of the partnership's tax return, sponsors could deliver the K-1s within a few days after the return is filed. However, the sponsor can also file for an automatic extension, which extends the filing deadline for the partnership's tax return to September 15. If they file for an extension, you might not get your K-1 until shortly after September 15.

Some sponsors are better than others when it comes to delivering K-1s. I've heard plenty of horror stories from investors who barely received their K-1s in time to file by the extension deadline in October! If sponsors really have their act together, they can often deliver their K-1s by the end or even the middle of March, which should allow you to have your return prepared in time to file by the deadline without an extension. This is not only great practice on the part of the sponsor, but great customer service. It's frustrating for investors to have to file for an extension because their syndication sponsor is late at issuing K-1s. When doing your due diligence on a sponsor, ask when they typically deliver their K-1s to their investors, and whether their investors have ever had to file for an extension because they were waiting for their K-1.

If you are invested in a fund that invests in offerings with other operating partners, there can be delays in getting your K-1 because first the operating partner must issue a K-1 to the fund, then the fund must complete its tax return and issue its K-1s to investors. If the operator is slow to issue K-1s to the fund and the fund is slow to issue its K-1s, your wait could extend beyond the extended tax filing deadline of October 15.

Sponsors should have an internal as well as an external accounting team. If the internal team is doing a good job, the external accounting team's job is far easier and much more efficient. It is typically the external accounting team's job to prepare the tax return and K-1s. If they aren't efficient at doing so, this could be a clue that the sponsor's internal accounting practices are lacking.

The bottom line is that, thanks to the legwork that has to occur before a K-1 can be generated, your K-1 is likely to be the very last item you receive prior to meeting with your tax preparer. This also means that an unfortunate by-product of investing in private offerings is that you may have to file for automatic filing extensions. Be sure to talk about K-1 delivery times before making your investment so you can set your expectations accordingly. Picking sponsors with a track record of early K-1 delivery can help you avoid tax filing extensions.

Property and Asset Management

Property management and asset management are two distinct roles. There are multiple ways to structure them and accomplish their tasks.

In a typical transaction, anywhere from days to weeks to months are spent trying to locate, underwrite, negotiate, and close on an acquisition. Once acquired, the property could be held anywhere from a number of years to decades. It's fair to say that the operational phase is far more important than the acquisition phase.

This doesn't mean that the acquisition phase is unimportant. The quality of the purchase is the foundation upon which the operational phase is built, so without a well-executed purchase, the plan is doomed from the outset. As the saying goes, you make your money when you buy, and while there is some truth to that, it could also be said that you can lose it while you hold. Let's discover the various ways sponsors tackle the challenge of property and asset management, the differences between the two, and what you should be looking for when interviewing sponsors.

Property Management

Property management is the process of tending to the day-to-day needs of a piece of real estate. This function is very hands-on and includes every aspect of property-level needs. Typical duties include marketing the property to prospective new residents, screening prospective residents, entering into leases, collecting rent payments, enforcing the rules, and maintaining the property and the grounds.

In addition to the mechanical aspects of overseeing the property, property management entails a high degree of administrative functions. These include conducting market surveys, receiving and categorizing invoices, processing invoice payments, hiring and supervising property staff, creating budgets, property-level accounting, and producing reports for the owner.

Syndication sponsors address property management in one of two ways: They hire a third-party management company or manage the property themselves.

There are advantages and disadvantages to each method:

THIRD-PARTY MANAGEMENT		SELF-MANAGEMENT	
Pros	Cons	Pros	Cons
Can select the top management company in the area	Lack of control	Sponsor has full control of the process	Lack of scale in geographical regions where they have few properties
Local market experts	Lack of integration of systems across multiple properties or regions	Complete integration across properties and regions	Less intimate knowledge of competitor properties
Can fire them if they do a bad job	No significant vested interest in the overall outcome	Significant vested interest in the overall outcome	Sponsors are unlikely to fire themselves if they are doing a bad job

Property management can be one of the most difficult businesses in the real estate industry. The nuances of managing both staff and residents—coupled with the challenges of maintaining occupancy, collections, and revenue, and containing expenses—make it an art form. These elements can easily overwhelm an inexperienced operator. In property management, experience isn't just desired, it's critical.

As you interview sponsors, it's important to understand not only how they will manage the real estate (third-party versus self-management) but who, specifically, will be in charge of this function. Who is the leader of the team, and what experience does this person have? What is the experience of the team as a whole? What is their experience in this area?

Experience has two components here: how long the managers have been in the business of managing real estate, and how many units or types of properties they have (meaning how many they have managed in the past, how many they currently manage, and how many of those are in proximity to the assets they are acquiring now).

Not all experience is created alike. A management company that specializes in apartments might be completely at a loss when managing an office building or retail strip center. Some managers have extensive experience managing Class A assets and do a fantastic job of it, but put them in charge of a Class D property and all hell breaks loose. Experience managing properties similar to the contemplated investment does matter, as does property size. Managers who specialize in 200-unit properties might struggle with managing a 50-unit property and vice versa. Most management companies and management executives have a sweet spot. Find out what it is as you are researching the company.

Property management is a hands-on function that requires adequate human resources. The proper amount of staff must be put in place: too few and the property will suffer, too many and the income will suffer. For multifamily properties, each property will need a minimum of two employees: a manager and a maintenance technician. As the size of the property increases, more staff needs to be put in place. This would include an assistant manager, leasing agents, assistant maintenance technicians, porters, and groundskeepers.

The business is also hands-on in dealing with residents. It isn't enough to just sign leases and collect rents. It is just as important to build a sense of community, give residents a sense of pride in where they live, and build relationships with property staff. These practices help build resident retention. Resident parties and functions, clubhouse gatherings, pool parties, neighborhood watch programs, and after-school programs all work to build relationships with residents. Good managers can also add value to their residents by offering bonuses such as financial education classes on how to improve their credit score or how to create a budget.

Other property types have unique management and staffing needs. Hotel properties are staffed by front-desk personnel, a night auditor, maintenance staff, housekeeping staff, and potentially concierges and shuttle bus operators. These properties are enormously complex to operate and specific experience is a must. On the other end of the spectrum, properties such as mobile-home parks and self-storage facilities might have just a single resident manager. Then there is the middle of the spectrum, such as office properties, which may have no staff at all, only part-time staff, or perhaps even full-time janitorial and maintenance staff. Some office properties go even further and have doormen and security in addition to the maintenance and janitorial staff.

Remote Management

Should operators invest only in the market where they are headquartered? Not at all. Many national operators do a fantastic job of operating their portfolios regardless of their corporate physical presence. To be fair, many are terrible operators too. The reality is that despite the hands-on nature of property management, it is entirely possible, and very common, to operate remotely.

This doesn't mean that a 300-unit garden apartment complex can have no leasing office and be run by the suits in the ivory tower five states away. But on-site staff can be supervised and all performance metrics monitored from anywhere if done correctly. As you are evaluating sponsors, it's a good idea to ask about their experience managing remotely and learn about their practices. Just because they are doing it doesn't mean they are doing it right.

Managing remotely requires robust systems, such as enterprise-grade property management software, remote-access video monitoring, integrated communication platforms, detailed reporting, and frequent travel for staff training and leadership.

Asset Management

If the property manager is the pilot, the asset manager is the air traffic controller. The asset manager sets the course, and the property manager executes the plan.

The asset manager's primary role is to maximize property value and investment returns. This means finding ways to reduce expenses and maximize revenue. It also means developing a capital improvement plan to improve the property and correct any physical deficiencies. The asset manager will work with the property manager to develop a budget, and ensure that the property manager and the staff stick to it. The asset manager would also be involved in insurance claims and reconstruction of the property in the event of severe damage resulting from fire, flood, wind, and such.

Imagine that you own a single-family rental home that is being managed by a property manager. As the owner you set the course for the property manager, monitor the manager's performance, and assist them in making major decisions, such as deciding when to refinance or sell. You are the asset manager.

Now let's assume that you sell the rental and invest the proceeds in a private offering that has acquired an apartment building. In this syndication there are twenty-five investors and one sponsor. The investors are the "owners" of the property, but it would be impractical for all the investors to oversee the property manager and dictate the strategy. What is needed is an asset manager, and generally the sponsor will fill this role.

In addition to overseeing the property manager, in the case of a syndication the asset manager performs additional functions that you as a rental home owner wouldn't have to. This includes things like investor accounting, making distributions to investors, verifying and comparing projected results to actual results, completing the entity tax return, and distributing tax reporting documents to investors. Besides performing accounting functions, the asset manager should also be involved in creating investor reports and communications.

SECTION III
EVALUATING REAL ESTATE

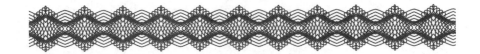

CHAPTER 5

REAL ESTATE BASICS

My friend Dan was a police officer and real estate investor. He would buy a house, move in, and start fixing it up—while living in it. It might take him two years, it might take him five, but when he was done the house would be amazing. Incredibly talented, he did all the work. But it would only be a matter of time, and usually not a lot, before he would put the house up for sale and then repeat the whole process on the next house. It did seem, however, that he kept each house a bit longer than the one before it, and he progressively stepped up to better houses and better neighborhoods. By the time he retired, he was able to buy his dream home. It was never his goal to be a landlord, yet he was still a bona fide real estate investor and it served him well.

My friend Bob was a radiologist and also a real estate investor. He owns a few rental homes but hasn't lived in any of them. He is hands-on with his rentals, often doing some of the repair work himself, collecting rent, and screening tenants. But that's not the only way he invests in real estate; he also buys farmland in Kansas and leases it out to farmers to grow crops. He is hands-on in the sense that he is involved in buying the property and depositing the checks, but aside from that the farmland is totally hands-off for him. The farmer does the farming and pays rent to Bob in exchange for using the land. Bob has an enviable income stream from residential and land rents, and a substantial net worth from the appreciated value of the properties.

My friend Isaac is a full-time active investor. He buys houses at foreclosure auctions on the courthouse steps, fixes them up, and sells them. He gets in and gets out. He also builds new homes and sells them, which supplements his fix-and-sell business for those times when it's too difficult to find houses at a discount.

The point is that there are a variety of ways to invest in real estate, a variety of desired outcomes, a variety of levels of involvement, and a variety of types of property to use to accomplish those outcomes. As you look at real estate syndications, it's important to remember that syndications don't have just one face either. They can take on many forms by investing in different sectors and with different strategies.

People often confuse sector and strategy. Just try asking a real estate investor what their strategy is and see if they get it all mixed up. They might say, "I invest in houses" or "I buy foreclosures." Neither is a strategy. The first is a sector; the second is a tactic. Let's clear up the confusion.

Real Estate Sectors

A sector is a type of property, sometimes also called an asset class. Dan, Bob, and Isaac invest in the single-family residential sector; some people invest in hotels or self-storage. All are examples of sectors or asset classes. When many people think about investing in syndications, often the first thing that comes to mind is large apartment buildings. That is one sector, and certainly a very common one, but it isn't the only sector that syndications operate in. Let's explore a few unique facts about various sectors.

Multifamily residential. Multifamily properties in a syndication need to be large enough to absorb the fixed costs of syndicating. This is more of a dollar-value threshold rather than a specific unit count, because values vary widely from one region to another. It might be common to syndicate one hundred units and larger in Texas, but in New York City you might see a syndication for a ten-unit building (and that building might be worth the same as a hundred units in Texas!). A fourplex in the Midwest is probably not large enough to support the costs of putting together a syndication offering.

Single-family residential. You won't typically see a single-house syndication. After being a predominantly mom-and-pop sector for most of modern history, single-family emerged into the limelight as a result of the residential real estate market collapse in 2005 to 2008. Large buyers came forward and bought up houses by the hundreds, many of which were syndication offerings. Now that pricing in the single-family market has returned to normal, you will likely see fewer syndication sponsors offering these opportunities, but they are still out there from time to time.

Office. Syndications in this sector might invest in anything from a single-tenant office all the way up to skyscrapers. Most commonly you'll see a neighborhood office, which is typically a multi-tenant building or small complex of buildings. Skyscrapers are more often owned by a REIT, although there are syndicate owners as well.

Industrial. There are a lot of subcategories of industrial property, including warehouses, manufacturing, distribution centers, and laboratories, among others. This sector is becoming more popular lately thanks to retail shifting to online retailers, who locate distribution centers in industrial areas and rely on shipping services that use industrial properties for sorting.

Retail. This sector includes single-tenant store buildings, neighborhood retail strip centers, large shopping malls, and everything in between. It's becoming more challenging due to online retailers taking market share from traditional shopping malls. Expect volatility here as consumer preferences shift.

Hospitality. Primarily hotels and resorts, syndications in this category could be anything from a single roadside motel all the way up to a portfolio of larger branded hotels. Expect some volatility here, since recessions that affect travel can cut a deep swath through hospitality revenue. But there can be a lot of value-add deals here as older hotels are upgraded or rebranded.

Self-storage. Considered by many to be recession-resistant, self-storage is a disposable necessity in the sense that people don't always need it but they want it. When the housing market suffers, people tend to move around, seeking smaller or cheaper homes, and use self-storage for items that don't fit in the new house. When the economy is going well, businesses expand and need space to store extra inventory, supplies, files, you name it. Storage is relatively efficient to build and operate, so many consider it to be a great alternative to residential syndications.

Mobile-home parks. These tend to represent affordability, and as a result they can continue to perform well even when other housing sectors are weak. Tenants tend to be sticky and income is steady because it's expensive to move a home from a park. (Just watch out for rent control, which can restrict the upside.) Although park expenses tend to be fairly low, when repairs are needed, they can be extremely expensive since the park's main responsibility is maintaining roads and underground utilities. Sometimes management rents the park-owned homes in addition to the spaces occupied by tenant-owned homes. Many investors find parks with park-owned homes to be less desirable because of the maintenance and upkeep costs on the homes, versus the simple and low-maintenance rental of only the spaces.

Land. You've probably heard the saying "Invest in land, because they ain't making any more of it." While that's true, land is the riskiest of all real estate sectors because it is at the mercy of markets, governments, federal and state agencies, and all sorts of other factors. Often there is no income to carry the investment, throw off a return, or reduce risk. Remember that raw land is valued by taking the value of whatever can be built on it and subtracting the cost to build whatever that is. As a result, land is one of the few real estate investments that can actually be worth less than zero. It can also represent an amazing opportunity if played right.

Specialty. This encompasses the "everything else" sectors: marinas, hospitals, parking lots/structures, stadiums, airports, transit centers. There are countless uses for real estate that present unique investment opportunities for those who have the right skill set and experience to navigate the idiosyncrasies of special-purpose real estate. If you are thinking of investing in these special-purpose sectors, consider sticking to those in which you have some experience of your own, such as medical offices or hospitals if you are a physician, or marinas if you are a boater. You should also consider investing smaller amounts in these sectors to spread out your risk. Going all-in on a special-purpose property could be disastrous if things go wrong. It's not as if there's an unlimited pool of potential buyers to take these off your hands.

Real Estate Strategies

When evaluating syndication sponsors, you should ask them about their strategy—not only because it's important to see if it's a good fit for you, but also to find out whether the sponsor can clearly articulate their own strategy, or even knows what their strategy really is. You'd be surprised how often they don't, and that's a big red flag. Let's talk about a few strategies.

Buy and hold. This is probably the most familiar because it's so time-tested and common: Buy a property, collect the checks, and hold for some period of time. Most syndication investments seek to hold for three to seven years, and occasionally for as long as ten or fifteen. Why such a short time? Three reasons, primarily. First, shorter terms tend to produce a higher return, especially in a value-add strategy (more on that in a moment). Second, investors want to know when they will get their money back. Most don't want to part with their money permanently, so having a defined investment period is more desirable than an open-ended one. And third, sponsors tend to receive the bulk of their income from the profits on the sale of the property, and sponsors want to get paid.

Buy and flip. If buy and hold wasn't the most familiar real estate investment strategy, buy and flip would be, thanks to all the TV flipping shows over the last decade or so. If you watch a lot of HGTV, you'll probably come to the conclusion that everyone is a house flipper. Flipping is easier said than done when there aren't many fixers on the market and you are competing against everyone who just watched a beginner make a killing on TV. But for those who are seasoned, this business can be sustainable in just about every point in a market cycle. Those with enough volume can syndicate the business with a *blind pool fund*. A blind pool fund is where investors invest in a single fund that purchases multiple properties over a period of time, and the properties to be purchased are not known at the time the investment is made.

Buy and watch. This one is my favorite, and not only because I invented the term but also because I think it works! The buy and watch strategy means you buy a property, renovate it, and add as much value as you possibly can. Then you watch the market for the most opportune time to exit. It might be as soon as the value-add improvements are complete, or it might be a year or even ten years later. The sooner you can exit, the better this works. But at least you have the flexibility to wait if conditions don't support an exit or if it looks like holding for longer will produce a lot of additional upside.

Development. Many consider this the riskiest real estate strategy out there. Development syndications are very common and can be very lucrative. They can also wipe out entire investments if they don't go according to plan. You might get a 100 percent annualized return, or you might suffer a 100 percent loss. Development projects can range from buying raw land and going through the entitlement process to obtain permits for a higher and better use, to buying already-entitled land and immediately beginning construction. Going straight to building is lower risk than entitlement projects, so consider these for your risk capital only, and commit only a small percentage of your overall investable assets.

The thing to remember about strategies is they can mix and match to sectors. In other words, you can buy and hold a mobile-home park, buy and flip a self-storage facility, and develop an apartment complex. When you ask a sponsor to tell you their strategy, "apartments" is the wrong answer. But if they say they develop apartments, they have articulated not only their strategy but their sector.

Sub-strategies

If sectors and strategies aren't enough variables, there are also sub-strategies. I call them sub-strategies because they also can be mixed and matched with strategies and sectors, creating a large number of potential combinations.

Core. Core assets are typically found in the urban core, but they might also be just outside the urban core and still be high-quality assets. For example, a high-rise in the central business district would be considered core, but a newer mid-rise ten miles outside of downtown could also be considered core. Core assets are favored by REITs and by syndication groups that have a fairly low cost of capital. In other words, the returns are typically lower than what more aggressive investors seek. But core assets are considered safe because they tend to be newer assets or very well located. On a risk-adjusted basis, the returns satisfy core investors because of the relative safety. These investors might brag to their friends about the trophy property they own a piece of, but they probably won't be bragging about their high returns. However, they probably sleep pretty well at night.

Core-plus. These assets aren't quite core, but they are close to it. These could include a newer property a bit farther out from downtown, or perhaps even in a secondary market. They could also include an older asset in the central business district that has some type of upside. Core-plus assets are a bit higher return than core. The risk profile is still very favorable but a notch higher than core. Investors in these assets might also brag about their property, but they won't be getting anybody too excited about their returns most of the time—unless, of course, the market gives them a major gift and they get a huge upside exit. This *can* happen, and it can be really exciting.

Value-add. This is probably the strategy most favored by many syndicators, for lots of valid reasons. Value-add means acquiring an asset and then making improvements, or adding value. Improvements could be as simple as implementing a proper marketing campaign to attract more prospects willing to pay higher rents, or changing management companies or on-site staff to better manage the property. The strategy could also mean making physical improvements, such as interior renovations and exterior improvements to enhance curb appeal and amenities. The best value-add opportunities encompass elements of all of these tactics. Value-add is higher risk than core and core-plus but is still a sound strategy when properly executed. The returns range from somewhat to considerably higher than core-plus.

Opportunistic. This sub-strategy implies a higher degree of risk and includes things like resurrecting partially completed development projects and deep value-add projects, such as mostly vacant properties and extreme repositioning projects. One thing to watch for is projects that are truly opportunistic being marketed as value-add, implying that the investment carries less risk than it actually does.

Subsidized housing. Why is this a strategy? Isn't it a property type or sub-type? Well, yes, but it is also a sub-strategy because there is a tactical play here. A subsidized housing property is typically an apartment complex that was built with tax credit money, special bond financing, or some other type of tax abatement or governmental assistance. This allows the developer to construct housing units that can be rented at a price that is below market and thus affordable to households meeting certain limited income thresholds. Without the subsidies, the costs to develop the property wouldn't allow it to be rented profitably at affordable rates.

There are two basic strategies with subsidized housing: one is to buy and hold; the other is to do a market-rate conversion. In a market-rate conversion, the property is converted from an income-restricted property to market-rate rents. When some subsidized properties are built or financed, there is a defined length of time during which the property must be rented to income-restricted residents. After that time frame the property can continue as it has, or it can go through a process to take it out of the program and rent the units at market rate. The strategy here is to acquire a property before the end of the income restrictions at a low price, convert the property to market rate, and then sell at a far higher price as a result of the substantially higher income. This complicated process can take a few years to complete, but when done properly, it can produce some pretty high returns.

Getting back to your interview with the sponsor, now when you ask about their strategy you'll know what they mean if they say they develop core office buildings, buy and hold core-plus apartments, or flip value-add mobile-home parks. Sectors, strategies, and sub-strategies create many options for you as an investor in syndications. You can invest in sponsors that are implementing the strategies you believe in, in the sectors you believe in. Just make sure that the sponsors can properly articulate their own business models; otherwise, you might not get the fit that you think you are getting.

Property Classes

If you haven't already, you will soon start seeing properties described by classes, using a scale from A to D. What do the classes mean? Which are best?

Class A properties. These are the highest-quality buildings in the most prime locations. As such, they command the highest rents. These properties are typically going to be in the best condition and have lower vacancy rates. They are seen as lower-risk steady workhorses for investors. Their premium ranking also means they are generally more expensive. The yields and cap rates are going to be lower than on other classes of property. They are more like a blue-chip stock. Their main risk factor is excessive new construction in the immediate area.

Lately, you may have even seen classes such as AAA or AAA+, which is really just marketing to differentiate the newest and best Class A properties. Maybe this is partly because the "lower tier" Class A properties really should be dropped to Class B.

Class B properties. These properties are the next step down from Class A. They are still in pretty good areas, but buildings are likely a little older and not as fancy, and rents may be a little lower. (Class A properties can fall to Class B through deferred maintenance and poor management.) Although Class B buildings may not be as prestigious as their A counterparts, they can often be brought up to A-class standards with retrofitting, new management, and better leasing, which can offer great value-add opportunities. They are still easy to finance and rent well, and they should deliver stable performance over the long term. Investors will often find that these properties offer better yield than Class A, albeit often with a higher-risk profile.

Class C properties. These properties are in less desirable areas than Class A and B. Buildings are normally at least thirty years old, and will generally benefit from significant updating and repairs. Rents will be lower, and vacancy rates may be slightly higher.

This all translates into lower acquisition prices, although these opportunities can deliver the best cash flow and returns if managed well. Over the long term they can grow in appeal and value very well. There is always a new neighborhood on the fringes that's the beneficiary of revitalization programs and dollars, and becomes the next trendy zone for artists and start-up businesses. Think of these as your Google or Uber stock when they started out, only with the advantage of brick-and-mortar security for your capital. One thing to watch for in real estate offerings is Class C properties being marketed as Class B, which is far more common than it should be.

Class D properties. Anything Class D and below is generally in a rougher neighborhood and needs a lot of work. We're talking aging buildings, often requiring substantial repairs or teardowns, and low rents, with crime being common. Vacancy and turnover rates can be high. Potential yields may be very appealing to offset the higher risk, but these properties will be management intensive. Class D properties are frequently represented as Class C in marketing brochures. Don't fall for it.

Spotting Property Classes

One way to identify property classes is by age. Older properties are often graded lower than newer properties. This test isn't absolute, but if you combine age with median income in the immediate area, you can zero in on the proper class. Newer properties in very-low-income areas are more likely to be Class B or C than Class A. Applying these tests will help you spot mis-classed properties in a sponsor's marketing. But remember, property classes are somewhat subjective and the lines are often blurry.

Markets

I'm often asked, "How's the real estate market these days?" The problem with this question is the word "the," as if there were such a thing as "the" real estate market! When it comes to real estate, every local area is a different market. Different states have different markets. Different counties have different markets, and different blocks have different markets. Real estate is a highly local business!

Many investors take the DIY approach to investing in real estate. This means they buy a property, manage it themselves, perhaps even to the point of fixing the toilets and collecting their own rents. For them, the expression "location, location, location" means buying the best property in the best neighborhood, or on the best block, or even on the best street corner. To make this work, they need to be within easy driving distance.

As a passive investor in real estate syndications, you have a lot more options. Because you aren't actively involved in the day-to-day operations of the property, you can literally invest anywhere. For you, "location, location, location" takes on a whole new meaning. Location can be anywhere in the world, anywhere in the country, anywhere in the state. There are no limits. But does this mean that where an investment is located doesn't matter? Hardly.

As it is true that each local market is different, so it is true that some markets have very favorable fundamentals. Others, not so much.

Markets Are Like Water

Imagine for a moment that you are camping in the remote wilderness— just you, your tent, and your rickety old raft. On one side of your campsite is a river; on the other side is a lake. At first the fish were biting but not anymore, so you realize that it's time to find a new camp. There are three other camps to choose from. All are two miles away but in three different directions: One camp is upstream on the river, the other is across the lake, and the third is downstream on the river. You board your trusty old raft to set sail for your new spot. But which spot did you choose?

If you answered, "Wherever the fish are biting," I like your thinking, but you don't know for sure which spot that is. The first option is across the lake. You board your raft and start paddling. Eventually you will get there, but if you get partway there and stop paddling, you stop moving. You aren't going anywhere unless you start paddling again. By the time you get there, you might not have much energy left to go fishing.

If you choose the upstream camp, you board your raft and start paddling. As you progress up the river the current gets a bit stronger, so you paddle harder. After a while you tire out and take a break for a few minutes. But the current is now taking you backward, farther away from your new camp. Maybe you have enough energy to actually make it all the way, or maybe you tire out before you ever get there and give up.

The third option is the camp downstream. You set your raft in the water, give yourself a few paddles to get going, and then sit back and let the current take you down the river. If you drift, give it a few paddles, maybe steer for a bit to get around a few tree stumps. You arrive at your destination in record time, all rested up to go fishing.

Selecting a market to invest in is a lot like picking your new camp. Some markets are simply stagnant; that is, rents aren't moving, occupancy isn't changing, and there's little job growth, no meaningful population growth, and no income growth. Such markets are like the campsite on the other side of the lake. You can make progress toward your goal, but every bit of it will require effort. If you stop making an effort, you stop making progress. You can be successful, but you'll be exhausted.

Then there are markets that are just going backward. Rents might be declining or vacancy rates rising. You might have negative population growth—more people are moving away than moving in. This could be because of lack of jobs, declining wages, or companies leaving town. Such markets are like the campsite upstream. Sure, you can get to where you're going, but you'll not only be exhausted, you'll be elated just to have actually made it. It will be a hard-fought battle, and if you ever look the other way you'll slide backward. The risk of failure, of not ever reaching your goal, is far greater than in any other market.

Finally, you have your emerging and growth markets. These are where jobs are expanding, incomes are growing, and people are moving in, not away. Such markets see high rent growth and high occupancy rates. They are like the downstream camp. You set the course and steer, and even without a ton of effort you can cover a massive distance. You'll have to steer around tree stumps and rocks while sailing downstream. In the context of a growth market this means that high rates of construction can cause inventory imbalances from the supply side, and you'll have to navigate that hazard. But you'll get to your goal, and it will take a lot more than just a little fatigue to cause you to fail.

The bottom line is that the market does matter. It is the environment you'll be operating in, and you need to know what that environment is like. As you evaluate potential syndication investments, your first questions should be about the market. As I said before, there is no such thing as "the" market, so as you consider your options you should be looking at the macro picture (the wide-angle-lens view) and the micro picture (the close-up view).

Top-Down Analysis

In stock investing there is a concept called "top-down analysis". Using this approach, you begin by looking at the big picture—how the overall economy drives the markets and stock prices. Next, you drill down to the performance of various industries and how that performance benefits from the big-picture factors. The theory is that if the industry is doing well, the stocks in that industry will also do well.

The top-down approach can also be applied to real estate by starting with a very wide view of the country as a whole. Which MSAs (metropolitan statistical areas, basically a fancy term for a metropolitan area) are growing? Which are stagnant? Which are declining? Find the growing markets, and narrow your focus on just those areas.

Next, examine the growing markets to locate which submarkets in the MSA are also growing. (Even a rapidly growing MSA can have a part of town that is declining.) This examination can continue to focus on smaller and smaller areas to home in on the best locations for investment. That said, most analyses don't have to be quite that specific. If you are Walmart looking to put in your next store, the specific block might make a tangible difference. If you are Starbucks, the side of the street might make or break you because you want to be on the side where morning traffic is flowing. But if you are buying apartments, the general area is usually specific enough.

The indicators to pay closest attention to are the "big three" of commercial real estate, especially commercial multifamily (large apartment complexes). These are job growth, income growth, and population growth. Each provides downstream current to the local economy and helps push you toward increasing revenues from your real estate investments. The big three support household formation, which is another important indicator of the health of residential real estate (and a topic we'll delve into shortly).

Supply-Side Risks

Growing markets also tend to breed development. This is healthy because a growing population places a demand on housing units, and as the population swells there will be a need for more housing. But sometimes developers get carried away, and overbuilding can become a serious problem. The problem is often mitigated by lenders, as they pull back availability of financing when overbuilding becomes concerning. This can result in a slowdown in construction.

Too much construction in the area can impact returns because it puts downward pressure on occupancy, rents, and income as the asset competes against newer projects. New projects frequently discount their rents as leasing begins in an effort to drive occupancy. These discounts cause prospects to choose the newer property because the rents aren't much higher than an older competitor's. This in turn causes the older property to offer rent concessions or lower rents in order to compete for prospects. Typically, this vicious cycle doesn't last long because once the competing property gets leased up, asking rents tend to rise. But if there are more new projects right behind the first one, this painful cycle can last a lot longer than anyone would like.

Investors often say things like, "I don't want to invest there because there is a lot of construction." What these investors are missing, however, is there are two sides to the construction story. If there is construction in a stagnant MSA, that's certainly a problem. But if there is construction in a rapidly growing MSA, where the population is increasing, that might not be a problem at all. In order to decide whether new construction is an issue, an analysis of the demand for new units is necessary. This will reveal another important indicator for commercial real estate: the construction/absorption ratio.

Construction/Absorption Ratio

This ratio is calculated by dividing the number of units built (construction) by the number of units leased (absorption), which provides a measurement of market equilibrium. Depending on the product type being evaluated, there are variations in how the construction/absorption ratio is composed. For example, construction and absorption could be expressed as the number of square feet in the case of commercial or industrial space, and absorption could be expressed as the number of units sold (instead of leased) in the case of for-sale housing.

The ratio is 1.0 when for every apartment built, one is leased, or when for every square foot of commercial space available, one square foot is leased. If 2,000 units were built and only 1,000 units were leased in a given time period, the construction/absorption ratio would be 2.0. If 1,000 units were built and 2,000 units were leased, the ratio would be 0.5. When this ratio climbs over 1.0 and stays there for a significant time, rents are likely to fall, concessions are likely to increase, and vacancies are likely to rise. If the ratio is above zero and below 1.0, more units are being rented than built. This leads to falling vacancy rates and ultimately supports rent growth.

If the ratio falls below zero, there is negative absorption. This means that vacancies are already rising. An example of a negative construction/absorption ratio would be if 1,000 units were built during the measurement period and there were 500 fewer occupied units at the end of the measurement period than at the beginning. Short periods of high (above 1.0) or negative construction/absorption ratios aren't fatal to a market, but the farther out of bounds the ratio is and the longer it persists, the more damaging it will be.

Details on the development pipeline and construction/absorption ratio can be found in various market reports available for free from large multifamily brokerage shops, or from paid independent market research firms such as REIS, Axiometrics, CoStar, Yardi Matrix, and others. Pipeline data and ratios can be found at the metro level and all the way down to the submarket level. Sponsors should be able to provide you with copies of this data upon request. If they are unable to provide it, you have to wonder if they even looked at the data themselves.

Development Is Submarket-Specific

Submarket reports are important because you can have a high construction/absorption ratio at the MSA level yet still have a submarket of that MSA with zero construction and positive absorption of in-place inventory. For that reason, it is important to understand the development landscape at the submarket level.

By way of example, I've bought a lot of apartments in MSAs with the highest levels of construction in the country, yet the submarkets where the properties were located had seen virtually no construction in several years and had no forecasted construction for the next two to three years. While understanding construction and absorption levels is very important, be sure to consider the complete picture before forming an opinion on how they will affect any particular investment.

"Everybody Needs a Place to Live" Is a Hoax

Let's dive deeper into household formation. A household is a group of people living together, and household formation means that a household has been created. In theory, you could have population growth without household formation. An example is when new births are creating population growth: Obviously the newborns aren't renting their own apartments. You can also have household formation without population growth, as when children become adults and move out on their own, or adult children that had once moved back home then move out again. Although population growth is important, household formation is even more important.

Back in the late 2000s the economy suffered a nearly unprecedented recession. During this recession many people were foreclosed out of homes and doubled up. Despite level or even rising populations, household formation was negative in a lot of markets, causing increasing vacancies, especially in single-family-home markets.

The next time you hear that owning apartments is the safest investment because "everybody needs a place to live," don't believe it! While it's true that everybody needs shelter, that doesn't mean it will be in your apartment unit. When the going gets tough, people absolutely will move in with family and friends, or relocate to cheaper areas.

Indicators to Watch

Beyond job, income, and population growth, the construction/absorption ratio, and space under construction as a percentage of inventory, there are other things to consider when evaluating a market.

Rent growth. Recent rent growth is considered by many to be the most important indicator. Keep in mind that recent high rent growth doesn't mean continued high rent growth. That doesn't make the statistic any less important, but it does expose its limitations. Reviewing forward-looking rent growth forecasts is very helpful but also has its limitations. Services that offer rent growth forecasts tend to cap their forecasts so that they aren't accused of overestimating. They also tend to avoid shooting too low so they don't risk alienating their paying client base, which is seeking third-party justification of their investment projections.

Market vacancy. Generally, markets with low vacancy rates hint at stronger fundamentals. Changes to vacancy rates can give some clues to future performance, assuming that increasing vacancies could lead to less rent growth and vice versa.

Long-term vacancy average. Looking at the average vacancy rate over an extended period, such as three to five years, gives you an idea on where to place vacancy rate assumptions when estimating the future income stream. If the sponsor is underwriting to a 3 percent vacancy factor and the long-term vacancy average is 10 percent, the sponsor is likely underestimating their vacancy rate, even if the market vacancy rate is currently at 3 percent. This is very common and is one of the ways that sponsors artificially inflate projected returns. Underwriting assumptions should be supported by a vacancy rate forecast by a third-party market research study. A good conservative practice is to model to future vacancy rates somewhere between the long-term average and the third-party vacancy rate forecast. This gives some downside protection if the forecast turns out to be wrong. Unless, of course, the vacancy rate forecast is higher than the long-term average. In that case, using the higher forecast number is appropriately conservative.

Adverse-cycle occupancy bottom. How low did occupancy go during the last adverse cycle? Or, stated the opposite way, how high did vacancy go? I wouldn't call this an underwriting guideline, but it does give some indication of how bad things can get. It would be interesting to apply this vacancy rate to the projected income and see if that throws the income below the break-even point. We'll cover this test more when we talk about secondary performance indicators in chapter 9 and performing a sensitivity analysis in chapter 14.

Median income. Most landlords apply an income standard of three times the rent (although in some markets it can be as high as four times). Comparing median household income to the forecasted rent can give clues as to how hard this property will be pushing the limit. It's important to remember, however, that median income means half the population earns less and half earns more. Just because the forecasted rents are above the one-third of median test doesn't mean that people can't afford to rent the units—it just means that half or more cannot. This might not be an issue if there is population growth in the area and higher-income arrivals are a major segment of the demand.

Employment base. Ideally you want to see a diversified employment base, which means that no particular employment sector exceeds 20 percent of the total employment base. It also means avoiding so-called one-horse towns, which have either one chief employer or one chief industry and little else. A great example would be Detroit, the once-growing "Motor City" that was home to a large concentration of automobile manufacturers. Structural changes in the auto industry led to the steady loss of manufacturing jobs over several decades, sending real estate into a tailspin.

Rent to cost of ownership. While not directly an indication of health, the comparison between the cost of renting versus the cost of owning can give clues to the stickiness of the tenant base. When the costs are close, you'll lose more tenants to homeownership than you would in a market where they are far apart. The cost of ownership can also give an indication of rent ceilings in the area.

Income to housing cost ratio. This ratio could also be described as rent as a percentage of household income, and it can vary widely. In many markets rents average 20 percent of income, while in some high-cost areas, like New York City, rents average more than 50 percent of income. The rental market in San Francisco is anything but weak, so a high percentage doesn't necessarily mean a bad rental market. But a low percentage does give the impression that rents have room to climb more than they could where the percentage is already high.

Market rankings. While not economic indicators, market rankings are useful because you can leverage the economic research of experts who interpret a multitude of economic indicators to rank markets in various ways. One of my favorites is the Milken Institute's annual *Best Performing Cities Index*.[3] This report produces rankings of the best-performing markets in the country for 200 major metros and 200 smaller metros. The rankings are based on the very economic indicators that are important to commercial real estate, including job growth, population growth, and income growth. The list also shows the biggest gaining and biggest falling markets, which tracks how many positions a market moved up or down from the previous year. Top markets and biggest gainers on the *Best Performing Cities Index* tend to be good markets for acquiring income-producing real estate.

PwC in cooperation with the Urban Land Institute has been publishing the annual *Emerging Trends in Real Estate*[4] report for more than forty years. This report gives some great information about various markets and ranks markets for various sectors of real estate. It's available for free online.

There are countless other lists with rankings based on various criteria. Some are more useful than others, but each tells a story. *Forbes* has produced lists of the most desirable cities to live in and the most

---

3 www.best-cities.org

4 www.pwc.com. In the search box, type "emerging trends in real estate," then look for the US and Canada report in the search results.

business-friendly states. Search online for "most desirable cities" or "business-friendly states" to find the latest information. Moving companies are also a great source for tracking migration trends. U-Haul[5] and Penske[6] truck rentals announce statistics each year ranking the cities with the highest one-way truck rentals, which is an interesting indicator of population movement.

Wrapping Up

No statistic stands on its own. All must be taken in context and used in conjunction with one another to measure the health of a market and forecast its potential. Be sure you are looking at statistics that are relevant to the property. Too often, sponsors will include market demographics in their packages for the metro market, but the property being acquired is outside of the metro. Finally, many remote markets have little to no data, so it is often difficult to judge the health of smaller or remote cities.

---

5 www.uhaul.com/About. Scroll down to "Migration Trends."

6 www.blog.gopenske.com. Search for "top moving destinations."

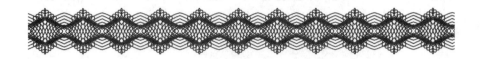

CHAPTER 6

BOTTOM-UP ANALYSIS

In the previous chapter we discussed the top-down approach to picking a market. The approach basically entails studying macroeconomic indicators to find the best places in the country to invest, based on the theory that properties in the best MSAs will benefit from the downstream current and perform better than those in stagnant or downward-trending areas.

In stock investing, there is a concept called the *bottom-up* approach to investing. Using this method, you examine the fundamentals of a stock regardless of market trends. You place less emphasis on overall market conditions, macroeconomic indicators, and industry fundamentals. Instead, you simply focus on how each company is performing as compared to other companies in the same industry.

When applying bottom-up analysis to real estate, the most important step is to compare the performance of the property against the performance of nearby comparable properties (what we in the industry call *comps*). What is the effective rent at the property? What is the average of the comps in the area? Making that comparison alone can be enough to see additional value very quickly and is the heart of bottom-up analysis. This comp analysis is called a *market study*.

Important Qualities for a Location

In addition to the market study, there are a few other bottom-up analysis points that shouldn't be ignored. Let's talk about some of them and how they might relate to various real estate sectors.

Visibility

Visibility can be a crucial element in a successful business plan. Let's say you are planning to invest in the ground-up development of a neighborhood retail center. The ability of people to find the center will be vitally important in securing major credit tenants to lease space at the center. Without major tenants it's hard to get minor tenants, and the plan is likely doomed from the start.

On the other hand, if you are investing in the ground-up development of a warehouse, visibility might not only be irrelevant, it might be undesirable. The tenant of the warehouse space might want to be out of sight and out of mind, at least to the general public, and almost certainly would be seeking lower-priced land in less-visible areas. Unless, of course, the warehouse is going to be a self-storage facility. This type of specialty property is highly reliant on drive-by traffic, and visibility can make or break performance.

Visibility used to be very important in the multifamily space, but it is becoming less so. A decade ago properties with high visibility attracted more prospects than those that were tucked behind other properties. While that is still somewhat true today, younger prospects are used to transacting virtually their entire lives online. Using smartphone apps and mobile-optimized websites, these prospects can shop for their next apartment from anywhere, and their phone's GPS can lead them right to the property. If they even bother to go—pictures and virtual tours give prospects unprecedented insight into the property and the units, and they can even fill out and submit a lease application right on the website. It's certainly possible that the first time they physically visit the property will be while driving their moving truck.

Hotels are another example of the shifting habits of a connected society. Decades ago roadside motels with lighted "(no) vacancy" signs were located in high-traffic areas near freeway off-ramps so passers-by could see whether there were rooms available. But now you see more smaller hotels tucked away in business parks or located a few blocks off the freeway. The use of online booking sites, smartphone apps, and GPS has reduced the mandate for high-visibility locations for hotels.

Traffic Count

Traffic count is a statistical method of quantifying visibility. A property could be located at a highly visible corner of two streets that only service a couple thousand cars per day, so all that visibility will do little good because there aren't many people traveling by.

However, a street with 50,000 cars per day would be a completely different story. These heavy arterial streets and highways bring lots of eyeballs to a high-visibility location. High-traffic-count areas, which to me means more than 20,000 cars per day, are the best locations for retail, restaurant, and self-storage uses. Multifamily can benefit too, just to a slightly lesser degree than they used to.

Finding traffic counts can be challenging. Sometimes cities have this data on their GIS (geographic information system) websites, or it is available from paid services on a broader scale. Often brokers will include traffic count data in the property's sales brochure.

Access to Transportation and Amenities

A neighborhood context map is a depiction of surrounding amenities like restaurants, shopping centers, schools, recreation areas, transportation hubs, and so on. Check the neighborhood context map for the investment you are contemplating to see whether the area helps or hurts the property's chance of success. Sponsors will often provide these in their marketing materials, or they can often get one from the real estate broker's sales materials. If the sponsor can't provide one, you can use your favorite online map website or app to make your own by searching the address and looking at the labels for various businesses in the area.

Hotel properties would benefit from easy access to recreation, entertainment, dining, and shopping. A self-storage property wouldn't benefit from any of those things, but might benefit from proximity to medical offices that need to store records, or businesses like plumbing contractors that might need space to store extra supplies. Most important, self-storage benefits from proximity to residential uses because the majority of their tenants will be nearby residents. Most people don't want to drive more than three miles to access their self-storage unit.

Multifamily properties benefit from easy access to transportation. Proximity to a commuter rail system or a bus stop (especially downtown express buses) can make it easier for residents to get to work. Proximity to freeways is also helpful; no one wants to drive 20 minutes just to get to the freeway.

Senior apartments benefit from proximity to bus lines, shopping, and medical offices, while downtown mid-rise apartments might benefit more from proximity to large office buildings and trendy restaurants.

Walkability Score

The walkability score[7] quantifies the ability to access amenities on foot. This score would be really important for a downtown apartment building but is unlikely to even be an afterthought for a suburban garden-style apartment complex in a secondary market with a cold climate. All those residents have cars. No one since my grandparents has walked ten miles each way to school, in the snow, uphill both ways.

Crime Rate

Crime rate is important, but it can be misleading and difficult to interpret. Multifamily investments in a very-high-crime area can be a management challenge, and come with heavy resident turnover and high delinquency losses. Those issues can be built into the budget but the headaches cannot. As an investor in a syndication, you have the luxury of a sponsor to absorb those headaches, but if the sponsor isn't experienced at managing in a high-crime area, even a great business plan can result in disaster.

Large multifamily properties by their very nature mean higher population density, and density brings a certain amount of crime just because of the quantity of people in the space. This makes it nearly impossible to acquire property with near-zero crime. The best interpretation of crime rate is the relative crime rate of the subject area as compared to other areas in the greater area.

By way of example, take a property we recently purchased in Atlanta. The crime rate in the immediate area was just more than double the national average. But the crime rate in Atlanta as a whole is nearly four times the national average, so in a relative sense this property was in a lower-crime area. You can find information on crime rates at www.city-data.com. Just type in the city name, then scroll down until you get to the crime statistics. For location-specific crime potential, there are good maps on www.trulia.com.

---

7 www.walkscore.com

I once purchased a property that had been the site of a recent homicide. An investor saw the report of the homicide and decided not to invest in the deal as a result of that incident. To add insult to injury (or in this case, death, I suppose), there was a relatively high crime area directly across the street. But a deeper look into the homicide revealed that it resulted from a domestic dispute in which the two parties knew each other and neither person lived at the property; they were visiting a resident there. It wasn't a random event.

We never had an unusual problem with crime at that property, and the financial performance exceeded our projections. The investor who declined to invest based on a single isolated event and a nearby high-crime area missed out. If you are squeamish about crime (and who isn't, really), investing in real estate might come with some discomfort at first. But that is why you are investing as a passive investor! Just be sure that the sponsor you are investing with has experience with addressing crime and resident safety.

School District

School rankings are important for the success of residential property but have little impact on commercial and industrial property, self-storage, and hotels. Nonetheless, be careful not to over-emphasize school rankings as you analyze multifamily investment opportunities.

Good schools don't necessarily mean better performance for a multifamily property. It might mean that the property can attract better residents and even achieve higher rents. But if the comps in the same school district are all getting $1,000 rents and the sponsor is projecting that this property can achieve $1,000 rents, low school ratings don't mean that the property won't achieve those rents. If the comps are located in similarly rated school districts, the school rankings are already baked into the pricing.

On the other hand, if the comps are all in great school districts and the subject property is in a bad school district, you shouldn't assume that the property will achieve the same rents as the comps, because the comps aren't truly comparable. The takeaway is to use school rankings with some context. They tell a story of potential performance relative to neighboring areas, but as a standalone indicator these rankings have limited value. You can find school rankings at www.greatschools.org.

Top-Down, Bottom-Up Real Estate Investing

In the previous chapter we talked about a *top-down* approach to investment analysis. Earlier in this chapter we talked about a *bottom-up* approach to investment analysis. If you are old enough to remember the commercials, you know that when you got your peanut butter in my chocolate, the peanut butter cup was born and candy was changed forever. (Well, maybe not quite, but those peanut butter cups are darn good.)

Why don't we just do the same thing here? Mix some top-down with some bottom-up, and you have the top-down, bottom-up approach to investing. This approach begins with a macro-level look at economic indicators to decide where to invest (top-down), then follows with a micro-level look at various properties and their comparables, visibility, traffic count, access to transportation, and such (bottom-up).

The beauty of this approach is that, if done correctly, it results in acquiring good real estate in good markets. That's what I call stacking the deck in your favor. I discovered this approach many years ago, and it completely changed the way I buy real estate. Once I used to be just a "deal chaser," which meant I spent most of my time chasing my own tail. But implementing this approach freed me to think nationally and cherry-pick my markets. No longer was I paddling across a lake or, worse, upstream. I could now just drift downstream and steer. You should try this too by investing with sponsors that use this approach; the views are pretty good from here.

Demographics

What do you know about your neighbors? If you are like most Americans, chances are you know very little. Maybe you know their names. You probably know what they drive. You can speculate on how much they make, but your guess may be way off.

Demographics are the socioeconomic statistical data points of the population, things like age, sex, education level, income, household size, and marital status, among others. Demographics are used a lot in real estate because they tell a story about the potential customer base of a store, the potential workforce of an office, and the resident base of a home or apartment.

Large retailers do extensive demographic research to determine where to place new stores. Housing developers use these statistics to size up demand for the finished product of their next vision. In some instances, demographic research is helpful; in others, it's misleading. The challenge is sorting out which is which. Unless you are a demographer or an economist, raw demographic data will be either useless to you or downright misleading.

If you are looking to invest in a retail development, demographics are vitally important. Hopefully the sponsor can supply you with a feasibility analysis and market study that will not only provide you with demographic data but interpret that data and tell you what is important. On the other hand, if that retail development is already fully leased before ground has been broken and before you make your investment, does the demographic data matter? Well, yes, because if the population doesn't support the tenants of the development once they open up, they'll go out of business and default on the leases, potentially causing a loss to investors.

Let's say you are investing in a 200-unit apartment complex, and the sponsor's business plan is to upgrade the interior finishes of the units and enhance the property's amenities with the hope that residents will be willing to pay higher rents.

The property you are looking to invest in has average rents of $800, and after upgrading the property, the sponsor says the units can rent for $1,000. Are there demographic data points that can predict the success or failure of this plan? There are some clues in the numbers, if you know where to look. The big one is median household income. If the area median household income is more than triple the projected post-renovation rents, you can presume that half the area population can afford the rent, given a three-to-one income-to-rent qualification ratio.

Age plays a role too. The largest age bracket among renters is the under-30 crowd. The second largest is 30 to 44. If you look at age demographic data, you can find breakdowns of the percentage of the population that falls into various age brackets. If the under-30 bracket makes up 50 percent of the population, you could assume that there should be very strong demand for rental housing. If the median income is more than triple the post-renovated apartment rents and there is a large percentage of under-30 folks in the same area as the property, you could conclude that there should be plenty of people to rent those apartments and they will be able to afford the prices.

But is it so? What if all the people under 30 fall below the median income, and those at or above the median income are in older age brackets that don't favor renting as much? You may never know which ages fall into which income brackets. This is why demographics are a useful tool, but not an absolute, for determining potential outcomes. The data placed in context before you can determine whether or not there will be demand at any given price level.

Consider a market that has our big three—population growth, job growth, and income growth. A growing population means that there is inward migration, and migration can add to the pool of qualified residents at any given price point. The incoming population may also have higher income which can create a deeper renter pool for your price point. It's also possible that the income level of the incoming population is lower than the median, and that can thin your renter pool. This makes it difficult to use demographic information alone to form an accurate opinion of pricing power.

When used as a backdrop to comps, rent growth, and vacancy rates, demographic data can be helpful as supportive data for rent, occupancy, and growth projections in a commercial real estate business plan. I don't suggest that you ignore demographic data in residential investments, but I believe this type of demographic data is a lot less relevant than comps and the "big three" economic indicators. For non-residential uses, demographic data can be as, if not more, important as comps. What you want to see is that the sponsor has thoughtfully laid out their case for how they arrived at their revenue conclusions, and has comp data and perhaps some demographic data to support their conclusions.

Market Studies

I cut my teeth in the real estate business by flipping houses. House flipping and commercial real estate might seem to be at opposite ends of the real estate universe, but they are actually far more similar than you'd think. Many people believe that buying commercial real estate is all about purchasing at a good cap rate (more on that later). If you are one of those people, this chapter might turn your thinking upside down. So will the discussion on cap rates in chapter 12.

I bought most of the homes on the courthouse steps at lender foreclosure auctions. This is a really unusual way to buy real estate, let me tell you. I'd walk up, listen to the auctioneer call out the opening bid, and place my bid. If I won the auction, I'd endorse a cashier's check for the full purchase price, and the auctioneer would hand me a carbon copy of a one-page handwritten receipt. Yes, really!

But bidding was the easy part. The hard part was figuring out how much to bid at the auction. Everyone has a different strategy at these auctions, so it can become a real zoo sometimes. Some buyers have absolutely no discipline. They just bid until they get the property, throwing money around as if it's not real. Other bidders would have fun with those guys because they'd just bid against them until they pushed the price so high that the sucker was sure to lose money on the deal. Other buyers, myself included, buy to make a profit and go to great lengths to buy at a price that makes sense. This all starts with setting a limit on how much to bid and sticking to it.

Whether buying a house to flip, an apartment complex to hold, or a strip mall to stabilize and resell in a few years, many buyers decide how much to pay by working forward. In other words, they decide how much to pay based on no data at all or on a gut feeling, telling themselves, "That's a good deal" or "That's a good cap rate" or "I wouldn't pay more than $75,000 per unit in that area." This works fine if you are holding forever, or if the market bails you out thanks to runaway rent growth or appreciation. But you can't bank on those things. You need a better system.

Fortunately, there is a better system, and I developed it back when I started buying houses at auction. The most important concept when setting a bidding limit is to *work backward*. Here is how that works.

The first thing I need to know is how much the house will sell for after it's fixed up. If I know that number, with absolute confidence and supported by data, I can work backward to decide how much to pay. To do that, I take the resale value and deduct three things:

- The cost to fix up the property
- The total of other costs, such as holding costs, closing costs, real estate commission, property taxes, insurance, utilities, and so on
- The profit I want to make

Remember, the most important part is to know how much I can sell the house for after it's fixed up. This is so important that it needs a Surgeon General's warning label: "Getting this wrong can be hazardous to your health!" You need a solid dose of respect for the sensitivity to movement in the resale value. In other words, if my estimate of the after-renovation resale value is wrong, a successful investment quickly becomes a failure and nothing can save it. If my goal is to earn a 10 percent profit on a house flip (which is pretty standard in the business) and my estimate of the resale value is 10 percent too high, I've wiped out my entire profit.

Establishing a resale value with relative certainty means that I have to do an in-depth market study on each house. This entails searching for similar properties that have recently sold, then making adjustments to account for the differences in size, quality, location, and physical condition of the neighboring properties compared to the subject property. It's a little bit science, a little bit art, and it takes a lot of practice to get it right.

Now that you understand how the house-flipping business works, let's connect this to the world of commercial real estate. In house flipping, the resale price is the driving factor behind everything. Buying an apartment complex, strip mall, office building, or hotel works the same way. You buy the property, fix it up, upgrade it, build on it, or improve it in some other way, and rent the units for a higher price than they were rented for before. Just as the after-renovation resale price of a house flip drives everything, the after-renovation rent you can achieve drives everything in a commercial investment.

The post-renovation rent will set the purchase price, and the accuracy of this estimate is the single most important factor in determining the outcome of the investment. Estimating too low will result in getting outbid by another buyer. Estimating too high will cause you to pay more than you should. Growing rents will move the needle more than anything else you can do to increase the income (and thus, the resale value) of commercial property. Let's face it, you can only save so much money on repairs, and you can only conserve so much water to cut utility bills. But you can make incredible shifts in income by growing rents.

The effect of rent on investment performance is dramatic. Just a $25 change in rents can drive the returns by a couple of percentage points in some cases. If the syndication sponsor is setting their purchase price by solving for a specific rate of return, an inaccuracy in the rent forecast could easily move their purchase price by a million dollars or even more.

This makes it even more surprising to see offering materials from a sponsor that include no market study or data to support their post-renovation rental rate thesis. More surprising still is that some sponsors don't even do a market study. If rental rates are the driving force behind everything, shouldn't more time be spent studying the market than, well, pretty much anything else? Yes, absolutely. But I see it often—sponsors focus their energy on cap rates, expense compression, and unsupported increases in revenue, and ignore the importance of a market study. If you see this happening, think twice before investing with this sponsor.

Rent Comps

The nuts and bolts of a market study is a survey of the nearby competition, or what we call *rent comps*. Rent comps are based on other similar properties in the area that are in comparable locations with comparable finish levels and amenities as the subject property. By looking at the rents those similar properties are achieving, you can make assumptions about what the units at the subject property can rent for if they are brought to a similar condition.

This means looking at the physical makeup of each of the competing properties. That includes age, level of amenities, and the general feel of the location and neighborhood (are these inferior or superior to the subject?). If the property is an apartment building, comparisons should be made to unit characteristics such as the number of bedrooms and bathrooms, square footage, and level of renovation.

Here is an excerpt from a market study on an actual multifamily acquisition. The property names were removed to protect the innocent.

NAME	PROPERTY QUALITY	LOCATION QUALITY	DISTANCE	YEAR BUILT	% OCC	# UNITS	TOTAL SF	SF/ UNIT	$/ UNIT	$/SF
Comp #1	Comparable	Comparable	4.4	1989	95%	324	353,484	1,091	$1,152	$1.06
Comp #2	Comparable	Comparable	3.3	1987	95%	316	322,320	1,020	$1,273	$1.25
Comp #3	Superior	Comparable	3.8	1993	97%	216	226,152	1,047	$1,207	$1.15
Comp #4	Inferior	Inferior	1.9	1991	94%	278	273,552	984	$1,111	$1.13
Comp #5	Comparable	Inferior	1.9	1990	97%	294	296,646	1,009	$1,050	$1.04
Comp #6	Comparable	Inferior	1.3	1989	98%	270	292,950	1,085	$1,005	$0.93
Totals*					96%	283	294,184	1,040	$1,133	$1.09
SUBJECT PROPERTY										
Subject (Current)				1985	98%	176	194,280	1,104	$894	$0.81
Subject (After Renovation)									$1,138	$1.03

*Weighted average based on number of units

This grid is a comparison of the various statistics on each of the comps, such as the distance from the subject property, year built, percentage of current occupancy, number of units at the property, total square footage of the property, the average square footage of the units at each property, the rent per unit, and the rent per square foot. Various sponsors may organize and display this data in different formats.

Next the grid shows the averages of the various statistics at the comps. In this example, you can see that the average square footage of all of the comps is 1,040 square feet, and the units are rented for an average of $1,133 per unit and $1.09 per square foot. The second-to-last shows the subject property, which has units averaging 1,104 square feet rented for $894, or $0.81 per square foot. It's evident that the rents are below market and have room to push higher if the units can be renovated to the level of the other properties.

The next step is to create a grid, noting the competitors' square footages, characteristics, and rental rates, and make adjustments to those rental rates to arrive at a rate for the subject property. If the other properties' two-bedroom units are renting for $1,000 and the two-bedroom unit at the subject property is 100 square feet smaller, an adjustment is made to the comparable properties' rents, let's say $50, to make the forecasted rent at the subject $950.

Price per Square Foot

Another method of interpreting comparable rent is to use the price per square foot. For example, if the rent at a nearby property is $1,000 for a 1,000-square-foot unit, the rent is $1 per square foot. If the subject property's units are 950 square feet, at $1 per square foot the rent should be $950. While this method might be useful for fine-tuning the rent assumptions, it doesn't always work.

Most tenants are more concerned with how much a unit costs. I don't think there's ever been a time when a prospect has come to the office of an apartment complex and asked how much the rent is per square foot! They ask how much it is to rent the apartment. They might not even notice the 50-square-foot difference in our units versus the neighbor's.

The value of space is a depreciating commodity. The more space, the less it's worth, and vice versa. Let's say that the neighboring apartment complex has one-bedroom units that are 1,000 square feet rented for $1,000, or $1 per square foot. The subject property has 600-square-foot one-bedroom units. At $1 per square foot the rent would be $600. But that would never happen. More likely, the smaller unit would rent for somewhere closer to $750 or $800, maybe even $850. That could bring the price per square foot up to $1.42! You can also be sure that the price per square foot of a 30,000-square-foot retail anchor space will be much lower than for a 1,000-square-foot retail suite. For that reason, comparing price per square foot is only useful for making minor adjustments between units of similar size.

The chart below is another excerpt from the market study in our earlier example. In this analysis, the comps are broken down by floor plan so that the rents can be estimated on a more granular level. Here we are comparing the square footage, rent per unit, and rent per square foot (PSF) for each floor plan. Below the comps, an overall average is computed. Finally, the subject property data is displayed showing the current rent and the forecasted rent after the renovation is complete.

COMP ANALYSIS						
	1 Bedroom			2 Bedroom		
Property	SQFT	Rent	PSF	SQFT	Rent	PSF
Comp #1	887	$1,064	$1.20	1,171	$1,220	$1.04
Comp #2	845	$1,193	$1.41	1,145	$1,326	$1.16
Comp #3	822	$1,105	$1.34	1,137	$1,276	$1.12
Comp #4	752	$995	$1.32	1,160	$1,211	$1.04
Comp #5	865	$925	$1.07	1,067	$1,100	$1.03
Comp #6	806	$875	$1.09	1,163	$1,028	$0.88
Comp Average	830	$1,026	$1.24	1,141	$1,193	$1.05
Subject (Current)	830	$844	$1.02	1,162	$905	$0.78
Subject (NEW)	830	$1,025	$1.23	1,162	$1,162	$1.00

In this example, the one-bedroom units are coincidentally the same square footage as the comp average. The future rent is set right in line with these comparables. The two-bedroom units are slightly larger than the comp average, and the future rent is set slightly below the average. These variances are normal and expected to a slight degree, as the future rent is set based not just on the average but also on a property-by-property analysis of the comparable individual units, features, amenities, location, and condition. The average is a good double-check just to be sure that the estimate isn't straying too far from the overall market where it becomes the high-price leader. It's better to acquire properties that won't stray too far ahead of the comp average.

Gross Potential Rent

The last step in the market study is to calculate the annual gross potential rent (GPR). GPR is the annual rent the property would receive if all units were rented at the market rate for the entire year. Using our market study, we already determined that we can rent one-bedroom units for an average of $1,025 and two-bedroom units for an average of $1,162. Determining GPR is now just a matter of tabulating the number of units in each unit type and multiplying by the average rent.

UNIT MIX/MARKET STUDY						
Bedrooms	# Units	Unit %	Size	Forecasted Rent	Total Monthly Rent	Total Annual Rent
1 Bedroom	31	17.6%	830	$1,025	$31,775	$381,300
2 Bedroom	145	82.4%	1,162	$1,162	$168,490	$2,021,880
Totals*	176	100%	1,104	$1,138	$200,265	$2,403,180

*Weighted average based on number of units

In this example, the gross potential rent for the property is $2,403,180. This annual potential rent is the starting point for building an income statement, which we will cover in detail in the next chapter and is hands-down the most important number in the entire analysis of a commercial property. This is where it all starts!

Floor Plan and Design

Recently I was looking to make an offer on a property that had very large units. The one-bedroom units had a single-car attached garage and the upstairs was a loft-style master bedroom with a gigantic walk-in closet. This walk-in closet was about ten-by-ten feet, or the size of a normal bedroom.

The property also had two-bedroom units. The odd thing was that the only difference from the one-bedrooms was they had no garage. Instead, that space was the second bedroom and bathroom. The square footage of the finished interior space was greater than the one-bedroom's, but the total square footage (including the one-bedroom unit's garage) was exactly the same, just used in different ways. Even worse, the master bedroom was still a loft-style room. That might be fine in a one-bedroom unit, but in a two-bedroom? No thanks.

The property also had three-bedroom units. These units were the exact same square footage as the two-bedrooms, the only difference being that the huge walk-in closet was used as a third bedroom by flipping the entrance. Here were three different unit types, same total square footage. How would you price the difference? How would you compare the value of these units against the competitors' when the competitors had conventional floor plans, with square footages that increased as the bedroom count got larger? There was simply nothing to compare these units to. Wasted square footage, loft-style master bedrooms, and odd floor plans are a bad combination, so I passed on the deal. No way to do an accurate market study on that one.

When studying competing units, it is important that the units be similar. If one property has ten-foot ceilings and the subject has eight-foot ceilings, they aren't similar. An adjustment needs to be made for the amenity of high ceilings. If the neighboring property has single-story casita-style walk-up units and the subject consists of three-story stacked flats, the rents would naturally be different, even for the same unit type and square footage. This is because the casita units have no upstairs or downstairs neighbors, and no stairs to climb.

Renovation level is also important. If the objective is to renovate units at the subject property and rent them out for a higher rent, the comparable properties should have renovated units that have similar finish levels to those planned for the subject property. If they don't, they aren't accurate comparables.

This doesn't mean that unrenovated units should be completely ignored. Studying unrenovated comps will determine the fair-market rent of the subject property's units in their unrenovated condition. It's possible that the owner hasn't been keeping up with rent increases and the market would support higher rents even without renovating. At the very least, this gives insight into how much of the projected rent increases are market based, and how much of the increase is renovation premium. Typically, renovations will produce $75 to $250 of added rent for the nicer finishes. If the sponsor is projecting to increase rents more than that, there should be some support for a portion of that amount being attributable to below-market in-place rents.

A great example of below-market rents is a property I bought in Houston. Upon studying the market, we concluded that we could increase rents $275. But it appeared that about $150 of that increase would be due to below-market rents. The seller had acquired the property at the top of the market, and had plans to renovate the property and increase rents. Then the great recession hit and threw their plans off-track. Because the property wasn't performing well, they burned through the capital they had set aside for renovations. Instead, they shifted course, deciding to be the low-cost leader in the submarket. As a result, they weren't keeping up with rent increases.

Fast-forward a decade and the rents had fallen pretty far behind. We knew that we could raise rents a lot higher with renovations, but we also knew that we could raise rents without doing anything at all to the property. The day we closed escrow our new management team took over the property, arriving at the office in the middle of the day. Every time a leasing prospect came to the office they would increase the asking rent by $25. They repeated this process with every prospect and didn't stop until a prospect decided not to rent there. The result? By the end of the day we were leasing units for $125 more than the previous owner without even touching the property. Once we completed exterior and interior renovations, we achieved our projected $275 increase and then some.

Class Cut

A class cut, not to be confused with cutting class, is a study of rent rates, growth rates, and occupancy rates between different classes of property. In the multifamily space, for example, a class cut would show that Class A properties were averaging $1,200 rents, 95 percent occupancy, and 3 percent rent growth, while Class B properties were averaging $900 rents, 97 percent occupancy, and 4 percent rent growth in a particular submarket.

Class cut data is useful because a market report talking about rents, growth, and occupancy without context doesn't tell the whole story. Sometimes Class A and B properties perform better than Class C properties—for example, during a recession, when people are moving out of lower-classed properties to the next-better tier (causing low occupancy in Class C) because the higher tier is cutting rents to attract occupancy. At other times Class B and C will outperform Class A—for example, during a strong economy, when builders are flooding the market with a bunch of new apartments and there aren't enough people moving to town to rent them. Those scenarios might seem counterintuitive, but this is exactly what I witnessed during the 2008 recession and subsequent recovery.

Yet another interesting statistic is the rent difference between classes. If Class A comps are renting for $1,500 and the Class B property being acquired is charging $800, there is a $700 difference between the two classes. This signals that there is a gap that can be filled by renovating the Class B property to a nicer finish level, competing with the Class A product yet still underpricing them. Perhaps the Class B property can rise to $1,100, a $300 increase that is still $400 cheaper than Class A. On the other hand, if the spread is only $200 you know there really isn't room to push the Class B property much higher than it already is.

The Bottom Line

The bottom line is that you are investing in *income* property, and income is indeed the name of the game. Establishing what the income will be sets the tone for everything that follows. The sponsor of the syndication you are investing in should have conducted a market study. The market study should support the forecasted post-renovation or post-purchase rental rates in the business plan.

The sponsor should show you this market study, and you should be able to arrive at the same conclusion as the sponsor after looking at the data. If you can't, this is either a red flag or at least a reason to have a conversation with the sponsor to learn how they arrived at their conclusions. If they don't have a market study, just remember that nothing moves the needle more than rent. If they can't establish the rent with a high level of certainty, all other projections, including return, cash flow, and the ultimate sale price, are pretty much useless.

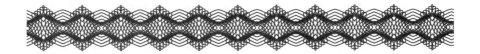

CHAPTER 7

UNDERSTANDING GROSS INCOME

If you're planning to invest in a real estate syndication, chances are you want something in return. Perhaps it's income, perhaps it's capital growth, and most likely it's both. Regardless of what your investment priorities are, understanding an income statement is at the heart of analyzing commercial real estate. But despite the importance of income statements, a lot of passive investors don't like to study them.

Basic knowledge of the various categories of income and expenses, and an understanding of what is normal and what is not, is critical to figuring out whether a sponsor's projected returns are achievable, conservative, or just flat-out pipe dreams. Depending on your affinity for numbers, operating statements are either a fun connect-the-dots puzzle or a tedious, boring, and overwhelming strain on your brain.

There's a lot to cover on the topic of income statements, so to make this more digestible I've broken it down into two chapters: one focused on income and another focused on expenses and cash flow.

I realize that there are numbers people, and there are people who hate numbers. If you aren't a numbers person, or you just can't stomach the thought of breaking down every detail of a spreadsheet, I have something just for you. Periodically throughout these two chapters you'll see shaded boxes with important tips. If you ignore everything else, that's fine—just don't ignore the shaded boxes! These tips will expose the biggest risks to underperformance, the boldest tricks that sponsors can play, and the biggest underwriting mistakes that you need to watch out for as you analyze investment opportunities.

Another way to use chapters 7 and 8 is to read through them but not worry about committing it all to memory. Instead, just bookmark them for future reference. Then, when you are analyzing your next private offering, go through the income statement one line at a time, and refer back to these chapters to get tips on what each line item means and what to look for. Eventually this will become second nature, so don't expect it to click on the first run.

I'll also explain how operating statements are built, even though you shouldn't be building them yourself. The sponsor should be doing this for you and including it in their offering materials. But you need to know the steps, because the best way to know if a house is built correctly is to know how to build one. Think of your role here not as the builder, but as the building inspector. You are looking at what the builder did to make sure it was done right.

Types of Operating Statements

Before we do a deep dive, let's first define some terms from the world of operating statements that you'll be coming across in this book and out in the real world.

- **Income statement.** Income is quantified using an income statement, also known in industry jargon as an operating statement, an annual property operating data (APOD, pronounced "A-pod"), a T-12, or simply trailing financials.
- **T-12.** This is industry jargon for "trailing twelve-month income statement," which means an income statement showing the last twelve months' historical income and expenses. This is usually presented with columns for each of the twelve months and one column for the total. The reason it's broken down by month is so you can see anomalies in the income stream, such as one-time income and expense items that will not be recurring in the future. Sponsors often will only include the total in their marketing materials, and that's fine, but they should also make available a month-by-month analysis of the historical income upon request. It's common practice for sellers to provide this to buyers, so it's likely that the sponsor already has a copy. The T-12 is the most

common trailing income statement used by buyers when evaluating income property.

- **T-3.** Similar to a T-12, T-3 stands for "trailing three months." However, this doesn't refer to creating an income statement with only three months of data. Instead, it means that whoever is analyzing the T-12 has extracted the trailing three months of data and annualized it (meaning they multiplied the three-month total by four). T-3 gross income is oftentimes more relevant than T-12 gross income, because property operations are always trending in one direction or the other. If rents are increasing and vacancy is decreasing, T-3 income would be higher than T-12 income. Conversely, if vacancies are increasing and the owner is now offering move-in concessions to encourage new leases, it's very possible that T-3 income will be less than T-12. Forecasting future income means using the most current income as a starting point, and T-3 income works very well for this purpose.

- **T-3/T-12.** One very common method for getting a true picture of the current income from a property is to use T-3 income and T-12 expenses. This works better than using T-3 expenses because expenses don't trend in quite the same manner as rents. For example, expenses can be seasonal. Imagine a property in Arizona, where you would expect electricity expenses to be higher in the summer because of the extra energy used for air-conditioning and extra water used to irrigate the landscaping. Annualizing T-3 expenses could inflate the influence of these seasonal variations in expenses. Thus, the best picture of net income is to use annualized T-3 income for a current snapshot of income and T-12 expenses for a true picture of expenses without seasonal influence. This is also called an "in-place" analysis because it's a snapshot of the most current in-place income.

- **T-1.** Similar to T-3, T-1 stands for "trailing one-month" and refers to annualized income from the most recent month (the last month's income multiplied by twelve). T-1 is often used by lenders to gauge the trend of the income. In other words, is the T-1 higher or lower than T-3? This can indicate whether operations are improving or declining. Lenders will sometimes use T-1 income to quote loan sizing under the assumption that the T-1 income will be the new baseline. If income starts declining between the time the loan was quoted and the closing date, the lender is likely to reduce the loan amount at the worst possible time.

Building the Foundation

Have you ever seen a house being built? If you have, you probably noticed that the first thing built is the foundation. That's no surprise, because everything else is built on top of it.

Building an income statement works the same way. First, you must start with a foundation: In this case, it's the first year of income and expenses. After that, each subsequent year is built on top of the first year, kind of like building a home in which the second story is built on top of the first story.

To build a foundation you'll need some building materials. For this project that means a market study and the property's historical actual income performance. In the previous chapter we covered the market study in detail, and to refresh your memory, that sample market study supported annual gross rental income of $2,403,180 once renovations are completed.

The property's historical performance is a look back to the income and expenses in the previous twelve months, and might also go as far back as the preceding two calendar years. I like to look at the T-12 and the T-3/T-12 side by side, and then build my first year adjacent to those two columns so that I can instantly see the historical and future income and expenses next to to one another. Hopefully the sponsor has already done this for you and included it in their investment package. If they did not, ask for it.

Here is a sample historical versus year 1 forecast analysis from the same actual property we used in chapter 6. This chart may seem a bit overwhelming at first, but we'll discuss every line item here and in the following chapter.

OPERATING STATEMENT	T-12		IN PLACE (T-3/T-12)		YEAR 1 FORECAST	
Gross Potential Rent	$1,925,700		$1,978,500		$2,403,180	
Loss to Lease	$(76,307)	3.96%	$(89,709)	4.53%	$(514,389)	21.40%
Vacancy	$(119,626)	6.21%	$(125,635)	6.35%	$(192,254)	8.00%
One-Time Concessions	$(69,647)	3.62%	$(75,834)	3.83%	$(30,040)	1.25%
Bad Debt	$(82,035)	4.26%	$(66,874)	3.38%	$(30,040)	1.25%
Non-revenue	$(9,900)	0.51%	$(10,200)	0.52%	$(18,024)	0.75%
Net Rental Inc./Econ. Vac.	$1,568,185	18.56%	$1,610,248	18.61%	$1,618,433	32.65%
Other Income						
Utility Reimb—Water/Sewer	$98,571	61.79%	$102,248	64.09%	$98,587	80.00%
Utility Reimb—Other	$1,141		$1,860		$—	
Pest Control Reimbursement	$—		$—		$2,534	
Trash Reimbursement	$—	$—	$—	$—	$6,336	
Miscellaneous Income	$87,150	$495	$99,033	$563	$87,150	$495
Total Other Income	**$186,862**	**$1,062**	**$203,141**	**$1,154**	**$194,608**	**$1,106**
Effective Gross Income	**$1,755,047**	**$9,972**	**$1,813,389**	**$10,303**	**$1,813,041**	**$10,301**
Operating Expenses		**Per Unit**		**Per Unit**		**Per Unit**
Property Management	$50,500	2.88%	$50,500	2.78%	$54,391	3.00%
Property Taxes	$162,384	$923	$162,384	$923	$222,974	$1,267
Insurance	$47,490	$270	$47,490	$270	$48,400	$275
Repairs and Maintenance	$320,290	$1,819	$320,290	$1,819	$88,000	$500
General/Admin	$67,335	$383	$67,335	$383	$39,600	$225
Marketing	$21,987	$125	$21,987	$125	$26,400	$150
Contract Services	$46,331	$263	$46,331	$263	$47,721	$271
Payroll	$97,892	$556	$97,892	$556	$211,200	$1,200
Utilities						
Electric	$21,797	$124	$21,797	$124	$22,451	$128
Vacant Electric	$1,577	$9	$1,577	$9	$1,624	$9
Gas	$683	$4	$683	$4	$704	$—
Water/Sewer	$159,526	$906	$159,526	$906	$164,312	$934
Total Utilities	**$183,583**	**$1,043**	**$183,583**	**$1,043**	**$189,091**	**$1,074**
Total Operating Expenses	**$997,793**	**$5,669**	**$997,792**	**$5,669**	**$927,777**	**$5,271**
Net Operating Income	**$757,254**		**$815,597**		**$885,264**	

Notice that the first column identifies the income and expense categories. The next set of columns shows the T-12 historical performance, and to the right of that is the annualized T-3 income with T-12 expenses. To the far right is our foundation—the forecasted first-year performance.

Income Statement: Line-by-Line Study

In order for you to properly understand the forecasts made by the sponsor, you first need to be familiar with all the line items you'll see in operating forecasts and historical comparisons. The income statement is broken down by income at the top and expenses at the bottom. Let's begin with each of the income line items and what to watch for.

Gross potential rent. We already covered this briefly, but let's go a bit deeper. Gross potential rent is the total amount of annual rent of all the units or square footage if everything was rented at the full-market rental rate. For example, with a 100-unit apartment complex in which all units are the exact same floor plan and rent for $1,000 per month, the gross potential rent (GPR) is $1.2 million per year.

$$100 \text{ units} \times \$1,000 \text{ each} \times 12 \text{ months} = \$1,200,000$$

If you are connecting the dots, this number should match the annual total rent shown in the sponsor's rent projections. To recap, here is our unit mix/market study for our sample property from chapter 6.

UNIT MIX/MARKET STUDY						
Bedrooms	# Units	Unit %	Size	Forecasted Rent	Total Monthly Rent	Total Annual Rent
1 Bedroom	31	17.6%	830	$1,025	$31,775	$381,300
2 Bedroom	145	82.4%	1,162	$1,162	$168,490	$2,021,880
Totals*	176	100%	1,104	$1,138	$200,265	$2,403,180

*Weighted average based on number of units

Notice that the "total annual rent," which is the same as GPR for the purposes of this discussion, is $2,403,180. That number carries down to the year 1 forecast in the operating statement. The first step in building an operating statement is to insert the first-year's GPR.

OPERATING STATEMENT	T-12		IN PLACE (T-3/T-12)		YEAR 1 FORECAST	
Gross Potential Rent	$1,925,700		$1,978,500		$2,403,180	
Loss to Lease	$(76,307)	3.96%	$(89,709)	4.53%	$(514,389)	21.40%
Vacancy	$(119,626)	6.21%	$(125,635)	6.35%	$(192,254)	8.00%
One-Time Concessions	$(69,647)	3.62%	$(75,834)	3.83%	$(30,040)	1.25%
Bad Debt	$(82,035)	4.26%	$(66,874)	3.38%	$(30,040)	1.25%
Non-revenue	$(9,900)	0.51%	$(10,200)	0.52%	$(18,024)	0.75%
Net Rental Inc./Econ. Vac.	$1,568,185	18.56%	$1,610,248	18.61%	$1,618,433	32.65%

 Look to make sure that the total annual rent of all the units matches the gross potential rent in the first year's operating statement.

Loss to lease. LTL is the difference between the GPR and the amount of all the actual leases added together. For example, let's say there are 100 units and the market rent is $1,000 per month. Ten of the units are rented for $900 per month, which is $100 below market rent for each of those units. The other 90 units are rented at the full $1,000 rate. The loss to lease is $12,000.

$$\$100 \times 10 \text{ units} \times 12 \text{ months} = \$12,000$$

The next step to building an income forecast is to align the first-year GPR with the current rent at the property. Let's begin by examining the actual rents in place at the property.

UNIT MIX/MARKET STUDY								
Bedrooms	# Units	Unit %	Size	Actual Average Rent	Total Actual Monthly	Forecasted Rent	Total Forecasted Monthly	Difference (Loss to Lease)
1 Bedroom	31	17.6%	830	$844.33	$26,174	$1,025	$31,775	$5,601
2 Bedroom	145	82.4%	1,162	$905.00	$131,225	$1,162	$168,490	$37,265
Totals*	176	100%	1,104	$894.31	$157,399	$1,138	$200,265	$42,866
Annual Rent/Loss to Lease					$1,888,791		$2,403,180	$514,389

*Weighted average based on number of units

The existing leases at the property average $894.31 per unit per month. When compared to the post-renovation forecasted rents of $1,138, there is roughly a $244 per unit difference. To calculate the annual loss to lease, add up the annual forecasted rents and subtract the annual actual rents.

OPERATING STATEMENT	T-12		IN PLACE (T-3/T-12)		YEAR 1 FORECAST	
Gross Potential Rent	$1,925,700		$1,978,500		$2,403,180	
Loss to Lease	$(76,307)	3.96%	$(89,709)	4.53%	$(514,389)	21.40%
Total					$1,888,791	

Notice that in our year 1 forecast the sum of the GPR and the LTL equals the current annual leases in place at the property. The objective going forward will be to reduce the LTL as units are renovated and rented out at higher rates to new tenants.

To see how phased-in renovations and rent increases work to bleed off LTL, see the future forecast for this property below, showing the first three years of GPR (increasing at 3 percent annually) and the compression of LTL as units are renovated and re-rented at the new rates. The objective is to have all units at the new rates within two to four years, where LTL will level out in the 1 percent to 3 percent range over the long term.

OPERATING STATEMENT	YEAR 1	YEAR 2	YEAR 3
Gross Potential Rent	$2,403,180	$2,475,275	$2,549,534
Loss to Lease	$(514,389)	$(264,910)	$(136,429)
Effective Rent	$1,888,791	$2,210,365	$2,413,105
Monthly Effective Rent (per unit)	$894	$1,047	$1,143

Notice that the LTL starts out very high—at $514,389. Then in the following year it is less, at $264,910. In year 3 the LTL has fallen to $136,429. That's because the GPR is calculated as if the rent had been increased to the post-renovation rate immediately. To estimate the ramp-up rate of new renovations and higher rental rates, each year's LTL is cut in half from the previous year.

This is a bit art and a bit science. We could assume that the property will receive some benefit from higher rental rates in the first year, not only from the renovations but from incremental rental rate increases imposed on existing tenants as their leases are renewed. As a result, this underwriting example is a bit ultra-conservative because the year 1 income could likely be higher than calculated here. Renovations could also proceed at a faster pace, compressing the LTL to a greater degree than in this example. There's nothing wrong with that, as long as the sponsor doesn't get too aggressive in the pace of increases. If they do, they probably won't meet those aggressive assumptions.

⚠️ Watch out for sponsors that calculate the forecasts as if they were to increase rents on every unit on the first day. This is impossible to accomplish in reality, not only because the units aren't renovated yet but also because tenants have leases, and rents can only be increased at specific times and with notice as required by local law. If the forecast shows gross potential rent jumping to post-renovated rates without an offsetting loss to lease, that's an enormous red flag and essentially guarantees that the projected performance will not be met.

Alternate method of addressing GPR/LTL. Another way to address rent increases on new leases of renovated units is to grow the GPR in parallel with the pace of expected renovations and increases. Using this method, the sponsor sets the GPR based on the current rates, and then creates a renovation schedule that maps out the number of renovations on a monthly basis. As units are counted as renovated, they replace the old rental rate with the new rental rate for the cumulative number of completed renovations. This will increase the GPR each month. Using this approach, the loss to lease generally stays relatively level throughout the period. You'll see different sponsors using one of these two approaches, and either approach essentially nets out to the same result.

Gain to lease. Gain to lease is the same as loss to lease but is applicable if the actual leases total greater than the GPR. For example, if our 100-unit property with market rent of $1,000 per unit has 90 units rented at $1,000 and 10 units are rented for $1,100, there would be a $12,000 gain to lease.

$$\$100 \times 10 \text{ units} \times 12 \text{ months} = \$12,000$$

The existence of a gain to lease really means nothing other than the management hasn't properly set their market rents. If 10 percent of the units are rented for $1,100, it's likely that the true fair-market rent for these units is $1,100, and the market rent in the property management software needs to be reset to $1,100. Doing so would increase the GPR to $1,320,000 ($1,100 × 100 units × 12 months), and it would wipe out the gain to lease and immediately create a $108,000 loss to lease ($100 below market × 90 units × 12 months). While the sum in either case is the same, having a larger loss to lease is preferable to any gain to lease from the perspective of optics and best operating practices.

Vacancy loss. Just what it sounds like, vacancy loss is the lost revenue attributable to units or square footage that was not rented for any period of time. Notice that the forecast below predicts an 8 percent physical vacancy loss. It is sometimes helpful to compare this percentage to the property's historical performance. However, the comparison is of only limited value because historical vacancy might be high due to the sponsor mismanaging the property, or it might be low because rents are below market.

Instead, it's better to compare this forecast to third-party market reports that show the occupancy performance of the submarket and projected future occupancy. You can ask the sponsor to provide you with a copy of a market study that reports submarket occupancy or forecasts future occupancy. The best-case scenario is to find that the forecasted vacancy rate is higher than the overall market study forecast, because an adverse market cycle could cause vacancy to rise. Creating a margin for safety by modeling to a higher vacancy rate than expected gives some insulation against the market turning against you.

OPERATING STATEMENT	T-12		IN PLACE (T-3/T-12)		YEAR 1 FORECAST	
Vacancy	$(119,626)	6.21%	$(125,635)	6.35%	$(192,254)	8.00%

As seen in our sample property above, the submarket vacancy forecast for the future is 8 percent. Notice that the property is currently operating at just over 6 percent vacancy loss historically. Despite the lower in-place vacancy loss, it is best practice to underwrite to market vacancy even though the property has performed better in the past. The historical performance could be due to stronger market conditions in the past, or because rents at the property are below market. Once rents are increased to market, vacancy should increase to market as well.

Recurring concessions. A recurring concession is when the landlord gives the tenant a discount on a recurring basis. For example, a leasing special might offer the tenant $50 off each month for the first six months.

One-time concessions. Just as the name says, these concessions occur only once. For example, a leasing special might offer half off the first month's rent. This one-time loss would be reflected here on the income statement. While it might be easy to assume that losses shown here on the income statement can be disregarded because they were one-time items, you shouldn't assume this. Sometimes the market is such that the only way to convert leasing traffic to tenants is to offer them some type of concession, which means that these one-time items may continue to recur, just with different tenants as units turn over and new tenants move in.

OPERATING STATEMENT	T-12		IN PLACE (T-3/T-12)		YEAR 1 FORECAST	
One-Time Concessions	$(69,647)	3.62%	$(75,834)	3.83%	$(30,040)	1.25%

In this example, one-time concessions have averaged 3.83 percent, which is abnormally high for most markets. This could be a sign of either bad management that is offering too many concessions or a weak market that requires heavy incentives to attract new tenants. In the case of this particular property, it was in rough physical condition with dated interiors and a lazy management staff, and that is the likely cause of the high concessions. Concessions in the overall market are closer to zero, so the forecasted concessions of 1.25 percent is likely feasible and perhaps even conservative if the property is to be renovated and properly managed. Many sponsors underwrite to no concessions, which I think is risky given that an adverse market cycle will quickly require concessions to attract tenants. To underwrite conservatively, planning for some concessions makes a lot of sense. One to 3 percent is appropriate for most markets most of the time. Entering a down cycle should result in modeling to higher concessions.

Bad debt. Income that is lost from tenants who fail to pay rent or obligations such as late fees, pet rent, or other charges is considered bad debt once it becomes uncollectable. Sometimes you will see this in the expense section, but most owners place it in the income section as a deduction from GPR.

OPERATING STATEMENT	T-12		IN PLACE (T-3/T-12)		YEAR 1 FORECAST	
Bad Debt	$(82,035)	4.26%	$(66,874)	3.38%	$(30,040)	1.25%

Bad debt losses at apartments tend to average between 0.5 percent and 3 percent depending on the class of property and quality of the tenants. Very high historical bad debt loss is a clue that the in-place tenant base is low quality (as in our example above), and a plan to renovate and improve the property and increase rents will require most of the tenants to move out. That's not unusual, and not necessarily a warning sign by itself, but it does signal that vacancy will rise temporarily while this all plays out. In theory, once units are renovated and better tenants move in, bad debt should normalize.

To digress for just a moment, after you make an investment in a private offering and you are reviewing the actual financial reports, there is one specific thing to watch for related to bad debt. Sponsors can hide bad debt losses by allowing the receivables to stack up on the balance sheet and not charging them off onto the income statement. What this means is the bad debt write-off on the income statement is lower than the actual bad debt losses. If you look at a balance sheet, which the sponsor should be providing you along with the periodic financial reporting, you'll see the "rent receivable" or "accounts receivable" line item growing from quarter to quarter. This is a warning sign that things might not be going as well as the sponsor is leading you to believe. Sellers can hide abnormally high bad debt loss from buyers in a similar way. The best defense is to ask for a *receivables aging report*, which will show all outstanding balances.

Non-revenue units. Units in an apartment complex that are unrentable are called non-revenue units. These might be apartment units converted into a leasing office or maintenance area, units down from fire damage, or staged model units used to tour leasing prospects. The rental value of these units is deducted from the GPR in the non-revenue units line item. Another example of non-revenue units are free units for site staff, such as for a resident manager, or discounted employee units where the discounted portion of the rent is deducted from GPR in the non-revenue units line item. It's common industry practice to have some employees live on-site with some portion of the rent waived as part of their compensation package. Non-revenue units at apartment complexes tend to run between 0.5 percent and 2 percent, with 1 percent being pretty common.

Net rental income. NRI is the GPR, minus loss to lease, plus gain to lease, minus vacancy loss, minus recurring and non-recurring concessions, minus bad debt, minus non-revenue units. Essentially, it is the total rental income actually received.

OPERATING STATEMENT	T-12		IN PLACE (T-3/T-12)		YEAR 1 FORECAST	
Gross Potential Rent	$1,925,700		$1,978,500		$2,403,180	
Loss to Lease	$(76,307)	3.96%	$(89,709)	4.53%	$(514,389)	21.40%
Vacancy	$(119,626)	6.21%	$(125,635)	6.35%	$(192,254)	8.00%
One-Time Concessions	$(69,647)	3.62%	$(75,834)	3.83%	$(30,040)	1.25%
Bad Debt	$(82,035)	4.26%	$(66,874)	3.38%	$(30,040)	1.25%
Non-revenue	$(9,900)	0.51%	$(10,200)	0.52%	$(18,024)	0.75%
Net Rental Income	$1,568,185	18.56%	$1,610,248	18.61%	$1,618,433	32.65%

Some inexperienced owners simply tally up the income they actually receive and lump it all into net rental income, instead of totaling the GPR and then deducting all the various categories of economic losses. The disadvantage to doing it this way is that anyone looking at the income statement cannot decipher how much the property is losing to loss to lease, vacancy, concessions, bad debt, and non-revenue units, and thus is unable to know exactly where to focus to improve operations. This method also makes it difficult to forecast future income because there is no visibility into why the property is presently performing as it is.

⚠️ When examining a comparison of historical versus forecast net rental income, pay close attention to the year 1 forecast as compared to the T-3 or in-place NRI. If you see a large jump here, it's likely that the sponsor will not meet the projected returns because it will take time for increases in income to build momentum. They can't just switch on higher rents property-wide on the first day.

Economic vacancy. This is a concept, not a line item. Economic vacancy is actually a combination of all the various economic loss factors discussed above: loss to lease, physical vacancy, concessions, bad debt, and non-revenue units. The thing to watch for here is the percentage of economic vacancy as compared to GPR.

OPERATING STATEMENT	T-12		IN PLACE (T-3/T-12)		YEAR 1 FORECAST	
Gross Potential Rent	$1,925,700		$1,978,500		$2,403,180	
Loss to Lease	$(76,307)	3.96%	$(89,709)	4.53%	$(514,389)	21.40%
Vacancy	$(119,626)	6.21%	$(125,635)	6.35%	$(192,254)	8.00%
One-Time Concessions	$(69,647)	3.62%	$(75,834)	3.83%	$(30,040)	1.25%
Bad Debt	$(82,035)	4.26%	$(66,874)	3.38%	$(30,040)	1.25%
Non-revenue	$(9,900)	0.51%	$(10,200)	0.52%	$(18,024)	0.75%
Net Rental Inc./Econ. Vac.	$1,568,185	18.56%	$1,610,248	18.61%	$1,618,433	32.65%

In our sample, the economic vacancy is shown on the bottom line next to the NRI. The first-year forecast is 32.65 percent. This number isn't all that meaningful because there is a large LTL as renovations ramp up. What is more meaningful here is to add up the other factors and a "stabilized LTL." A stabilized LTL would typically be between 1 percent and 3 percent, so in our example we could substitute 2 percent LTL and add the 8 percent vacancy, 1.25 percent concessions, 1.25 percent bad debt, and 0.75 percent non-revenue units to arrive at an economic vacancy of 13.25 percent.

> ⚠️ For a multifamily property, stabilized economic vacancy should average between 8 percent for a Class A property in a hot market to 15 percent or even more for a Class B or C property in an average market. But watch out: You'll see sponsors underwriting to a 5 percent economic vacancy on Class B and C properties. When you see that, run the other way. Unless the property is Class A+ in the hottest submarket of an area in a housing crunch, 5 percent economic vacancy is rarely achieved.

Utility reimbursements. It's common for multifamily properties to charge utility fees to their tenants. For example, when there is only one water meter for a property and the owner pays the water bill, tenants may be charged a fee based on the size of the unit, or a specially installed "sub-meter" reading, or a formula based on how many residents live in the unit. Other utility reimbursements could include trash collection reimbursement, cable television, electricity (in the case of master-metered properties), sewer, storm drainage, and pest control.

OPERATING STATEMENT	T-12		IN PLACE (T-3/T-12)		YEAR 1 FORECAST	
Utility Reimb—Water/Sewer	$98,571	61.79%	$102,248	64.09%	$98,587	80.00%
Utility Reimb—Other	$1,141		$1,860		$—	
Pest Control Reimbursement	$—		$—		$2,534	
Trash Reimbursement	$—	$—	$—	$—	$6,336	

In our example underwriting, notice that the historical financials do show some historical utility income for water and sewer, and a small amount for "other." They do not appear to be collecting any pest control and trash reimbursements. The first-year forecast includes pest control and trash because the plan would be to implement those charges.

Notice that there is a percentage shown next to the water/sewer reimbursement. This percentage represents the recovery rate of the actual utility bill. The seller is collecting just over 60 percent of their actual water bill. The plan is to grow this to 80 percent. It will take time to get there, which is why you'll notice that the actual income amount in the first year is in line with the historical amount. If you see big jumps here in the first year, it's unlikely that those projections will be achieved.

CAM charges. Common area maintenance charges are amounts charged to tenants of a commercial property under triple-net leases to pay for common area maintenance, including landscaping, insurance, common area utilities, and such. You don't typically see CAM charges in multifamily properties, but they are common in office buildings and retail centers.

Miscellaneous income. Sometimes called "other income," this line item is actually multiple smaller line items all lumped together. It might include late fees, application fees, administration fees, pet fees, parking charges, storage units (except at storage facilities where rent for storage units is tabulated in gross potential rent), forfeited security deposits, bounced check fees, vending and laundry room income, and even miscellaneous fees and income that just can't be categorized anywhere else. When I underwrite miscellaneous income, I tend to go with the lower of the T-12 number and the T-3 number, which you can see in the sample underwriting where the year 1 forecast is $87,150, the same as the T-12 but less than the T-3. Sometimes, however, there is justification for forecasting either higher or lower. Lower would be appropriate if an examination of the historical miscellaneous income includes items that are doubtfully sustainable. Higher would be appropriate if they aren't charging for things that can easily be charged for, such as pet rent, parking charges, and the like.

Effective gross income. EGI is the net rental income plus utility reimbursements, miscellaneous income, and, in the case of office and retail property, CAM charges. EGI is essentially the total of all income actually received by the property.

OPERATING STATEMENT	T-12		IN PLACE (T-3/T-12)		YEAR 1 FORECAST	
Gross Potential Rent	$1,925,700		$1,978,500		$2,403,180	
Loss to Lease	$(76,307)	3.96%	$(89,709)	4.53%	$(514,389)	21.40%
Vacancy	$(119,626)	6.21%	$(125,635)	6.35%	$(192,254)	8.00%
One-Time Concessions	$(69,647)	3.62%	$(75,834)	3.83%	$(30,040)	1.25%
Bad Debt	$(82,035)	4.26%	$(66,874)	3.38%	$(30,040)	1.25%
Non-revenue	$(9,900)	0.51%	$(10,200)	0.52%	$(18,024)	0.75%
Net Rental Inc./Econ. Vac.	$1,568,185	18.56%	$1,610,248	18.61%	$1,618,433	32.65%
Other Income						
Utility Reimb—Water/Sewer	$98,571	61.79%	$102,248	64.09%	$98,587	80.00%
Utility Reimb—Other	$1,141		$1,860		$—	
Pest Control Reimbursement	$—		$—		$2,534	
Trash Reimbursement	$—	$—	$—	$—	$6,336	
Miscellaneous Income	$87,150	$495	$99,033	$563	$87,150	$495
Total Other Income	$186,862	$1,062	$203,142	$1,154	$194,608	$1,106
Effective Gross Income	$1,755,047	$9,972	$1,813,390	$10,303	$1,813,041	$10,301

You don't want to see a large jump from the in-place income to the first-year forecast. Notice that here there is no jump at all. You might think that we would get some benefit from an increase, right? In some cases, yes, especially on a stabilized property. But this one isn't stabilized, and there are clues to this, such as poor management and high bad debt losses indicating a subpar resident profile, so using a flat income projection in this case is prudent.

Notice that there is a large jump in GPR. This means that there will be some significant rental increases. These clues lead me to believe that implementing a renovation plan and accompanying rent increases will require most units to eventually turn over to new tenants, which would mean either that the increases will be slow to materialize, or the occupancy will have to be drawn down initially. Either way, the first year is unlikely to see a large jump in income. It'll get there eventually, but if the sponsor is forecasting an immediate large jump, everyone is likely to be disappointed with the actual performance.

> ⚠️ Watch out for large jumps in the first-year effective gross income as compared to the property's historical performance. A reasonable increase is feasible, but a large increase is very unlikely to be achieved. If a large increase in year 1 EGI is in the forecast, the projected returns are very unlikely to be met.

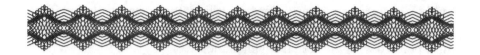

CHAPTER 8

NET INCOME AND CASH FLOW

Wouldn't it be nice if properties had money coming in and no money going out? Unfortunately, it doesn't work that way, no matter how much we all dream that it did. In the previous chapter we ended at effective gross income. From there, expenses will get paid, which brings us to net income, and after that we will pay the mortgage and invest in improvements to the property. Only then will we be able to count the money that goes to investors.

Expense Statement: Line-by-Line Study

Let's walk through the various components of expenses and cash flow so we can finish building our foundation—the first year's operating statement. Building this forecast can be a bit tricky because it's somewhat subjective, varies from one geographical area to another, and even varies among property types. We'll delve into an example from the multifamily acquisition we used in the previous chapter, so a lot of this will lean heavily toward multifamily, but the concepts can also be applied to other property types. However, the averages and ranges used in this book will be different from what would be appropriate for nonresidential properties.

In other words, normal payroll expenses quoted here for a multifamily property would be miles off if you were looking at a hotel investment.

If you are looking at property types other than multifamily, ask the sponsor if they can provide you with some actual expenses from other similar properties they own, or perhaps excerpts from the property's appraisal that outline expenses at comparable properties. The goal is to see if the assumptions made in their underwriting are supported by data, because it's very easy to fudge these expense assumptions to manipulate the returns.

Expense Items

Operating expenses are the costs associated with operating and maintaining a property. They do not include improvements to the property or capital expenses that are made to extend the life of a property. On an operating statement, expenses are often broken down by dollars per unit per year, as in the example below, so that one property's operational cost can easily be compared to other properties'.

OPERATING STATEMENT	T-12		IN PLACE (T-3/T-12)		YEAR 1 FORECAST	
Operating Expenses		Per Unit		Per Unit		Per Unit
Property Management	$50,500	$287	$50,500	$287	$54,391	$309
Property Taxes	$162,384	$923	$162,384	$923	$222,974	$1,267
Insurance	$47,490	$270	$47,490	$270	$48,400	$275
Repairs and Maintenance	$320,290	$1,819	$320,290	$1,819	$88,000	$500
General/Admin	$67,335	$383	$67,335	$383	$39,600	$225
Marketing	$21,987	$125	$21,987	$125	$26,400	$150
Contract Services	$46,331	$263	$46,331	$263	$47,721	$271
Payroll	$97,892	$556	$97,892	$556	$211,200	$1,200
Utilities						
Electric	$21,797	$124	$21,797	$124	$22,451	$128
Vacant Electric	$1,577	$9	$1,577	$9	$1,624	$9
Gas	$683	$4	$683	$4	$704	$4
Water/Sewer	$159,526	$906	$159,526	$906	$164,312	$934
Total Utilities	$183,583	$1,043	$183,583	$1,043	$189,091	$1,074
Total Operating Expenses	$997,792	$5,669	$997,792	$5,669	$927,777	$5,271

This is useful for sponsors that own several properties in the market, because they can apply their operational costs from their portfolio to estimate future operating expenses at a property they are considering purchasing. Appraisers will also often include "expense comps" in their appraisal reports. These expense comps show the operating expenses per unit from similar nearby properties to use as a point of comparison for the forecasted expenses at the subject property.

You'll often see a large disparity in a comparison of historical expenses and forecasted expenses. At first glance it might seem like an error or bad underwriting. Sometimes it is, but other times it's the result of the sponsor applying their market experience or expense comps to make their estimates because the property's historical expenses are outside of norms thanks to bad management or other factors. Let's discuss the various expense categories and what to watch for in each.

Property management fee. This is the cost of the compensation for the property management company. It is typically calculated as a percentage of the effective gross income. (You'll find a detailed discussion of property management fees in chapter 17.) Comparing forecasted property management fees to historical is of little value because the fees are a percentage of income, and the forecasted income is likely to be higher than the historical income at some point in the future.

OPERATING STATEMENT	T-12		IN PLACE (T-3/T-12)		YEAR 1 FORECAST	
Operating Expenses		Per Unit		Per Unit		Per Unit
Property Management	$50,500	$287	$50,500	$287	$54,391	$309

Property taxes. These include taxes imposed by the city, county, school district, and any other taxing authority. Often they will include special assessments for items such as hospital districts, infrastructure bond repayments, and storm water districts as well. A look at the current owner's latest property tax bill will show these add-ons.

OPERATING STATEMENT	T-12		IN PLACE (T-3/T-12)		YEAR 1 FORECAST	
Operating Expenses		Per Unit		Per Unit		Per Unit
Property Taxes	$162,384	$923	$162,384	$923	$222,974	$1,267

Property taxes are calculated differently from one jurisdiction to another but are generally the result of multiplying a tax rate, called a "mil rate," by an assessed value, which is a property value established by the local tax assessor's office. For example, if the assessed value is $1 million and the mil rate is 1 percent, the annual property tax would be $10,000.

The similarities stop there. Many states reassess new owners at a higher assessed valuation than the previous owner was assessed prior to the sale. Some states reassess the value of properties every year, whether the property was sold or not. Other states reassess every few years, and still others don't reassess at all; they just increase the assessed value each year by a set or variable percentage.

As a result of these variations in assessment methodology, there's often little relationship between historical and future property tax expenses. California might be the most extreme example. The property tax system there sets the initial property tax at 1 percent of the value of the property at the time it is sold, and limits increases of the assessed value to 2 percent per year. If a property has been under the same ownership for 50 years, the assessed value is likely to be far below the actual market value of the property. On the day the property sells to a new owner, the assessed value will increase to 1 percent of the property's new value. As a result, the historical property tax expense will be far below the future property tax expense.

Determining the mil rate and current assessed value is easy—just look at the most current property tax bill. In some jurisdictions, you can get a quick check of the property tax forecast by using the tax rate shown on the bill and multiplying that rate by the purchase price of the property. In other jurisdictions, this calculation won't even come close. The best approach is to ask the sponsor how property taxes are calculated in the jurisdiction where the property is located, and what calculations they used in their forecasts.

> ⚠ Are the projected property taxes higher than the trailing property taxes? Does the expense reflect a reassessment after the purchase if the tax calculations of the area include a practice of reassessing the property? Does the proforma calculation method of projected tax expense conform to the practices of the local taxing jurisdictions?

Insurance. This line item refers to insurance that covers loss of the structures and fixtures on the property, as well as liability claims. It usually does not include worker's compensation insurance, which is typically included in the payroll line item. The insurance expense is often equal to or slightly higher than the historical insurance expense at the property, but this doesn't have to be the case. Sometimes the buyer or the seller has a large portfolio and gets deep discounts on insurance, resulting in a disparity in future insurance costs as compared to previous.

Another reason for a disparity is when the seller has a much smaller loan than the buyer will have: The lender's insurance requirements are lower because their exposure is lower. An owner buying only the minimum amount of insurance required by their lender might have a very low insurance bill, whereas the buyer's bill will be higher thanks to their lender's requirement for higher limits or lower deductibles.

Insurance expenses vary widely. In an area with few natural disasters, such as Arizona, insurance expenses would be relatively low, sometimes even as low as $150 per unit per year. Areas at higher risk for natural disasters, such as Houston or coastal areas of Florida, might see insurance rates closer to $500 per unit per year or more.

OPERATING STATEMENT	T-12		IN PLACE (T-3/T-12)		YEAR 1 FORECAST	
Operating Expenses		Per Unit		Per Unit		Per Unit
Insurance	$47,490	$270	$47,490	$270	$48,400	$275

 If you are concerned about the insurance cost forecast, ask the sponsor if they have an insurance quote to support the forecast.

Repairs and maintenance. This category includes materials and supplies for the upkeep of the property. It would also include any outside contractors, such as plumbers or heating/AC contractors, that respond to the property to address maintenance requests. This item should not include capital improvements, such as interior or exterior renovations and ongoing replacements that extend the life of the property. This topic can get quite convoluted; there are fine lines between what constitutes a repair, what is an operating expense, and what constitutes a capital improvement, which is not an operating expense.

Here are a few examples of repair expenses and capital improvements.

REPAIR	CAPITAL IMPROVEMENT
Fixing a pothole in the parking lot	Applying a seal coat over the entire lot
Fixing a roof leak	Replacing a roof
Replacing a broken cabinet door	Installing new cabinets
Planting seasonal flowers	Replacing the landscaping
Painting a scratched front door	Repainting a building

Anything in the left-hand column above would be included on the income statement. Anything from the right-hand column would not. Instead, those items would be subtracted from cash flow rather than income. Although this may seem like splitting hairs, there's a logic behind all this, and once you get deeper into this book, that logic will become more evident.

Comparing historical to future repair and maintenance expenses is often difficult. With a stabilized property that is being properly maintained, the two might be very similar. For a mismanaged property, or one that is not properly maintained, or one with unsophisticated owners, the future and historical repair expenses might be miles apart.

OPERATING STATEMENT	T-12		IN PLACE (T-3/T-12)		YEAR 1 FORECAST	
Operating Expenses		Per Unit		Per Unit		Per Unit
Repairs and Maintenance	$320,290	$1,819	$320,290	$1,819	$88,000	$500

A case in point is our example above. Here, the historical repair and maintenance expense is very high, more than $1,800 per unit per year. A stabilized property in this area would typically expect to see repair and maintenance expenses between $450 and $550 per unit per year.

A poorly maintained property might have historical R&M expenses that are below average, because the maintenance needs aren't being properly met. Conversely, a mismanaged property might instead have high R&M expenses because management neglected things for so long that problems are now getting expensive to fix, or high turnover is causing units to require a lot of make-ready work to be done after tenants move out. Unsophisticated owners often run other expenses through the property, such as repairs on their own home or repairs on other rentals. They also frequently improperly expense capital improvements as R&M. Any of these practices will greatly inflate R&M expenses above typical ranges.

The business plan for this sample property is to renovate it. These renovations will include new appliances, plumbing and lighting fixtures, and so on. As a result of these new components, R&M expenses should drop because these improvements are less likely to fail.

Turnover expenses. This category is similar to repairs and maintenance but includes materials, supplies, and contractor costs that are attributable to making a unit or space rent-ready after a tenant moves out. Turnover expenses are commonly lumped in with repairs and maintenance, so ask your investment sponsor how they categorize these expenses.

General and administrative. Phone bills, internet for the office, staff uniforms, the alarm system: All these costs are typical general and administrative (G&A) expenses. Other items might include credit check fees, training for staff, office supplies, postage, printing, dues for local trade associations, business licenses, travel, bank fees, and anything that doesn't fit anywhere else.

OPERATING STATEMENT	T-12		IN PLACE (T-3/T-12)		YEAR 1 FORECAST	
Operating Expenses		Per Unit		Per Unit		Per Unit
General/Admin	$67,335	$383	$67,335	$383	$39,600	$225

Forecasted G&A expenses are typically similar to historical G&A but could be higher or lower if the sponsor has other units in the market and is underwriting to their known cost structure. Some sponsors use more sophisticated property management software, which raises their G&A costs. Typically, I see G&A ranging from $200 to $300 per unit per year for an experienced operator in most markets.

⚠ If G&A costs are abnormally high, it's good to investigate why. Perhaps the property is in a homeowner's association and the dues are lumped in here, or maybe the seller is paying themselves abnormal fees and charging them off to the property. It's time well spent to learn the reason for high historical G&A expenses. That way you can determine if those expenses are likely to continue or can be eliminated, and judge whether the forecasted expense rate is appropriate.

Marketing. This category includes all advertising costs as well as other marketing costs, such as resident pool parties and events, and fees to professional apartment locators or leasing agents. Typical marketing costs are $75 to $200 per unit per year. If historical marketing costs are abnormally low, that might be a clue as to why the property is in trouble—the management hasn't been marketing. Implementing a marketing program might be an immediate value-add opportunity. On the other hand, if the sponsor of an offering you are examining is forecasting an abnormally low marketing expense, it could be a signal that they won't be properly marketing the property. It might also signal nothing, especially for a property located on a busy corner in a hot market. In such a case marketing might not be necessary.

Contract services. Any recurring contractual cost would fit into this category. The most common example is fees paid to a company that has a contract to maintain the landscaping. Other examples include the cost of pest control service, pool service, snow removal service, and trash collection (although some owners categorize trash collection as a utility expense). Watch out for owners incorrectly categorizing repairs performed by an outside plumber, painter, or heating/AC contractor as contract services when they should really be repair and maintenance expenses. Contract services should include only contracts that regularly recur on a monthly, quarterly, or annual basis.

OPERATING STATEMENT	T-12		IN PLACE (T-3/T-12)		YEAR 1 FORECAST	
Operating Expenses		Per Unit		Per Unit		Per Unit
Contract Services	$46,331	$263	$46,331	$263	$47,721	$271

Contract services is one expense category that tends to stick with the property to a large extent. When I underwrite, I typically forecast the first-year contract services expense by growing the property's historical contract services expense for the previous twelve months by 3 percent. The theory is that whatever service contracts are in place are assumed by the new owner and the same contractors will continue to perform the services, theoretically at the same price or with a small increase.

However, this isn't always the case. Some sponsors terminate all service contracts when purchasing the property and seek new bids from existing and competing vendors. This can result in cost savings, making the above method of underwriting future expenses conservative. There are other ways to save on contract services. For example, the new owner could eliminate a security patrol that carries a high monthly cost, choosing to install a security gate and cameras instead.

Payroll. This includes salaries and wages for any on-site staff, prorated reimbursement for off-site staff (such as regional managers, if charged, or a shared maintenance person), and any bonuses. In addition to wages, the payroll category would include employer-paid employment taxes, health insurance and other fringe benefits, and worker's compensation insurance.

OPERATING STATEMENT	T-12		IN PLACE (T-3/T-12)		YEAR 1 FORECAST	
Operating Expenses		Per Unit		Per Unit		Per Unit
Payroll	$97,892	$556	$97,892	$556	$211,200	$1,200

Note that the property has been paying $556 per unit per year for payroll. This is an exceptionally low number. Generally, adequate payroll starts at $1,000 per unit per year and ranges up to $1,400 per unit per year, and even more in high-cost coastal or downtown markets. If the sponsor is underwriting to less than $1,000 per unit per year for payroll, ask to see a staffing plan. As a rule of thumb, you need two employees for every 100 units: one person in the office and one person for maintenance. This means that a 200-unit property should have four people: two in the office and two for maintenance. Some properties of this size might even require five or six people.

Taking a 200-unit property as an example, a $1,200 payroll would be $240,000. Twenty percent of payroll is fairly typical for covering costs such as worker's compensation insurance, employer taxes, health insurance, and other fringe benefits. This leaves $200,000 for salaries and bonuses, or $50,000 per employee for a four-person staff, which is about $24 per hour. The local labor market will determine whether that's enough to attract quality staff. A payroll allowance of $800 per unit would leave only $16 per hour for the staff in this example, and there's virtually no chance that wage will attract the high-quality staff required to operate a 200-unit property.

So how does the 176-unit property in our example survive with $556 per unit payroll expense? Well, they don't, which is why the owner was selling the property, and why the property is drastically underperforming. The owner drove the expense this low by operating the property with less staff than required, and paid this skeleton crew an under-market wage.

This is a great example of why the historical income at a property can't be taken at face value when analyzing a purchase. Historical income must be taken in context, and forecasted income has to include reasonable assumptions and allowances for not repeating previous owners' mistakes and mismanagement.

⚠️ Is the payroll enough to pay for an adequate staff? As crazy as this may sound, underestimating payroll expense is a common mistake among inexperienced sponsors and a common manipulation among sponsors trying to inflate their estimated returns. Say, for example, an apartment complex has historically expensed $800 per unit per year for payroll expenses, but the property is underperforming and there is a lot of deferred maintenance. The sponsor of the offering you're analyzing is projecting $800 per unit per year for payroll expenses and is promoting their plan to better manage the property and improve maintenance, but they have made no increase to the low payroll expense. If the property's problems are caused by inadequate staffing levels, or unqualified and underpaid staff, these problems cannot be remedied without increasing the payroll expense.

Utilities. Common-area electricity, electricity for vacant units, natural gas for the common area and vacant units, water, sewer, sub-meter reading fees, and other utilities are included in this category. Some owners include trash as a utility expense, and some include trash removal as a contract service.

OPERATING STATEMENT	T-12		IN PLACE (T-3/T-12)		YEAR 1 FORECAST	
Operating Expenses		Per Unit		Per Unit		Per Unit
Utilities						
Electric	$21,797	$124	$21,797	$124	$22,451	$128
Vacant Electric	$1,577	$9	$1,577	$9	$1,624	$9
Gas	$683	$4	$683	$4	$704	$4
Water/Sewer	$159,526	$906	$159,526	$906	$164,312	$934
Total Utilities	$183,583	$1,043	$183,583	$1,043	$189,091	$1,075

Sometimes sponsors will project reductions in water and electricity costs as a result of a plan to implement energy-saving improvements, such as low-flow showerheads, faucets, and toilets, or LED lighting or solar panels. If you notice a reduction of utilities expense on the projected income statement, ask the sponsor why they are forecasting a reduction and look in the capital improvement plan for money in the budget to complete the contemplated retrofits.

In this sample underwriting, the water and sewer expense of $906 per unit is quite high, which indicates that the property has likely not implemented any water-saving improvements. There is some low-hanging fruit here: Installing low-flow showerheads and faucet aerators at a very low cost could result in significant savings on water and sewer expenses. Nevertheless, this underwriting forecasted an increase in water and sewer costs for the first year, which is a conservative approach given the easy opportunity to save. If those improvements are made, the resulting savings will be a bonus that will drop to the bottom line. Typical water and sewer expenses are in the range of $300 to $600 per unit in many areas but can be higher in some water-constrained markets, such as California.

Before you get too excited about the prospects of huge upside by reducing utilities expense, remember that in our forecast we projected an 80 percent recovery rate on water and sewer expenses as tenants are charged for water and sewer. This mutes the upside because a reduction in water expense will result in a reduction of water income. In this example, the property would benefit from only 20 percent of the savings because the tenants pay 80 percent of the cost.

There's a silver lining, however. If tenants evaluate their total cost for the apartment, a savings in water charges reduces their cost of living at the property. If low-flow fixtures save tenants $10 in monthly water charges, this opens up the possibility of charging $10 more for rent. Indirectly, the property truly can benefit from water savings. This is another example of art versus science in analyzing income property.

> ⚠️ Are the forecasted utility expenses higher than the trailing expenses? They should be, because utility rates don't often go down. The cost of electricity, gas, water, and sewer is always on the rise, and the sponsors should be planning for this and building it into their proforma.

Total expenses. Just like it sounds, this line item is simply a total of all of the various expense categories. I wish I could say that you should look for expenses to go up or go down, but in reality, they could go either way. Increases in property taxes, the cost of utilities, and contract service rates should force future expenses higher than historical. But if the seller is expensing capital improvements as a repair and maintenance cost, running the property with too many overpaid employees, and wasting a lot of money on general and administrative expenses, it's entirely possible that the new owner's total expenses could be lower than the historical amount.

I have no statistics to back this up, but after underwriting thousands of properties over my career I'd guess that about 75 percent of the time future expenses will be higher than historical, and 25 percent of the time they'll be lower. Anyone saying that reducing expenses is an easy way to increase net income is oversimplifying.

Net operating income. NOI is one of the most important measurements in income property investing. It is simply the effective gross income minus total expenses. NOI is the measurement that drives the value of the property and is one of the components of computing a property's resale value using the capitalization rate formula. (There's an entire chapter dedicated to cap rate coming up). Note that the cost of debt service and capital improvements to the property are not subtracted from effective gross income when arriving at NOI. Those come in later.

OPERATING STATEMENT	T-12		IN PLACE (T-3/T-12)		YEAR 1 FORECAST	
Effective Gross Income	$1,755,047	$9,972	$1,813,390	$10,303	$1,813,041	$10,301
Total Operating Expenses	$(997,793)	$5,669	$(997,793)	$5,669	$(927,777)	$5,271
Net Operating Income	$757,254		$815,597		$885,264	

In some cases, such as this one, the first year's NOI is higher than the historical NOI. Here, there were significant savings in repair and maintenance cost because of the way the seller was accounting for capital improvements. That created overall savings in operating expenses. Coupled with effective gross income, the NOI increased.

In other cases, operating expenses might increase, and a flat EGI will result in less NOI in the first year than in the previous year. Whether first-year forecasted NOI is higher or lower than the previous year isn't relevant to the quality of the underwriting. The underwriting quality is dependent on the factors described up to this point in this chapter. If all the component parts are underwritten properly, the NOI will land wherever it lands.

The Multi-Year Forecast

The foundation has now passed your inspection—it's safe to build the house on it. The next step involves building a multi-year income forecast and cash flow statement. Building a multi-year forecast is fairly simple: Take the first-year forecast and grow the component parts to account for rent increases and expense inflation.

Forecasted income is typically displayed by ownership anniversary-date year, which means that if the property was acquired on March 1, the income forecast would show income from March 1 to February 28 of the following year. Here is an example of a multi-year forecast for our sample property.

OPERATING FORECAST	YEAR 1	YEAR 2	YEAR 3
Income			
Gross Potential Rent	$2,403,180	$2,475,275	$2,549,534
Loss to Lease	$(514,389)	$(264,910)	$(136,429)
Vacancy Loss	$(192,254)	$(173,269)	$(178,467)
Concessions	$(30,040)	$(30,941)	$(31,869)
Bad Debt	$(30,040)	$(30,941)	$(31,869)
Non-revenue Units	$(18,024)	$(18,565)	$(19,122)
Net Rental Income	**$1,618,433**	**$1,956,649**	**$2,151,778**
Utility Reimb—Water/Sewer	$98,587	$133,421	$136,090
Pest Control Reimbursement	$2,534	$3,430	$3,498
Trash Reimbursement	$6,336	$8,575	$8,746
Miscellaneous Income	$87,150	$88,893	$90,671
Total Other Income	$194,608	$234,319	$239,006
Effective Gross Income	**$1,813,041**	**$2,190,969**	**$2,390,783**

OPERATING FORECAST	YEAR 1	YEAR 2	YEAR 3
Operating Expenses			
Property Management	$54,391	$65,729	$71,724
Property Taxes	$222,974	$247,346	$257,242
Insurance	$48,400	$49,368	$50,355
Repairs and Maintenance	$88,000	$89,760	$91,555
General/Admin	$39,600	$40,392	$41,200
Marketing	$26,400	$26,928	$27,467
Contract Services	$47,721	$48,675	$49,649
Payroll	$211,200	$215,424	$219,732
Utilities	$189,091	$192,873	$196,730
Operating Expenses	**$927,777**	**$976,495**	**$1,005,654**
Net Operating Income	**$885,264**	**$1,214,473**	**$1,385,129**
Growth Assumptions			
Rent Growth	3%	3%	3%
Other Income Growth	2%	2%	2%
Expense Growth	2%	2%	2%
Property Tax Growth	4%	4%	4%

After the first year is built, subsequent years expand on the previous year by applying a growth factor to the GPR, other income, and expenses. This growth factor can be as simple as a single factor, such as 3 percent to gross potential rent, other income, and all expenses. Or it could be as detailed as different growth factors for every unit, different factors for every expense category, and different factors for every unit type and every expense category for every year.

The sky is the limit as to how detailed these growth factors can be, but most sponsors keep it simple because growth factors are nothing more than educated guesses. The more detail you use, the more educated guesses you have to make, and the less accurate these guesses are likely to be.

The forecasted income statement should include as many years as the property is intended to be held. It's not necessary to forecast further out than the intended hold period, but it sure is beneficial. If things don't go according to plan and a sale at the intended year isn't possible or practical, it's nice to have some baseline for understanding potential performance beyond the intended hold period. The other benefit to longer-range forecasting is that you can evaluate performance across a variety of hold periods to determine the optimal point of exit. It is also prudent to stress test the numbers beyond the anticipated hold period, and you can't stress test the performance if it isn't even forecasted. For all these reasons, ten-year forecasts are highly desirable.

If you are double-checking my math, you've probably noticed that several categories don't add up when applying a growth factor. Before you think I've messed this all up, let's discuss those issues. Here are the categories that don't precisely follow the growth rate.

OPERATING FORECAST	YEAR 1	YEAR 2	YEAR 3
Other Income			
Utility Reimb—Water/Sewer	$98,587	$133,421	$136,090
Pest Control Reimbursement	$2,534	$3,430	$3,498
Trash Reimbursement	$6,336	$8,575	$8,746
Operating Expenses			
Property Management	$54,391	$65,729	$71,724
Property Taxes	$222,974	$247,346	$257,242
Growth Assumptions			
Other Income Growth	2%	2%	2%
Expense Growth	2%	2%	2%
Property Tax Growth	4%	4%	4%

The income items follow the growth rate from year 2 forward. They don't follow the growth rate from the first year to the second because there is an increase to be implemented relative to the historical rates, and that increase is to be phased in over the first year as leases come up for renewal.

Property management fees don't follow the 2 percent expense growth rate because they are tied to a percentage of the effective gross income.

Property taxes are a bit complicated. This sample property was modeled with a mid-year purchase, but property tax assessments run on a calendar year. This means that the first half of the first year benefits from a lower property tax assessment (this local jurisdiction doesn't issue supplemental property tax bills for the period between the sale and the end of the tax year). As a result, there is a large jump from the first year to the second year. After that, the assessment grows at the 4 percent projected growth rate.

Forecasting Cash Flow

The final step in analyzing an operating statement is to look at the cash flow statement. The operating forecast brought the income from the gross potential rent all the way down to the net operating income. The cash flow forecast picks up where the operating forecast left off.

CASH FLOW FORECAST	YEAR 1	YEAR 2	YEAR 3
Net Operating Income	$885,264	$1,214,473	$1,385,129
Replacement Reserves	$(52,800)	$(53,856)	$(54,933)
Sponsor Asset Mgmt. Fee	$(18,130)	$(21,910)	$(23,908)
Before-Debt Cash Flow	$814,334	$1,138,707	$1,306,288
Debt Service	$(476,091)	$(453,637)	$(626,323)
After-Debt Cash Flow	$338,243	$685,070	$679,965

Notice here that each year's NOI from the operating forecast is the starting point. From there, the deducting begins.

Replacement reserves. Buildings and their components and systems don't last forever. Eventually they will need new roofs, windows, siding, appliances, water heaters, and heating/AC systems, as well as parking lot resurfacing. These capital improvement items can be recurring, such as ongoing appliance replacement, or one-time, such as a total roof replacement.

Lenders will typically require owners to set aside funds to ensure that there is money available when replacements become necessary. To accomplish this, lenders generally collect a fixed amount with the monthly mortgage payment and deposit it into a lender-controlled account. If a roof needs to be replaced, for example, the lender will pay for the cost of the roof by drawing against the funds in the reserve account. The replacement of the roof doesn't impact the cash flow, but the monthly deposits to the reserve account do, so this amount is reflected on the cash flow forecast. With a multifamily property, replacement reserves generally run between $200 and $500 per unit per year, and are determined by conducting an analysis of the remaining useful lives of the various building components when the loan is originated.

Sponsor asset management fee. This is a fee charged to the partnership by the sponsor for ongoing asset management. I'll go into more detail on this in a later section on sponsor fees. The fee shown here is 1 percent of the effective gross income on the operating statement. These fees are not operating expenses, so they do not appear on the operating statement forecast and they are not an expense that makes up part of the NOI calculation. Nonetheless, they impact the cash flow, so they need to appear on the cash flow statement.

> ⚠️ If the sponsor is charging fees, which they certainly are, they should be reflected in the cash flow forecasts. This may sound obvious, but you would be surprised how frequently they are not.

Debt service. This is the cost of making loan payments and includes both interest and principal. Notice here that there is a significant increase in debt service cost from year 2 to year 3. In this example, the debt was modeled to include two years of interest-only payments. In the third year, the loan begins amortizing, which means that principal payments are now due each month. As a result of the added principal payments, the debt service increased.

CASH FLOW FORECAST	YEAR 1	YEAR 2	YEAR 3
Debt Service	$476,091	$453,637	$626,323

One common question is whether debt service is an expense that reduces the NOI. It does not; it is deducted from cash flow after the NOI has already been calculated. That's because NOI is used for calculating the cap rate of the property (more on this in an upcoming chapter). Cap rate is a measurement used to compare the value of income streams from one property to another, and every property can be financed differently. If financing costs were included in the NOI, the cap rate concept wouldn't provide the answers for the questions it is designed to answer.

After-debt cash flow. NOI minus replacement reserves, minus sponsor fees, minus debt service equals after-debt cash flow. This is the cash flow generally available to be distributed to investors and the sponsor, unless it is needed for non-recurring capital improvement items or other specific company needs.

Refinances

If the property is to be refinanced at a point during the hold period, the effect of the refinance should be shown on the cash flow statement. Here is an example of a cash-out refinance of our example property.

CASH FLOW FORECAST	YEAR 1	YEAR 2	YEAR 3
Net Operating Income	$885,264	$1,214,473	$1,385,129
Replacement Reserves	$(52,800)	$(53,856)	$(54,933)
Sponsor Asset Mgmt. Fee	$(18,130)	$(21,910)	$(23,908)
Before-Debt Cash Flow	$814,334	$1,138,707	$1,306,288
Debt Service	$(476,091)	$(473,821)	$(690,994)
Loan Fees	$—	$(587,250)	$—
Loan Payoff	$—	$(10,725,000)	$—
Added Loan	$—	$16,000,000	$—
Net Debt Effect	$(476,091)	$4,213,929	$(690,994)
After-Debt Cash Flow	$338,243	$5,352,636	$615,294

Net debt effect. This is the before-debt cash flow, minus debt service, minus fees for originating the new loan, minus the payoff amount of the existing loan, plus the proceeds from a new loan. Notice that in this example there is a large amount available for distribution in year 2 as a result of a cash-out refinance. What happens to the after-debt cash flow will be covered in detail in chapter 16, so stay tuned.

Wrapping Up

As you evaluate syndication investments, you should pay special attention to the sponsor's projected income statement. Since the property's income determines the performance of the investment, this forecast is the most important analysis for evaluating any syndication investment, except for due diligence on the sponsor.

Sponsors should provide you with a way to analyze the historical financials and compare them to the sponsor's forecasts. Some sponsors will simply supply the raw historical financial statement with the due diligence materials, while others will provide a representation of the historical financials in the marketing package or offering documents—either by itself or, better yet, with a side-by-side comparison with the first year's financials, as I've shown in this chapter. This takes the work out of it for you. Major variations between historical and projected performance of any income or expense category are good topics for discussion with the sponsor.

It will take two to four years to fully stabilize a value-add multifamily property. It can take even longer for office and retail properties that have longer-term leases. Hotels and self-storage can be stabilized faster because of the short-term nature of the tenancies.

Income is everything, and projected income is based on a variety of assumptions. Assumptions include future rental rates, vacancy rates, bad debt loss, concessions, timing of rent increases, income and expense growth rates, future property tax expense, and all other operating expense categories. Making reasonable and conservative assumptions is the foundation upon which all income and expense assumptions are built. If this foundation is weak or improperly constructed, anything that is built on top of it is at risk of structural failure.

It is all too common for syndication investors to scan through a variety of private offerings and simply select the one projecting the highest returns. They do this without examining what assumptions were employed to arrive at the projected income and resale price that resulted in the promised returns. Aside from selecting a sponsor that is a blatant criminal, this could be the biggest mistake you can make.

As you analyze assumptions and the comparison between historical and projected performance, one quick test you can employ to determine if a sponsor is using reasonable assumptions takes less than a few seconds. Simply look at the T-3 EGI and compare this figure to the year 1 projected EGI. If you see a large increase in year 1 versus T-3, you should either pass on the investment or, if you want to give the sponsor the benefit of the doubt, have a conversation with them to learn how they intend to produce a large jump so quickly.

This underwriting fail is one of the most common that I see among newer or inexperienced sponsors. Sometimes it's evidence of outright fraud, other times it's a sneaky maneuver to juice the returns in an effort to attract investors, and still other times it's just due to ignorance or inexperience. Very rarely is a large increase achievable in the first year. Subsequent years are built on the first year, so the bad foundation results in a bad building.

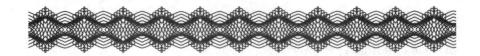

CHAPTER 9

PERFORMANCE INDICATORS

Imagine for a moment that you are driving to the office. You are traveling fifty miles per hour in a fifty-miles-per-hour zone. Could you be ticketed for speeding?

The correct answer is yes! Most states have a prima facia speed law that says something to the effect that you cannot travel faster than is safe for the conditions. If it's foggy outside and visibility is only twenty feet, traveling at fifty miles per hour would be unsafe regardless of the speed limit. But what if it's a clear, dry, sunny day? Yup, you can still get a ticket. Imagine that there's a car stopped in the roadway, waiting as a pedestrian crosses the road. You strike the rear of that car at fifty miles per hour. The safe speed for the conditions was zero miles per hour because of the stopped car ahead of you. Sign your ticket.

We like numbers because they paint us a picture. However, the problem with numbers is that they can tell an inaccurate story and influence our behavior in inappropriate ways. Performance indicators in private offerings also tell stories and influence behavior. Everyone wants investing in real estate to boil down to a few simple numbers: numbers that you can use at a glance to form an opinion, compare options, and make decisions. This seems natural enough because numbers are used this way all the time.

There are two primary scores for real estate syndications: the return and the multiple. The return is the annual percentage of your committed investment that was made in profits. When you exclaim, "I got a 10 percent return!" you're saying you made 10 percent of your investment amount each year. Multiple is how many times you multiplied your investment, as in, "I doubled my money!"

That's where the simplicity stops and the problems begin. It's human nature to want to compare the return and/or the multiple of one syndication against another, then choose the one with the highest number. Just like in sports, the most points wins, right? Well, not so fast. To make an informed decision, you need context for the projections. In private offerings, the context comes from the assumptions behind the score.

In baseball, if the batter hits the ball and runs all the way around the bases, the team gets a point—there's little room for interpretation. But a syndication isn't that cut and dried. You must examine what is behind the score to determine how likely it is that the score is real, that your capital will be preserved, and that the investment will meet your expectations and needs. Then you must consider the added context of risk. In the previous chapter, you learned how to assess assumptions. Now let's move on to learning about each of the performance indicators you'll see—as well as the ones you might not see but that are nevertheless important.

Types of Performance Indicators

Performance indicators come in two varieties: primary and secondary. Primary performance indicators tell you the direct results of your investment. Think of them as a speedometer: At a quick glance you know exactly how fast you are going. These primary indicators include:

- Annualized return
- Internal rate of return
- Cash-on-cash return
- Equity multiple

A secondary performance indicator is more like a tachometer. Instead of telling you how fast your investment is going, a secondary performance indicator will tell you how hard the engine is working and how much power remains in reserve. You can redline your tachometer by revving your engine too hard in the wrong gear even if you aren't going very fast.

Secondary performance indicators include:
- Break-even ratios
- Debt service coverage ratios
- Expense ratios
- Physical and economic vacancy rates

Primary Performance Indicators

Annualized Return

Annualized return is a simple calculation: Take the total profit you received and divide it by the amount of money you contributed, then divide the result by the number of years you held the investment.

$$Annualized\ Return = \left(\frac{Total\ Profit}{Amount\ Invested} \right) \div Years\ Invested$$

This method of gauging return can be highly misleading because it's unable to account for the timing of cash flows. As an extreme example, let's say that you contributed $100,000 to an investment, and the next day you got your $100,000 back. Five years later you got a profit of $100,000. If you use the annualized return calculation, you received a 20 percent return on your money ($100,000 ÷ $100,000 ÷ 5 = 20%). But you received your money back the very next day, so your real return on investment is actually much higher because your capital was only committed for a day and you doubled your money. It just took five years to get paid. During those five years you could have invested your principal in another investment and earned another return on the same funds.

Because timing is important, annualized return is not an accurate measurement of the performance of a real estate investment. There are other factors that limit the usefulness of annualized return:
- Sporadic timing of cash flows
- Varying distribution amounts from one period to another
- The potential for negative cash flows, where the investor must put additional money in
- Varying amounts of capital committed to the deal if some or all capital is returned during the investment period, or if capital to be invested is called or invested over time rather than all at once

Internal Rate of Return

Internal Rate of Return (IRR) is considered by most to be the gold standard for measuring and comparing returns in real estate syndications.

IRR is defined as the discount rate that makes the net present value of all cash flows equal to zero. There, that's out of the way. Now you can forget that part, because just like the new math they teach kids in school these days, you'll never use the definition in the real world.

If the definition of IRR isn't confusing enough, calculating it is virtually impossible without using a spreadsheet. Fortunately, a spreadsheet makes calculating IRR easy with its built-in IRR function. Just enter the formula into a cell like this:

	A	B	C	D	E	F	G
1		Year 0	Year 1	Year 2	Year 3	Year 4	Year 5
2	=IRR(B2:G2)	$(1,000,000)	$60,000	$80,000	$90,000	$100,000	$1,500,000

Year 0 is a negative number, representing the amount invested. It's negative because it's a negative cash flow to you—cash is going out of your pocket and into the partnership's account. Next to year 0 are each of the five years that the property is to be held. The final year's cash flow includes both operating cash flow and proceeds from the sale of the property. Years 1 through 5 are positive numbers because the cash flows are positive to you—they are coming out of the partnership's account and into your account.

What makes IRR superior to other methods of calculating return is that it takes into account all cash flows, whether positive or negative, as well as the timing of those cash flows to arrive at a rate of return. Why is this important? Because that's how real estate investments work, and you want a measurement that takes all that into account so you can compare one investment option to another. Plus, timing is important because a dollar received today is more valuable than a dollar received five years from now.

Let's compare a set of cash flows, and compare an annualized return and IRR. This first example calculates the annualized return using the following formula: $830,000 profit, divided by $1,000,000 invested, divided by five years held.

ANNUALIZED RETURN	TOTAL CASH FLOW	YEAR 0	YEAR 1	YEAR 2	YEAR 3	YEAR 4	YEAR 5
16.6%	$830,000	$(1,000,000)	$60,000	$80,000	$90,000	$100,000	$1,500,000

This results in a 16.6 percent annualized return. The problem is that this calculation cannot distinguish that most of the cash flow was received in the fifth year. Annualized return always assumes that cash was spread evenly over the investment period. Let's look at the IRR using the same set of cash flows. This was calculated using Microsoft Excel's built-in IRR function.

IRR	TOTAL CASH FLOW	YEAR 0	YEAR 1	YEAR 2	YEAR 3	YEAR 4	YEAR 5
14.3%	$830,000	$(1,000,000)	$60,000	$80,000	$90,000	$100,000	$1,500,000

Notice that the IRR is 14.3 percent, which is significantly lower than the 16.6 percent annualized return. It's lower because IRR recognizes that most of the cash flow came at the end of the investment. Now let's examine what happens if there is a refinance during the investment period, and some of the invested capital is distributed back to you when the refinance is completed.

IRR	TOTAL CASH FLOW	YEAR 0	YEAR 1	YEAR 2	YEAR 3	YEAR 4	YEAR 5
17.7%	$830,000	$(1,000,000)	$60,000	$80,000	$790,000	$100,000	$800,000

As you can see in the chart above, you invested $1 million. Three years later the property was refinanced and you got $700,000 of your capital back, along with $90,000 in operating cash flow. Then the investment was held another two years and sold. This results in a 17.7 percent IRR, higher than the previous example because $700,000 of your money was returned after only three years. Your return is higher because during the last two years, you are receiving the same distributions but have only $300,000 invested instead of $1,000,000. Better yet, you can invest the $700,000 that you got back in another investment and earn a second return on it. This is one of the most powerful aspects of investing in real estate offerings.

In all three examples above, the total cash flow was $830,000. The only thing that changed was the timing of the cash flow. No matter the timing, the annualized return would be the same because annualized return cannot understand timing, nor can it understand having less money in the deal for portions of the investment period. IRR understands both.

Critics of IRR will argue that it isn't a good comparison of investment alternatives because it assumes that you are re-investing your distributions at the same rate of return as the investment is generating. Maybe so, but that's not the point. The best use of IRR is for comparing one real estate private offering to another. IRR is an excellent tool for making this comparison because it accounts for the timing, amount, and direction of cash flows, and it's commonly available. Most syndication investment offering memorandums will provide IRR projections, and if they don't, you can calculate it yourself using a spreadsheet and the formula outlined above.

The real danger with IRR is that it can be manipulated. Sponsors can tweak assumptions to forecast a higher IRR. They can alter the timing of projected cash flows. They can, deliberately or unintentionally, project too small of a capital raise so that the IRR is higher (due to less money being initially invested), and then later raise more money without revising the projected IRR to reflect the additional injection. And they can manipulate assumptions such as economic and physical vacancy, rent and expense growth, expense amounts, and debt interest rates to juice IRRs.

As if all of that weren't problematic enough, there's another issue. One sponsor might calculate their IRR using annual cash flows while another might use monthly or quarterly cash flows, even if both sponsors are actually distributing at the same frequency. Therefore, even if the annual amounts are identical, these two sponsors would project two different IRRs. They wouldn't be wildly different, but if you based your investment choice solely on IRR, you would select the investment with the higher number even though the end result to you would be identical.

For all those reasons I feel like a broken record when I once again say that comparing one investment offering to another involves more than just choosing the one with the highest projected IRR. More important are the assumptions made in the operating statement, market study, rent roll, and financing that, all together, make up the forecasted cash flows that will ultimately result in a forecasted IRR. Assuming that you agree with all the assumptions, comparing IRRs is perfectly acceptable. Just keep in mind that risk plays a role, too. A 15 percent IRR with high risk isn't necessarily better than a 13 percent IRR with low risk. Your tolerance for risk should be directing your steps.

Varieties of IRRs

After discussing all the great and not-so-great things about IRR, let's add a few more guests to the party. IRRs come in several forms: gross or net, and levered or unlevered.

Gross IRR is asset-level IRR. If you were to buy the property yourself, with your own money and no other investors, the resulting IRR would be the gross IRR. It is the IRR thrown off by the real estate.

Net IRR is investor-level IRR. In a syndication investment, the sponsor will charge certain fees, and they will be entitled to a share of the profits. The amount distributed to the investors is therefore less than the amount of cash flow thrown off by the real estate. Plus, the amount of money invested in the deal is higher than if the real estate had been acquired without sponsor fees. Net IRR is the IRR to the investor, considering the extra money invested to cover sponsor fees, the fees themselves, and the sponsor's profit split.

When looking at the projected IRR of a syndication opportunity, it is important to note whether the IRR being shown to you is the gross IRR or the net IRR because there is a material difference and you want to compare apples to apples. Sometimes the type of IRR is obvious and clearly spelled out, and sometimes it isn't and you are left to guess. And some sponsors will show both.

In the context of a syndication, the sponsor's gross IRR shouldn't factor in the sponsor's profit split, but it may or may not include the impact of sponsor fees. The only way to know for sure is to ask. The answer matters—if one sponsor is forecasting a gross IRR with the fees stripped out and the other is forecasting with the fees baked in, they will project two different IRRs. This is another way of making sure you are comparing apples to apples.

Most real estate investments use leverage (debt), and syndicated real estate investments are no different. For that reason, most IRRs are levered IRRs, meaning that they are showing the IRR of the investment with the assumption that part of the purchase price will be paid with borrowed money and the cash flows will be burdened by debt service. This is fine because it is the best estimate of the return that you'll actually receive.

Some people like to compare one piece of real estate against another, and a levered IRR is not helpful in doing so because different financing can be employed from one asset to another. For example, you could purchase a property with fixed-rate financing with thirty-year amortization, or you could use floating-rate financing with two years of interest-only payments and twenty-five-year amortization. In this case the same property would throw off two different levered IRRs because the debt service for the two financing vehicles would be different.

This is where unlevered IRR comes into play. Unlevered IRR removes the cost of obtaining financing (such as loan points and lender's title insurance) from the initial investment amount, removes the debt service payments from the cash flow statement, and assumes that the entire purchase price is paid in cash. This method of calculating IRR allows you to compare one property against another because the variability of financing is taken out of the equation. Oftentimes sponsors do not display an unlevered IRR. If they don't, try asking for it. If they don't know how to calculate it, this gives you a clue to the sophistication of their modeling tools or skills.

Cash-on-Cash Return

Cash-on-cash return (CoC) is a measure of the actual cash received divided by the amount of cash that remains committed in the investment. For example, if you invested $100,000 and in the first year you received distributions totaling $5,000, the CoC for that year was 5 percent.

$$\frac{\$5,000\ Received}{\$100,000\ Invested} = 5\%\ CoC$$

Unlike IRR, CoC doesn't account for proceeds from sale and refinancing (except to reduce the amount of invested capital). This is purely a measure of how much income you are receiving from operations. One thing to watch out for is sponsors counting the return of capital from a cash-out refinance as a distribution in their CoC calculation. Doing so artificially inflates the CoC and is an improper use of the calculation. For example, if in year 3 you receive distributions totaling $35,000, and $30,000 was received from the proceeds of a refinance, your CoC that year is still 5 percent on your $100,000 investment, not 35 percent. Now let's say that in year 4 you receive distributions totaling $5,000. Your CoC for year 4 is 7.14 percent because in year 3 you received $30,000 of your capital back, leaving only $70,000 of unreturned capital.

$$\frac{\$5,000\ Received}{\$70,000\ Remaining\ Capital} = 7.14\%\ CoC$$

CoC can be expressed in a few different ways. It can be expressed year by year, allowing you to see the projected return in each of the years that the investment will be held, or as an average by taking the average value of each of the individual year's CoC returns. It's helpful to see both, because each tells a different story. For someone depending on the income from their investments, an average CoC doesn't help them much if the first two years' cash flow is zero.

If the CoC is negative, this means the investment has negative cash flow. The sponsor will need to raise additional capital at the beginning, to be held in reserve and applied to offset the negative cash flow. Otherwise, investors might be asked (or even required, depending on how the partnership agreement reads) to contribute additional capital to cover the negative cash flow.

Many real estate investment plans involve acquiring an underperforming asset, making some type of improvements, and increasing the income. Oftentimes these "value-add" investments will have little to no cash flow in the early years of the investment. Investors who depend on the income from their investments might want to avoid offerings with low cash flow in the early years. On the other hand, more aggressive investors who are seeking capital growth over income might be attracted to these value-add opportunities because they tend to ultimately yield a higher IRR and equity multiple than a property that was already stabilized prior to acquisition.

Stabilized properties tend to have more consistent CoC. The distributions will likely rise slowly over time as the market allows for rent increases, but they are unlikely to experience a significant boost unless unusual economic forces are at play. On the other hand, value-add opportunities tend to have lower cash flow initially but can rise quickly, and ultimately rise above the level of a similar asset that was acquired already stabilized.

Equity Multiple

Who doesn't want to brag about going to Vegas and doubling their money— or even tripling it? Talking like that is fun. Talking about equity multiples, however, is boring. But it turns out that when we speak of doubling or tripling our money, equity multiples are exactly what we're talking about.

The equity multiple is a numerical expression of how much you have multiplied the cash you invested. Like IRR, it can only be calculated after the property has sold, or projected as of the time of the anticipated sale, because it depends on receiving all cash distributions, including refinances and sale.

To calculate equity multiple, simply divide all the distributions you received during the life of the investment by the amount you invested. Here's an example:

$$\frac{\$150,000\ Received}{\$100,000\ Invested} = 1.5\ Equity\ Multiple$$

While it might be possible to quadruple your money in Vegas, it's hard to do that with real estate investments, so most multiples you'll see in forecasts are expressed with a decimal, and usually fall somewhere between 1.5 and 2.5. Anything much higher than that should be viewed with some amount of skepticism, as the sponsor might be a bit too optimistic with their projections. We all know what they say about things that sound too good to be true.

Because income from real estate tends to grow over time and properties tend to appreciate, longer hold times tend to produce higher multiples than shorter hold times. To illustrate this, imagine that an investment produced a 10 percent annualized return after factoring in operating cash flow and proceeds from the sale (I'm not using IRR here for simplicity's sake). On a $100,000 investment that is $10,000 per year. If the investment was held for one year, the equity multiple would be 1.1. If the investment was held for five years, the equity multiple would be 1.5. If it was held for ten years, the equity multiple would be 2.0.

For this reason, equity multiple isn't all that useful by itself. Certainly some investors will think it is, saying they won't do any investment that doesn't result in a 2.0 multiple. But applying such a myopic line in the sand would cause them to miss an opportunity that yielded a 50 percent IRR in one year because that investment would result in only a 1.5 multiple. It's hard to argue that a 2.0 multiple in ten years is better than a 1.5 multiple in one year, but to each their own.

Incidentally, this basic premise is also why IRR isn't the best yardstick all by itself. An investment yielding a 25 percent IRR for six months might sound great, but you've earned only a 1.125 multiple. Sometimes such a low multiple isn't worth the hassle and risk of making the investment.

However, take IRR and multiple together, then consider the CoC on both a year-by-year and average basis, and these three primary performance indicators give you a very telling picture of the performance of the contemplated investment.

But watch out: Just like IRR, equity multiple can be expressed as a gross multiplier and a net multiplier. Gross means the total dollars received from the real estate divided by the total dollars invested. This says nothing about what the investors themselves received because the sponsor is entitled to fees and a split of the profits. These sponsor payments reduce the distributions to the investors, so the investors' net equity multiple would be less than the gross multiple. When comparing multiples among various investment alternatives, be sure to compare net to net and gross to gross. Some sponsors like to show gross numbers because they are higher and might attract investors. Don't fall for it.

One handy thing about equity multiple is that it can instantly tell you how much money you'll get back from the investment (if the cash flow was to be exactly as projected). For example, if you invest $100,000 and the equity multiple is 1.65, you'll get $165,000 back, and so on.

Secondary Performance Indicators

Secondary performance indicators come in lots of shapes and sizes, and no one is significantly more important than another, per se. But every investor is different, and some people have hot buttons they don't want pressed, either because they've been scarred in the past or have seen calamity unfold as a result of someone else doing something foolish. My hot button is economic vacancy. It drives me nuts to see investment prospectuses based on 5 percent vacancy factors with no other economic losses in the forecast. It's simply misleading to propose that properties can be expected to operate that way for an entire ten-year investment plan.

But enough about my frustrations. Let's delve into secondary performance indicators to watch for.

Break-even occupancy. This is the economic occupancy rate that results in zero cash flow. Dropping below break-even occupancy will result in negative cash flow; rising above it will result in positive cash flow. This metric is useful for comparison to the projected economic occupancy rate so you can see how much slack there is between forecasted performance and break-even performance. Upon stabilization, a break-even occupancy of more than 80 percent can be risky. The calculation is:

$$\text{Break-Even Occupancy} = \frac{\text{Operating Expenses} + \text{Debt Service}}{\text{Gross Potential Rent}}$$

Keep in mind that the occupancy rate that results from this calculation is the economic, not the physical, occupancy rate. For example, let's say the break-even occupancy is 85 percent and physical occupancy is 90 percent. Loss to lease, bad debt, concessions, and non-revenue units total 6 percent, meaning that the economic occupancy rate is 84 percent. The property has fallen below the 85 percent break-even occupancy rate.

Cap rate. I'm bringing this up just so you don't think I forgot it—but that's the only reason. Don't worry: There's an entire chapter coming up about cap rate, so how about we just agree to table the discussion for now?

Default ratio. Also called *break-even ratio*, the default ratio is the percentage of its effective gross income a property needs to break even or, in other words, for the income to equal costs. When the default ratio climbs above 85 percent, the risk increases because the income can only fall 15 percent before the property breaks even.

$$Default\ Ratio = \frac{Operating\ Expenses + Debt\ Service}{Effective\ Gross\ Income}$$

Default ratio is different from break-even occupancy because it is expressed as a percentage of effective gross income, meaning that all economic vacancy has been factored in. The practical, if subtle, difference is that the default ratio is telling you how much the *income* can fall versus how low the economic *occupancy* can go. People tend to favor one over the other, with investors tending to be drawn to break-even occupancy and lenders tending to be drawn to default ratio. You can choose which one makes more sense to you—there's no right or wrong answer here.

Debt service coverage ratio. DSCR is the ratio of cash flow to debt service, and is used primarily by lenders to limit the size of a loan. It's also called debt coverage ratio (DCR) and is displayed as a decimal, such as 1.25. A 1.25 DSCR means that the NOI is 1.25 times the annual debt service. Different lenders have different requirements for DSCR minimums, with 1.15 to 1.25 being common, but some are higher and some lenders' limits are lower. The calculation is:

$$DSCR = \frac{Net\ Operating\ Income}{Total\ Annual\ Debt\ Service\ (Principal\ \&\ Interest)}$$

The way it works is the lender calculates the loan payments for the year and then calculates the DSCR. If the DSCR is lower than the lender's required level, they will not approve the loan at the requested loan amount. Instead, they will approve a lower loan amount that results in a DSCR that meets their required minimum. This is why borrowers are often unable to borrow at the maximum loan-to-value ratio. For example, sometimes a loan at 75 percent LTV results in a DSCR lower than the lender's minimum, which results in the lender dropping the loan size to 70 percent. Such loans are called "coverage constrained" because the loan amount is limited, or "constrained," by DSCR instead of LTV. In markets trading at low cap rates, such as below 6 percent, coverage constraint becomes very common.

I frequently hear investors discussing their preference for specific DSCR levels that make them comfortable. Personally, I don't think it matters as much as break-even ratio or default ratio. What is important is how much operations can suffer before seeing negative cash flow. Those indicators tell that story better than DSCR in my opinion, but your mileage may vary.

Debt service ratio. This is the percentage of the effective gross income that is used for debt service. If half the property's income is used to service the loan, the debt service ratio is 50 percent. For the most part, this isn't a particularly useful performance indicator. I bring it up here only so you'll know what it is if you hear or see the term.

$$Debt\ Service\ Ratio = \frac{Total\ Debt\ Service}{Effective\ Gross\ Income}$$

Economic vacancy. This indicates income lost due to *physical vacancy* (units that are not rented), *loss to lease* (the difference between asking rent and the actual lease rent), *concessions* (discounts given to attract residents), *bad debt loss* (income not received because the tenant failed to pay and the debt became uncollectable), and *non-revenue units* (units that are not in rentable condition or units that are not rented because they are used by management for employee units or a leasing office).

> ⚠️ Watch out for sponsors projecting unachievably low economic vacancy. In many markets economic vacancy less than 8 percent is difficult to achieve, and often 12 percent or even 15 percent is more appropriate. Yet time and again you'll catch sponsors forecasting negligible economic vacancy, such as 5 percent.

Expense ratio. The percentage of the effective gross income that is used to pay operating expenses is known as the expense ratio. Multifamily properties tend to have expense ratios in the 40 to 50 percent range. If the sponsor is showing an expense ratio lower than 40 percent, you should be suspicious and dig deeper into the assumptions to determine whether it is realistic. The sponsor may be underestimating expenses.

$$Expense\ Ratio = \frac{Operating\ Expenses}{Effective\ Gross\ Income}$$

NOI ratio. This is the percentage of the effective gross income that is left over after operating expenses, or net operating income. The NOI ratio is always the inverse of the expense ratio, and the two combined will always equal 100 percent. For example, if the expense ratio is 45 percent, the NOI ratio would be 55 percent, meaning that 45 percent of the EGI was used to pay operating expenses and 55 percent of EGI dropped down to net operating income. Remember, debt service comes after NOI, so it is not a part of the expense ratio and NOI ratio calculations.

$$NOI\ Ratio = \frac{Net\ Operating\ Income}{Effective\ Gross\ Income}$$

Physical vacancy. The number or percentage of units that are not rented.

Physical vacancy loss. Related to physical vacancy, but with a subtle difference, this refers to the percentage of gross potential rent that is not collected because of vacant units. Let's say that a property is half one-bedroom and half two-bedroom units. If 10 percent of the one-bedroom units are vacant, the physical vacancy is 5 percent because 5 percent of the total units are vacant. But the physical vacancy loss is most likely less than 5 percent because the one-bedroom units rent for less per month than the two-bedroom units. Given that all the physical vacancy consists of one-bedroom units, the loss of income would be less than if the vacancies were spread evenly between the two unit types.

Percentage of IRR from cash flow versus reversion. If you prioritize cash flow over appreciation, you might be interested in knowing how much of the IRR is attributed to cash flow and how much is attributed to the sale of the property, or reversion. This would be expressed as "65 percent of the

IRR was from cash flow and 35 percent was from reversion." Investments where the majority of the IRR comes from the sale are considered more speculative, because there may or may not be profit from the sale depending on market conditions. Conversely, if the majority of the return comes from cash flow, the investment would be considered less speculative.

Yield on cost (and development spread and development lift). Yield on cost (YoC) is the NOI at the time the project has stabilized, divided by the total project cost. YoC differs from cap rate because cap rate is NOI divided by the purchase price, not total project cost. Total project cost includes the purchase price, capital improvements, acquisition closing and financing costs, and sponsor fees. Stabilized NOI could be year 2, 3, or even 4 depending on how long it is expected to take for the project to be renovated and fully stabilize. The year when rental rates have been increased to the new market rates and economic vacancy levels off is the stabilized year.

$$Yield\ on\ Cost = \frac{Stabilized\ NOI}{Total\ Project\ Cost}$$

YoC is used to calculate the difference between the market cap rate and the actual yield on the total project cost. In real estate development circles, the difference between the YoC and the market cap rate is called the *development spread*. For example, if a project's YoC is 8 percent and the market cap rate is 6 percent, the development spread is 200 bps because there is a 200 basis point spread (2 percent) between the 8 percent YoC and 6 percent market cap rate. The greater the spread, the more potentially feasible the development project would be.

This concept isn't restricted to ground-up development, however. Value-add multifamily deals are small development projects, in a sense, as the property is acquired, and then significant money is injected into the project to make improvements. Examining the YoC and development spread in a value-add multifamily plan can measure the amount of value that is added, and is a common "quick check" test for institutional investors.

Oftentimes investors view a specific development spread as a minimum test that an investment opportunity must pass; for example, a "good deal" must have a 150 bps development spread. That is a poor measurement, however, because the point spread is really irrelevant by itself.

More relevant is the *development lift*. This is the development spread expressed as a percentage of the market cap rate, and tells you how much the value of the property is "lifted" over the total project cost. A 20 percent development lift means that the improvements created 20 percent more property value than the total cost.

$$Development\ Lift = \frac{(Development\ Spread \div 100)}{Market\ Cap\ Rate}$$

Using the previous example of a 6 percent market cap rate and an 8 percent YoC, providing a 200 bps development spread, the development lift is 33 percent of the market cap rate. This essentially means that the value-add improvements resulted in a 33 percent increase in property value (development lift) over the total invested in the property. On the other hand, the same 200 bps development spread where the market cap rate is 4 percent would equate to a 50 percent development lift. In a 4 percent cap rate market, a 100 bps development spread produces the same development lift as a 200 bps development spread would in an 8 percent cap rate market.

Let's use this in a practical example. You acquire a property for $7.5 million in a market where similar properties are selling for a 6 percent cap rate. Closing costs are $500,000 and the renovation costs $2 million. This makes the total project cost $10 million. After the property is stabilized, the YoC is 7.2 percent, making the development spread 120 bps (1.2 percent). At a 6 percent cap rate the property is worth $12 million. You have created $2 million of value or, said another way, 20 percent of added value over the $10 million total cost. This coincides with the development lift, which is 20 percent (1.2 divided by 6 = 0.2 or 20 percent).

Now that you've learned about yield on cost, you'll laugh the next time you hear someone say they bought a property at a 6 percent cap rate and turned it into an 8 percent cap rate. Not only is that an incorrect application of cap rate, but the concept they are trying to convey is irrelevant given that it takes an infusion of capital to improve the property, and that capital isn't counted in their "transformed cap rate." If a sponsor wishes to articulate the value they have added, they should talk about YoC and development lift, not cap rate.

Point-of-Sale Metrics Versus Running Metrics

Many performance indicators can take two different forms, point of sale and running. A point-of-sale indicator shows you a measurement as of the time of the sale of the property. A good example is the internal rate of return, which can be calculated only if it includes all cash-flow events, including the sale of the property. Equity multiple is another performance indicator that can be used only as a point-of-sale metric. You will never know the IRR or the equity multiple during the hold period of the investment.

Running indicators can be calculated along the life of the investment. An example would be debt coverage ratio. This can be calculated each year or even each month of the investment by simply dividing the net operating income by the debt service.

Some indicators can be used as either point of sale or running. An example would be cash-on-cash return. At the end of each year, or even each month, you can calculate your exact cash-on-cash return by dividing the amount of cash you received during the year by the amount of capital you have remaining in the investment. You can also use it as a point-of-sale measurement by averaging the cash-on-cash return for the entire hold period.

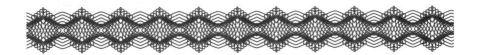

CHAPTER 10

DEBT STRUCTURE

Debt: It's just a simple word to some, a nemesis to others. When it comes to evaluating real estate investments debt is a tool, and like any tool, it can be dangerous as well as useful. Debt comes in all shapes and sizes, and one size does not fit all. As you evaluate syndication opportunities, you should pay close attention to the debt structure proposed by the sponsor. The structure they elect to use could negatively or positively affect the risk profile and returns, and it could even cause a total failure of the investment.

Think back to all the news about real estate foreclosures during the great financial collapse. Most foreclosures were encumbered by debt that exceeded the value of the property. I remember one house I bought at a foreclosure auction that was worth about $600,000 had an outstanding loan balance of $1.1 million! I bought it for $355,000, so the bank took a serious loss on this one. This type of improper use of debt isn't limited to single-family homes.

I've bought several foreclosed apartment complexes throughout the market cycles. These properties were encumbered by massive debt, all exceeding the market value, and on a couple of occasions, the debt was more than double the market value. Trouble is, memories are short and many newer syndicators these days have never seen this firsthand. Fortunately for them, lenders have become more disciplined. However, even lenders aren't foolproof.

When evaluating a syndication investment opportunity, ask the sponsor if they have a term sheet in hand from a lender. Oftentimes you'll find that the sponsor is still working out the terms of the debt or hasn't decided on a lender yet. That's fine in the beginning, but once they select a lender and debt structure, the underwriting and projections can change if the terms of the loan are different than first expected. Be sure that the sponsor is updating their underwriting and that you have seen the updated projections, based on a final lender's term sheet, before you make your final investment commitment.

It's easy for sponsors to use high-leverage loans to juice returns. But that can dramatically increase risk. Low-leverage loans are much safer but result in lower returns because more capital needs to be raised. You have to decide which is more important to you—risk or return. It's difficult to have the best of both.

Interest Rates and Prepayment Penalties

Interest rates fall into two primary categories: fixed rate and floating rate. A fixed-rate loan is one where the percentage of interest charged on the outstanding loan balance is set when the interest rate is locked in during the origination process, usually just a few days before the loan is funded. Once the rate is locked, it never changes. Homeowners often opt for fixed-rate loans on their homes because knowing that their payment will never change gives them a sense of security.

The interest rate of a fixed-rate loan is typically established by applying a "spread" rate to an "index" rate. Often this index is the ten-year Treasury rate. This rate is constantly changing as trades occur in the bond market. Lenders seek to earn a profit on the money they lend, so they apply a spread rate on top of the index, and that spread rate will differ from lender to lender, property to property, and loan to loan. As the lender perceives higher risk in a particular loan, they'll apply a higher spread rate.

A floating-rate loan is one in which the interest rate is not fixed; instead, it adjusts periodically as the index adjusts. Most of the time the interest rate on a floating-rate loan will adjust monthly, but it could also adjust annually or even daily depending on the terms agreed to by the lender and the borrower. Just like a fixed-rate loan, a floating-rate loan uses an index rate plus a spread to determine the borrower's interest rate. In the past, the index rate most often used was the thirty-day LIBOR

(London Interbank Offered Rate). At the end of 2021, LIBOR will be retired and replaced by SOFR (Secured Overnight Financing Rate), so it is likely that you will start seeing floating-rate loans indexing to SOFR as well.

At first glance a fixed-rate loan appears more advantageous than a floating-rate loan because the interest rate doesn't change. Most important, it doesn't go up. For most homeowners who plan to stay in their home for a long period of time, fixed rate is likely the best choice.

But what if you are contemplating an investment in an apartment syndication? Which is better, fixed or floating? Before you think the answer is obviously fixed rate, let's cover two concepts that are unique to commercial lending.

Defeasance

The thirty-year fixed-rate mortgage on your home is usually backed by one of two government-sponsored enterprises (GSEs), Freddie Mac or Fannie Mae. These GSEs securitize the loans by packaging them and selling them on the bond market. If you pay off your loan, the terms of these bonds allow for that payoff, and oftentimes there is no penalty for paying off the loan early, whether through a sale, refinance, or winning the lottery.

Many loans secured by multifamily properties are also backed by the same GSEs and then sold, but the terms of the bonds are different, partly because the loan sizes are so large. An early payoff of a large GSE loan on an apartment building is problematic for the issuers of the bonds because the high dollar amount really moves the needle.

The issuers address this in two different ways. The first is defeasance. Defeasance means that you are not permitted to pay off the loan early. Instead, if you sell or refinance you have to use the proceeds that would have been used to pay off the loan to purchase securities, such as Treasury bonds, and hold those securities until the end of the loan term. You then pledge the securities as collateral to the lender to replace the real estate collateral.

Perhaps this sounds simple enough, but it comes at a cost. A consultant is typically employed to manage the transaction and form an entity to hold the securities. However, there's a bigger cost, because the securities are likely to throw off a yield that is lower than the loan's fixed interest rate, and the borrower is responsible for covering the difference. That can get very expensive, unless you are lucky and bond yields have skyrocketed since you took out your fixed-rate loan. In that instance, it is possible that you could pay nothing to defease, or even make money. In a rapidly rising rate environment, a fixed-rate loan with defeasance might be a good option. In a falling or steady-rate environment, fixed-rates loans become much less desirable.

Yield Maintenance

Yield maintenance differs from defeasance in that you are allowed to pay off the loan prior to the maturity date. The only problem is, you must ensure that the lender receives the interest on the loan that they would have been entitled to if you had not prepaid the balance.

This doesn't mean that if you have five years left on your loan term you have to send in payments for five more years even though you paid off the loan. What it does mean is that the lender will calculate the present value of the interest through the remaining loan term and charge you a prepayment penalty in that amount. Just as with defeasance, if interest rates have inflated significantly, it is possible that the yield maintenance penalty could be zero. But in a stable- or falling-rate environment, a yield maintenance penalty could be disastrously high.

I once purchased a property where the seller was paying a yield maintenance penalty of nearly $2 million (on a $12 million loan), and the penalty can go much, much higher depending on the size of the loan.

Fixed Versus Floating Rate: The Great Debate

The choice between fixed and floating interest rates centers primarily on risk. The obvious risk is rising interest rates. A fixed-rate loan eliminates that risk because the rate is locked in at the beginning. But thanks to prepayment penalties, defeasance, and yield maintenance, fixed-rate loans introduce a separate and less-appreciated risk factor not present in floating-rate loans. That is, it can cost you big money to get out of them.

Floating-rate loans transfer interest-rate risk to the borrower, and the theory is that the borrower gets paid for taking that risk because the starting rate on the floating-rate loan is typically lower than the starting rate on a fixed-rate loan. For example, let's say that fixed-rate loans are priced at 4.5 percent and floating-rate loans are priced at 3.25 percent. There is a 1.25 percent difference between the two loans, and the interest on the floating-rate loan is going to cost less than on the fixed-rate loan.

If rates rise 0.5 percent, the interest rate on the fixed-rate loan will still be 4.5 percent, but the floating-rate loan will adjust upward to 3.75 percent. Let's say that happens after the first year. After the second year, rates go up another 0.5 percent, bringing the floating rate to 4.25 percent. The rate is still 0.25 percent lower than the fixed-rate loan, and as a result the borrower is still "getting paid" for taking interest-rate risk from the lender.

Let's say interest rates go up another 0.5 percent after the third year. Now the rate on the floating loan is 4.75 percent, which is 0.25 percent higher than the fixed-rate loan. Many people would be quick to point out that the floating rate is costing more that the fixed rate, which means that the fixed-rate loan would have been the better choice. However, let's not forget that the borrower with the floating rate saved 1.25 percent for the first year, 0.75 percent for the second year, and 0.25 percent for the third year. If the business plan is to fix the property up and sell after three years, the floating-rate loan in this example clearly wins.

On the other hand, if the business plan is to hold the property for ten years and interest rates continue to climb, the fixed-rate loan will cost less from a total interest cost standpoint.

Let's introduce yield maintenance into the discussion. Most floating-rate loans can be prepaid with just a small exit fee, perhaps 0.5 percent to 1 percent of the loan amount, and in certain cases that exit fee can be waived, such as when refinancing with the same lender, for example.

A fixed-rate loan cannot be prepaid in the same manner. Let's go back to our example of a business plan to fix up the property and sell in three years. If the property was financed with a floating-rate loan, the sponsor could sell the property, pay the 1 percent exit fee, and distribute the capital and profits to the investors. If the property was financed with a fixed-rate loan with a ten-year maturity, the sponsor would have to pay the yield maintenance penalty. With seven years left on the loan, let's just say, for argument's sake, that the yield maintenance penalty is 15 percent of the loan amount. If the improvements made to the property increase its value by 25 percent, after factoring in the costs of the improvements and the costs to sell the property, the yield maintenance penalty could soak up the entire profit.

Looking at another example, let's say that the plan is to improve the property and refinance after three years, pulling cash out to return to the investors. If the property is acquired with floating-rate debt, no problem. The sponsor pays the 1 percent exit fee (or not, if it's waived) and gets a new loan with a higher starting balance based on the higher property value. The sponsor can now make a distribution to the investors to return some capital.

If the property was originally financed with a fixed-rate loan, it's possible that the entire amount of capital earmarked for returning money to investors could be soaked up by the yield maintenance penalty for the old loan. The plan fails. Or does it?

Supplemental Loans

There is an alternative in this situation. In some cases, the sponsor can obtain what's called a "supplemental," which essentially is a second mortgage. A supplemental is written by the same lender as the original loan and provides for a mechanism to pull cash out of the property after improvements have been made and income has increased. Placing a supplemental does not pay off the original loan; it just adds another loan behind the original, thus there is no yield maintenance to ruin your day.

However, this isn't a perfect solution. Supplementals come with a higher price tag in the form of a larger spread on the interest rate. This further increases the overall interest cost on the debt, and when compared to a new floating-rate loan or even a new fixed-rate loan, it is possible (and even likely) that the total interest cost would be higher using the existing loan with a supplemental.

Loan Assumption

Another method of avoiding yield maintenance is the loan assumption. This is where the property is sold and the new buyer assumes the existing loan, taking over the payments. Most commercial fixed-rate loans allow this, as long as the lender qualifies the new buyer and the new buyer pays an assumption fee, usually 1 percent of the loan amount. Since the loan did not pay off, there is no yield maintenance penalty. Let's go back to our example of the property that was fixed up and sold after three years. The new buyer takes over the existing loan and has seven years left before the loan matures. The seller gets to sell without paying yield maintenance.

This might sound like the perfect solution, but again, there is no such thing. Two problems arise when executing a sale with a loan assumption. The first is that the property increased in value. While this may not seem like a problem, it is, despite the fact that this increase was the entire motivation behind the seller's original acquisition in the first place.

Let's say that when the property was purchased the loan was originated at 75 percent of the purchase price. Now let's assume that the property increased in value by 25 percent. For example, the property was bought for $10 million with a $7.5 million loan and is now worth $12.5 million.

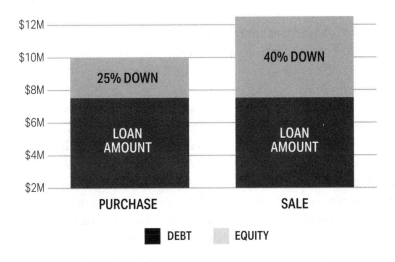

The new buyer is now assuming a loan that is only 60 percent of the purchase price. While the first owner put 25 percent down, the second owner is putting 40 percent down. In order for the second buyer to get a similar return on their invested dollar, they would have to buy at a below-market price, which is a problem for the seller.

Assumption/Supplemental Combination

A solution here could be an assumption with a supplemental, where the supplemental brings the total debt up to 75 percent of the purchase price. This solves the problem we just discussed but introduces another: The blended interest rate is higher because of the higher-rate supplemental loan. So again, the buyer will be seeking to purchase the property for a lower price to offset the higher interest rate.

The second problem introduced by the assumption sale is that the new buyer will also be looking at the yield maintenance risk on the loan. If their business plan is to sell prior to the loan maturing, they'll have to pay the yield maintenance due at that time. This could cause the buyer to subtract that expected yield maintenance premium from the purchase price, again resulting in a lower price to the seller.

So which is better, fixed or floating? This comes down to using the right tool for the job. Debt is a tool, and as we've just seen, the wrong tool can cause a complete failure of the business plan, turning a would-be profit into a break-even or even a loss. Using long-term fixed-rate financing with yield maintenance penalties might not be the right tool for a short-term business plan, just as using short-term financing for a long-term plan introduces loan maturity risk. Use the right debt for the right plan.

The way I see it, floating rate exposes you to the risk of interest rate movement. Fixed rate exposes you to the risk of yield maintenance penalties or defeasance costs.

On the other hand, floating-rate loans give the sponsor flexibility to react to the market and sell whenever the timing is right, without the gun to their head of a looming yield maintenance penalty influencing their decision. For some business plans, this might not be a factor. In any event, runaway interest rates can be mitigated by purchasing an interest rate cap. An interest rate cap is generally set a couple of percentage points above the rate at the time the loan is originated, giving some disaster insurance if rates go on a steep climb. Rate caps aren't all that expensive, at least not when compared to yield maintenance. A three-year cap is generally available for somewhere between a quarter and half a percent of the loan amount.

Common Loan Terms

In addition to those related to interest rates, there are other loan terms you should pay attention to. Let's cover a few.

- **Loan term.** This is the period of time before the loan matures. A ten-year term means that the loan will be due in full at the end of the tenth year. If the sponsor is financing with a three-year-term loan and the plan is to hold for ten years, you should have a discussion with the sponsor about what the plan is for refinancing the loan before it matures so that the investment can be held for the intended period. You should also be prepared for the possibility that financing will be unfavorable at that time, which presents a risk of foreclosure when the loan matures. Short loan terms were one of the things that caught many owners off-guard during the great financial collapse and resulted in many foreclosures of commercial property.

- **Amortization period.** This is the period over which the loan would be fully paid off. A thirty-year amortization period means that if principal and interest payments are made for thirty years, the loan balance at the end of thirty years would be zero. It is common for commercial loans to have a shorter loan term than amortization period, such as a thirty-year amortization with a ten-year term. Principal and interest payments will be made for ten years, which will reduce the loan balance, and at the end of the tenth year the remaining balance is due in full.

- **Interest-only period.** Also called the IO period or I/O period, this is a segment of time in the beginning of the loan when interest-only payments are due. No principal payments are due during this period. This allows for lower debt service payments in the early part of the loan. At the end of the IO period, payments increase because they now include both principal and interest going forward. IO periods are commonly one or two years but are sometimes as long as five years. There are even full-term IO periods, which last for the entire loan term.
- **Loan-to-value ratio.** Expressed as a percentage, LTV is the size of the loan relative to the purchase price of the property when used at the time of the purchase, or relative to the current market or appraised value of the property when used after the time of purchase. For the purposes of defining value at the time of purchase, the lower of the purchase price or the appraised value would be used by a lender determining the maximum loan size when LTV is the constraining measurement.

$$LTV = \frac{Loan\ Amount}{Purchase\ Price\ or\ Appraised\ Value\ or\ Market\ Value}$$

For example, a $7.5 million loan for a $10 million acquisition would be 75 percent LTV. As the LTV increases, the risk increases. Most lenders will not lend above 80 percent LTV except for a renovation or an unstabilized property, which we'll cover in a moment. Many sponsors and passive investors alike prefer to have an LTV at or below 75 percent at the time of purchase, and some prefer 65 percent or lower as a defense against adverse market cycles. When evaluating an offering, pay close attention to the LTV at the time of acquisition, but also note the LTV throughout the hold period as the property's value increases and the loan amount decreases.

- **Loan-to-cost ratio.** Similar to LTV, LTC is the loan amount expressed as a percentage of the total cost to acquire and renovate the property. An LTC of 100 percent would mean that the entire project was financed with no money from the sponsor. You'll almost never see this because, except in the rarest of circumstances, lenders will require that the owner have some money in the deal.

$$LTC = \frac{Loan\ Amount}{Purchase\ Price + Renovation\ Cost}$$

For example, a $9 million loan on a property acquired for $10 million with $1.25 million of planned capital improvements is 80 percent LTC and 90 percent LTV. These types of loans are common in renovations when the sponsor is acquiring an underperforming property, improving it, and increasing the income. The lender is willing to lend above 80 percent LTV because they believe that after the improvements are completed the LTV will drop below 80 percent, but they don't want to finance the total project cost so they cap the loan amount at 80 percent LTC instead of LTV.

Recourse

Recourse means the ability of the lender to pursue the assets of the borrower in connection with the repayment of the loan or the property's obligations. Loans are either full recourse, partial recourse, or non-recourse. A full-recourse loan means that if the borrower defaults on the loan and the lender suffers a loss, the lender can sue the borrower and seize other assets belonging to the borrower in an effort to recapture that loss.

Recourse loans are common from banks and on smaller commercial loans, development loans, and loans made to inexperienced borrowers. These loans are also sometimes referred to as loans with a personal guarantee.

In the case of a non-recourse loan, the lender cannot, in most instances, pursue the borrower's other assets in the event of a borrower default. This means that the lender can only look to the collateral property in an effort to collect, and if they foreclose on the collateral and suffer a loss, that loss is the lender's loss to bear.

Non-recourse loans aren't completely non-recourse, however. They usually have partial guarantees, called "bad boy carve-outs" or just "carve-out guarantees." Under these guarantees the borrower or their key principal (KP) personally guarantees that the lender won't sustain a loss as a result of certain specified acts. These usually include fraud committed by the borrower, diversion of funds that should have been used to pay senior obligations such as property taxes, diversion of money that was to be set aside for the renovation of the property, and the filing of a bankruptcy petition. Commission of any of these acts can turn the non-recourse loan to full or partial recourse.

A partial-recourse loan lies somewhere between recourse and non-recourse, and usually means that the borrower has personally guaranteed a portion of the loan. The portion might be 10 percent of the loan amount, 50 percent of the loan amount, or whatever number is mutually agreed to in the negotiation when the loan is originated.

One benefit for investors in a syndication is that there is typically no recourse to the passive investor related to the debt financing. In other words, in the event of a foreclosure and loss to the lender, the lender cannot come after you and your assets in an effort to collect the balance.

There can be exceptions to this from certain lenders, however. The most common exception is for investors taking a large stake of the equity, usually 10 to 20 percent. An investor taking such a large position can be considered a KP by some lenders, who may require that the investor either sign a personal guarantee or sign on to the bad boy carve-outs. This wouldn't be done without the investor's knowledge; the investor would have to sign specific lender documents agreeing to this prior to closing escrow. Other times, the investor would need to have some element of control rights, such as the ability to kick out the sponsor, in order for the lender to require the investor to be a guarantor on the loan. In some instances, the requirement for a passive investor to sign on carve-outs can be negotiated out of the loan terms, so even a large investor wouldn't be required to be a guarantor.

Types of Lenders

There are many different types of lenders for commercial property. Here are the major ones.

- **Agencies.** An agency loan is one that is backed by a GSE, either Fannie Mae or Freddie Mac.
- **Bridge.** Bridge lenders come in many shapes and sizes. Debt funds and banks are the most likely to call themselves bridge lenders or offer bridge lending products. Bridge loans are relatively short-term, typically three to five years, and offer higher LTVs because they tend to

limit loan proceeds to an LTC ratio. Interest is usually floating rate with a higher spread than agency loans. Bridge loans are a great tool for acquiring unstabilized value-add property, where agencies would be most restrictive and cap out at relatively low LTVs. Despite the higher interest cost, bridge loans can allow investors to receive a higher return because they contribute less cash than in an agency lending scenario.

- **HUD.** The United States Department of Housing and Urban Development offers financing for certain income-restricted properties with longer amortization periods. The time it takes to originate such loans, the onerous reporting requirements, and restrictions on distributions make them a lot less popular than they would be if they were faster to get and easier to deal with.

- **Banks.** Bank loans are more common for smaller multifamily properties but tend to be less competitive for larger properties, especially stabilized properties, where the agencies dominate the landscape. Bank loans are more useful in specialty lending situations, such as unstabilized properties, development projects, smaller assets, and office and retail sectors.

- **CMBS.** Although the letters stand for commercial mortgage-backed securities, CMBS loans are originated by lenders that specialize in making loans and then selling (or "securitizing") them as commercial mortgage-backed securities. CMBS loans were really popular before the great financial collapse, or GFC, because the lenders would make crazy loans at high LTVs and long IO periods, which from the lens of a borrower was more competitive than most other options. After losing their shirts in a rash of foreclosures after the GFC, CMBS lenders got more disciplined, and now their programs are less competitive than the agencies in many cases.

- **Life insurance companies.** These companies make commercial loans, generally focusing on larger loans against newer properties. You are less likely to encounter life insurance companies when looking at a syndication of an older value-add property.

Case Studies

You can see that there are a lot of options for structuring debt. Choice of structure, lender, and terms will have a positive or negative effect on the risk and financial performance of an investment. To help sort that out, here are a few case studies.

In the earlier chapter on analyzing operating statements we used a sample property that produced a sample set of cash flows. Let's use the same deal to model out a few different debt scenarios, assuming a $16.5 million purchase price. After you see these scenarios you'll understand why two different sponsors could syndicate the same property and come up with vastly different forecasted returns if they were using different debt structures. This is yet another example of why simply comparing returns without context can steer you in the wrong direction.

Agency Fixed 75 Percent LTV

Let's start by examining a fixed-rate agency loan with a five-year term, thirty-year amortization, and 75 percent LTV, which is a loan amount of $12,375,000 at a 4.5 percent interest rate.

OPERATING STATEMENT	YEAR 1	YEAR 2	YEAR 3	YEAR 4	YEAR 5
Before-Debt Cash Flow	$814,334	$1,138,708	$1,306,288	$1,440,589	$1,503,800
Debt Service	$(752,428)	$(752,428)	$(752,428)	$(752,428)	$(752,428)
After-Debt Cash Flow	$61,906	$386,280	$553,861	$688,162	$751,372

Note that the after-debt cash flow in year 1 is very low. In fact, the DSCR is only 1.18 in year 1. Many lenders' DSCR minimums fall between 1.15 and 1.25. Also, notice that the default ratio is very high here in year 1—more than 92 percent. This would be problematic if the first-year performance were to suffer, as there is little room for error. But it does fall into lower-risk territory in year 2 and beyond.

	AVERAGE	Year 1	Year 2	Year 3	Year 4	Year 5
SECONDARY PERFORMANCE INDICATORS						
Debt Coverage Ratio	2.03	1.18	1.61	1.84	2.02	2.11
Break-Even Occupancy (%GPR)	66.52%	69.92%	69.85%	68.96%	68.05%	67.07%
Default Ratio (%EGI)	71.25%	92.67%	78.91%	73.54%	69.89%	68.48%

This debt might be achievable, or the low DSCR might be a signal that this loan would be coverage constrained, and the lender would only approve a smaller loan amount. I'll discuss the implications of this in a bit, but stick with me here. The purpose of this exercise is to compare debt options and how they impact the primary performance indicators. To that end, the next step is to analyze a sale in year 5.

SALE ANALYSIS	YEAR 5
Next Year's NOI	$1,636,911
Exit Cap Rate	5.90%
Sale Price	$27,744,260
Cost of Sale	$(832,328)
Loan Balance	$(11,325,797)
Working Capital Return	$372,662
Net Sales Proceeds	$15,958,798

The final step is to add the net sales proceeds to the year 5 after-debt cash flow, and then lay out the initial investment and each year's cash flow as below.

IRR	MULTIPLE	TOTALS	YEAR 0	YEAR 1	YEAR 2	YEAR 3	YEAR 4	YEAR 5
Investor Cash Flow								
20.33%	2.39x	$10,700,378	$(7,700,000)	$61,906	$386,280	$553,861	$688,162	$16,710,170
Cash-on-Cash Return								
6.34%	←— Average		Yearly —→	0.80%	5.01%	7.19%	8.93%	9.75%

Notice that this debt scenario requires $7.7 million of investment capital and results in a 20.33 percent IRR, 2.39 equity multiple, and 6.34 percent average cash-on-cash return. You can also see each year's CoC return along the bottom row under each year's cash flow. Note that for the purpose of comparing loan options in these case studies these performance indicators are gross numbers, which means before the sponsor has received a split of the profits. Sponsor fees are included in all the calculations in this chapter, however.

Agency Fixed 65 Percent LTV

Next, let's model out the same fixed-rate agency loan, but this time at 65 percent LTV, which is a $10,725,000 loan amount at 4.5 percent interest.

OPERATING STATEMENT	YEAR 1	YEAR 2	YEAR 3	YEAR 4	YEAR 5
Before-Debt Cash Flow	$814,334	$1,138,708	$1,306,288	$1,440,589	$1,503,800
Debt Service	$(652,104)	$(652,104)	$(652,104)	$(652,104)	$(652,104)
After-Debt Cash Flow	$162,230	$486,604	$654,184	$788,485	$851,696

SALE ANALYSIS	YEAR 5
Next Year's NOI	$1,636,911
Exit Cap Rate	5.90%
Sale Price	$27,744,260
Cost of Sale	$(832,328)
Loan Balance	$(8,815,691)
Working Capital Return	$359,788
Net Sales Proceeds	$17,456,029

IRR	MULTIPLE	TOTALS	YEAR 0	YEAR 1	YEAR 2	YEAR 3	YEAR 4	YEAR 5
Investor Cash Flow								
18.35%	2.19x	$11,099,228	$(9,300,000)	$162,230	$486,604	$654,184	$788,485	$18,307,725
Cash-on-Cash Return								
6.33%	← Average	Yearly →	1.74%	5.23%	7.03%	8.48%	9.16%	

Under this scenario, the required investment capital rose to $9.3 million. The IRR went down roughly 2 percent, the equity multiple is down 20 basis points, but the average CoC return wasn't impacted much.

	AVERAGE	Year 1	Year 2	Year 3	Year 4	Year 5
SECONDARY PERFORMANCE INDICATORS						
Debt Coverage Ratio	2.35	1.36	1.86	2.12	2.33	2.43
Break-Even Occupancy (%GPR)	62.86%	65.74%	65.79%	65.02%	64.22%	63.36%
Default Ratio (%EGI)	67.31%	87.14%	74.33%	69.34%	65.97%	64.69%

This financing scenario resulted in a 1.36 DSCR in the first year, so it is likely that this scenario would be easily approved by the lender, as opposed to our 75 percent LTV scenario that resulted in a DSCR lower than what would likely be approved.

Interest-Only Period

Next, let's model the exact same loan, but with two years of interest-only payments, after which the loan will amortize with thirty-year amortization. An interest-only period is common in the agency lending space, and it's popular because it reduces the debt service during the early years when income is the lowest. Interest-only periods range from one year to all the way to the end of the loan term. One to two years is very common; longer interest-only periods tend to be restricted to loans with a lower LTV. In the operating statement, notice that the debt service jumps in year 3 when the debt rolls from interest-only to principal and interest payments.

OPERATING STATEMENT	YEAR 1	YEAR 2	YEAR 3	YEAR 4	YEAR 5
Before-Debt Cash Flow	$814,334	$1,138,708	$1,306,288	$1,440,589	$1,503,800
Debt Service	$(490,669)	$(489,328)	$(652,104)	$(652,104)	$(652,104)
After-Debt Cash Flow	$323,665	$649,380	$654,184	$788,485	$851,696

SALE ANALYSIS	YEAR 5
Next Year's NOI	$1,636,911
Exit Cap Rate	5.90%
Sale Price	$27,744,260
Cost of Sale	$(832,328)
Loan Balance	$(10,204,079)
Working Capital Return	$359,787
Net Sales Proceeds	$17,067,641

IRR	MULTIPLE	TOTALS	YEAR 0	YEAR 1	YEAR 2	YEAR 3	YEAR 4	YEAR 5
Investor Cash Flow								
18.65%	2.19x	$11,035,051	$(9,300,000)	$323,665	$649,380	$654,184	$788,485	$17,919,336
Cash-on-Cash Return								
7.03%	◄— Average		Yearly —►	3.48%	6.98%	7.03%	8.48%	9.16%

This financing structure results in a slightly higher IRR and average CoC return but a substantially higher year 1 cash flow. Some people see interest-only periods as increasing the risk profile of the investment. I suppose in some cases that could be true, but more often I view a short interest-only period as reducing risk. As you can see in this example, the DSCR in the first year is higher as a result of the interest-only period, jumping from 1.36 in the previous scenario to 1.8 in this scenario. The break-even occupancy and default ratio are also lower. The extra cash flow provides a cushion during that critical first year, when the bulk of the value-add heavy lifting is in progress.

	AVERAGE	Year 1	Year 2	Year 3	Year 4	Year 5
SECONDARY PERFORMANCE INDICATORS						
Debt Coverage Ratio	2.45	1.80	2.48	2.12	2.33	2.43
Break-Even Occupancy (%GPR)	61.53%	59.02%	59.22%	65.02%	64.22%	63.36%
Default Ratio (%EGI)	65.68%	78.24%	66.90%	69.34%	65.97%	64.69%

The key things to look for in this scenario are the DSCR, break-even ratio, and default ratio in the year that the payments increase from interest-only to amortizing. What you want to see is that the DSCR doesn't get too low and the default ratio doesn't get too high (more than 85 percent). Notice in this example that the DSCR and default ratio with fully amortizing payments are actually more favorable than they were in the first year, when the loan was interest-only. If things don't go according to plan, however, these favorable measurements won't be as favorable. Nevertheless, at least you have a way to quantify the risks by examining these ratios in the forecast, if the sponsor is providing them. If they aren't, you can calculate them yourself using the formulas in chapter 9.

Yield Maintenance

Next, let's examine this same loan, but instead of a five-year term let's model a ten-year term. Longer amortization periods are preferable for mitigating refinance and loan maturity risk, and many investors like to see the extra wiggle room in case an adverse economic cycle makes a sale at the end of the fifth year undesirable or impossible.

OPERATING STATEMENT	YEAR 1	YEAR 2	YEAR 3	YEAR 4	YEAR 5
Before-Debt Cash Flow	$814,334	$1,138,708	$1,306,288	$1,440,589	$1,503,800
Debt Service	$(490,669)	$(489,328)	$(652,104)	$(652,104)	$(652,104)
After-Debt Cash Flow	$323,665	$649,380	$654,184	$788,485	$851,696

SALE ANALYSIS	YEAR 5
Next Year's NOI	$1,636,911
Exit Cap Rate	5.90%
Sale Price	$27,744,260
Cost of Sale	$(832,328)
Loan Balance	$(10,204,079)
Yield Maintenance	$(985,000)
Working Capital Return	$359,787
Net Sales Proceeds	$16,082,641

Because we are selling in year 5 and paying off the ten-year loan early, we are forced to pay a yield maintenance penalty. This estimated yield maintenance penalty was calculated with an online yield maintenance estimator.

IRR	MULTIPLE	TOTALS	YEAR 0	YEAR 1	YEAR 2	YEAR 3	YEAR 4	YEAR 5
Investor Cash Flow								
17.43%	2.08x	$10,050,051	$(9,300,000)	$323,665	$649,380	$654,184	$788,485	$16,934,336
Cash-on-Cash Return								
7.03%	←— Average		Yearly —→	3.48%	6.98%	7.03%	8.48%	9.16%

The nearly million-dollar cost of the yield maintenance reduces the IRR by 1.22 percentage points and reduces the equity multiple by 11 basis points. Because the yield maintenance is paid from the proceeds of the sale, it has no impact on CoC return. If you had invested $100,000 in this offering, this yield maintenance penalty would cost you roughly $11,000 in profits on the sale. If the property wound up being sold in year 3 instead of year 5, the yield maintenance penalty would have risen to $1,396,000 (using the same online yield maintenance estimator). This would have had a much more substantial impact to the IRR.

Floating Rate

To eliminate yield maintenance, a floating-rate loan could be used. Let's examine a scenario with a seven-year 65 percent LTV agency loan priced at thirty-day LIBOR plus 180 basis points, which is a starting interest rate of roughly 4 percent, although it varies monthly. To forecast the variation, I've used a ten-year LIBOR forecast that predicts the rate each month for ten years. The actual rate may be higher or lower than the forecasted rate depending on market movement. This loan is also 65 percent LTV and has twenty-four months of interest-only payments.

OPERATING STATEMENT	YEAR 1	YEAR 2	YEAR 3	YEAR 4	YEAR 5
Before-Debt Cash Flow	$814,334	$1,138,708	$1,306,288	$1,440,589	$1,503,800
Debt Service	$(454,284)	$(431,889)	$(611,429)	$(617,504)	$(625,480)
After-Debt Cash Flow	$360,050	$706,819	$694,860	$823,085	$878,320

SALE ANALYSIS	YEAR 5
Next Year's NOI	$1,636,911
Exit Cap Rate	5.90%
Sale Price	$27,744,260
Cost of Sale	$(832,328)
Loan Balance	$(10,158,977)
Working Capital Return	$359,787
Net Sales Proceeds	$17,112,743

IRR	MULTIPLE	TOTALS	YEAR 0	YEAR 1	YEAR 2	YEAR 3	YEAR 4	YEAR 5
Investor Cash Flow								
19.09%	2.21x	$11,275,876	$(9,300,000)	$360,050	$706,819	$694,860	$823,085	$17,991,063
Cash-on-Cash Return								
7.45%	◀— Average	Yearly —▶	3.87%	7.60%	7.47%	8.85%	9.44%	

In this scenario, you get the highest IRR, equity multiple, and average CoC out of all the scenarios we've tested thus far, except for the 75 percent LTV fixed-rate scenario—but that scenario might be impossible because the DSCR is below some lender minimums.

	AVERAGE	Year 1	Year 2	Year 3	Year 4	Year 5
SECONDARY PERFORMANCE INDICATORS						
Debt Coverage Ratio	2.55	1.95	2.81	2.27	2.47	2.54
Break-Even Occupancy (%GPR)	60.62%	57.51%	56.90%	63.43%	62.91%	62.38%
Default Ratio (%EGI)	64.67%	76.23%	64.28%	67.64%	64.61%	63.69%

Notice that the floating-rate scenario also results in a higher average DSCR, and lower average break-even occupancy and default ratio than you saw in the earlier fixed-rate scenarios. That's because in this model the interest rate is lower than in the fixed-rate scenario. Certainly it is possible that floating-rate debt could rise above fixed-rate levels and swing the pendulum in the opposite direction. One common defense mechanism is to purchase a rate cap, which essentially puts a ceiling on the interest rate at a point where the debt service would result in a 1.0 DSCR using the lender's first-year underwriting.

Cash-Out Refinance

Using the same floating-rate 65 percent LTV loan scenario, let's take this one step further and introduce a cash-out refinance at the end of year 3. For the new loan, we'll use a loan amount of $16 million, which is about 63 percent LTV of the capitalized value of the income at the time the loan is made. This time the interest rate will be LIBOR plus 200 basis points, which is roughly 4.2 percent interest. We will get another twenty-four months of interest-only payments with the new loan.

OPERATING STATEMENT	YEAR 1	YEAR 2	YEAR 3	YEAR 4	YEAR 5
Before-Debt Cash Flow	$814,334	$1,138,708	$1,306,288	$1,440,589	$1,503,800
Debt					
Debt Service	$(454,284)	$(431,889)	$(618,178)	$(688,059)	$(726,728)
Loan Fees	$—	$—	$(585,556)	$—	$—
Loan Payoff	$—	$—	$(10,555,563)	$—	$—
Added Loan	$—	$—	$16,000,000	$—	$—
Net Debt Effect	$(454,284)	$(431,889)	$4,240,704	$(688,059)	$(726,728)
After-Debt Cash Flow	$360,050	$706,819	$5,546,992	$752,530	$777,072

SALE ANALYSIS	YEAR 5
Next Year's NOI	$1,636,911
Exit Cap Rate	5.90%
Sale Price	$27,744,260
Cost of Sale	$(832,328)
Loan Balance	$(16,000,000)
Working Capital Return	$359,787
Net Sales Proceeds	$11,291,133

IRR	MULTIPLE	TOTALS	YEAR 0	YEAR 1	YEAR 2	YEAR 3	YEAR 4	YEAR 5
Investor Cash Flow								
20.41%	2.09x	$10,134,596	$(9,300,000)	$360,050	$706,819	$5,546,992	$752,530	$12,068,205
Cash-on-Cash Return								
10.78%	←— Average		Yearly —→	3.87%	7.60%	7.99%	16.94%	17.50%

This debt scenario significantly boosts performance, because in year 3 nearly $4.86 million of capital is returned (the rest is operating cash flow). This means that the CoC is increased in the final two years because there is significantly less money remaining committed to the deal. The equity multiple goes down slightly, primarily because of the extra interest on the larger loan after the refinance.

	AVERAGE	Year 1	Year 2	Year 3	Year 4	Year 5
SECONDARY PERFORMANCE INDICATORS						
Debt Coverage Ratio	2.02	1.95	2.81	2.24	2.21	2.18
Break-Even Occupancy (%GPR)	67.04%	57.51%	56.90%	63.69%	65.59%	66.12%
Default Ratio (%EGI)	71.25%	76.23%	64.28%	67.92%	67.37%	67.51%

The key things to watch for in a cash-out refinance scenario are the DSCR, break-even occupancy, and default ratio in the first year after the refinance. Because the debt on the property is increasing, there will be increased drag on the cash flow. This could result in reintroducing elements of risk that would be nearly distant memories if the debt were left alone. But notice in this scenario that the DSCR is more favorable in the first year after the refinance than it was during the first year after purchase.

Some might argue that increasing the size of the loan introduces more risk. Conversely, others might argue that receiving more than half of your capital back after the refinance reduces your risk because it limits your downside. You can no longer lose all your money, only half of it. Maybe that makes you feel better, maybe it doesn't, but one thing is for sure: You can certainly earn more money. Not only does this debt scenario increase your return, but after year 3 you can invest half of your original investment in another offering, and essentially earn two sets of returns on the same dollars.

Bridge Loan

In our final case study let's examine a bridge loan scenario. This loan will be 80 percent LTC (notice this is *to cost*, not *to value*, so this includes purchase price plus renovation). The purchase price is $16,500,000 and the renovation budget is $2,387,000. Let's use a loan amount of $15.1 million at LIBOR plus 3.5 percent, which is a starting interest rate of around 6 percent.

Bridge loans are typically floating rate, and often have a three-year term (although some are shorter and some are longer) and interest-only payments to maturity. Bridge loans carry higher interest rates in exchange for the higher LTV. They typically have lower DSCR limits too, sometimes even less than 1.0, as in this scenario. Notice the negative cash flow in year 1 that is covered by an interest reserve (money placed on deposit to subsidize negative cash flow).

To pay off the loan at the end of the term, let's model for an agency loan refinance using the same terms as the refinance in our previous case study.

OPERATING STATEMENT	YEAR 1	YEAR 2	YEAR 3	YEAR 4	YEAR 5
Before-Debt Cash Flow	$814,334	$1,138,708	$1,306,288	$1,440,589	$1,503,800
Debt					
Debt Service	$(900,576)	$(868,333)	$(850,221)	$(688,059)	$(726,728)
Loan Fees	$—	$—	$(631,000)	$—	$—
Loan Payoff	$—	$—	$(15,100,000)	$—	$—
Added Loan	$—	$—	$16,000,000	$—	$—
Net Debt Effect	$(900,576)	$(868,333)	$(581,221)	$(688,059)	$(726,728)
Interest Reserve	$86,242				
After-Debt Cash Flow	$0	$270,375	$725,067	$752,530	$777,072

SALE ANALYSIS	YEAR 5
Next Year's NOI	$1,636,911
Exit Cap Rate	5.90%
Sale Price	$27,744,260
Cost of Sale	$(832,328)
Loan Balance	$(15,980,587)
Working Capital Return	$399,108
Net Sales Proceeds	$11,330,453

IRR	MULTIPLE	TOTALS	YEAR 0	YEAR 1	YEAR 2	YEAR 3	YEAR 4	YEAR 5
Investor Cash Flow								
23.03%	2.61x	$8,555,498	$(5,300,000)	$0	$270,375	$725,067	$752,530	$12,107,525
Cash-on-Cash Return								
8.83%	◄— Average		Yearly —►	0.00%	5.10%	8.66%	14.96%	15.45%

The bridge scenario reduces the required investment capital from $9.3 million to $5.3 million. But with less equity comes higher risk: loan maturity risk, higher interest rates, higher LTV, lower DSCR, and potentially even negative cash flow.

	AVERAGE	Year 1	Year 2	Year 3	Year 4	Year 5
SECONDARY PERFORMANCE INDICATORS						
Debt Coverage Ratio	1.73	0.98	1.40	1.63	2.21	2.18
Break-Even Occupancy (%GPR)	71.57%	76.08%	74.53%	72.79%	65.59%	66.12%
Default Ratio (%EGI)	76.67%	100.84%	84.20%	77.63%	67.37%	67.51%

Notice that the highest risk is the first year. Because of the negative cash flow, extra money needs to be raised to cover the debt service. It would also be prudent to raise even more cash reserves than normal, just to have on hand in the event that things didn't go exactly to plan, as any hiccup can cause major problems in this scenario. After the second year, assuming that the plan to increase income was effective, the risk normalizes. In the right circumstances, bridge loans can serve a useful purpose. Only you can decide if the risk is acceptable to you, and if the potential reward of higher returns offsets the potential downside of thinner safety margins.

Case Study Comparison

We've examined several debt scenarios here, all of them with the same set of operating cash flows. As you have seen, each of these scenarios resulted in a different value for each of the primary performance indicators. Let's examine all the scenarios at a glance.

	IRR	MULTIPLE	COC
Fixed Rate 5-Year	18.35%	2.19	6.33%
FFixed Rate 5-Year with 2 Years I/O	18.65%	2.19	7.03%
Fixed Rate 10-Year with 2 yYears I/O	17.43%	2.08	7.03%
Floating Rate with 2 Years I/O	19.09%	2.21	7.45%
Floating Rate with Year 3 rRefinance	20.41%	2.09	10.78%
Bridge Loan with Year 3 Refinance	23.03%	2.61	8.83%

The point of all this is not to advocate for one method of financing over another. Instead, it is to show how financing impacts cash flow using a comparison of several financing structures with the same set of operating cash flows. It's interesting to note that in this case the ten-year fixed-rate loan performs the worst and the bridge debt performs the best, albeit with the trade-off of higher risk. A noteworthy compromise is the floating rate with year 3 refinance. This provides a high return with less risk than bridge, and returns some capital to reinvest in another investment two years early.

As discussed earlier in this chapter, debt is a tool, and the right tool must be used for each job. Every type of financing comes with advantages and disadvantages, and as of yet, there is no single "perfect" debt vehicle.

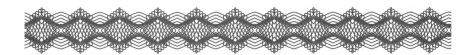

CHAPTER 11

CAPITAL IMPROVEMENTS

There is one certainty for real estate owners: Sooner or later you are going to have to spend money replacing a major component. Maybe it's a roof or maybe it's appliances, but with so many systems that have limited useful lives, capital improvements are part of the deal.

What is a capital improvement? And how is it different from a repair?

A repair is the correction of a routine defect, such as replacing a broken light switch. Every operating budget should have a line item for routine repairs, except perhaps triple-net commercial investments where the tenant is responsible for all repairs.

Capital improvements, also known as capital expenditures or replacements, are different from repairs because they extend the useful life of the property. Fixing an air conditioner is a repair. Replacing an air conditioner is a capital improvement. A new roof, new windows, new doors, new siding, upgraded interiors, and new pool furniture are all examples of capital improvements.

Capital improvements are often referred to as "CapEx," "cap-ex," or "capX"—all abbreviations for "capital expenditures." There are two forms of CapEx, immediate and routine. Immediate CapEx is performed near the time of acquisition, typically either as part of a renovation program or to correct deferred maintenance. Routine CapEx can occur at any time and would include things like replacing an old water heater, sealing and restriping the parking lot, painting the exterior, and plastering the swimming pool.

Improvement Plans

Value-add investments typically involve some level of property renovation. With apartments, the most common are upgrading interior finishes, such as cabinet faces, countertops, flooring, lighting and plumbing fixtures, and appliances. In hotels they might involve flooring and paint, new shower and bath tile, upgrading fixtures, and replacing furniture. For office property they would include foyer improvements, landscaping, new flooring, and paint in the hallways. Retail shopping center value-add investments usually include parking lot improvements, lighting, and facade improvements to modernize curb appeal.

Plans for these types of renovations are established as part of the business plan. A renovation budget is set and the funds for making the improvements are raised along with the other funds needed to acquire the property. The offering documents for the investment should include a renovation budget showing how the money will be spent and how much will be spent.

The budget might be broken into two parts, interior and exterior. Interior renovation budgets are often discussed as a price per unit. For example, light renovations at a Class C apartment complex might be expressed in the budget as $3,500 per unit. On the other hand, a Class A multifamily budget might be $15,000 per unit because of higher-end finishes such as granite countertops, travertine tile, and stainless-steel appliances. The cost per unit will depend on the scope of the interior renovation, the size of the units, and the quality of materials to be used. Some sponsors might itemize the interior upgrades, attaching a cost for each item and then estimating how many of each of those items will be needed. Because the interiors of the units tend to vary considerably, there's no right or wrong answer here as long as the sponsor has done the proper due diligence to not get caught off-guard by finding the units in worse condition than they expected.

Where the property is located can also have a big influence on renovation cost. In Houston, I can renovate an entire Class B apartment for about $7,500. But in California I just paid that for kitchen countertops alone.

The exterior renovation budget may include correction of deferred maintenance as well as amenity enhancements. Deferred maintenance includes replacement of dry-rotted wood siding, new roofs, sealing the parking lot, plastering the swimming pool, replacing pool pumps, and fixing broken stair treads.

Examples of amenity enhancements are new fitness center equipment, clubhouse upgrades, new pool furniture, installing an outdoor kitchen and barbecue grills, adding a dog park, and upgrading playground equipment. These items are typically shown as an itemized list, with each item having a projected cost.

Routine Replacements

Aside from improvement plans, the other type of CapEx is the routine replacement. Refrigerators only last so long. Air conditioner pumps wear out. Tennis court surfaces fade. All will need to be replaced over time. These things don't usually have to be replaced all at once; instead it's a water heater here, a stove there. At a large apartment complex, hardly a month goes by without something having to be replaced.

These replacements are budgeted for on an annual basis. You don't see these items on the income and expense statement because they're not expenses, they're capital improvements. Since they aren't related to the normal operation of the property, these items don't impact the net operating income, but they still cost money, which impacts the cash flow.

Sponsors have two ways of dealing with this. One is to simply hold back cash from distributions to save up for future routine capital replacements. The more common way is forced upon the sponsor by the debt lender. Lenders know that all real estate will need routine replacements, so they require the borrower to deposit money into a lender-controlled reserve account. Each month, as the mortgage payment is made, anywhere from hundreds to thousands of dollars are deposited into this reserve account. The borrower cannot access the funds without producing receipts to the lender showing that a capital improvement was made. This is designed to prevent borrowers from letting the property go and keeping all the cash flow, only to later let the property go into foreclosure, leaving the lender owning a property with a ton of deferred maintenance and failed systems.

Physical Inspections

As part of the due diligence process, the sponsor should inspect the property to determine its physical condition. Every single unit should be entered and inspected, and the condition noted. Major mechanical systems should be tested and inspected, and estimates should be made of the remaining useful life of those systems.

Structural components—including the foundation, roof, windows, siding, plumbing, wiring, circuit breaker panels, and underground utilities—should be checked. These due diligence inspections are done to identify any need for immediate CapEx. As problems are identified, specialists should be engaged to estimate the cost of correcting any adverse findings. Then the items can either be added to the budget, or a credit or repair can be negotiated between the buyer and the seller.

Plumbing is a difficult system to inspect because it's invisible, hidden either underground, under floors, or in walls. But clues to plumbing problems can still be discovered. The most obvious is evidence of leaks. A less obvious (but expensive) approach is hiring a plumbing contractor to feed a camera through the plumbing lines to look for defects from the inside. At least one inspection can be completed without even visiting the property: looking at the financials. An unusually high water bill can be a clue to potential water leaks. Unusually high ongoing plumbing repair expenses can be a clue to failing sewer lines, leaking supply lines, or aging fixtures.

Capital Improvement Considerations

As you review offering memorandums of private placements, take a close look at the renovation plan, renovation budget, and replacement reserves. Ask the sponsor whether the renovation budget is based on contractor bids, their past experience, or just a wild guess.

Also look to see if there is a line item in the budget for contingencies. No matter how thoroughly the property is inspected, something unexpected always crops up. Perhaps there's a budget for replacing the roof, but what if they strip off the roof and discover rotted roof sheathing underneath the shingles? How about if they go to replace bathroom floor tile and discover dry rot in the subfloor? There could be other issues as well, such as materials or labor price increases, or other surprises that cost additional money. A contingency allowance can absorb these things. If the sponsor doesn't have a contingency budget, there's a good chance that the renovation plan won't be completed as planned, or they'll have to raise additional money to complete it, or they'll need to siphon operating cash flow that otherwise could have been distributed to investors.

In what order does the sponsor plan to complete the improvements? If the exterior has poor curb appeal, starting with interior renovations isn't the best plan. No one will even see the beautiful interiors if they drive right by the property thanks to the exterior appearance. Better to start enhancing the outside first and then move to the inside.

How long will the improvements take? Exterior construction is disruptive to tenants and can cause move-outs, and make leasing more difficult. The faster it is completed, the better. If the exterior renovation is extensive, a higher vacancy factor should be used for the duration of the work. Check the sponsor's vacancy assumptions to see if they allowed for this.

Finally, try to judge the "fit" of the renovation plan. If the sponsor is planning to do a major renovation of the exterior and renovate the interiors to Class A standards, but the property is located in a low-income neighborhood, the plan might be doomed from the start. The renovation must provide a return on investment for it to be practical, and if the community cannot afford the rents needed to provide that return on investment, the property will experience either high vacancy or very little rent growth for the money invested. There are some areas where you invest in granite countertops, and some areas where you don't. Nice renovations can be done at a lower cost if the scope of the renovation is properly tailored to what is affordable for the area.

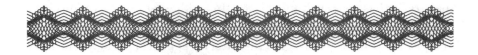

CHAPTER 12

CAP RATE AND VALUATION

Perhaps no topic is more misunderstood or debated than cap rate. Cap rate is short for "capitalization rate," which is a mathematical formula used by appraisers to measure the value of income-producing real estate.

If you've never heard of cap rate, you're in luck because you're coming into this with no misconceptions. If you already know what cap rate is, I'm about to unwind everything you've been taught, and you'll have a lot of bad habits to forget.

Cap rate is calculated by dividing the net operating income (NOI) by the property's purchase price (or sale price, depending on which side of the table you are sitting on). For example, if the property produces $100,000 of NOI, and is purchased for $1 million, the cap rate is 10 percent. If the purchase price is $2 million, the cap rate is 5 percent.

$$\frac{NOI}{Purchase\ Price} = Cap\ Rate$$

$$\frac{\$100,000}{\$1,000,000} = 10\%\ Cap\ Rate$$

That's simple enough, but the easy part ends right there. Commercial real estate investors have an odd love affair with cap rate, which leads to all sorts of opinions on what cap rate is and what it means for their investment strategy. Here's a list of the most common statements I hear about cap rate:

- "Cap rate is equivalent to the return I receive if I pay cash for the property."
- "I need to buy at a high cap rate to get the returns I'm looking for."
- "A high cap rate means I'm getting a better deal."
- "If interest rates rise by 1 percent, cap rates have to increase by 1 percent, too."

What do these four statements about cap rate have in common? They are all wrong. Yes, every one of them.

In this chapter, I'll debunk all these misconceptions and show you what cap rate really does. To avoid disappointment, I'll warn you now: It doesn't do much. Stick with me, though, because you'll be told a lot of things about cap rate as you explore real estate, and it's important to know the truth.

Myth Busted: The All-Cash Return

"Cap rate is the equivalent to the return I receive if I pay cash for the property." If you follow any online real estate discussion forums or read blog posts about cap rates, you've probably seen this statement more times than you can count. But it's wrong. How can that be? At the beginning of this chapter we learned that cap rate equals the NOI divided by the purchase price. If you recall our discussion of NOI in chapter 8, NOI doesn't account for the cost of debt service. If you pay the $1 million purchase price in cash and the property is producing $100,000 of NOI, the cap rate is 10 percent. Your annual return is also 10 percent, right? For the purposes of a simple theoretical discussion in a textbook, yes. But in the real world, no.

To purchase this $1 million property, you will need to put up more than $1 million. At the very least, you'll have to pay closing costs too. Adding closing costs makes your $1 million investment closer to $1,050,000, which drops your return to 9.5 percent. You'll probably have to put some money into fixing up the property as well. Maybe it's in immediate need of a paint job, or the parking lot has to be resealed and restriped. That adds to your investment. Let's say those things cost an additional $200,000, which means you've put up $1.25 million for $100,000 NOI, so your return is now 8 percent. That's still a 10 percent cap rate, but only an 8 percent return. So no, cap rate does not equal your return, even if you pay all cash.

Let's take it one step further. You now spend another $100,000 and make improvements to the interiors of the units, which allows you to raise rents 25 percent. If the rental income is $200,000 per year and the expenses are $100,000 per year, you have $100,000 of NOI. A 25 percent rent increase brings the rental income up to $250,000. For argument's sake let's say expenses stay the same (in reality, they won't quite), so now your NOI is $150,000. Your investment has gone from $1.25 million to $1.35 million, so your return is now 11.1 percent ($150,000 divided by $1,350,000). Still not 10 percent, despite the 10 percent cap rate!

Now let's go even deeper. Assuming this last scenario, you've increased the NOI from $100,000 to $150,000, which is a 50 percent increase. Working the cap rate calculation in reverse, at a 10 percent cap rate the property is now worth $1.5 million. If you sell it in three years and it costs you 5 percent of the sale price to get it sold, you'll net $1,425,000. You paid a total of $1,350,000, so you made a $75,000 profit on the sale. That is a 5.5 percent total return on your $1.35 million investment over three years, which is 1.83 percent per year. Add that to the 11.1 percent return you received from cash flow and your total return is now 12.95 percent annually. That's right, still not 10 percent!

What good is cap rate then? The most important thing to understand is that cap rate is not a measurement of performance; it's a measurement of market sentiment. Cap rate gives us a way to numerically quantify how the market is valuing an income stream—not the return on investment from that income stream. Let's explore what that means.

Estimating Market Value

If you live in a home in a housing tract where every fourth house has the same floor plan, it's easy to figure out how much your house is worth. Simply look at the most recent sales for your exact floor plan and you'll come pretty close to the fair-market value. You could even look at other floor plans in the same neighborhood and make adjustments for square footage, lot size, upgrades, and so on, and still get a fairly accurate estimate of value. Appraisers call this the comparable sales approach to appraising market value.

Now try to do the same thing with an apartment complex. This is difficult because no two apartment complexes are the same: The floor plans, square footage, amenities, and neighborhood all result in different rental rates in any given area.

Don't get me wrong; people will still try to use comparable sales, saying things like, "The property next door sold for $75,000 per unit, so this property must be worth $75,000 per unit." That's not necessarily true.

To complicate matters even more, the expenses at each property are different because one has water-saving plumbing fixtures, resulting in lower water bills, and the other has a master gas meter feeding all the apartments' heating systems, and the owner is paying the gas bill. There are just too many differences between one property and another for the comparable sales approach to be accurate at measuring the value of the property.

This same difficulty exists with self-storage, hotels, warehouses, and industrial properties. While one hotel might seem comparable to another, the income they produce can be wildly different. Let's say you are going to buy a self-storage facility and there is another self-storage facility right next door. Both facilities have the exact same total square footage. Couldn't you just take the sale price of the property next door and use the comparable sales approach, just like you did for your personal residence? Nope. Your facility is all 5-by-5 units, and the neighbor facility is all 10-by-20 units. You can't use price per square foot to compare the two because 5-by-5s rent for a higher price per square foot than 10-by-20s. You can't use price per unit, because there's no way a 5-by-5 is worth the same as a 10-by-20.

One thing all these apartment buildings and self-storage facilities have in common is that they produce income. An investor in income-producing real estate is investing in the property because of the income it's producing, so why not measure the value of the property by simply measuring the income? Well, that is exactly what cap rate does. Divide the income by the price a buyer was willing to pay and you get a cap rate.

Textbooks that cover real estate appraisal concepts will teach you that the value of the property is estimated by working the cap rate calculation in reverse. To determine the value of a property, you take the NOI and divide it by the cap rate. If the NOI is $100,000 and the cap rate is 5 percent, dividing the income by the cap rate results in a value of $2,000,000.

$$\frac{\$100,000 \; NOI}{.05} = \$2,000,000$$

Who's in Charge Here?

People often think that cap rate is whatever they decide it to be. You might hear someone say, "I want to buy at a 10 percent cap rate, so I'll pay $1 million for this property because the NOI is $100,000." Why do they want to buy at a 10 percent cap rate? Only they can answer that. Either they are just making up a number in their head, or they misunderstand cap rate to mean that it has something to do with investment returns, or they just generally misunderstand how cap rate is properly used. They're probably thinking that a 10 percent cap rate is better than a 7 percent cap rate, so that's what they want.

But cap rate is not about you. It doesn't care what you want to pay or what returns you expect. Cap rate cares about only one thing: What is the market willing to pay for a given income stream for this type of property, in this condition, in this area?

If every apartment complex with similar features is selling, after reasonable exposure to the market, between a willing buyer and seller (neither under any pressure to buy or sell), at a 5 percent cap rate, the cap rate for other similar properties is 5 percent. This means that the market cap rate for the property you want to buy is also 5 percent. No matter what any investor wants or expects, that's the market. What about our guy who wants to buy this property at a 10 percent cap rate? What he is essentially saying is that he wants to buy it for half its market value. Yeah, who doesn't? It's unlikely this investor will be successful at acquiring anything, because other bidders are willing to pay twice as much, so no seller will accept such a low offer.

Cap Rates Versus Performance

Cap rates work in the opposite direction of prices. Think of it like a see-saw: For the same income stream, as price goes up, cap rate goes down, and as price goes down, cap rate goes up.

Cap rate is calculated using net *operating* income, which is the effective gross income minus the property's *operating* expenses. Debt service is not included in this calculation, and for good reason. Cap rate is intended to be used as a method to compare one property against another, and each property can be, and is, financed differently. Including financing as any component of the cap rate calculation throws off the direct comparison of two or more properties against one another. There are other methods for comparing the performance of properties that include the impact of debt. You probably remember those from chapter 9—IRR, CoC, and equity multiple.

Remember the list of incorrect statements about cap rate? The second one was "I need to buy at a high cap rate to get the returns I'm looking for." Consider these two examples.

Example 1: An 8 percent cap rate on a stabilized property in a stagnant market with no rent growth, no job growth, a slowly declining population, and no ability to push rents with renovations.

Example 2: A 6 percent cap rate in a market with above-average population growth, job growth, and income growth, with stable occupancy and high rent growth. The property is underperforming relative to nearby comps. With some minor cosmetic improvements, rents can be increased 20 percent on each unit that is rented to a new resident in upgraded condition.

In nearly every case, over the long term, example 2 will outperform example 1 despite example 1's higher cap rate.

A Better Deal?

"A high cap rate means I'm getting a better deal on the property." This statement by itself is false. Our examples above illustrate this point across two different markets, but even within the same market you could have a property selling at an 8 percent cap rate that could be a worse deal than another property in the same market selling at a 6 percent cap rate.

Example 1: An 8 percent cap rate on a fifty-year-old property in which all the interiors have been recently renovated and the seller has pushed the rents to $25 higher than the comps. The property doesn't need a thing; it is totally turnkey.

Example 2: A 6 percent cap rate on a twenty-year-old property that hasn't been touched since it was built, except that the owner just put on a new roof. Interiors are original, rents are $150 below market, and renovated comps are getting $100 more than the non-renovated comps.

Example 2 is more likely to be a better deal despite the lower cap rate. There's nothing you can do to push the income in example 1; it's been pushed as far as it can go. Example 1 is fifty years old, so despite the upgrades, the maintenance bills are likely to increase substantially over time. There could also be big-ticket items in your future, such as a new roof, foundation repairs, new windows, and new heating and cooling systems; the list goes on and on.

But at example 2, you have multiple opportunities to increase income. The low-hanging fruit is just bringing the rents to market rate, in line with non-renovated comps. Then you have the option to go to the next level by performing minor interior cosmetic improvements to push rents further, to the level of the renovated comps in the area.

Now let's really blow it up with another example: a property with $200,000 rents and $100,000 expenses, which is $100,000 NOI. You invest $350,000 in closing costs and improvements so you can increase rents 25 percent to $250,000—bringing the NOI to $150,000. The property is resold after three years. We touched on this example earlier in this chapter, but let's now look at it with two different market cap rates.

CAP RATE	10%	5%
Purchase Price	$1,000,000	$2,000,000
Total Cash Invested	$1,350,000	$2,350,000
Annual Income	$150,000	$150,000
Cash-on-Cash Return	11.1%	6.4%
Sale Price	$1,500,000.00	$3,000,000.00
Cost of Sale (5%)	$(75,000.00)	$(150,000.00)
Sale Proceeds	$1,425,000.00	$2,850,000.00
Cash Invested	$(1,350,000.00)	$(2,350,000.00)
Gain on Sale	$75,000.00	$500,000.00
Total Return From Sale	5.6%	21.3%
Hold Period	3 Years	3 Years
Annual Return From Sale	1.87%	7.1%
Total Annual Return	**12.97%**	**13.5%**

(Cash-on-cash return plus annual return from sale)

Notice that the 10 percent cap rate example produced a higher return from cash flow than the 5 percent cap rate example. But the total annual return is greater on the 5-cap deal.

At the risk of sounding like a broken record, the important takeaway here is not that one cap rate is better than the other, but that cap rate is a measurement of market sentiment. It is not a measurement of performance or return.

Think of cap rate as a thermometer measuring the market. As the market heats up, buyers place a higher value on the income stream because they see upside, and that pushes cap rates down. This is called *cap rate compression.* As the market cools off, buyers back off and are only willing to buy the same income stream for a lower price. This causes cap rates to decompress, or rise. Cap rates are not static; they move as market sentiment shifts. They also are not uniform across markets or property types. Apartments built in 1980 in a good neighborhood might be selling at a 5 percent cap rate in Dallas, but a 4.5 percent cap rate in San Francisco and a 6.5 percent cap rate in Kansas City. Newer properties tend to sell at lower cap rates than older ones, and better neighborhoods command lower cap rates than war-zone neighborhoods.

Sectors all have their own cap rates. In the same neighborhood, you might find apartments selling at a 6 percent cap rate, office buildings at a 7 percent cap rate, industrial at 8 percent, retail at 9 percent, and hotels at 7.5 percent. The cap rate depends on how these sectors are performing and many other factors.

With all these variables affecting cap rates, what good are they? If used properly, cap rates are helpful for evaluating one thing and one thing only: the ultimate exit price of the property, or the price the sponsor can sell the property for at the intended point of sale. Cap rate is also used to estimate the sale price of the property for the lender, in the event that the borrower stops paying the mortgage, and the lender is forced to foreclose and resell the property.

How to Use Cap Rate

As you evaluate potential syndication opportunities, look for how the sponsor is using cap rate. Cap rate should be used to estimate the sale price of the property, not to arrive at a purchase price. If they are using it improperly, that is probably a good reason to have a conversation with the sponsor to understand their approach. It might also be a red flag that the sponsor doesn't know what they are doing.

In the example below, you can see the forecasted NOI for each year, and below that you see a projected exit cap rate for each year. By dividing the projected income by the projected exit cap rate, you can calculate the expected sale price for each future year.

SALE ANALYSIS	YEAR 1	YEAR 2	YEAR 3	YEAR 4	YEAR 5
T-12 NOI	$885,264	$1,214,473	$1,385,129	$1,522,187	$1,587,444
Exit Cap Rate	5.50%	5.60%	5.70%	5.80%	5.90%
Sale Price	$16,095,709	$21,687,018	$24,300,509	$26,244,603	$26,905,831

Where does the projected exit cap rate come from? That's a great question without a great answer. The task is to predict what market sentiment will be in the future—at what level buyers will value the income stream at that time. Doing this is part art, part science. The first step is to determine where the market cap rate for this type of property in this specific area is today. For example, if this is a Class B multifamily property, and other Class B multifamily properties in the area have sold at a 6 percent cap rate, the 6 percent cap rate is the best starting point, even if the purchase price of the subject property calculates to a 5 percent cap rate.

From this starting point of 6 percent, the sponsor next needs to have an opinion on where cap rates are likely to go in the future. If the market is super hot, cap rates and interest rates are near historic lows, and buyers are chasing after real estate like there's no tomorrow, it's a safe bet that cap rates are more likely to rise than to fall. In such a market you should look for sponsors to be forecasting exit cap rates that are higher than market cap rates today. Just how much higher is a matter of opinion, though, as no one truly knows how far cap rates will rise or when. This is where the art comes in, and the sponsor must make an educated guess as to what the increase will be.

On the other hand, if the overall market climate isn't that good, chances are cap rates have room to compress in the future when the economy and markets rebound. In that case, sponsors might forecast level or even compressing cap rates.

⚠ Here's one dirty little secret in the syndication business: Sponsors know they can manipulate the projected performance of an investment by playing with the exit cap rate. Sometimes you'll see the exit cap rate set to equal the rate at the time of purchase, even though the market is about as good as it can get. Sometimes you'll see the exit cap rate set to equal the acquisition cap rate, which could be lower than the current market cap rate. Manipulating the cap rate will alter the sale price assumptions, which will influence the projected investment returns. There's really no definitive exit cap rate; nobody can predict exactly what will happen with cap rates, so an educated guess is necessary. But are the sponsor's assumptions reasonable? Do they make sense?

Cap rates on stabilized properties tend to be higher than cap rates on properties that have a value-add component. Let's say that the overall market cap rate is 6 percent but the sponsor is buying at a 5.5 percent cap rate. Does that mean they are paying too much for the property? Not necessarily. If the property has below-market rents, is mismanaged, or could absorb rent increases if it were to be renovated, the upside in income will drive investment returns. This means that a buyer can pay more for the existing income stream than they could if the existing income stream were as good as it gets. In other words, all other things being equal, value-add properties tend to trade at lower cap rates than stabilized properties.

Having said that, when the property is fixed up and resold it will be sold as a stabilized property, and the upside will have been taken out of it. You would expect the cap rate on the exit to be higher than the cap rate on the purchase, typically around 0.25 percent, not even counting adjustments for overall market movement. This is why the starting point for the exit cap rate assumption should be the stabilized market cap rate, not the value-add cap rate or the cap rate of the purchase of the property itself.

Sometimes you'll notice that sponsors don't say anything at all about cap rate, or only show the cap rate that the property is being purchased for, so you have no idea at all what assumptions the sponsor is making about the cap rate upon sale. This should prompt questions from you on what assumptions were made in estimating the future sale price of the property.

To estimate the future price, apply the exit cap rate to the forecasted income in the year of sale as shown on the proforma income statement. As an alternative, you could do as in the example below, which capitalizes the value of the following year's NOI. In other words, in the year 3 column, the $1,522,187 NOI is actually the year 4 forecasted NOI, not the year 3 NOI. Why can this NOI be used to calculate a sale in year 3? Isn't value based on trailing income? Yes, but in a competitive market, buyers estimate income aggressively. The most aggressive measurement is T-3 income, or even T-1 income, either of which is higher than T-12 income if performance is continuing to trend upward. Buyers frequently base their purchase price on forecasted income too. While aggressive, this assumption is often accurate. To take a more conservative approach, use the NOI from the year of sale instead of the following year.

SALE ANALYSIS	YEAR 1	YEAR 2	YEAR 3	YEAR 4	YEAR 5
Next Year's NOI	$1,214,473	$1,385,129	$1,522,187	$1,587,444	$1,636,911
Exit Cap Rate	5.50%	5.60%	5.70%	5.80%	5.90%
Sale Price	**$22,081,327**	**$24,734,446**	**$26,705,035**	**$27,369,724**	**$27,744,254**

⚠ In areas where property taxes are reassessed upon sale, it's important that the NOI be adjusted for future property taxes. Otherwise, the forecasted sale price will calculate higher than is likely to be achieved.

The final step is to estimate the future sale proceeds. First, calculate the sale price. Then subtract the costs of the sale (commissions, closing costs, etc.) and the payoff balance of the loan. Finally, add back any cash reserves and the remaining balance of lender impound accounts (funds held in trust by the lender for future payment of property taxes and insurance, or reserves for capital improvements). The result is the cash received from the sale. This cash is then split between the investors and sponsor in accordance with the splits defined in the operating agreement.

SALE ANALYSIS	YEAR 1	YEAR 2	YEAR 3	YEAR 4	YEAR 5
Next Year's NOI	$1,214,473	$1,385,129	$1,522,187	$1,587,444	$1,636,911
Exit Cap Rate	5.50%	5.60%	5.70%	5.80%	5.90%
Sale Price	$22,081,336	$24,734,453	$26,705,044	$27,369,724	$27,744,260
Cost of Sale	$(662,440)	$(742,034)	$(801,151)	$(821,092)	$(832,328)
Loan Balance	$(10,725,000)	$(10,725,000)	$(10,547,567)	$(10,365,083)	$(10,178,982)
Working Capital/Reserves	$359,787	$359,787	$359,787	$359,787	$359,787
Net Sale Proceeds	$11,053,683	$13,627,206	$15,716,113	$16,543,336	$17,092,737

Notice in this example that the sale price and sale proceeds have been calculated for each year for five years. Going out ten years is even better. This is helpful because you can see the exit price trajectory at a glance, and by comparing each year's jump in value, you can find the optimal year to exit. In this example, the largest increase is between years 1 and 3. After year 3, the increase in sale price is more muted. This leads to the conclusion that a sale at the end of year 3 might produce the highest return.

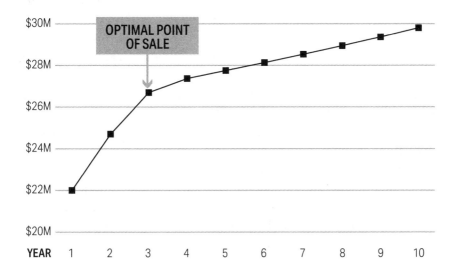

Cap Rate Compression and Decompression

It is often said that cap rates move when interest rates move. You might hear people say things like, "If interest rates rise by 1 percent, cap rates have to increase by 1 percent, too." There are two concepts at play that give people reason to believe this.

Investment return. The thinking is that if someone can invest in risk-free Treasury bonds at 3 percent interest, why would they invest in real estate at a 4.5 percent cap rate? There isn't enough of a risk premium to justify investing in real estate at such a low yield.

Hopefully by now you already see why this argument is a red herring. Cap rate is not a measurement of investment return; it is a measurement of market sentiment. Under the right conditions, it's entirely possible to capture a 20 percent return from a 4 percent cap rate property. As a result, comparing risk-free yields to real estate cap rates is like comparing apples to oranges.

Borrowing costs. The thinking here is that if interest rates rise, it costs more to borrow money. Therefore, you have to buy at a correspondingly higher cap rate in order to preserve investment returns. There are two reasons why this usually isn't true.

First, the debt represents only a portion of the purchase price, such as 75 percent, and the remainder of the purchase price is cash. This mutes the effect of a higher interest rate on the borrowed money to some extent.

Second, if interest rates are increasing, it is also likely that the economy has momentum and perhaps inflation. Rents tend to rise during inflationary times, which in turn increases the income from the property, perhaps to an even greater extent than the increased borrowing cost takes from it.

The bottom line is that cap rates compress and decompress at the whim of market sentiment. When real estate becomes less popular, prices go down, which means cap rates go up. When real estate is highly sought after, prices go up, which means cap rates go down. Cap rates can also move when outside factors alter investment returns. For example, if rent growth slows or operating expenses go up, the only way to achieve the same desired investment return is to pay a lower price for the property, which means buying at a higher cap rate. Interest rates are only one of the many inputs in solving for returns.

How Purchase Prices Should Be Calculated

Cap rate should not be used to establish a purchase price. It's the desired investment return that drives the purchase price. Let's examine how this works.

Only you know what IRR, CoC, and equity multiple fulfill your investment objectives. First, the cash it takes to do the deal, the cash flow received from it, and the proceeds from the sale are all modeled out. Next, you slide the purchase price up and down to solve for the values you are looking for in the primary performance indicators that are important to you. Because different investors have different objectives as well as different performance indicators that are most important to them, each can arrive at a different purchase price for the same property. A price that makes sense to one investor might not make sense to you because your investment objectives wouldn't be fulfilled.

By way of example, in the table below we have a purchase price of $16.5

million that requires a total of $9.3 million in cash to close, and the rest is financed with a loan from an institutional lender. Here you see cash flows each year after all sponsor splits. This results in an IRR of 15.06 percent, an equity multiple of 1.88, and an average cash-on-cash return of 7.26 percent over a five-year hold. If your goal is to achieve a 15 percent IRR, this purchase price will produce that return if all the assumptions are met.

IRR	MULTIPLE	TOTALS	YEAR 0	YEAR 1	YEAR 2	YEAR 3	YEAR 4	YEAR 5
Investor Cash Flow								
15.06%	1.88x	$8,207,621	$(9,300,000)	$338,242	$685,071	$679,965	$808,115	$14,996,227
Cash-on-Cash Return								
7.26%	← Average		Yearly →	3.64%	7.37%	7.31%	8.69%	9.28%

Next, let's see what happens if we increase the price to $17 million. This requires $9.5 million to complete the purchase, and the IRR drops to 14.27 percent, the equity multiple to 1.83, and the CoC to 6.85 percent. If your goal is to achieve a 15 percent IRR, this price is too high.

IRR	MULTIPLE	TOTALS	YEAR 0	YEAR 1	YEAR 2	YEAR 3	YEAR 4	YEAR 5
Investor Cash Flow								
14.27%	1.83x	$7,883,150	$(9,500,000)	$319,545	$663,829	$653,191	$780,841	$14,965,744
Cash-on-Cash Return								
6.85%	← Average		Yearly →	3.36%	6.99%	6.88%	8.22%	8.79%

But what if your objective is to double your money in five years? This would require a purchase price of $15,450,000 to achieve a 2.0 equity multiple on $8,890,000 invested to acquire the property.

IRR	MULTIPLE	TOTALS	YEAR 0	YEAR 1	YEAR 2	YEAR 3	YEAR 4	YEAR 5
Investor Cash Flow								
16.78%	2.00x	$8,891,801	$(8,890,000)	$377,513	$729,680	$736,196	$865,393	$15,073,020
Cash-on-Cash Return								
8.13%	← Average		Yearly →	4.25%	8.21%	8.28%	9.73%	10.17%

For syndication sponsors, establishing a purchase price is a bit of a challenge. They have to guess what their investors are seeking and solve for that when setting their purchase price for a property. Active sponsors likely have a good read on the appetite of their investors, while newer or less active sponsors might have no idea. This can be a problem for these sponsors, because they might pay too much for the property, and then struggle to raise the capital from investors seeking higher returns than the sponsor is projecting. Or worse, the sponsor might attempt to correct for their error by manipulating the assumptions to project a higher return in an effort to attract investors. This is yet another reason why comparing returns without validating the assumptions used as a basis for those projections is just a bad idea.

Other Valuation Methods

There are three primary methods appraisers use to estimate the value of real estate.

- **Comparable sales approach.** Earlier we talked about the comparable sales method of estimating market value. While this approach works for single-family homes, it doesn't work for most income real estate for the reasons we've outlined. Looking at comparable sales is still a useful exercise, however. Most investors find value in knowing that other properties have sold for similar prices as the contemplated investment. Looking for similar apartment complexes that have sold for a similar price per unit and are capturing similar rents helps validate the purchase price. It's not definitive data, but it's supportive. Looking at the price per room for hotels and the price per square foot for office, industrial, retail, or self-storage facilities can also give a point of reference to pricing in the market. It just isn't precise, and a competitive market climate requires precision.
- **Income approach.** Because of the limitations of the comparable sales method for valuing income real estate, appraisers tend to favor the income approach, which is to estimate the income at the property and value the property by dividing that income by a market cap rate. Essentially, this is doing exactly what I just told you not to do. That's okay, though. As a passive investor you are a buyer, not an appraiser. Your objectives are to earn a return, not to identify the potential sale price of the property for the lender, which is what an appraiser does.
- **Cost approach.** Another method for appraising value is called the cost

approach. Using this method, the appraiser establishes a value for the property by estimating the value of the land and the cost to construct the improvements on the land. This approach is mostly useful for newly constructed properties and development projects, and has little use in appraising existing stabilized income property.

Estimating replacement cost might not be useful for appraising the value of the property being purchased, but it is still useful in evaluating a potential investment. If the replacement cost of the property is higher than the purchase price, you gain some comfort from the knowledge that the property couldn't be duplicated for a lower cost. While future costs of construction aren't easy to estimate, if the projected resale price of the property is above a reasonable estimate of the future replacement cost, it could point to a forecasted exit price that is too high.

Wrapping Up

Cap rate is not the driver; it is the passenger. Rather than saying cap rates went up so prices went down, it's more accurate to say that prices went down, so cap rates went up.

Cap rate shouldn't be the primary factor in your selection of real estate investments, nor should you set your purchase price based solely on cap rate. Cap rate is simply a way of measuring, after the price has been decided, how much you were willing to pay for the property's income stream so that people (including you) can make relative comparisons between this acquisition and other similar acquisitions in the same area.

Cap rate is most useful for estimating the price that the property will later be sold for, so that you can estimate the proceeds from the sale. The sale proceeds will be an important part of calculating the IRR and equity multiple.

IRR, cash-on-cash return, and equity multiple—not cap rate—should be used to determine the right price to pay, and to decide the quality and suitability of a real estate investment.

SECTION IV
EVALUATING OFFERINGS AND STRUCTURE

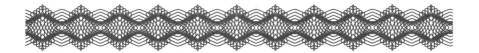

CHAPTER 13

INVESTMENT STRUCTURE

You could say that there are as many different structures as there are investments. Setting aside the concept of "structure" as it relates to fees that are charged and how profits are divided (we'll get to that later), the structure of most private offerings can be divided into four major categories: debt, equity, identified asset, and funds. Let's dive into each of these.

Debt

Most people probably think of debt as borrowing money from banks. While syndications almost always borrow money from lenders to provide leverage to the invested capital when buying real estate, I'm not talking about debt in that sense.

When I discuss debt in this chapter, I'm talking about the syndication borrowing money *from you*. This can be as simple as you making a loan against a property, for example, by lending a house flipper money to finance the purchase and renovation of a property. It can also be a private offering specifically structured so that the investors are given promissory notes for their investment instead of equity interests in the partnership. This is not all that common, but you might see it once in a while.

If you are making the loan directly to the borrower, it should be secured by the real estate with either a deed of trust or a mortgage. This gives you recourse if the borrower fails to make the payments as agreed, and you can initiate foreclosure and hold a public auction to recover the unpaid balance. If no one bids at the foreclosure auction, you instruct the auctioneer to enter a bid on your behalf and then you'll own the property, which can then either be resold or held.

The advantage to this type of investment is that you have security for your investment, and assuming that nothing goes terribly wrong, you should receive the return (interest) specified in the promissory note. The downside is that you have no upside—in other words, you don't typically share in the profits and get the opportunity to make a larger return than expected. You also don't receive the tax benefits of real estate ownership, as you would if you invested in an equity offering.

Another way to invest in debt without lending money directly to borrowers is through debt funds. With this structure, you invest money into a managed fund, and the fund makes the loans to borrowers. This could be real estate related, such as hard money loans to house flippers or even apartment syndicators. Or it might not involve real estate at all, such as a fund organized to purchase defaulted credit card debt. These investments could be debt investments, where you are issued a promissory note by the fund and receive interest, or equity investments, where you own a percentage of the fund.

If you are investing in a debt fund that is making loans to others, the fund receives the real estate collateral when they make the loan to the borrower. You don't receive the collateral directly. The upside? If there is a foreclosure the fund will own the real estate and carry the responsibility of reselling the property, rather than you having to do that yourself.

Equity

Most people think of equity as the value of their home that exceeds the amount of their mortgage. But in syndications the term is more likely being used to describe the money required to fund the business plan that is not debt and not secured by the real estate. In other words, it's the money invested by you in the syndication.

Most syndication investments are equity investments. You contribute money to a company (usually an LLC or limited partnership), and the company then purchases the real estate and obtains financing from a lender. The equity is used for the down payment, closing costs, property renovations, working capital, and sponsor fees. The money you invest in the company is exchanged for *units* in a limited liability company or *partnership interests* in a limited partnership, which is similar to you being a stockholder in a corporation. The equity is not secured by the real estate, and you have no ability to foreclose on the property. Instead, you are an owner of the company and the company is the owner of the real estate. You have no more ability to foreclose on your equity investment than you would have to foreclose on your own home.

Equity can also be placed into different classes. Two common classes are *preferred equity* and *common equity*. Preferred equity has priority over common equity, either by being first in line to receive cash flow, first to receive return of capital, or both.

Most investments made into syndications are common equity. If preferred equity has preference over common equity, you might wonder why you wouldn't invest only in preferred equity. There are preferred equity offerings out there, but they aren't all that common, at least not from the syndication sponsors themselves. You might occasionally see them from crowdfunding platforms, however. Many syndication sponsors don't use preferred equity because it places their common equity in a subordinate position, or they simply don't need it.

Preferred equity has limited upside for the investor. Because preferred equity is in a priority position to common equity, the returns typically mimic debt but at a higher interest rate. Terms often involve payments to be made on a monthly or quarterly basis, called a "current pay." Additional payments accrue until the preferred equity is paid off; this is called a "deferred pay." For example, 6 percent would be paid while the preferred equity is committed, and 6 percent would be paid when the equity is paid back—basically, it's like an unsecured loan at 12 percent interest with half the payments to be made and the other half to be added to the principal until repayment. Preferred equity doesn't usually get a share of the profits beyond the current pay and deferred pay amounts. However, structures differ and some preferred equity structures include a small percentage of the profits.

Capital Stack

The money required to facilitate a real estate acquisition and business plan is called a *capital stack*. When you view the various components of the capital, they look like a stack, with debt at the bottom, preferred equity in the middle, and common equity at the top, as in the following image.

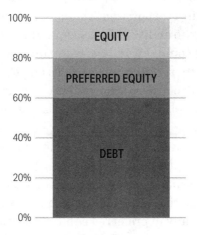

Debt is considered to be the safest portion of the capital stack because there is equity behind it. Many investors stick to making only debt investments so that they live in the safest part of the stack—a defensive strategy similar to investing only in bonds and staying away from stocks. Debt also has the lowest expected return, starting at just a few percent and climbing up to as much as 8 to 10 percent for higher-risk loans.

The next safest portion of the capital stack is preferred equity. It is subordinate to debt and can only receive cash flow that doesn't go to servicing debt. Because it is less safe than debt, it comes with a higher return, typically somewhere between 8 and 14 percent. The only collateral is the shares in the company; it is not secured by the real estate itself.

The least safe portion of the capital stack is common equity. It is subordinate to debt and preferred equity (if any), and can only receive cash flow that doesn't go to servicing debt or current-pay requirements of preferred equity. When the property is sold, the debt must first be paid off, then the preferred equity is paid off, then common equity. If the property is sold at a loss, it's entirely possible that the debt will be fully repaid, the preferred equity will be fully repaid, and the common equity will experience a partial or even total loss.

Because common equity bears the highest risk, it also commands the highest return. Typically, equity owners will receive the majority of the profits generated by the property. If preferred equity is also used, common equity holders expect to earn a higher return for taking on the additional risk than they would if preferred equity were not used.

Offering memorandums should include a "Sources and Uses of Funds" table. We'll go into more detail in a later chapter about what to look for on these, but for now you should know that such tables show where the money for the business plan is coming from and what the money will be used for. You should see the entire capital stack—the debt, preferred equity (if any), and common equity.

Identified-Asset Syndications

The simplest form of syndication is an identified-asset syndication. In this vehicle, the sponsor has identified one or more properties to be acquired using the money raised and debt from one or more lenders. Often this is for a single property, but identified-asset syndications can also be used to acquire multiple properties, such as a portfolio of office buildings or apartment complexes.

The advantage of identified-asset syndications is that you can underwrite not only the sponsor but the assets to be acquired. You can usually view the historical financials of the asset, the renovation plan and budget, and future projections before you decide to invest. You can also pick and choose which asset classes to invest in, which properties to invest in, and even which markets to invest in simply by selecting a syndication that is investing in what you are looking for. The disadvantage is that you get less diversification, unless the syndication is acquiring a large multi-property portfolio with assets located in different areas.

Funds

You can also invest in funds. A fund is a pooled vehicle where a large amount of equity is raised for the purpose of acquiring multiple assets in the future. Funds can be set up as a "blind pool," where you give the sponsor complete discretion as to which assets to acquire. Or they can be set up as a "semi-blind pool," where you give the sponsor free rein to buy properties that fit into a predefined box, such as apartment complexes between 100 and 300 units built after 1990 in Atlanta.

The advantage of pooled funds is that you get some diversification because the fund is buying multiple properties, perhaps even in different areas. The disadvantage is that you don't get to see the properties prior to making your investment. You are completely relying on the sponsor to make all decisions on what to buy, and if they buy a property that you don't like, you are stuck with it. The other disadvantage is that you cannot underwrite the assets, or see the financials or the projections before you make your investment. The pros and cons of syndications versus funds are shown below:

	SINGLE-ASSET SYNDICATIONS	MULTI-ASSET SYNDICATIONS	BLIND POOL FUNDS	SEMI-BLIND POOL FUNDS
Can underwrite assets	Yes	Yes	No	Sometimes
Can choose assets to invest in	Yes	Yes	No	Somewhat
Diversification	No	Yes	Yes	Yes

Operators Versus Joint Venture Funds

Before you decide to invest in a fund, it is important to understand the sponsor's business model. Some sponsors are operators, meaning they buy the real estate, make improvements, manage the property, and eventually sell. When you make your investment, you are an owner of the company that owns the real estate, and you will split the profits with the sponsor.

Other sponsors manage joint venture funds. From all outward appearances these seem to be either blind pool or semi-blind pool funds. The key difference is that they invest in joint ventures with operators instead of buying properties directly. You are investing in a company managed by a sponsor who is investing the equity from the fund in another sponsor's offering.

I once had a conversation with a potential investor who was looking to place a large amount of capital in one of my offerings. He was researching multiple options and contemplating either investing in our offering or investing in the offering of another sponsor. He was favoring investing with the other sponsor because the profit split and fees being offered by the other sponsor were more favorable.

Even though this investor was leaning toward the other sponsor in order to get a lower fee structure and a higher profit split, he would actually receive higher fees and a lower profit split. How could that be? The other group he was looking to invest with was a joint venture fund—he would invest his money in the fund, and the fund would invest in the offerings of other sponsors, like me. Looking at the structure in reverse, a sponsor like me would buy a property and get the equity from a joint venture fund. I would charge fees and get a split of the profits. The joint venture fund would also charge fees and get a split of the profits, and *then* the investors in the joint venture fund would get their split of the profits. In other words, those investors are getting a split of the split, because the operator got part of the profits and the rest went to the fund. Then the fund took part of the profits, and the rest went to the fund's investors. This is called a "double promote."

By way of example, let's say that an operator's syndication is giving its investors 70 percent of the profits and a joint venture fund is giving its investors 80 percent of the profits. If an investor who doesn't know any better is comparing the two, the joint venture fund will seem more attractive because of the more favorable profit split. What this joint venture fund investor might not realize is that instead of getting 80 percent of the profits generated by the real estate, they would actually receive only 56 percent of the profits, because they would be getting 80 percent of 70 percent, not 80 percent of 100 percent.

This doesn't mean joint venture funds are bad investments. They serve a purpose if you would rather have someone else select sponsors to invest with and underwrite those investment opportunities for you. This is somewhat like choosing to invest in a mutual fund instead of picking stocks individually. What's important is that you make your investment in a joint venture fund knowing that a double promote (and double fees) are likely in play.

Types of Entities

Most private offerings are structured as limited liability companies. LLCs are a form of business entity that are somewhat of a hybrid of a corporation and a partnership. The "members" of the LLC, which is what you will be as an investor, benefit from limited liability similar to that offered to corporate shareholders, and also pass-through tax treatment, just like that offered by partnerships. Pass-through tax treatment means that the LLC does not pay income tax; instead, the members report their share of the LLC's income on their own tax returns.

LLCs are favored entities for syndications because of the limited liability, the flexibility allowed in the structure of the partnership, and the ability to have a "managing member" that is in charge of it all. This managing member, sometimes called a "manager," typically has the authority to carry out the partnership's business activities, such as buying and selling real estate and borrowing money. The manager typically does not need separate approval from the investors to carry out these tasks as long as the manager is acting within the authority given by the LLC's operating agreement.

Investors like LLCs for the limited liability, meaning their losses are limited to the amount they invested. Sponsors like LLCs because they also enjoy limited liability, plus they have control over the business. Lenders like LLCs because they can't be burdened by the debts levied against the individual members and the manager, plus there is one party in control of the company.

Limited Partnerships

Limited partnerships (LPs) are business entities in which investors, called limited partners, get limited liability similar to that offered by LLCs, plus the same pass-through tax treatment. LPs also have a general partner, which is similar to the managing member of an LLC in that they have control of the company as defined by the terms of the limited partnership agreement. Unlike a managing member of an LLC, however, a general partner of a limited partnership does not have limited liability. To achieve limited liability, sponsors often use a corporation or LLC as the general partner of the limited partnership.

The reason for using a limited partnership instead of an LLC is usually tax-driven. Some states, such as California, charge LLCs a disproportionate and punitive gross receipts tax, so some sponsors use an LP in these states to avoid that tax.

Limited partnerships have been around a lot longer than LLCs, which means that a lot of common lingo from back in the day when LPs were the only game in town lives on. You'll often hear investors called LPs and sponsors called GPs, even though those terms don't apply to LLCs. You'll also hear the term "partnership agreement" in reference to LLCs, but the agreement governing an LLC is called an LLC agreement, company agreement, or operating agreement. It's all semantics, I know. But if you are going to live in this world, you should know the lingo.

Tax-Deferred Exchanges

I'll go into more detail about tax-deferred exchanges (also known as 1031 exchanges) later in this book, but for now suffice it to say that real estate owners can sell their property and use a special procedure to defer paying tax on the gain from the sale of the property if they invest the proceeds in another property.

People often wonder if they can invest the proceeds from their 1031 exchange in a private offering, thus deferring the tax without having to endure the hassle of locating another property to buy. This is a really common pain point, especially among long-term real estate owners who want to get out of the business of actively owning real estate, and would rather invest in a passive syndication and let someone else do the work.

Unfortunately, with syndications typically being structured as LLCs or LPs, this type of exchange is not allowed. These exchanges must be for like-kind property, which means that if real estate is sold, other real estate must be bought. An investment in a syndication isn't a purchase of real estate from the lens of the passive investor—it is a purchase of units in an LLC or of partnership interests in an LP. Even though the syndicate is purchasing real estate, it isn't like-kind for the investor's exchange.

This age-old problem needed a solution, so it was only a matter of time before someone figured out a way around this limitation. There are two ways to go about it, and I'll detail both.

Tenants in Common

Tenants in common, or TIC, is a form of joint ownership of real estate by two or more parties. With this method of co-ownership, each owner can individually deed their interest in the real estate, and each owner can own a different percentage of the real estate. The idea is that each investor can buy a fractional interest in the real estate itself instead of units in an LLC. This accomplishes the goal of like-kind property for the exchange, because the investor is in fact purchasing real estate and is even on title.

Back when TICs were popular, sponsors managed the property through property and asset management agreements, and were compensated with an array of fees rather than a split of the profits. Investors liked the structure because they could get like-kind treatment for their exchange. Sponsors liked the structure because they could attract large amounts of capital from tired real estate owners looking to switch from active to passive. Lenders liked the structure because they were making loans and their loan officers were making fees.

But there were two major problems. First, there was a lack of centralized control because you could have up to thirty-five owners of a single piece of real estate, which meant that a major decision could require unanimous consent. In order to sell the property, every owner was required to deed their interest. A lone holdout could cause a major problem. Sponsors tried to mitigate this and other issues, with varying degrees of success, by placing restrictions in the TIC agreement by which they could compel owners to sign. Investors would also have to sign the loan documents and likely would also be required to participate in any loan guarantees.

The second issue with TICs was that the sponsor's interests were only minimally aligned with those of their investors. Because sponsors weren't allowed to have a typical split of profits, their compensation was generally through fees that were paid whether the deal was performing or not. This led to a lot of problems. Lenders came to dislike TICs because these problems began leading to disputes, poor performance, and projects being abandoned by sponsors and left to investors to sort out. Many ended up in foreclosure, leading to massive investor and lender losses.

Despite the TIC industry largely dying after the 2008 recession, the TIC model does still exist. Nowadays, the lessons of TICs past have led to lenders often limiting TICs to two to four owners. These smaller TICs are far more manageable, and despite the lack of centralized control, a small group can usually work out any issues.

Many sponsors are unfamiliar with how to navigate the TIC space, so they stay out of it. A few have figured it out and are able to accept two or three TIC investors plus the syndication entity. The syndication entity is just one of the TIC owners, but within the syndication there can be an unlimited number of conventional investors, just as in any other syndication. The syndication LLC owns its percentage of the property, and that percentage of income is passed through to the LLC. From that point on, the LLC functions as any other LLC syndication. For the portion of the real estate owned by the TIC investors, the sponsor would have a management and fee agreement, and receive compensation via fees designed to mimic what they otherwise might have expected to earn in a conventional syndicate structure.

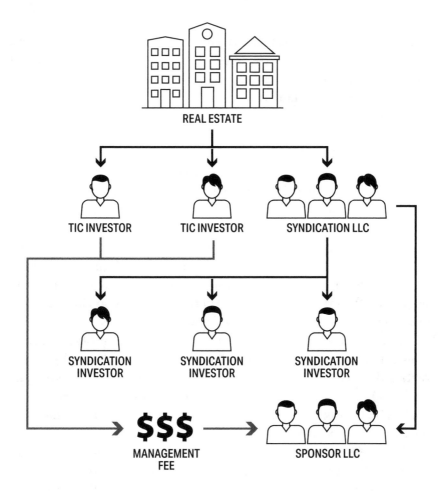

REAL ESTATE

TIC INVESTOR

TIC INVESTOR

SYNDICATION LLC

SYNDICATION INVESTOR

SYNDICATION INVESTOR

SYNDICATION INVESTOR

$$$
MANAGEMENT FEE

SPONSOR LLC

For example, let's say that the sponsor is raising $5 million to purchase a property. You have $1 million coming from a 1031 exchange. The sponsor could let you invest as a 20 percent tenant-in-common owner. They raise the other $4 million from their syndication investors, who all invest in the syndication LLC, and that LLC becomes an 80 percent tenant-in-common owner.

The challenge to making this work is that you have to find a sponsor willing to do this. The sponsor would need to have a property in their acquisition pipeline that is a fit for the size of your 1031 exchange, and the timing of the closing has to fit with the statutory time constraints of your 1031 exchange from both an identification aspect (45 days from the sale of your property) and closing of escrow (180 days from the sale of your property).

This strategy works best with larger exchanges, as making this work is somewhat complex and expensive. As a result, some sponsors might not be inclined to accommodate you for smaller amounts of capital. Each sponsor's ability to execute this process and willingness to accept this type of capital varies, so ask around.

Delaware Statutory Trust

A Delaware statutory trust (DST) is an unincorporated association recognized as an entity under Delaware law. In 2004, the IRS issued Revenue Ruling 2004-86, which permitted the use of the DST to qualify as like-kind property in a tax-deferred exchange.

The DST concept was a response to the downsides of the TIC structure. It solved the issue of decentralized control by holding the property in a trust (the Delaware statutory trust, specifically), and the investment sponsor (or an affiliate) is the trustee of the trust. Now you have a structure in which the sponsor has control of the asset and the investors own beneficial interests in the trust, just as investors own units in an LLC. Using this vehicle, a sponsor can create a syndicated offering by selling fractional beneficial interests in the trust to a variety of investors, just like in an LLC syndication. Thanks to the IRS ruling, beneficial interests in a DST are considered like-kind to real estate, and thus qualify as replacement property in an exchange.

This might seem like the holy grail of real estate syndication, since you get the benefits of traditional syndications and the tax treatment of 1031 exchanges both going in and coming out. You'd think that every syndication would use the DST structure to capture these incredible benefits.

But not so fast! In real estate there is no perfect solution to every problem, and the DST is no exception—it comes with its own limitations and downsides. The regulatory framework surrounding the DST structure is very specific and also very restrictive. The primary limitations are known as "the seven deadly sins." There really are seven of them, but I'll just focus on a few key "sins" that influence the way DSTs are used.

First, sponsors cannot raise any additional capital once all original beneficial interests are sold. If they raise enough in the beginning, they should be fine. But if something comes up that requires more capital than the trust has available, the sponsor can't raise more money to address the issue without consequences. The sponsor is forced to make one of two choices: run out of money, which could lead to foreclosure or other problems, or convert the DST to an LLC (this is called a "springing LLC") and then raise more money in the LLC. Sounds simple enough, but this conversion can have tremendous tax consequences to the beneficial owners of the DST, so sponsors and beneficial owners alike strongly wish to avoid this option. Just because you saved a lot of taxes by investing in a DST doesn't mean there's no risk that Uncle Sam won't come knocking at your door. In this scenario, he'll be kicking you while you're down.

Second, the sponsor cannot refinance the property and take out cash, nor can they renegotiate the terms of any existing loans. Once the loan is put in place, that's it.

Third—and I think this is one of the most constraining factors—sponsors are limited to making capital expenditures only to the extent required for normal repair and maintenance, and minor non-structural capital improvements. This means no heavy value-add projects and major rehabs.

Finally, DST sponsors can't receive a split of the net profits. Instead, they have to earn their compensation with fees. The structure of a DST investment is complex, with the trust owning the property, an LLC to act as trustee of the trust, another LLC to execute a master lease on the property, and another to act as property manager.

Because of these limitations, most DST offerings are stabilized Class A multifamily properties that don't need major rehab, or single-tenant triple-net leased industrial properties, such as distribution centers, FedEx sorting facilities, or large retail stores. The properties are generally nice enough to brag about, but you probably won't be bragging about the high returns. DST investments tend to have low cash-on-cash returns and IRRs, especially compared to many other syndication investment alternatives.

Thinking Outside the Box

If you are in the position of exchanging and are looking to DSTs or TICs as a solution, you might also want to run the numbers on the outside-the-box alternate scenario of (gasp) paying the tax on your gain and investing what's left in a conventional syndication that performs at a higher return. At first blush this might sound like a preposterous suggestion, but in some circumstances, it might make a lot of sense. Before you start sending hate mail, allow me to explain.

A challenge with 1031 exchanges is the tight time frame. If you don't find a property in forty-five days, your 1031 gets blown, so you are just as motivated, if not more so, by your desire to avoid taxes as by your desire to find a good investment. This means that if you are seeking a replacement property, you are essentially buying with a gun to your head.

A challenge with DSTs is that the returns tend to be in the mid-single digits. Thanks in part to the high fee load of DSTs, many offerings struggle to throw off a 6 percent CoC and single-digit IRRs. This is due to most DSTs investing in coupon-clipper-style deals that don't have much of a value-add component, if any at all. Investing in a syndication that produces a 16 percent IRR on the money you have left over after paying taxes might be a better option than an 8 percent IRR from a DST with pre-tax dollars.

At the end of the day, you might find that you end up with more money with the conventional syndication. On the other hand, you might not—it depends on many factors surrounding your basis in the property you are selling, and other factors that your tax advisor can assist you in examining. Certainly this option isn't for everyone, but you shouldn't automatically rule it out. Run the numbers and see how well it works for you.

People tend to either dismiss this option or not even think of it, because their investment decision is motivated more by tax considerations than investment considerations. Don't let the tax tail wag the investment dog. You should evaluate both side by side and make the best decision supported by the evidence.

Alignment of Interest

You've just arrived at the grocery store and found a great parking spot right out front. You need to pick up only a couple of things, so you know you won't be long. Would you leave your car unlocked with the keys in the ignition? For most people, the answer is absolutely not, but why not? Probably because your car won't be there when you finish shopping, and no one is going to feel all that sorry for you, because, hey, you left the keys in the ignition!

What's so wrong with that? Stealing your car would be illegal. As true as that statement is, we live in a world where some people disregard the laws and seek to profit from the misfortune of others. I lost count of how many stolen vehicle reports I took back in my law enforcement days. Heck, if everyone obeyed the law, I probably wouldn't have had that job to begin with.

Why would a thief steal your car? Two reasons, really.

First, his interests aren't aligned with yours. He needs a ride and sees an opportunity, so he'll take your ride. You need a ride too, but your need for a ride doesn't matter to the car thief.

Second, the thief lacks moral character. He is willing to disregard the law for his own gain. He knows full well that taking your car is against the law, but because of his character, he doesn't care.

You are now about to invest your hard-earned money in a real estate syndication. This means you are going to willingly hand your money over to an investment sponsor and hope that when it's time, the sponsor gives you your money back and then some. But how do you know the sponsor will do that? You don't, so you look for two things to manage the risk: first is good moral character, and second is alignment of interest. Often what constitutes either is misunderstood.

The problem with real estate syndications is that they are illiquid. Unlike publicly traded stocks, this is an investment you can't exit at the click of a mouse when you don't like the way things are going, and there is no way around that. You want to maximize the odds that the sponsor is looking out for you and minimize the odds that they will take unnecessary risks, make bad decisions, or disappear with your money.

How do you ensure that the sponsor's interests are aligned with yours? I hate to be the one to break this to you, but you can't. The difficult reality here, and it is the reality that no one wants to acknowledge, is that the sponsor's interests are *not* aligned with yours.

Of course investment sponsors will say they have alignment of interest, and they'll point out all the ways that they establish it. Many of the things they point out certainly contribute to keeping sponsors on the straight and narrow—and many are just fluff. Let's sort them out.

Sponsor Investment in the Deal

I read article after article preaching that you ask the investment sponsor whether they are putting money in the deal. "If they are putting money in the deal, their interests are aligned with yours," these articles say. "Investing alongside you means the sponsor has skin in the game," they say.

There's nothing wrong with asking the sponsor if they are investing in the deal; I take no issue with that at all. My problem with this advice is the insinuation that having money in the deal checks the box in the "Skin in the Game" column and solves for alignment of interest, so now you can move on to other due diligence concerns. Just as false is the insinuation that if the sponsor is not investing in the deal, there is no skin in the game and no alignment of interest.

The practice of sponsors investing in their own deal alongside investors is called "co-investment." The co-investing strategy was first introduced in the late 1980s and early 1990s, when Wall Street investment firms used it to coax investors into real estate portfolios that the firms had bought from the Resolution Trust Corporation, a federal program instituted to liquidate real estate and other assets held from failed savings and loans associations. The idea was that having the managers share risk with the investors gave the investors comfort in an uncertain time.

Have you ever suffered from a cold that dragged on seemingly forever? Let's say you go to the doctor and walk out with a prescription for antibiotics. After a few days you start to feel better. The reality is that a cold is a virus, and antibiotics don't kill viruses, they kill bacteria. But you feel better because you have a prescription from the doctor. Knowing that you were doing something gave you comfort. The same applies to investors who want to see sponsors put money in their own deals. Whether or not it has any true impact, co-investment gives investors comfort. They feel better if the sponsor loses money alongside them. But does it influence whether or not money is lost to begin with?

There is little evidence to support that it does, nor is there substantive evidence that co-investment improves performance or even suppresses risk-taking on the part of investment managers. However, there is evidence to support the counterargument that co-investment does little to suppress risk-taking. Think back to the great financial collapse of 2008: Many of the principals of Lehman Brothers, including its two top executives, had substantial percentages of their personal net worth invested in the company. And many of the real estate sponsors who lost substantial amounts of their capital had posted substantial co-investments.

Let's bust a few myths as we dissect this further.

Myth: The sponsor won't abandon the investment if they have money in it too.

Bust: There could be a lot of reasons why the sponsor wouldn't want to abandon the project, and we'll explore them in more detail later in this chapter. For now, consider this: Only a sponsor with a character flaw would abandon an investment. Remember that the sponsor also controls the company's checkbook. It would not be hard at all for an unscrupulous sponsor to raid the company accounts and siphon off the property's cash flow to recover the money they put in before abandoning the project. Abandonment is about character, not about money.

Myth: The sponsor won't take aggressive risks because they could lose their money.

Bust: Sponsors generally earn a percentage of the profits, called a "promote," after investors have achieved a specific level of return, called the "preferred return," or "pref." Until the investment has fully distributed the pref that investors are entitled to, there is no promote to be paid to the sponsor. This means that their promote is "out of the money."

Let's say the sponsor's promote is out of the money and they are faced with a decision that could either substantially increase or decrease the property's income, and both outcomes have equal probability. If the income rises, the sponsor's promote would go in the money, meaning that the preferred return would be fully met and they would start to receive a percentage of the profits. The sponsor might take this risk in an attempt to receive their promote, even though there's an equal chance that the income will fall substantially, because for them the upside is greater than the downside. The reduction of the return on their co-investment is smaller than the increase of return on their co-investment plus their promote, so the 50/50 odds, to them, aren't really 50/50. But they are to you, which is partly why I say that it's impossible for the sponsor's interests to be fully aligned with their investors', whether they have money in the deal or not.

Myth: The sponsor will make better decisions if their money is also at stake.

Bust: Sometimes markets move against you. Take the great financial collapse as an example: Massive business and job losses resulted in residential and commercial tenants that couldn't pay their rent. Vacancies and bad debt rose, and landlords offered concessions to lure tenants in an attempt to curb vacancy losses. Many owners lost their properties to foreclosure, including syndicates that had sponsors with significant co-invest capital in the deal. Why didn't their capital investment cause them to make better decisions? Perhaps it was partly because sponsors, like their investors, were drinking the Kool-Aid. Operators either had skill or they didn't. They either made good decisions or they didn't. Or maybe their decisions were sound but the negative market forces were just too powerful to survive. No amount of incentive, no amount of at-risk capital, could overpower Mother Nature or incompetence.

Myth: I'll earn higher returns because the sponsor will try to maximize their return.

Bust: Not likely. Sponsors recognize that the majority of their income is derived from their fees and promote. Returns on their capital are little more than background noise representing such a small portion of the total that they are unlikely to drive decisions. Imagine that the sponsor has invested $100,000 in the deal and the projected return to the investors is expected to be 15 percent over a three-year period, or roughly $45,000, but the sponsor's promote is expected to be $500,000. If they are the type to let self-interest drive the bus, it is more likely that the sponsor's decisions would be based on what might increase their promote rather than what might increase the return on their capital. This might mean taking outsized risks that could result in the opposite of the desired outcome. If you believe that the sponsor is motivated by greed, you probably don't want to be investing with them anyway. If you believe that the sponsor is *not* motivated by greed, then the argument that investment returns will be higher because they have money in the deal fails for lack of foundation.

Creating Misalignment

There may be instances where co-investment capital actually causes the sponsor to be further misaligned from the investors. One common belief is that the sponsor should co-invest a "meaningful" amount of capital, that is, an amount large enough to be important to the sponsor. The idea is that this creates greater alignment because a small, meaningless amount would have little influence on the sponsor. While there may be some truth here, beware of unintended consequences.

For instance, consider a shopping center in the early stage of the business plan with a sponsor who has a substantial portion of their net worth co-invested alongside their investors. The plan is to lease out the vacant anchor space, which would increase foot traffic, which in turn would drive sales at the smaller retail spaces. Once that happens, rents can be increased at the smaller suites to further drive property value.

But right as the lease is signed for the anchor space, the sponsor's elderly parents fall ill, requiring around-the-clock care. The sponsor's capital is tied up in the shopping center, and they are faced with a tough choice. Do they continue with the business plan, or do they sell the property to recover the cash needed to take care of their family? The investors' best interest is to continue with the business plan, but the co-invest has now misaligned the sponsor with their investors.

So why do so many people advise that co-investment should be the definitive test of alignment? They're just making it important because they can measure it, not measuring it because it's important. Don't misunderstand: There's nothing wrong with sponsors investing in their deals, and there's nothing wrong with investors feeling good about them doing so. But there *is* something wrong with believing that it really matters. If you accept this, you can focus on other forms of skin in the game that matter just as much, and arguably more.

Reputation Risk

Skin in the game takes on many forms besides money. Unfortunately, those other forms are subjective, much harder to quantify, and harder to verify, but that doesn't make them any less real.

The most powerful form of skin in the game is the sponsor's reputation. If this is the sponsor's first syndication, they have little to lose, so they can screw up and start over.

On the other hand, if the sponsor has been in business for a long time, has a long list of investors, and has raised a lot of money in the past, they cannot just walk away from a deal and start over. The trust they have built with their investors has taken an entire career to build and can take only seconds to destroy. That is a far deeper level of skin in the game than any amount of sponsor capital put into the deal.

Many sponsors build their business through word of mouth and referrals. In today's world of social media and websites dedicated to discussion of real estate topics, word of one wrong move will spread like wildfire and could spell the end of the road for a sponsor. The sponsor's interests align with the investors' when the sponsor is aware that their performance will have an impact on their future fundraising efforts. Sponsors with a brand to protect have far more alignment than those who don't.

One thing to notice is length of time the sponsor has been in business. If they have been operating for many years, there's a good chance that they act with their investors' best interests in mind. If they didn't, they would likely be out of business. If they have survived market cycles, there's a good chance that they are good investors and good operators, and make good decisions—or at least they've learned a lot of lessons from any bad decisions.

Loan Guarantees

Lenders require certain guarantees in connection with making real estate loans. If the loan is a recourse loan, someone has to guarantee the loan. If it is a non-recourse loan, someone has to sign on to the carve-out guarantees, which give the lender personal recourse against the guarantor in the event of specific violations, such as fraud or misappropriation of funds. Who is signing this guarantee? This may seem like a silly question, but the answer is not necessarily the sponsor.

Some sponsors don't have the net worth or liquid capital to qualify as a guarantor, so they "hire it out" by giving up a portion of either fees or promote to a third party. This transfers the guarantor risk from the sponsor's shoulders. If the sponsor's principals are guaranteeing the loan or the carve-outs, they are placing themselves at risk if they default on the specified lender obligations. This gives the sponsor tangible skin in the game—hiring it out does not.

Deal Structure

The way a deal is structured can provide some level of alignment or misalignment, so you can't overemphasize the importance of deal structure. Consider the case of a sponsor charging an asset management fee based on a percentage of the amount of equity raised, a fairly common practice in funds that purchase multiple properties over time. The sponsors get paid the same fee regardless of performance, or lack thereof.

Not that asset management fees are bad, but there are other ways to calculate this fee that tie it to performance, for example, basing it on a percentage of income or a percentage of the property value, which should rise as income rises.

Moral Character

The most important factor in alignment is the moral character of the key executives. Remember that car thief? He wouldn't be stealing cars if he had good moral character. Laws are no deterrent. Neither is the prospect of losing his freedom if he gets caught. The only thing that could keep him honest would be good character.

Unfortunately, good or bad character is difficult to identify and even harder to quantify. But given that it's the most important factor in alignment, it's worth exploring. Character is so important, in fact, that the entire second section of this book is dedicated to digging into the sponsor, the way they act, and the way they think. If you follow the advice in that section, you'll be well on your way to learning a lot about the sponsor's character.

Real alignment is elusive. When you invest in a syndication you will be given a document chock-full of disclosures related to conflicts of interest. The structure of the deal can incentivize the sponsor to act in the best interests of the investors, but in reality, how well sponsors manage the various conflicts of interest is directly related to the quality of their character. This underscores the importance of selecting trustworthy sponsors, and illustrates why I'll always argue that the sponsor is more important than the deal itself. You can't simply rule the sponsor as aligned or not aligned based solely on the presence or absence of a co-investment.

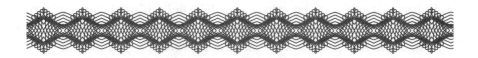

CHAPTER 14

UNDERWRITING AND PROJECTIONS

Section 3 of this book was dedicated to discussing various aspects of underwriting a commercial real estate investment, including market rent and occupancy forecasts, debt structure, operating statements, cap rates and values, performance indicators, market studies, and capital improvements. This chapter is where we put it all together and learn how to apply that knowledge when evaluating whether a particular investment is a good fit for you.

Projecting a return is an exercise in financial engineering. Sponsors pull on different levers until there aren't any left to pull, in an effort to increase the projected return to make it more attractive to investors. Some sponsors pull the levers harder than others, at times boosting the projected returns artificially. Investors often fall for it, choosing the offering with higher projected returns just to find themselves disappointed once the deal is all over. That's why it's critical to examine and question the assumptions that the underwriting and the projected returns are based on.

Another issue with comparing IRRs, cash-on-cash returns, and equity multiples is that some sponsors might be showing you gross values while other sponsors are showing you net values. We talked about this in chapter 9, so this is just a reminder to be sure to compare apples to apples. The net returns are most important to you because they tell the story of what you are projected to receive after the sponsor receives their fees and profit split.

What is a good return? There are as many opinions as there are investors. Some would be thrilled with an 8 percent return; others wouldn't get out of bed for less than 20 percent. Each investor's needs, goals, objectives, and risk tolerance dictate what is acceptable to them. Some investors focus on the cash-on-cash return because they want or need the income. Other investors focus on the IRR because they are most interested in the overall return. Yet other investors focus on equity multiple because they are looking to build capital.

Having said that, what should investors expect? This varies too. At the time of this writing, a value-add multifamily investment should produce a 12 to 17 percent net IRR depending on the level of potential risk, quality of the property, and length of the hold period. These offerings tend to produce cash-on-cash returns averaging 6 to 9 percent over the hold period, but they typically experience lower cash-on-cash returns during the first one to three years as the property is improved and income is increased. For that reason, a planned three-year hold might have a low average cash-on-cash return because the property is sold right after the income stabilizes at a higher level. Net multiples typically fall between 1.6 to 2.0, depending on the length of the expected hold. A longer hold should produce a higher multiple but a lower IRR than a shorter hold. This makes sense when you think about it—a 14 percent IRR over ten years would produce a higher equity multiple than a 16 percent IRR over three years.

A stabilized Class A multifamily or office investment might be closer to the 11 to 15 percent IRR range. Average cash-on-cash return is typically around 5 to 8 percent, but unlike in value-add properties, the cash on cash in the first couple of years tends to be higher. Multiples typically fall in the 1.5 to 2.0 range.

Ground-up development projects tend to project higher returns because of the risks of development. Expect to see IRR projections of 20 percent and higher, but don't expect much, if any, cash flow. Multiples can be high compared to value-add business plans of similar duration, but they tend to stay relatively low compared to other longer-term hold investments, just because of the short duration. But once you receive your capital back, you can invest in something else and maximize the multiple over the long term. Ground-up development projects come with higher risk than stabilized properties, however.

Very high projected returns for a value-add multifamily opportunity are a red flag. I once saw an offering from a sponsor where they were projecting a 25 percent IRR over a ten-year hold. I've underwritten thousands of value-add multifamily properties in my career, and I can't recall a single one where I would have been comfortable projecting a 20 percent IRR over a ten-year hold. Most often they are quite a bit below 20 percent. Obviously something was wrong with this sponsor's calculations, assumptions, enthusiasm, competence, or all of the above. They said they'd found a smoking-hot deal. It would take a lot of convincing to get me to believe that. You shouldn't believe it either, and using the tools and skills you've learned from this book, you should be able to dissect the sponsor's underwriting to find the problem.

Why would a sponsor project such a high return? Setting aside the possibility that they just made mistakes in their underwriting, they might use high returns as a strategy to attract capital from investors who are simply comparing projected returns and selecting the offering showing the highest number. This strategy will ultimately backfire on the sponsor, however, as one day they will run up against reality. The property will be sold, the money will be counted, and the final results will be tabulated. If the deal fails to perform to the sponsor's lofty projections, their investors won't be happy, and unhappy investors don't reinvest. This means that the sponsor will constantly have to look for new investors because the old ones will have fled—not a good recipe for longevity.

Smart sponsors will often under-project their returns. They do this for two reasons: First, they have a loyal enough following, so they don't need to over-project in order to win the "highest projection" game. Second, they like to under-promise and over-deliver, recognizing that this builds loyalty with their investors over the long term. Consider this: If a sponsor projects a 17 percent IRR and delivers a 15 percent IRR, they've missed their target and some of their investors will be disappointed. But if they projected a 14 percent IRR and deliver a 15 percent IRR, their investors will be thrilled. Same return, two different expectations.

Your mission is to try to figure out if the sponsor's projections are aggressive, realistic, or conservative. Using the knowledge from section 3 of this book and the techniques in this chapter, you should be able to get a good idea of how the offering stacks up. Let's take it one step at a time, starting at the top, with income.

Returns Versus Risk

It's important to keep in mind that all IRRs aren't created equal. An 18 percent IRR isn't necessarily better than a 12 percent IRR. For example, if the sponsor is using a lot of leverage (debt), such as a bridge loan where they are borrowing 85 percent of the cost of the property and improvements, it's easier to get a higher IRR because there is less investor cash in the deal. But this tactic comes with added risk because of the high debt load. On the other hand, if the sponsors are using low-leverage debt, such as 65 percent of the purchase price, they'll need to raise more equity, and as a result, the returns are likely to be lower. But the lower debt load makes the deal a lot less risky. While high returns are nice, you have to balance how much risk you are willing to take for the returns you are seeking.

Unit Mix and Market Study

The sponsor's offering materials should contain a unit mix and market study. Here is a simple example of a unit mix for a sample apartment complex:

RENT ROLL													
					Effective Rent (Actual Avg)			Newest Leases			Future Market Rent		
BD	BA	# Units	SF	Total SF	Per Unit	PSF	Total	Per Unit	PSF	Total	Per Unit	PSF	Total
1	1	31	800	24,800	$844	$1.06	$26,174	$875	$1.09	$27,125	$1,025	$1.28	$31,775
2	2	145	1,000	145,000	$905	$0.91	$131,225	$975	$0.98	$141,375	$1,125	$1.13	$163,125
Total*					$894	$0.93	$157,399	$957	$0.99	$168,500	$1,107	$1.15	$194,900
Change to Future/Total Annual					$213		$1,888,791	$150		$2,022,000			$2,338,800

*Weighted average based on number of units

What you see here is a unit mix with 31 one-bedroom, one-bathroom 800-square-foot units, and 145 two-bedroom, two-bathroom 1,000-square-foot units. The weighted average rent is $894 but the newest leases have been capturing an average of $957. The plan is to increase rents to $1,107 on average ($1.15 per square foot) once the units are renovated, representing a $213 increase over the in-place average and $150 above the average newest leases.

When you analyze an offering, pay close attention to this unit mix because what you see here, and what you don't, can reveal opportunity as well as potential problems. The unit mix can also reveal fundamental flaws in the sponsor's underwriting, or worse, an attempt to mislead investors. I've seen all four, so it pays to look closely at this.

Start with the unit mix and examine the rents that the property is currently achieving on average for each floor plan. Note the difference between that average and the average of the newest leases that are being signed (assuming the sponsor is even showing you this—if they aren't, I'll explain how to work around that in a minute).

If there is a big spread between the overall average rate and the rate of the newest leases, this is a sign that either rents are increasing (opportunity) or the property hasn't kept up with rent increases, but has now woken up and started charging market rates (also opportunity). It could also be a sign that the seller is pumping up the rents to try to get a higher sale price either by letting in unqualified residents (warning), or by setting a high rental rate and a recurring concession to effectively charge the tenant a lower rate "behind the scenes" (also a warning). If the newest leases are going out lower than the in-place average, that could be a signal that rents are declining (another warning).

Next, look at the sponsor's market study and rent comps to see what neighboring properties are getting for similar floor plans, noting differences for unit size. The rent comps should at least support the property's current average lease rates for each of the various floor plans. If the comp average is close to the in-place average, there's probably not much room for rent increases at the property. If the sponsor is projecting large increases, that plan is likely unachievable if the comps don't support higher rates than are currently in place.

If the rent comps support the rates being charged on the property's newest leases, this can be an indicator that these rates might in fact be real, and not just an artificial effort to juice the income for the sale. But if the rent comps don't support a rate higher than the newest leases, this is an indicator that the property is already getting rents about as high as they'll go, and the only play here is bringing the rest of the older leases up to the level of the newest leases. If that's what the sponsor's business plan is, that's fine. But if the sponsor is projecting to go even higher, this plan could also be doomed from the start.

As you examine the comps in the market study, pay close attention to the price per unit and less attention to the price per square foot. Sponsors often will justify lofty rent projections based on price per square foot that skew the price per unit because of different unit sizes. What you want to see is that the rent comps support the projected future rents. If they do, you're off to a good start. If they don't, there's not much reason to continue analyzing the underwriting any further because the rent drives the return more than any other variable. If the sponsor's underwriting begins with faulty rent assumptions, the outcome of the underwriting is inherently flawed. As the old saying goes, "garbage in, garbage out."

Rent Roll

A rent roll is a table of units at the property along with information about the tenancy in each unit. Most important, the rent roll should show the actual rental rate for each unit and the move-in date. Most often, sponsors will not include a rent roll in their offering package. They may, however, provide it in their due diligence materials. If you don't see the rent roll, ask for it. The sponsor should be willing to provide you a copy or provide excerpts that include unit number, square footage, actual lease rate, recurring concessions, and move-in date.

The reason you want to see the rent roll is to verify the unit mix data in the sponsor's offering package. This is important because the square footage of the units, the number of units, and the in-place rents have a tremendous impact on the outcome of the investment. Think of it as "trust, but verify." If the data doesn't match up, you have good reason to question other data in the offering materials.

If the sponsor isn't showing you the average rental rate of the newest leases in the unit mix, you can calculate it yourself using the data in the rent roll. Highlight the units where the move-in date is within the last ninety days and average them for each floor plan to see what the newest leases are. If you are truly ambitious, you can average all the leases in each floor plan and compare that number to the in-place rents shown in the unit mix in the offering circular.

One big trap to watch out for is when sponsors report the rent for each unit size as the "asking rent" or "market rent" for each floor plan. This is just the "street price," in other words, the price you would be quoted if you walked into the office today and asked to rent a unit. In no way does the asking or market rent represent the actual lease rates at the property. If sponsors are representing the market rent as the in-place rent in their unit mix, then highlighting only the amount of increase they are proposing above such market rent once they renovate, they could be grossly misrepresenting the amount of increase truly necessary to bring the units up to the future forecasted rent. If you see this, consider it a red flag.

Income Statement

Assuming that you were able to substantiate the projected rental rates, the next step is to examine the income statement to see whether the projections are reasonable. This requires a four-step approach.

Step 1. Verify that the gross potential rent matches the total annual rent from the unit mix. Next, examine the rent growth assumptions and ensure that they are reasonable and supported by third-party data.

Step 2. Examine the various economic vacancy factors to see that:

1. There is a phasing in of rent increases as renovations are completed, typically over two to three years before normalizing at the projected rents in the unit mix and market study.
2. They align with the market averages, third-party data, and the property's historical averages.
3. The assumptions are conservative enough to allow for the market to underperform yet still achieve projections. For example, if market vacancy rates are 5 percent, are they underwriting to 5 percent, or are they underwriting to 6 or even 7 percent—or better yet, to a long-term average?

Step 3. Examine the other sources of income, such as utility reimbursements, late fees, and vending income, to ensure that the projections align with the property's historical performance. Note that sometimes there are opportunities for increase here, for example, when a property doesn't charge for basic things like pet rent and covered parking, and the sponsor plans to implement those charges. In such cases, these miscellaneous income items could be higher than the property's historical numbers but should phase in over time.

Step 4. Examine the projected expenses to ensure that they are appropriate, and that the expense growth rates are reasonable. Refer back to chapter 8 for guidance on each of the various expense categories and what assumptions are reasonable.

Third-Party Data

How do you know if the economic vacancy factors and rent growth rates used in the underwriting are appropriate? One way is to seek some third-party validation. There are firms that specialize in assembling data for the commercial real estate industry. These firms produce reports that include historical data and future forecasts for rent growth, vacancy rates, and concessions. Seeing data from these reports can provide third-party validation of the sponsor's underwriting assumptions. Sponsors should be able to provide these reports or excerpts from them that support their assumptions.

In the multifamily industry, these reports are written by REIS, Axiometrics, CoStar, and Yardi Matrix, among others. In addition to these specialized sources, other sources of third-party validation are news articles from major media outlets and websites, and market survey data from the major brokerage firms' research teams.

Debt Structure

Assuming that the underwriting has passed the tests so far, the next test is to examine the debt structure and the debt service. How is the sponsor financing the acquisition and any renovations? Or for a ground-up construction investment, how are they financing the construction?

Does the financing match the business plan? In other words, does the debt mature too soon, or is the loan a long-term fixed-rate loan with big exit fees even though the business plan is to sell in three years?

What is the LTV and the LTC? Is the interest rate fixed or floating? Is there an interest-only payment period, and if so, for how long? What is the amortization period? Are there large fees associated with paying off the loan, and if so, are those costs accounted for in the model?

Cash Flow Forecast

The income statement should end with the net operating income (NOI), which is the effective gross income minus operating expenses. The NOI should then carry over to the cash flow forecast. The cash flow forecast should show the cost of debt service and any other debt-related cash flows, such as loan payoffs, new loans, cash-out refinances, loan exit costs, and payments to preferred equity. If there is a cash-out refinance, the cash flow forecast should show the amount of excess cash from that transaction.

In addition to debt-related costs, the cash flow forecast should also show routine capital expenditures. These are typically shown as a monthly or annual reserve amount rather than an itemized list. The amount of the reserve is typically between $200 and $400 per unit, per year for a multifamily property.

The cash flow forecast should also show the proceeds from the sale of the property and any sale-related costs. In the year of the sale, the cash flow would include both operating cash flow and sale proceeds. The bottom line of the cash flow forecast is the after-debt cash flow. This amount then flows to the investor waterfall, where it will be divided up between the investors and the sponsor (more on that in a later chapter).

Sale Assumptions

Sale assumptions are forecasts of the future resale price of the property. The sales prices can be calculated for each year of the intended hold period as well as beyond the hold period so that multiple exit strategies can be examined. In the sale assumptions, look for the NOI being used and compare that to the NOI in the income statement forecast. Is the NOI consistent with that shown in the forecast for the year of the sale (or perhaps the year following the sale)?

What exit cap rate is the sponsor using for calculating the exit price? Is that exit cap rate reasonable? If today's cap rates for this type of property in this area are 5 percent and the sponsor's cap rate upon sale ten years later is also 5 percent, you can reasonably conclude that the sale forecast is questionable because there is an assumption that cap rates will not change. Whether exit cap rates should be higher, lower, or the same as the current cap rates depends on where the market cycle currently sits at the time the purchase is made. If the market is hot and interest rates are low, it's unsafe to assume that cap rates won't rise given that the market could cool. On the other hand, if the real estate market in the area is slow and buyers are scarce, it could be safe to assume that cap rates will not rise, and might even fall, as the market heats up.

Stress Tests

Life is good when everything goes according to plan. But the only certainty in the syndication investment space is that things never go according to plan. I'd bet my next distribution that no one could ever show me actual income and cash flow statements that match the projections to the dollar. Actual performance will either be slightly higher or lower than forecast, or massively higher or lower than forecast. How does that affect the return?

The obvious answer is that income falling below projection will cause the return to decrease, and income above projection will cause the return to settle above the projected return. But by how much? The answer is probably a lot more, or a lot less, than you'd think.

This question can be answered with a sensitivity analysis. A sensitivity analysis is a table or tables that show the projected return for various alternative performance scenarios. This might be exit cap rates that are higher or lower than forecast, or income that is higher or lower than forecast, or vacancy that is higher or lower than forecast. The best sensitivity analyses will show a variety of combinations of all those factors, and even show variances for different hold periods, in case the property is held for more or less time than forecast.

The benefit of a sensitivity analysis is that you can see where the deal really starts to get stressed, and perhaps even discover ways to maneuver around that stress. You can also see some best-case versus worst-case scenarios. Here are a couple sensitivity analyses comparing various exit cap rates and vacancy rates that vary above or below projection.

LEVERED IRR MATRIX—PHYSICAL VACANCY VS. EXIT CAP RATE—HOLD PERIOD 3 YEARS

Physical Vacancy ⟶

Exit Cap Rate	2.46%	3.46%	4.46%	5.46%	6.46%	7.46%	8.46%	9.46%	10.46%	11.46%
5.40%	34.24%	32.93%	31.60%	30.27%	28.92%	27.56%	26.21%	24.80%	23.40%	21.98%
5.65%	31.58%	30.28%	28.96%	27.63%	26.29%	24.94%	23.59%	22.18%	20.78%	19.37%
5.90%	29.05%	27.75%	26.44%	25.11%	23.77%	22.43%	21.08%	19.68%	18.28%	16.88%
6.15%	26.63%	25.33%	24.02%	22.70%	21.37%	20.03%	18.68%	17.28%	15.89%	14.48%
6.40%	24.31%	23.02%	21.71%	20.39%	19.06%	17.72%	16.37%	14.98%	13.59%	11.92%
6.65%	22.08%	20.79%	19.49%	18.17%	16.84%	15.50%	14.15%	12.59%	10.89%	8.92%
6.90%	19.93%	18.64%	17.34%	16.03%	14.70%	13.27%	11.66%	9.80%	7.84%	5.04%
7.15%	17.86%	16.57%	15.27%	13.95%	12.37%	10.68%	8.79%	6.44%	3.57%	0.57%
7.40%	15.86%	14.57%	13.11%	11.54%	9.71%	7.82%	5.07%	2.17%	-0.84%	-4.01%
7.65%	13.85%	12.32%	10.63%	8.79%	6.50%	3.74%	0.86%	-2.19%	-5.37%	-8.74%

Notice that the baseline scenario is a 6.46 percent average vacancy rate and a 6.4 percent exit cap rate with a three-year hold. The net investor IRR is shown where those two baseline assumptions intersect. Returns increase greatly as vacancy and exit cap rates decrease. Conversely, performance suffers when exit cap rates and vacancy climb. Notice that as you approach the lower right corner of the sensitivity analysis, investors could suffer a loss.

A sensitivity analysis can also reveal alternative exit scenarios. Take, for example, the scenario of a 10.46 percent vacancy rate and an exit cap rate of 7.4 percent. In this three-year hold scenario, that would result in a negative investor IRR of 0.84 percent, in other words, a small loss. Now take a look at a five-year hold sensitivity analysis for the same property.

LEVERED IRR MATRIX—PHYSICAL VACANCY VS. EXIT CAP RATE—HOLD PERIOD 5 YEARS

Exit Cap Rate ↓ / Physical Vacancy →	2.46%	3.46%	4.46%	5.46%	6.46%	7.46%	8.46%	9.46%	10.46%	11.46%
5.70%	20.60%	19.47%	18.36%	17.27%	16.19%	15.13%	14.09%	13.05%	11.88%	10.70%
5.95%	20.11%	19.03%	17.97%	16.92%	15.89%	14.88%	13.88%	12.87%	11.71%	10.55%
6.20%	19.68%	18.65%	17.63%	16.63%	15.63%	14.66%	13.70%	12.68%	11.56%	10.36%
6.45%	19.31%	18.32%	17.34%	16.37%	15.41%	14.48%	13.57%	12.54%	11.41%	10.17%
6.70%	18.98%	18.02%	17.08%	16.17%	15.28%	14.37%	13.46%	12.40%	11.27%	10.00%
6.95%	18.69%	17.81%	16.94%	16.07%	15.17%	14.27%	13.35%	12.27%	11.14%	9.84%
7.20%	18.56%	17.71%	16.85%	15.97%	15.08%	14.17%	13.26%	12.15%	11.01%	9.69%
7.45%	18.48%	17.63%	16.76%	15.88%	14.99%	14.08%	13.15%	12.03%	10.89%	9.55%
7.70%	18.40%	17.54%	16.68%	15.80%	14.90%	13.99%	13.04%	11.92%	10.76%	9.41%
7.95%	18.32%	17.46%	16.60%	15.72%	14.82%	13.91%	12.94%	11.82%	10.63%	9.28%

Note that in this analysis the same 10.46 percent vacancy rate and 7.4 percent exit cap rate would result in a positive IRR of close to 10.89 percent (a 7.4 percent exit cap rate isn't an option on this table, so the closest alternative is 7.45 percent). Comparing these two sensitivity analyses tells us that if the property is underperforming in year 3, holding for an additional two years could turn it around, even if the vacancy rate and cap rate don't improve.

Look for a good sensitivity analysis to see a menu of potential performance and how variations in performance outside of the sponsor's projections will affect you. Good underwriting, with a clear vision of alternative performance scenarios, should give you a high level of understanding of potential outcomes.

Due Diligence

Buying real estate isn't as simple as locating a suitable property, making an offer, and then completing the purchase. The four walls of a building don't just shelter its occupants from the elements; they also shelter hidden defects and complex operational challenges. Any buyer of real estate needs to do a thorough investigation before completing the purchase. This investigation is known in the business as due diligence.

In the world of syndicated commercial real estate investments, it's the sponsor's responsibility to conduct thorough due diligence on the property. Your job, as a passive investor, is to protect yourself by ensuring that the sponsor has in fact conducted proper due diligence, because if they didn't, it will be you who pays the hefty price.

Most sponsors will share their due diligence results with prospective investors as part of the subscription documents. Some do it as a matter of procedure; others will do it when asked. If the sponsor refuses to share the due diligence materials, that could be a red flag. It's possible that they didn't conduct proper due diligence, or there were unfavorable findings that they don't want investors to know about. Neither is good, and either might be a reason to pass on this particular investment.

All this information and documentation can amount to a pretty thick package. Fortunately, today's technology allows nearly everything to be made available in electronic format and shared through a variety of online file-sharing services.

The following is a partial list of due diligence items that the sponsor should receive and share with investors.

Appraisal. The lender will obtain an appraisal. If the property doesn't appraise high enough to support the loan, the lender won't make the loan. The lender may or may not share the appraisal with the sponsor before closing, so the appraisal might not be available to share with the investors.

Bank statements. A year of bank statements can support the collections shown on the operating statement. Oftentimes sellers are not willing to share bank statements, so they might not be available to share with investors. Requesting bank statements is more common on smaller properties where owners can be perceived as less trustworthy than the more sophisticated owners of larger properties.

Capital improvements made. A list of capital improvements made in the recent past, such as the previous two years, or even better, during the seller's entire period of ownership, can give insight into what replacements have been made. It can help to establish the age of major components such as roofs and mechanicals.

Certificates of occupancy. These certificates establish that the property is in compliance with codes and is authorized to be occupied. They are typically issued by the building department at the time that building construction is completed. Check with the municipality to see whether they issue certificates of occupancy. If the municipality requires certificates of occupancy to be renewed periodically, it's important that the certificates be current. In most offerings, you likely wouldn't need to research certificates of occupancy yourself because the lender will be engaging a zoning consultant to conduct research to ensure that the property complies with zoning codes and all required certificates.

Debt term sheet. This isn't really a due diligence item; it's more of a disclosure item to show the investors the exact terms of the debt to be used to acquire the property.

Environmental report. The lender will require a report identifying any environmental risks, such as underground storage tanks, former dry-cleaning businesses, or spills and other hazards. This is commonly called a Phase I report because it's a fairly simple search of historical records. If the Phase I identifies a potential hazard, a Phase II report can be required. In that case, the inspector will visit the property and might take samples of the soil and water, among other things, and issue a report describing their findings.

Financial statements. This includes the T12 as well as the complete calendar year financials for the previous two to three years. The calendar year financials can be compared to one another, and to the T12, to look for inconsistencies in the income or expenses.

Insurance loss runs. Insurance carriers keep a record of all insurance claims, and upon request will provide that list, called a "loss run." Copies of the loss run will be required by the new insurance carrier, and they also provide insight into potential problem areas. For example, if there are a lot of slip-and-fall claims, perhaps the sidewalks or stair-wells are in need of repair. If there are a lot of fire claims, it could signal problems with the building or indicate a careless resident profile. Claim history by itself doesn't mean the property will be a bad investment, but it can be a clue for things to watch for or address—and could mean premiums might be higher than if there were a clean loss history.

Maintenance records. Recurring problems can often be discovered by reviewing the maintenance records. For example, repeated maintenance requests due to water leaks might signal that the plumbing inside the walls is failing. Or a high volume of air conditioner repairs might be a hint that the mechanical components are aging and will soon need replacement.

Notices of violations. Copies of any records related to building code or municipal code violations show issues that need to be corrected or, if already corrected, can be a clue to possible recurring problems.

Pending or threatened litigation. The insurance loss runs may reveal litigation, but the seller should disclose any pending litigation even if an insurance claim wasn't filed. The seller should also disclose any threatened litigation they are aware of. Litigation isn't necessarily a red flag—baseless and malicious lawsuits against landlords are fairly common. If you were to believe every tenant lawsuit, you'd think that every apartment in the country was infested with rats, cockroaches, termites, and bedbugs, and none of them met basic habitability standards. But some allegations could be true, so the presence of a pending lawsuit should trigger further investigation to determine what effect, if any, it could have on new ownership. Generally, the lawsuit itself would have no effect on a new owner, but the precipitating incident in the case could be a concern if the underlying issue still remains or could recur.

Permits and licenses. The seller should provide all issued permits and licenses. Oftentimes cities or counties issue permits for swimming pools, or they might require a license of some sort to operate a rental housing property.

Personal property inventory. This is a list of personal property that comes with the property, such as desks, computers, lawn mowers, golf carts, and so on.

Plans and drawings. If the current owner has the architectural drawings, site plans, or as-built drawings, they should be delivered to the buyer.

Property condition report. This lender-required report is prepared by an engineering firm after conducting an inspection of the property.

The inspector looks at the major systems and components of the property, and identifies material physical deficiencies. The inspector will also provide an assessment of the needed capital expenditures over the term of the loan and call out any immediately necessary repairs.

Lenders will likely require that repairs identified as immediately necessary be corrected shortly after closing. The sponsor should have these items in their renovation budget or have a contingency budget with enough room to accomplish the repairs. If they don't, they'll have to siphon money from cash flow or issue a capital call to the investors for more money to accomplish the rest of the planned renovation. I say "the rest of the planned renovation" because the lender will require the sponsor to deposit capital at least equal to the estimated cost of the immediate repairs into a lender-controlled reserve account to make sure that those repairs are made. This would impact the sponsor's intended renovation plan budget if they didn't account for such contingencies. If they have to raise more money or siphon from cash flow, this will affect the projected performance.

Property tax records. Two or three years of previous property tax bills can corroborate the property tax expense shown on the operating statements, as well as show the most current assessed value and mil rates. The bills should also show the parcel numbers and will reveal whether the property consists of multiple parcels.

Rent roll. A current rent roll is part of standard due diligence. The rent roll will show the current rents and occupancy rate, as well as security deposits and ancillary charges. Watch out for recurring concessions, as these sometimes are used to hide the "real" rent achieved by the property. For example, the rent roll might show that the rent is $1,000, but there is a $50 recurring concession. This means that the effective rent is really $950. If the sponsor's plan is to renovate units and increase rents by $100 to $1,100, this $50 recurring concession means that the rents really need to increase by $150 to get to $1,100.

Most of the time, comparable renovated properties are used to determine the price the subject property can get for renovated units. But once in a while, the property can be its own best comp. Let's say that the current owner has renovated 10 percent of the units, and the post-renovated rent forecast is based on the property's own post-renovated rates on the small sample of upgraded units. That's fine, but if the property is offering recurring concessions on the renovated units, it's important that the effective rent be used as the baseline.

Service contracts. Larger properties tend to have a variety of contracts with vendors. Some of these contracts, such as those for fire alarm monitoring or landscaping maintenance service, can be canceled with thirty days' notice, while others, such as those for trash collection or laundry equipment leases, cannot be canceled prior to the expiration of the contract term. Cancelable contracts aren't typically a problem because the sponsor can cancel these contracts and put them back out to bid to get lower pricing. Non-cancelable contracts, such as a laundry room contract where the coin-laundry vendor is receiving an unfavorable split of the laundry income, can be a material issue. If the plan is to increase laundry income, an in-place contract could derail that plan.

Survey. A survey is a plot plan of the property showing lot lines, building footprints, parking areas, setbacks, and easements. The survey will help to identify problems such as building setback violations and violations of required parking ratios, as well as easements that might interfere with improvement plans. For example, if the plan was to add a swimming pool but the electric utility has an easement crossing through the intended location, the pool is unlikely to be built.

Title report. The title company will issue a title report, also called a "title commitment," because it is a commitment to issue title insurance. The title report will identify all easements of record and any other liens and encumbrances on the property. The sponsor's legal counsel should be reviewing the title report and objecting to items on title that could present a problem. Objected-to items can either be removed or insured around. If all else fails, they could kill the deal. If you see something on the title report that is concerning, you can ask the sponsor whether they'll share their counsel's title objection letter and the seller's response to it.

Utility bills. One year's worth of utility bills will confirm that the utility expenses shown on the income statement are accurate. Since utilities are one of the few expenses that will remain roughly the same before and after the sale, ensuring an accurate expense amount in the trailing financials is important for forecasting future utility expense. Keep in mind that properties that are suffering from low occupancy will have an increase in water and sewer expenses when occupancy increases. There could be a small decrease in electric bills if each unit has its own electric meter, because the incoming tenants would typically be responsible for the electric bill once they move in. The decrease in electric expense is likely to be offset by the higher water and sewer expenses, however. The trick is accurately estimating what the utilities will be in these circumstances, which is easier said than done.

Warranties. If a roof was recently replaced, it might be under warranty. The same goes for new siding, windows, boilers, and such. The sponsor should be receiving copies of these warranties in case issues arise during the warranty period.

Zoning report. The lender will typically require a zoning report, where a consultant will examine records and talk to the local building, fire, and zoning departments to determine whether the improvements are legally conforming. The consultant will examine the certificates of occupancy and search for outstanding building, fire, and zoning violations.

Knowing When to Sell

I've often said that the first thing I want to know before getting into an investment is how I'm going to get out of it. People often complain about how hard it is to find good deals. But how often do you hear people complain about how hard it is to get out of a bad deal? Not nearly as often—not because it isn't hard or painful, but because it's so painful that no one wants to talk about it.

My need to know my exit strategy probably comes from my background of flipping houses. Since I would only own the house for a few months, the first thing I needed to know was what it would be worth after it was fixed up and how I would sell it. I carried this over to my multifamily investing—and I think you should too. As you are browsing the glossy investment prospectus, try to look past all the pretty pictures and hype about how great the opportunity is, and find out what the plan is to get out of it.

People sometimes ask why syndications have a life cycle of around three to five years. The answer is because sophisticated investors want to know when they will get their money back, which is why you don't see many syndications where the business plan is to hold in perpetuity. The plan is usually to get in, make some type of improvements, and then sell. On the other hand, you sometimes will see sponsors of larger or more institutional offerings buying stabilized assets in great markets with some type of macro growth story, and holding for several years before selling—but even they nearly always have an exit strategy.

An exception is long-term holds where the cash flow is relatively high and the business plan is just to enjoy the income. The exit plan is simply to have low leverage so that there is downside protection, and hold for years or even decades. These are typically stabilized Class A properties with long remaining useful lives meant to mimic the performance of a bond. They don't offer a lot of upside, just a fair cash return, like an annuity. There's nothing wrong with that if that's what you're looking for.

But a large percentage of high-net-worth syndication investors are looking for upside. Some want a mixture of cash flow and upside; others place a higher priority on upside and a lesser emphasis on cash flow. It just depends on your goals.

Value-Add Phases

When investing in so-called value-add opportunities, your exit strategy is very important. Generally, the exit plan is to hold for a few years, usually three to five, and then sell. Why three to five years?

A value-add business model consists of two phases. Phase 1 is where the sponsor is adding value. This means making improvements, changing the resident profile, improving the management, and most important, increasing the income. Doing this takes two to three years. There are renovations to be done, new residents to be recruited, and leases to be signed. Once those things are done, it takes another six months to a year for the income to prove out. In the graph below, you can see where the property's value is climbing steeply during phase 1; then it starts to level off. The point where this line turns the corner to rise less steeply is the beginning of phase 2.

Phase 2 is where any additional performance improvements come primarily from market forces. Every value-add deal has this inflection point, where the improvements in the income stream shift from active improvement (renovations and management) to passive improvement (supply-and-demand drivers). In most cases, when that shift happens the most optimal exit point is reached. Investors can then take their money out and roll it into the next opportunity where the forced value can happen again. The plus side is that this results in less dependence on the market (less, not none). The downside is that it's not a tax-efficient business model. I'd argue that, done properly, the higher returns of rolling from value-add to value-add offsets the tax burden, but that's up to you to decide.

Disaster Planning

What is the exit plan if there is an adverse market cycle? One thing you'd rather not do is buy at the top and sell at the bottom. Unfortunately, there really is no way of knowing exactly where the top is until it's too late. What happens if it turns out that you bought at the top or at the start of a plateau? If the sponsor's plan is to sell in three years, and when three years rolls around the market is in the toilet, what would you want them to do?

What if the property just happens to be in a short-term blip when sale time comes around? In most cases, assuming that the property is cash flowing and you can hang on, you'd probably want to wait for conditions to improve rather than selling when performance is suffering.

This happened with one of our properties in Houston. As we were approaching the time to sell, a hurricane came through town and caused a lot of damage. Fortunately for us, our property suffered only very minor damage. Many businesses were heavily damaged, forcing them to close and lay off staff. Many closed temporarily either because of damage or due to lack of business when customers literally had to use a boat to get there. Those layoffs and job losses impacted our residents, which ultimately resulted in evictions and difficulty leasing units once they were vacated.

The courthouse was also heavily damaged, causing it to close. This delayed evictions, so getting people out for non-payment became a months-long exercise. Word spread, which emboldened other tenants to stop paying rent. This created enormous delinquencies on top of the vacancies. Surely this would have been the worst time to sell! It took about a year and a half to get back to the performance level we saw before the hurricane. Delaying the sale was the right thing to do and resulted in performance in line with our business plan; it just took longer.

Does the sponsor have a plan for such an event or for an adverse market cycle? If their plan is to hold for three years and the operating agreement doesn't allow for any additional time, the sponsor might be stuck, perhaps even forced into a sale at the worst possible time. Look in the offering materials for income projections going out ten years, showing that the sponsor has thought about what performance could look like if the property is held longer than planned. Next, look to see whether the operating agreement allows the sponsor to hold for longer than planned if the timing isn't right.

I call this style "buy-and-watch" investing. It means you buy, improve the property, then watch the market for the optimal exit point. In a typical value-add deal, this could mean selling in three years if you can, five years if you need to, or ten years if you have to. To do this right, the sponsor should have a three-year projection, a five-year projection, and a ten-year projection, along with stress tests and sensitivity analyses to project performance under a variety of scenarios.

Exit Strategies

There are five primary exit strategies.

1. Outright sale
2. Refinance and return some (or all) capital to investors
3. Hold for cash flow for the long term
4. Recapitalize
5. REIT roll-up

The first three are essentially self-explanatory. One caution with the refinance is to watch out for sponsors that alter the deal terms after capital is returned. In other words, they either refinance you out, keeping the deal for themselves, or change your ownership percentage or profit split after capital has been returned to you. Don't let them get away with that, and don't invest in deals where the operating agreement allows a sponsor to do that. You invested in the deal at the riskiest point—the beginning. It's not fair for your upside to be shifted to the sponsor after the deal is de-risked.

A recapitalization, also known as a recap, is when the sponsor is essentially re-syndicating the deal to new investors and selling the property to the new venture, giving the original investors their capital back plus a profit, similar to an outright sale to a third party. Once the property is stabilized and the value has increased, the original investors' return on equity decreases (because the property is worth more, there is now more capital tied up in the deal). This makes holding longer less attractive to the sponsor's value-add investors, but it is very attractive to institutional investors, such as pension funds and retail investors, that are just looking for a stabilized bond-like return with a long hold time.

The original investors get a sale at or above the projected exit price in the promised three- to five-year time frame. They now have their original investment plus the profits to invest in the next value-add opportunity. The new investors get to acquire a stabilized property with lower risk (but lower returns) than a value-add property. The sponsor retains control of the property because they are the sponsor of the new syndication, or they retain the property management contract, or both. When done correctly, the idea is that all three sides win.

The key in a recap scenario is whether the exit price for the original syndication is market price. If sponsors are going to do a recap, they should disclose this to the investors and produce appraisals to support the value of the transfer. This is often done by obtaining two or three appraisals, and going with the average of the two or the middle of the three. As long as it is fair to everyone, a recap can be done without being shady. Just be sure you are paying attention when and if this type of transaction is contemplated. In theory, the sponsor should want the recap to trade at the highest fair price because their promote is dependent on it. There usually isn't an incentive to trade under market in this scenario as it's likely that the institutional recap has less favorable promote terms to the sponsor than the original value-add syndication.

A REIT roll-up is when the syndication is converted, or rolled up, into a REIT (real estate investment trust) controlled by the sponsor. This gives both the sponsor and the investors liquidity, and preserves the tax basis for existing investors who don't want to cash out of the investment. Both the sponsor and the investors typically have the option to convert their partnership interest for publicly traded REIT shares, which they can then sell through the exchanges whenever they want. They can also hold the shares, and enjoy the cash flow and returns from the REIT.

Wrapping Up

Let's revisit the concept of investors who talk about how difficult it is to buy property and how hard it is to find good deals. For many, the solution is to go to markets where there is less competition, under the assumption that they can get a better deal if they don't have to bid against others to win.

No matter how attractive that may sound, what these investors forget to account for is the exit plan. If there is no one bidding against them to buy the property, how many bidders do they expect to make offers when they sell the property? Seemingly the only ones will be those looking in less competitive markets so they can get a better deal. Funny thing, though: The sponsors promoting these deals seem to forget that the knife cuts both ways. They don't get a less competitive deal on the buy and sell for top dollar in a bidding war. I call these "high barrier to exit" markets. If we all realize that it's actually harder to get out of a deal than to get into one, we won't perceive these markets as producing such great deals after all.

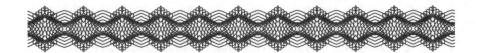

CHAPTER 15

SOURCES AND USES OF FUNDS

I'm not much of a cook. If it weren't for my wife's excellent cooking, pizza delivery, and In-N-Out Burger, you wouldn't be reading this book because I would have starved to death long ago. That doesn't mean I haven't tried to cook: I've pulled out a cookbook once or twice and attempted to prepare a meal. I gather the ingredients, follow the recipe, and *voilà!* I have some unidentifiable result that looks nothing like the picture.

A real estate syndication offering is much like a cookbook. You see the picture of a delicious meal and you want it. In this case it's not pizza or burgers; it's IRR, equity multiple, and cash-on-cash return. Instead of consuming a meal, you are consuming investment performance. The sponsor's business plan and the assumptions they make in their underwriting are the recipe instructions. What about the chef's skill? That's not in the book—they either have it or they don't. The same goes for the sponsor's skill, background, and experience.

What's missing? If you said "the ingredients," you are correct! Without ingredients, no chef, despite their skill, can cook anything at all. Because of this simple fact I doubt you'll find a recipe anywhere that doesn't begin with a list of ingredients.

So why do syndication sponsors leave out their list of ingredients? What is a list of ingredients in a real estate investment anyway? It's called a "sources and uses of funds" table, often referred to as a sources and uses, or even just S&U. Because the ingredient in an investment is money, where the money is coming from and how it will be spent are fundamental.

Sources of Funds

The "sources" portion of the table illustrates how much money is needed and where that money will come from. It could be as simple as one line if the purchase is all cash, or there could be several entries if the money comes from several sources. The table below is an example of the sources of funds in an all-cash transaction, where all the funds are coming from investors.

SOURCES	AMOUNT
Investor Equity	$27,900,000
Total	$27,900,000

If the sponsor is obtaining a loan to purchase the property and obtaining the rest of the funds from investors, the sources of funds will have two entries, as in the example below.

SOURCES	AMOUNT
Investor Equity	$9,900,000
Acquisition Loan	$18,000,000
Total	$27,900,000

The sources of funds shows you the components of the capital stack. In the two previous examples, the "stack" isn't much of one at all. But commercial real estate can get complicated, as in the example below.

SOURCES	AMOUNT
Investor Equity	$1,580,000
Joint Venture Equity	$6,320,000
Preferred Equity	$2,000,000
Supplemental Loan	$3,000,000
Assumed Loan	$15,000,000
Total	**$27,900,000**

Generally speaking, the higher you are on the capital stack, the more risk you are taking, and the higher the rewards should be in exchange for taking that risk. As you can see above, the lowest spot on the capital stack is a loan that is already in place on the property and being assumed by the buyer. This is the lowest-risk position on the stack because the lender can foreclose and resell the property, and if the property is worth $20 million in a foreclosure sale and the debt is $15 million, there is plenty of equity behind the loan to recover the capital that was lent.

The supplemental loan is the next lowest on the stack. There is more risk here, because there is less equity behind the debt and there is a senior loan that has priority over this one. As a result, this loan would come at a higher interest rate. Next up on the stack is preferred equity. This slice is not secured by the property. Instead of foreclosure rights, the preferred equity investor more likely has control rights, and perhaps the ability to foreclose on the units in the LLC to take control of the company. There is $18 million of debt ahead of them in line, but there is also $7.9 million of equity behind them. The risk is higher, so the preferred equity gets a higher return than the supplemental loan.

Next up are the joint venture equity and investor equity. Joint venture equity is usually from a single large investor, such as an institutional investment fund or a family office. In this example, the joint venture partner is bringing 80 percent of the common equity and the investors in the syndication are bringing 20 percent of the common equity.

There are two approaches to this type of funding. In one structure, the joint venture equity has priority over the syndication investors. If this is the case, it is important to understand exactly how the priority works because it can have a profound impact on the risk you are taking. If the deal goes south, it would be entirely possible for everyone in the capital stack to get all their money back except for the syndication investors. You could suffer a total loss.

In the other structure, the joint venture and syndication equity are "pari passu," which means that they hold the same priority in the capital stack and the same right to cash flow. Their claim on cash flow is in the same percentage as the amount of equity contributed, so in this example, the joint venture partner would get 80 percent of the investor cash flow and the syndication investors would get 20 percent.

The bottom line is that it is important to see how much money is being raised and where the money is coming from because it can have an affect on your risk. A complex capital stack could explain why the project is forecasting very high rates of return to the syndicate. What once seemed very attractive might now seem like just a fair risk-adjusted return. If the risk is greater than you are willing to assume, it might not be worthwhile for you to go after the higher return. An alternative with a lower-risk profile, and perhaps a lower return, might be more appropriate for you.

As I've said before, a high forecasted return is nice and all, but you really need to understand how the sponsor has arrived at that return. It isn't just underwriting assumptions that can breed a high return. The makeup of the capital stack can as well, and it can do so with a higher-risk profile. Not all high returns are created equal.

Uses of Funds
The sources of funds is all about understanding where the money is coming from, and your position in the capital stack. The uses of funds is all about knowing how the money will be spent. People have a tendency to oversimplify a syndication investment as consisting of only the amount needed to cover the down payment. It's much more than that.

I've lost count of how often I've heard would-be syndication sponsors say things like, "I want to buy a property for $1 million and I can get $750,000 from the bank, so I need to raise the other $250,000 from investors." This is a clear sign of someone who has lost sight of the many costs beyond the down payment that are associated with a real estate investment. If the sponsor you are thinking of investing with is saying things like that, be aware that there's a lot they're not accounting for and their plan won't play out as projected.

Using the same example from the previous discussion about sources, the below uses of funds shows how the $27.9 million will be spent.

USES	AMOUNT
Purchase Price	$24,000,000
Renovation	$2,737,900
Working Capital	$216,767
Escrows (Insurance, Taxes)	$103,380
First Month's Debt Service	$87,553
Property Due Diligence	$38,900
Real Estate and Securities Legal	$52,000
Financing Origination	$240,500
Title	$16,000
Start-up Costs	$47,000
Sponsor Acquisition Fee	$360,000
Total	**$27,900,000**

You see here that the purchase price of the property is $24 million. If you recall from the sources table, there was $18 million in debt, which means that the down payment is $6 million. Notice that you don't see the down payment on the uses of funds. That's because you see the entire purchase price instead. If the down payment were listed in addition to the purchase price, you'd be double-counting it. If the down payment were listed instead of the purchase price, the total uses of funds would not equal the total sources of funds.

It all boils down to $9.9 million of equity being raised and a $6 million down payment. This leaves $3.9 million of other costs, illustrating my point about the need to raise much more than just the down payment. Not raising enough money is a common mistake among syndication sponsors. Your best defense is to scrutinize the sources and uses to see if the sponsor's assumptions are reasonable and thorough.

Let's walk through the various line items shown on the uses of funds table and what to look for in each.

Purchase price. This is the price being paid to acquire the property. It should match the price shown in the real estate purchase contract. Ask the sponsor whether the price shown here is the price being paid to the seller of the property. Every now and then you see sponsors "mark up" the real estate, buying it from the seller at one price and syndicating it at a higher price. I suppose there's nothing wrong with this if it's clearly disclosed and investors are okay with it, but if it's not disclosed, it's just a sneaky sponsor fee. In some instances, marking up the property is standard practice, as in the case of a Delaware statutory trust (DST) investment. This is usually because the sponsor fees and all other closing costs are wrapped into the price paid by the DST.

Renovation. If the business plan is to make improvements to the property, such as upgrading interiors, enhancing amenities, or correcting deferred maintenance, there should be a budget for completing those improvements. The total amount of that budget would be shown in the uses of funds, assuming that the work is to be financed from cash on hand, not by funds siphoned from the operating cash flow.

The rehab budget should match the business plan. For example, if the plan is to spend $7,500 per unit to remodel apartments, the uses of funds should reflect an amount high enough to cover that, as well as any exterior work plus a contingency for hidden damage and unknowns. If the plan includes renovations and there is no renovation budget in the uses of funds, the only place where the money can come from is cash flow. In that case, check the cash flow projections to make sure the cost of renovations is being accounted for there, and that the amount of the total deductions from cash flow is enough to complete the renovations as described.

Working capital. Working capital is just what it sounds like. It's extra money that isn't earmarked for any specific purpose—a cushion in the bank account and some cash reserves in case things don't go according to plan. The more working capital, the better, but there is a tug-of-war between working capital and investment performance. Assuming the same income and sale proceeds from the property, the more money raised, the lower the returns, so raising too much working capital is a drag on returns. However, raising too little increases risk. I've found that a good balance is between 0.5 percent and 2 percent of the purchase price, with the lower percentages applying to higher-priced stabilized properties, and the higher percentages applying to lower-priced or unstabilized properties.

Escrows. Lenders are a very cautious breed. They do everything possible to protect themselves, and that starts with protecting the property secured by their loan. If the sources of funds includes a loan, it's safe to assume that the lender will require an impound account for insurance because they want to make sure that the property will be insured if there is a fire or other covered loss. They will also want to prevent getting foreclosed by anyone else holding a lien that is a higher priority than their loan. Usually there is only one, the property tax. To make sure the property tax is paid, they will require that an impound account be put in place.

The way this works is that the lender will estimate the cost of the insurance and property tax for one year, and divide that amount by twelve. They then add that amount to the monthly loan payment, and when the borrower makes a loan payment, the lender will strip out the impound amount and put it in a lender-controlled account. When the tax or insurance bill comes, the lender pays it from that account. But there's a catch: The lender will want an initial deposit into that impound account so they have a cushion equivalent to about three months of the estimated annual impound. The sponsor should be planning for this and have a spot for it on their uses of funds. If they don't, they might get caught short and have to raise more money, diluting you; or take it from the working capital, which increases risk; or do a capital call, which means that everyone has to contribute more money.

Another item to include in the escrows category is utility company deposits. The first time I bought a large multifamily property, I called to set up the electric service and the utility provider wanted an $18,000 deposit to open the account. I was caught completely off-guard and had to take the money from working capital to pay it. That drew my working capital down to nearly nothing, which made it really difficult for the first few months. Never again! Sponsors should budget for utility company deposits and include them somewhere in their uses of funds.

First month's debt service. Some lenders require borrowers to deposit the first debt service payment into an impound account, and they deduct it when the first payment comes due. If the sponsor hasn't planned accordingly, it can catch them off-guard and short of funds. Not all lenders do this, so if the first month's debt service is missing from the uses of funds, it could mean that the lender won't be following this practice. Or it could mean that the sponsor forgot, doesn't know about it, or is planning to use working capital for this purpose, with the understanding that they will essentially get the money back when the first payment is made from the impound instead of from cash flow.

Property due diligence. This item covers various sponsor and lender inspections, such as a property condition report, fees to a due diligence firm, inspection fees, surveys, environmental reports, zoning reports, insurance consultants, travel, and anything else that relates to conducting pre-purchase due diligence. Sometimes sponsors will itemize each line item; other times the items will be grouped together.

Legal fees. Large commercial property transactions generate a lot of legal fees. Unlike residential transactions, agreements to purchase and finance commercial real estate are drafted by attorneys and are specific to each transaction. In addition to legal fees for negotiating the purchase agreement, reviewing the condition of title, and negotiating the terms of the loan documents, syndications have the additional burden of fees for securities lawyers, who will draft the private placement memorandum and subscription agreement for the investors. Fees can vary widely depending on the complexity of the transaction. For most commercial property syndicates, transaction and securities legal fees range from $15,000 to $75,000.

Financing. If you've ever bought a house, you know about the smorgasbord of fees that lenders charge to make the loan. Commercial loans aren't immune from these fees; the main difference is that the dollar amounts are higher. Expect to see one to two points on the loan (1 to 2 percent of the loan amount), underwriting fees, application fees, and an appraisal. Remember the legal fees we just talked about? The lender has legal fees too, and the borrower pays for them. The lender might also do some of their own due diligence, such as a site visit by one of the lender's executives, and the borrower pays for the travel costs. Floating-rate loans might require the purchase of a rate cap (these typically cost between 0.2 and 0.5 percent of the loan amount), and some states might have a mortgage tax. All of this must be accounted for and included on the uses of funds table.

Title. This includes title insurance for the buyer and the lender, recording fees, escrow fees, transfer taxes, and any other title insurance and escrow-related expense. If the seller is paying for the owner's title insurance policy, which is customary in some areas, this might be a small amount. But if the buyer is paying for the owner's title policy, this cost can be quite high. Large commercial transactions generate some hefty title insurance premiums.

Start-up costs. This is somewhat of a catchall, and not all sponsors include it. Sometimes they itemize the start-up items elsewhere; sometimes they plan to fund them from cash flow. Inexperienced sponsors might forget about them or fail to plan for them. Start-up costs can include office expenses, such as new computers or furniture (often what's there is outdated or near the end of its life), set-up costs for installing property management software or other systems, new furniture for model units, or a new website for the property.

Sponsor fees. Sponsors charge a variety of fees, and any fees that are to be paid at the time of the purchase must be accounted for on the uses of funds. Sponsor fees are covered in detail in chapter 17, but for the sake of this discussion, just make sure they are shown on the uses of funds and that the amount matches what is specified in the operating agreement. If the sponsor isn't presenting their various fees as a percentage of the purchase price (or loan amount, in the case of loan fees), you can calculate the percentage yourself by dividing the fee shown in the uses of funds by the purchase price or loan amount.

Total. This may seem self-explanatory, but there's an important point to watch for here. Make sure the total uses of funds matches the total sources of funds. If the two don't match, there is money unaccounted for, and that's never a good thing!

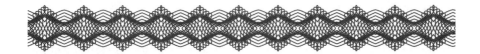

CHAPTER 16

WATERFALLS

One of the things I love about Maui is the beautiful waterfalls. They're among the most amazing in the world. Back here in the office, I'm lucky enough to look at waterfalls every day. No, my view isn't overlooking the rain forest—it's a spreadsheet. And there's not a drop of liquid in these waterfalls!

In the syndication world, "waterfall" is slang for the division of profits. One of the ways syndication sponsors make money in exchange for all they do is to share in the cash distributions. We've spent a lot of time going through how real estate makes money, and how to calculate and forecast the money the property will make. But what happens next? That cash flow gets divided, and how it's divided can get extremely complicated. As the money flows downhill, it fills up a variety of buckets, hence the term "waterfall." Let's dive into the different types of waterfalls and how they work.

Profit Split

The simplest waterfall is a straight division of profits. For every dollar out, the investors get a percentage and the sponsor gets a percentage. The sponsor's portion is also called a "promote" because their interest in the deal is "promoted," meaning they are receiving more proceeds than they would have if they were just an equal owner along with the other investors.

The "division of profits" waterfall dates back to an old partnership concept: "You bring the money; I do all the work; we split the profits." At what ratio the cash flow is split depends on whatever the parties agree to. For investors who flip houses, it isn't uncommon to see straight 50/50 profit splits because flipping houses is a lot of work.

As the scale of the projects increases, the need for capital grows and the potential profits also increase. For these reasons, the simple 50/50 profit split becomes very rich to the sponsor on larger projects. For example, a $250,000 house flip making a 10 percent profit that is split 50/50 results in a profit of $12,500 for the sponsor and $12,500 for the investor. Let's assume that $125,000 was contributed by the investor and the rest was borrowed from the bank. The investor made $12,500 on their investment in four months, which is a 30 percent annualized return. The flipper made $12,500 for four months' work. It's a fair deal for both parties.

Now let's assume that the venture is buying a $10 million apartment complex with the plan to fix up the property, increase the income, and sell in five years. The venture borrows $7.5 million from a bank, and an investor contributes $5 million to cover the down payment, capital improvements, and all other costs. If the venture makes a $5 million profit that's split 50/50, the sponsor makes $2.5 million and the investor makes a 10 percent annualized return. This is imbalanced because the return isn't high enough to justify the risk, and the sponsor's profit is too high relative to the investor's reward. If the property made only a $2.5 million profit, the sponsor would have made $1.25 million and the investor would have earned a 5 percent annualized return. I doubt many investors would be happy with that outcome.

Another problem is that the sponsor makes a healthy profit even if the investor earns very little, which doesn't incentivize the sponsor to perform at their best. In the previous example, if the profit was only $500,000, the investor would still have made a $250,000 profit but the investor would have earned a measly 1 percent return. There has to be a better way—and there is.

Preferred Return

The most common way to prevent the previous scenario is a structure that gives the investors preference over the earliest cash flow. Said another way, the investors receive a minimum rate of return, called a "preferred return," before the sponsor gets any split of the cash flow. A preferred return is not a guaranteed return; it is simply a preferred position in the waterfall. The water has to fill your bucket before it overflows and spills cash to the sponsor's.

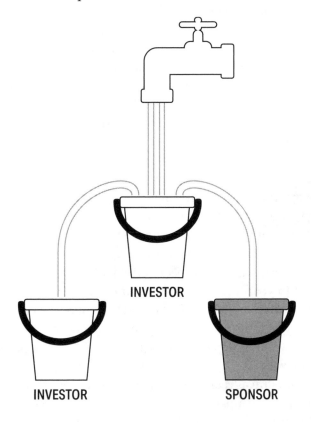

To calculate a preferred return, simply multiply the capital invested by the preferred return rate. Let's say the investors are contributing $1 million and the preferred return is 8 percent.

$$\$1,000,000 \times .08 = \$80,000$$

The investors must receive $80,000 each year before the sponsor receives anything. If the distributions for the year are less than $80,000, the sponsor receives nothing. What happens to the shortfall depends on how the partnership agreement is worded. There are a number of different ways this is handled. Let's look at some examples of language from a partnership agreement.

Cash flow shall be distributed in the following order and priority:

- *First, until the Investors have received an eight percent (8%) Annual Rate of Return on their unreturned Capital Contributions, to the Investors on a Pro Rata basis;*

This language outlines the preferred return. It may be short but it is actually saying several things. Let's break it down. The first thing to note is that some of the terms are capitalized. In a partnership agreement, any capitalized term should be defined somewhere in the partnership agreement, and you should consult the definition to learn exactly what the term means.

In this example, "Annual Rate of Return" is capitalized, so we must go to the partnership agreement's definition of that term. There are a few different ways that the return can be calculated, and how this is done will change the actual dollars at stake.

This agreement specifies "unreturned Capital Contributions," which means that the preferred return is calculated on the capital invested in the deal, not on capital that has been returned to investors. For example, let's say that in year 3 the sponsor refinanced the property. From the proceeds of the new loan, half of all investor capital was returned. From that point forward, the preferred return would no longer be 8 percent of $1 million; it would be 8 percent of $500,000, or $40,000 per year from that point forward.

The partnership agreement also specifies "to the Investors on a Pro Rata basis." This means that the distribution is divided among all the investors in the same proportion as the amount that each invested. Let's say that you invested $100,000 of the total $1 million from all the investors combined. You own 10 percent of the total capital, so 10 percent of each distribution meant for the investors as a whole will go to you.

Tracking the Preferred Return

In order to properly account for preferred return payments, the amount of accrued preferred return must be tracked. This is typically done on a spreadsheet that tracks the preferred return due and the preferred return distributed for each period. In the partnership agreement language above, the preferred return is "an eight percent (8%) Annual Rate of Return," which could be defined a number of ways.

The agreement could define the annual rate of return as "cumulative," which means that if in any year the preferred return hasn't been fully satisfied, the balance due will carry over to the next year, as in the example below. Notice that the investors are receiving the entire cash flow each year because it takes all three years to get to a cumulative 8 percent return on the capital. The sponsor is receiving nothing.

	YEAR 1	YEAR 2	YEAR 3
Project Cash Flow	$40,000	$80,000	$120,000
Starting Balance	$0	$40,000	$40,000
Required for 8% Pref	$80,000	$80,000	$80,000
Preferred Return Distribution	$(40,000)	$(80,000)	$(120,000)
Ending Balance	$40,000	$40,000	$0
Investor Net Cash Flow	$40,000	$80,000	$120,000

The agreement could also define the annual rate of return as "non-cumulative," which means that if the distributions in any given year do not satisfy the preferred return, the shortage will not carry over to the next year. This treatment is uncommon, but you might come across it, so be sure to check the language in the partnership agreement in order to understand exactly what is happening. A non-cumulative preferred return would look like this:

	YEAR 1	YEAR 2	YEAR 3
Project Cash Flow	$40,000	$80,000	$120,000
Starting Balance	$0	$0	$0
Required for 8% Pref	$80,000	$80,000	$80,000
Preferred Return Distribution	$(40,000)	$(80,000)	$(80,000)
Ending Balance	$40,000	$0	$0
Investor Net Cash Flow	$40,000	$80,000	$80,000

Note that in the above example there is still $40,000 remaining in year 3 because there was $120,000 of cash flow but only $80,000 in preferred return. I'll cover what happens to that $40,000 later in this chapter.

The definition of annual rate of return might also specify that the preferred return is "compounding," which means that any unpaid preferred return from one year not only carries over to the next year, but adds to the balance of the invested capital and earns an annual rate of return as well—preferred return on the preferred return, so to speak. It would look like this:

	YEAR 1	YEAR 2	YEAR 3
Project Cash Flow	$40,000	$80,000	$120,000
Starting Balance	$0	$40,000	$43,200
Required for 8% Pref	$80,000	$83,200	$83,456
Preferred Return Distribution	$(40,000)	$(80,000)	$(120,000)
Ending Balance	$40,000	$43,200	$6,656
Investor Net Cash Flow	$40,000	$80,000	$120,000

Note that the $40,000 that carried over from year 1 to year 2 earned 8 percent, just like the $1 million that was invested, so the total preferred return due was $83,200 instead of $80,000. The same goes for the $43,200 from year 2 that carried over to year 3. In this example, compounding the preferred return would result in $6,656 of additional preferred return over a non-compounding preferred return. A preferred return calculated from an annualized return is usually cumulative and non-compounding, but it could also be non-cumulative, or cumulative and compounding. Whatever it is, not all annualized rates of return are created alike, so you need to study the definitions in the operating agreement.

Cash Flow Split Above Preferred Return

Preferred return gives investors the first claim on cash flow. That means investors get 100 percent of the cash flow until the preferred return has been fully satisfied. But what happens next? That depends on the waterfall language in the partnership agreement. Typically, one of two things will occur: The surplus is distributed to the investors to incrementally return their invested capital, or it is split between the investors and the sponsor in some fashion. Let's examine a couple of sample partnership agreements.

Cash flow shall be distributed in the following order and priority:

   a. *First, until the Investors have received an eight percent (8%) Annual Rate of Return on their unreturned Capital Contributions, to the Investors on a Pro Rata basis;*

   b. *Second, (i) seventy percent (70%) to the Investors on a Pro Rata basis and (ii) thirty percent (30%) to the Manager.*

In this agreement, subsection (a) is the preferred return and subsection (b) is the split of the remaining cash flow. Plainly stated, this is an 8 percent preferred return followed by a 70/30 split. Let's assume that annual rate of return is defined as cumulative but non-compounding. The waterfall would look like this:

	YEAR 1	YEAR 2	YEAR 3	YEAR 4	YEAR 5
Project Cash Flow	$40,000	$80,000	$100,000	$120,000	$140,000
100% UNTIL REACHING 8% RETURN					
Starting Balance	$0	$40,000	$40,000	$20,000	$0
Required for 8% Pref	$80,000	$80,000	$80,000	$80,000	$80,000
Preferred Return Distribution	$(40,000)	$(80,000)	$(100,000)	$(100,000)	$(80,000)
Ending Balance	$40,000	$40,000	$20,000	$0	$0
Remaining Cash	$0	$0	$0	$20,000	$60,000
70/30 THEREAFTER					
Investor Share (70%)	$0	$0	$0	$14,000	$42,000
Sponsor Share (30%)	$0	$0	$0	$6,000	$18,000
Investor Net Cash Flow	**$40,000**	**$80,000**	**$100,000**	**$114,000**	**$122,000**

Let's walk through this one year at a time.

Year 1. There is $40,000 to distribute. This is less than the preferred return due for the year, so the investors get all of it. Forty thousand dollars of undistributed preferred return carries over to next year.

Year 2. The investors are owed $40,000 in undistributed preferred return from year 1, plus another $80,000 for this year, which comes to $120,000. There is $80,000 to distribute. The distribution is less than the preferred return due, so the investors get all of it. Forty thousand dollars of undistributed preferred return carries over to next year.

Year 3. The investors are owed $40,000 in undistributed preferred return from year 2, plus another $80,000 for this year, which comes to $120,000. There is $100,000 to distribute. The distribution is less than the preferred return due, so the investors get all of it. Then, $20,000 of undistributed preferred return carries over to next year.

Year 4. The investors are owed $20,000 in undistributed preferred return from year 3, plus another $80,000 for this year, which comes to $100,000. There is $120,000 to distribute. The distribution is greater than the preferred return due, so the investors get $100,000 to satisfy the preferred return. Twenty thousand dollars remains, and that is split 70 percent to the investors and 30 percent to the sponsor. There is no undistributed preferred return to carry over to next year. The investors receive $100,000 in preferred return and $14,000 in excess cash, or $114,000 total.

Year 5. There is no undistributed preferred return from year 4. Eighty thousand dollars of preferred return is due for this year. There is $140,000 to distribute. The distribution is greater than the preferred return due, so the investors get $80,000 to satisfy the preferred return. Sixty thousand dollars remains, and that is split 70 percent to the investors and 30 percent to the sponsor. The investors receive $80,000 in preferred return and $42,000 in excess cash, or $122,000 total. There is no undistributed preferred return to carry over to next year.

Treatment of Sale Proceeds

Most often proceeds from the sale are treated just like any other cash flow, except that it is first applied to returning investor capital, and after that it follows the rest of the waterfall rules. A common way to handle this in the operating agreement is with a simple provision saying: *"Capital received from the sale of the property is to be distributed to the Investors on a Pro Rata basis to the extent of their unreturned Capital Contributions."* This provision might be spelled out in the same subsection as the distribution provisions or it might be located elsewhere.

This is what the waterfall would look like if the property was sold in year 5 and $2 million was received from the proceeds of the sale, plus there was $140,000 of operating cash flow in year 5.

	YEAR 1	YEAR 2	YEAR 3	YEAR 4	YEAR 5
Project Cash Flow	$40,000	$80,000	$100,000	$120,000	$2,140,000
100% OF SALE PROCEEDS UNTIL ALL CAPITAL RETURNED					
Starting Capital	$1,000,000	$1,000,000	$1,000,000	$1,000,000	$1,000,000
Capital Distributions	$0	$0	$0	$0	$(1,000,000)
Ending Capital	$1,000,000	$1,000,000	$1,000,000	$1,000,000	$0
Remaining Cash	$40,000	$80,000	$100,000	$120,000	$1,140,000
100% UNTIL REACHING 8% RETURN					
Starting Balance	$0	$40,000	$40,000	$20,000	$0
Required for 8% Pref	$80,000	$80,000	$80,000	$80,000	$80,000
Preferred Return Distribution	$(40,000)	$(80,000)	$(100,000)	$(100,000)	$(80,000)
Ending Balance	$40,000	$40,000	$20,000	$0	$0
Remaining Cash	$0	$0	$0	$20,000	$1,060,000
70/30 THEREAFTER					
Investor Share (70%)	$0	$0	$0	$14,000	$742,000
Sponsor Share (30%)	$0	$0	$0	$6,000	$318,000
Investor Net Cash Flow	**$40,000**	**$80,000**	**$100,000**	**$114,000**	**$1,822,000**

The only difference with our previous example occurs in year 5. Notice that of the $2 million of sale proceeds and $140,000 of cash flow that are distributed, the first thing that happens is the return of $1 million of investor capital. This leaves $1,140,000 of cash flow. Of that, $80,000 goes to the investors to satisfy this year's preferred return. That leaves $1,060,000 to be split 70/30 between the investors and sponsor. The investors receive $1 million plus $80,000 plus $742,000 for a total of $1,822,000. The sponsor receives $318,000, representing 30 percent of the remaining cash after the investors' capital is returned and preferred return is paid.

Calculating IRR, CoC, and Equity Multiple

Now that you've seen how a waterfall calculates the division of cash flow, let's add in some performance indicators so you can see how all this translates into calculating your returns. As you may recall from chapter 9, the three primary performance indicators are IRR, cash-on-cash return, and equity multiple. Let's assume the cash flow scenario outlined in our previous example.

INVESTOR NET CASH FLOW	$40,000	$80,000	$100,000	$114,000	$1,822,000

The only way to calculate IRR is with a spreadsheet using Microsoft Excel's IRR function. The function is "=IRR(Year 0:Year 5)," where Year 0 refers to a cell populated with a negative number reflecting your initial investment, and Year 5 refers to a cell containing the fifth year's cash flow. In between each of those cells is each year of cash flow. The result of this spreadsheet calculation is an IRR of 18.2 percent.

	A	B	C	D	E	F	G
1	=IRR(B1:G1)	($1,000,000)	$40,000	$80,000	$100,000	$114,000	$1,822,000

Now let's calculate the cash-on-cash return for each year, and the average. This can be done with a calculator: Simply divide the cash flow each year by the amount invested. In this example, there is $1 million invested in each of the years.

AVERAGE	YEAR 1	YEAR 2	YEAR 3	YEAR4	YEAR 5
9.1%	4%	8%	10%	11.4%	12.2%

The only tricky one here is year 5. There was $1,822,000 received in year 5, but some of that was return of capital, some was profit from the sale, and some was operating cash flow. Including either the return of capital or profit from sale would be improper for calculating a CoC return, so those cash flows must be excluded. To properly calculate the CoC for year 5, recall that the cash flow from operations was $140,000 in our very early examples. Take that number and set aside the $80,000 in preferred return, leaving $60,000 to flow to the next tier. The preferred return was fully satisfied, so $60,000 was split 70/30 with the sponsor. This means that the investors received $42,000. Add the $80,000 preferred return distribution to the $42,000 investor share of the excess, and you get $122,000 of investor operating cash flow. Divide that by $1 million and you get 12.2 percent.

$$\$140,000 \text{ Cash Flow} - \$80,000 \text{ Pref} = \$60,000$$

$$\$60,000 \times 0.7 = \$42,000$$

$$\$42,000 + \$80,000 = \$122,000$$

$$\frac{\$122,000}{\$1,000,000} = 12.2\%$$

Next, let's calculate the equity multiple. To do this, simply add up all the cash flow received. In this case it is:

$$\$40,000 + \$80,000 + \$100,000 + \$114,000 + \$1,822,000 = \$2,156,000$$

Next, divide $2,156,000 by the amount invested, which was $1 million.

$$\frac{\$2,156,000}{\$1,000,000} = 2.16 \text{ Equity Multiple}$$

Now let's put it all together and attach it as a footer on our waterfall tables so we can compare the performance of the rest of our waterfall examples.

INVESTOR NET CASH FLOW		$40,000	$80,000	$100,000	$114,000	$1,822,000
CoC	9.1% (Avg)	4%	8%	10%	11.4%	12.2%
IRR	18.2%					
Equity Multiple	2.16					

Return of Capital After Preferred Return

Previous examples have illustrated a waterfall where the sponsor and investors split the cash flow after the preferred return has been satisfied. This is a fairly common arrangement but not the only one possible. It all depends on what the partnership agreement says. Consider this example:

Cash flow shall be distributed in the following order and priority:
  - *First, until the Investors have received an eight percent (8%) Annual*

Rate of Return on their unreturned Capital Contributions, to the Investors on a Pro Rata basis;

- *Second, to the Investors on a Pro Rata basis to the extent of their unreturned Capital Contributions;*
- *Third, (i) seventy percent (70%) to the Investors on a Pro Rata basis and (ii) thirty percent (30%) to the Manager.*

In this waterfall, first the preferred return is satisfied, then the remaining capital gets distributed to the investors until they have received all their invested capital back. Chances are they won't receive all their capital back until the sale of the property, which also means that the sponsor won't receive any profit split until the property is sold either.

		YEAR 1	YEAR 2	YEAR 3	YEAR 4	YEAR 5
Project Cash Flow		$40,000	$80,000	$100,000	$120,000	$2,140,000
100% UNTIL REACHING 8% RETURN						
Starting Balance		$0	$40,000	$40,000	$20,000	$0
Required for 8% Pref		$80,000	$80,000	$80,000	$80,000	$78,400
Preferred Return Distribution		$(40,000)	$(80,000)	$(100,000)	$(100,000)	$(78,400)
Ending Balance		$40,000	$40,000	$20,000	$0	$0
Remaining Cash		$0	$0	$0	$20,000	$2,061,600
100% UNTIL ALL CAPITAL RETURNED						
Starting Capital		$1,000,000	$1,000,000	$1,000,000	$1,000,000	$980,000
Capital Distributions		$0	$0	$0	$(20,000)	$(980,000)
Ending Capital		$1,000,000	$1,000,000	$1,000,000	$980,000	$0
Remaining Cash		$0	$0	$0	$0	$1,081,600
70/30 THEREAFTER						
Investor Share (70%)		$0	$0	$0	$0	$757,120
Sponsor Share (30%)		$0	$0	$0	$0	$324,480
Investor Net Cash Flow		**$40,000**	**$80,000**	**$100,000**	**$120,000**	**$1,815,520**
CoC	9.2% (Avg)	4%	8%	10%	12%	12.2%
IRR	18.2%					
Equity Multiple	2.16					

For the first three years this waterfall is essentially the same as our previous example. But in year 4, things get different. Instead of the surplus cash being split 70/30, all of it is distributed to the investors and deducted from their capital balance. In year 5, the preferred return drops from $80,000 to $78,400 because the capital balance has dropped from $1 million to $980,000. The investors receive $6,000 more in year 4 but receive $6,480 less in year 5.

Some investors like the idea of receiving their capital back before the sponsors receive any compensation, but many don't realize that this privilege comes at a cost. Everything in the syndication world is a trade-off, and changing the priority of the return of capital is no exception.

What is interesting is that this waterfall and the previous example are both structured as an 8 percent preferred return and a 70/30 split, but simply switching the order of the return of capital results in $480 less total cash flow to the investors. That's because there is $1,600 less preferred return due in year 5. So why wasn't the total cash flow $1,600 less? Because of the 70/30 split. The investors recover 70 percent of the reduction in preferred return when the surplus cash drops to the 70/30 split tier. While a reduction in preferred return sounds bad, it isn't quite as bad as it sounds because a loss of preferred return isn't a dollar-for-dollar loss of cash flow. It simply changes the dollars from preferred return to surplus cash, dropping them down to the next split tier.

Another interesting thing to note: The actual dollar difference wasn't enough to move the needle much on the calculations of the performance indicators.

Return of Capital Before Preferred Return

Waterfalls can be as creative as the sponsor wants them to be, and the details matter. Take, for example, the following language.

Cash flow shall be distributed in the following order and priority:
- *First, to the Investors on a Pro Rata basis to the extent of their unreturned Capital Contributions;*
- *Second, until the Investors have received an eight percent (8%) Annual Rate of Return on their unreturned Capital Contributions, to the Investors on a Pro Rata basis;*
- *Third, (i) seventy percent (70%) to the Investors on a Pro Rata basis and (ii) thirty percent (30%) to the Manager.*

All we did here was switch the order of (a) and (b). Now the cash flow first goes toward returning investors' capital. After that, cash flow goes to the investors to satisfy the preferred return. Only after that is cash flow split with the sponsor. While this might sound desirable, there is no free lunch here either. This is what the waterfall looks like:

		YEAR 1	YEAR 2	YEAR 3	YEAR 4	YEAR 5
Project Cash Flow		$40,000	$80,000	$100,000	$120,000	$2,140,000
100% UNTIL ALL CAPITAL RETURNED						
Starting Capital		$1,000,000	$960,000	$880,000	$780,000	$660,000
Capital Distributions		$(40,000)	$(80,000)	$(100,000)	$(120,000)	$(660,000)
Ending Capital		$960,000	$880,000	$780,000	$660,000	$0
Remaining Cash		$0	$0	$0	$0	$1,480,000
100% UNTIL REACHING 8% RETURN						
Starting Balance		$0	$80,000	$156,800	$227,200	$289,600
Required for 8% Pref		$80,000	$76,800	$70,400	$62,400	$52,800
Preferred Return Distribution		$0	$0	$0	$0	$(342,400)
Ending Balance		$80,000	$156,800	$227,200	$289,600	$0
Remaining Cash		$0	$0	$0	$0	$1,137,600
70/30 THEREAFTER						
Investor Share (70%)		$0	$0	$0	$0	$796,320
Sponsor Share (30%)		$0	$0	$0	$0	$341,280
Investor Net Cash Flow		$40,000	$80,000	$100,000	$120,000	$1,798,720
CoC	9.1% (Avg)	4%	8%	10%	12%	11.4%
IRR	18.0%					
Equity Multiple	2.14					

Notice that each year the remaining capital is reduced by the amount distributed, which results in a smaller preferred return accumulation for the subsequent year. In the year of the sale, the remainder of the capital is returned and all of the preferred return is paid. Because of the smaller accumulation of preferred return, the total cash flow to the investors is less than in any of the previous examples, but only marginally so, because the difference in preferred return dropped down to the 70/30 split tier. All performance indicators dropped slightly. Having the investors receive their capital back first resulted in the lowest performance of all methods so far.

Annualized Return Versus Internal Rate of Return Waterfalls

All the waterfalls we've shown up until now have been based on achieving an annualized return to meet the preferred return. However, there is another common method of calculating waterfalls, and that is for the required return to be an internal rate of return, or IRR. The difference in the operating agreement is so slight that it is almost imperceptible.

Cash flow shall be distributed in the following order and priority:
- *First, until the Investors have received an eight percent (8%) Annual Internal Rate of Return on their unreturned Capital Contributions, to the Investors on a Pro Rata basis;*
- *Second, (i) seventy percent (70%) to the Investors on a Pro Rata basis and (ii) thirty percent (30%) to the Manager.*

That's right, changing just one word in the agreement changes the math in the calculation of the waterfall. Using this waterfall, the test is to meet an 8 percent IRR instead of an 8 percent annualized return, which is similar but slightly different. To achieve an 8 percent IRR, a few things must happen by definition. First, the preferred return must be cumulative and compounding. Second, the invested capital must be returned. This means that there is no need for a provision in the operating agreement providing for a return of capital. You might still see one, though, because either the sponsor or the attorney who wrote the agreement wasn't aware that you can't achieve a positive IRR without returning the capital, or they just wanted the redundancy for the comfort of investors who are reading the operating agreement and aren't aware of this.

Another unique feature of IRR-based waterfalls is that the invested capital and the preferred return are tracked together, with the preferred return adding to the invested capital and all distributions being deducted from it. Whether preferred return or capital is returned first is moot, because they are one and the same in this case. This is what an IRR-based waterfall would look like:

		YEAR 1	YEAR 2	YEAR 3	YEAR 4	YEAR 5
Project Cash Flow		$40,000	$80,000	$100,000	$120,000	$2,140,000
100% UNTIL REACHING 8% IRR						
Starting Balance		$1,000,000	$1,040,000	$1,043,200	$1,026,656	$988,788
Required for 8% Pref		$80,000	$83,200	$83,456	$82,132	$79,103
Preferred Return Distribution		$(40,000)	$(80,000)	$(100,000)	$(120,000)	$(1,067,891)
Ending Balance		$1,040,000	$1,043,200	$1,026,656	$988,788	$0
Remaining Cash		$0	$0	$0	$0	$1,072,109
70/30 THEREAFTER						
Investor Share (70%)		$0	$0	$0	$0	$750,476
Sponsor Share (30%)		$0	$0	$0	$0	$321,633
Investor Net Cash Flow		$40,000	$80,000	$100,000	$120,000	$1,818,367
CoC	9.2% (Avg)	4%	8%	10%	12%	12.2%
IRR	18.2%					
Equity Multiple	2.16					

The main point here is to show that not all 8 percent preferred returns with 70/30 splits are created alike. Cumulative versus non-cumulative preferred returns, compounding versus non-compounding preferred returns, measuring preferred return to IRR versus annualized rate of return, and the priority of the return of capital will all affect the dollars, and returns, received.

Refinance Proceeds and Effect on Future Cash Flow

A very common question is "What happens if the sponsor refinances the property and returns some or all of my capital?" This is a great question with no single answer. What *should* happen is not much. But what actually happens depends on what the partnership agreement says. It's important to review the agreement to find out.

Some sponsors will use a return of capital event to capture your ownership position. In other words, they seek to "buy you out" by refinancing. They either shift the cash flow to themselves by changing the profit split after you've received your capital back, or they alter the split of the sale proceeds. Whichever tactic they use, don't fall for it. These sponsors, often inexperienced, are counting on investors who don't know any better. You, however, have read the book on how to invest in syndications, so you *do* know better. Don't invest in deals where sponsors cap your upside by refinancing you out of a deal.

Let's assume the partnership agreement doesn't play any of those tricks, and just reads like this:

Cash flow shall be distributed in the following order and priority:
- *First, until the Investors have received an eight percent (8%) Annual Rate of Return on their unreturned Capital Contributions, to the Investors on a Pro Rata basis;*
- *Second, (i) seventy percent (70%) to the Investors on a Pro Rata basis and (ii) thirty percent (30%) to the Manager.*
- *Distributions from capital events including refinances or sale shall be distributed to the Investors on a Pro Rata basis to the extent of their unreturned Capital Contributions.*

Subsection (c) might be located in the cash flow distributions section of the partnership agreement or might be located elsewhere in the agreement. If section (a) says "Internal Rate of Return" instead of "Annual Rate of Return," the return of capital doesn't need to be addressed because it's included by definition.

Here is what the waterfall based on the above language would look like if there was a cash-out refinance at the end of year 3, producing $500,000 of distributable cash.

	YEAR 1	YEAR 2	YEAR 3	YEAR 4	YEAR 5
Project Cash Flow	$40,000	$80,000	$600,000	$100,000	$1,620,000
100% OF REFINANCE AND SALE PROCEEDS UNTIL ALL CAPITAL RETURNED					
Starting Capital	$1,000,000	$1,000,000	$1,000,000	$500,000	$500,000
Capital Distributions	$0	$0	$(500,000)	$0	$(500,000)
Ending Capital	$1,000,000	$1,000,000	$500,000	$500,000	$0
Remaining Cash	$40,000	$80,000	$100,000	$100,000	$1,120,000
100% UNTIL REACHING 8% RETURN					
Starting Balance	$0	$40,000	$40,000	$20,000	$0
Required for 8% Pref	$80,000	$80,000	$80,000	$40,000	$40,000
Preferred Return Distribution	$(40,000)	$(80,000)	$(100,000)	$(60,000)	$(40,000)
Ending Balance	$40,000	$40,000	$20,000	$0	$0
Remaining Cash	$0	$0	$0	$40,000	$1,080,000
70/30 THEREAFTER					
Investor Share (70%)	$0	$0	$0	$28,000	$756,000
Sponsor Share (30%)	$0	$0	$0	$12,000	$324,000
Investor Net Cash Flow	$40,000	$80,000	$600,000	$88,000	$1,296,000
CoC	12.3% (Avg)	4%	8%	10%	17.6%	22%
IRR	20.0%				
Equity Multiple	2.10				

Notice that in year 3 there is $600,000 to distribute: $500,000 of that comes from the refinance, and $100,000 of that is the same operating cash flow we've used in our previous examples. You'll also notice that the cash flow has been reduced by $20,000 in years 4 and 5 because of the additional interest payments to the lender on the additional $500,000.

You'll see that $500,000 has been returned to the investors as a return of capital, leaving $500,000 still in the deal. In years 4 and 5, the preferred return accrual is cut in half, to $40,000, because it is now 8 percent of $500,000 instead of 8 percent of $1 million. In the year of the sale there is only $500,000 of equity remaining to be returned. Add to that $40,000 of preferred return to distribute, and the rest is split 70/30.

Focusing on the performance indicators, notice that in years 4 and 5 the CoC return jumps. That's because there is only $500,000 remaining in the deal, in contrast to all our earlier examples, where there was $1 million committed in years 4 and 5. Returning capital has a profound effect on CoC return.

Refinancing also has a profound effect on IRR. Because IRR takes into account the timing of cash flows, returning half of the invested capital sooner increases IRR. With no change in operational performance, the IRR has risen from between 17 and 18 percent to 20 percent. The equity multiple has gone down, but only slightly, meaning that this refinance resulted in the investors receiving fewer total dollars than if the refinance hadn't been done. On first glance, this appears to be a bad thing. But consider that the investors will have $500,000 available to invest in other investments two years sooner, so they can more than make up for this difference if they make a good investment with the money soon after receiving it. It's like having your cake and eating it too, because investors get to earn a second return on their money. This is a powerful feature of real estate syndications.

Now let's look at an example where all the investors' capital is returned as a result of a refinance. This is somewhat unusual but theoretically possible, so we should at least run the numbers so you understand how the waterfall would work if this were to happen.

		YEAR 1	YEAR 2	YEAR 3	YEAR 4	YEAR 5
Project Cash Flow		$40,000	$80,000	$1,100,000	$80,000	$1,100,000
100% OF REFINANCE AND SALE PROCEEDS UNTIL ALL CAPITAL RETURNED						
Starting Capital		$1,000,000	$1,000,000	$1,000,000	$0	$0
Capital Distributions		$0	$0	$(1,000,000)	$0	$0
Ending Capital		$1,000,000	$1,000,000	$0	$0	$0
Remaining Cash		$40,000	$80,000	$100,000	$80,000	$1,100,000
100% UNTIL REACHING 8% RETURN						
Starting Balance		$0	$40,000	$40,000	$20,000	$0
Required for 8% Pref		$80,000	$80,000	$80,000	$0	$0
Preferred Return Distribution		$(40,000)	$(80,000)	$(100,000)	$(20,000)	$0
Ending Balance		$40,000	$40,000	$20,000	$0	$0
Remaining Cash		$0	$0	$0	$60,000	$1,100,000
70 / 30 THEREAFTER						
Investor Share (70%)		$0	$0	$0	$42,000	$770,000
Sponsor Share (30%)		$0	$0	$0	$18,000	$330,000
Investor Net Cash Flow		**$40,000**	**$80,000**	**$1,100,000**	**$62,000**	**$770,000**
CoC	Infinite	4%	8%	10%	Infinite	Infinite
IRR	22.2%					
Equity Multiple	2.05					

Notice that all the capital is returned in year 3, so there is no preferred return due in years 4 and 5. The cash flow has been reduced by another $20,000 to account for the additional interest on the larger loan. The CoC return is now infinite because there is no cash left in the deal for the last two years. IRR has gone up to 22.2 percent, and the equity multiple has gone down slightly.

Investors often think that receiving their capital back is a bad thing because the preferred return is reduced or goes away. However, it's important to think this all the way through. In this example, the loss of preferred return is $80,000 per year. But that $80,000 simply drops down to the 70/30 split tier, so the investors receive $56,000 instead of $80,000, which is a loss of $24,000. There is additional interest on the now-borrowed $1 million, which at a 4 percent interest rate comes to $40,000. At a 70/30 split, the investors take a $28,000 hit due to the interest. Add the $24,000 loss of preferred return and the investors are out $52,000.

But they have all their money back, so their downside risk is all house money, and they can use that $1 million to invest in something else. You would have to earn only a 5.2 percent return on your $1 million to make up for the $52,000 reduction of cash flow in this example. Completing this loop, let's now assume that you invest your $1 million in another syndication that duplicates the performance of this example. With each of these investments yielding a double-digit return, for two years you are earning a double-digit return on the same dollars twice. That's a very favorable trade-off for the sacrifice of some preferred return, and this demonstrates the power of compounding at its best.

Multi-Tier Waterfalls

So far, we have covered simple profit splits and two-tiered waterfalls with a preferred-return tier and a profit-split tier. While you'll encounter these often, there's another type of waterfall that we need to cover because it's just as common. Consider a scenario in which the sponsor believes the property has a lot of upside if they implement their plan properly. If they hit a grand slam, they want to be rewarded for doing so. But what if they don't? The investors would be right to be concerned that they'd be stuck giving the sponsor a large slice of the pie for lackluster performance. How do you satisfy both interests?

The "multi-tiered waterfall" provides a solution. With this structure, the sponsor's promote increases with better performance and decreases with weaker performance. It starts with a preferred return. After the preferred return is met, the remaining cash flow is split, just like in our earlier examples. But this time there is a second rate of return, called a "hurdle." Once that return is met, the split shuts off and the remaining cash flow drops to a subsequent tier that has a different profit split. This can happen once, twice, three times, or as many times as desired, but usually you'll see two to four tiers.

Here's how it looks in the partnership agreement:

Cash flow shall be distributed in the following order and priority:

- *First, until the Investors have received an eight percent (8%) Annual Rate of Return on their unreturned Capital Contributions, to the Investors on a Pro Rata basis;*
- *Second, until the Investors have received a twelve percent (12%) Annual Rate of Return on their unreturned Capital Contributions, (i) seventy percent (70%) to the Investors on a Pro Rata basis and (ii) thirty percent (30%) to the Manager.*
- *Third, until the Investors have received a fifteen percent (15%) Annual Rate of Return on their unreturned Capital Contributions, (i) sixty percent (60%) to the Investors on a Pro Rata basis and (ii) forty percent (40%) to the Manager.*
- *Fourth, (i) fifty percent (50%) to the Investors on a Pro Rata basis and (ii) fifty percent (50%) to the Manager.*
- *Distributions from capital events including refinances or sale shall be distributed to the Investors on a Pro Rata basis to the extent of their unreturned Capital Contributions.*

In this example, you get an 8 percent preferred return. After that, you get 70 percent of the profits until you have reached a 12 percent return. After that, you receive 60 percent of the profits until you reach a 15 percent return. After that, anything left over is split 50/50 between you and the sponsor. Note that only the surplus cash flow left over after satisfying any given tier is split at the next tier's ratio. This means that if you receive a 20 percent return, you are not splitting 50 percent of all cash flow with the sponsor. The only cash flow that's split 50/50 is the cash left over after you have received a 15 percent return.

This complicated structure requires what is called a "lookback," which means the sponsor must look back to all previous cash flows to ensure that each tier is met so as not to over-distribute their portion of the profits and short the investors. A lookback is easy to calculate; it works just like a preferred return. Track the amount of money invested and how much is required to be distributed to achieve the hurdle. In this example, the investors receive 70 percent of the cash flow until the remaining accrual is reduced to $0. Let's see what that looks like.

	YEAR 1	YEAR 2	YEAR 3	YEAR 4	YEAR 5
Project Cash Flow	$40,000	$80,000	$600,000	$100,000	$1,620,000
100% OF REFINANCE AND SALE PROCEEDS UNTIL ALL CAPITAL RETURNED					
Starting Capital	$1,000,000	$1,000,000	$1,000,000	$500,000	$500,000
Capital Distributions	$0	$0	$(500,000)	$0	$(500,000)
Ending Capital	$1,000,000	$1,000,000	$500,000	$500,000	$0
Remaining Cash	$40,000	$80,000	$100,000	$100,000	$1,120,000
100% UNTIL REACHING 8% RETURN					
Starting Balance	$0	$40,000	$40,000	$20,000	$0
Required for 8% Pref	$80,000	$80,000	$80,000	$40,000	$40,000
Preferred Return Distribution	$(40,000)	$(80,000)	$(100,000)	$(60,000)	$(40,000)
Ending Balance	$40,000	$40,000	$20,000	$0	$0
Remaining Cash	$0	$0	$0	$40,000	$1,080,000
HURDLE #1—70% UNTIL REACHING 12% RETURN					
Starting Balance	$0	$80,000	$120,000	$140,000	$112,000
Required for 8% Pref	$120,000	$120,000	$120,000	$60,000	$60,000
Preferred Return Distribution	$(40,000)	$(80,000)	$(100,000)	$(60,000)	$(40,000)
Hurdle #1 Distribution	$0	$0	$0	$(28,000)	$(132,000)
Ending Balance	$80,000	$120,000	$140,000	$112,000	$0
Investor Share (70%)	$0	$0	$0	$28,000	$132,000
Sponsor Share (30%)	$0	$0	$0	$12,000	$56,571
Remaining Cash	$0	$0	$0	$0	$891,429
HURDLE #2—60% UNTIL REACHING 15% RETURN					
Starting Balance	$0	$110,000	$180,000	$230,000	$217,000
Required for 8% Pref	$150,000	$150,000	$150,000	$75,000	$75,000
Preferred Return Distribution	$(40,000)	$(80,000)	$(100,000)	$(60,000)	$(40,000)
Hurdle #1 Distribution	$0	$0	$0	$(28,000)	$(132,000)
Hurdle #2 Distribution	$0	$0	$0	$0	$(120,000)
Ending Balance	$110,000	$180,000	$230,000	$217,000	$0
Investor Share (60%)	$0	$0	$0	$0	$120,000
Sponsor Share (40%)	$0	$0	$0	$0	$80,000
Remaining Cash	$0	$0	$0	$0	$691,429

		YEAR 1	YEAR 2	YEAR 3	YEAR 4	YEAR 5
HURDLE #3—50/50 THEREAFTER						
Investor Share (50%)		$0	$0	$0	$0	$345,714
Sponsor Share (50%)		$0	$0	$0	$0	$345,714
Investor Net Cash Flow		$40,000	$80,000	$600,000	$88,000	$1,137,714
CoC	11.8% (Avg)	4%	8%	10%	17.6%	19.2%
IRR	18.0%				Total Invested	$1,000,000
Equity Multiple	1.95				Total Received	$1,945,714

This one looks like a monster, doesn't it? But it's also somewhat simple if you ignore most of it! If you refer back to the previous example—not the one where we refinanced out all investor cash but the one before that, with the $500,000 received in year 3—you'll notice that the investor net cash flow is identical for the first four years. The reason nothing changes is because up to that point the investors have received less than a 12 percent return.

Prior to reaching an 8 percent return, the investors receive all of the distributions. After reaching an 8 percent return and before reaching a 12 percent return, the investors receive 70 percent. Nothing different here yet. The difference is all in year 5 in this example, because it is not until the profits from the sale are received that the investors cross the 12 percent hurdle. If you look at the hurdle #1 section in the table, you can see that the $40,000 remaining in year 4 after the preferred return is split 70 percent to the investors, which comes to $28,000. At that point there is nothing left to drop to the next tier.

But in year 5, there is $1,080,000 left after the investors' capital is returned and the preferred return is paid. First, $132,000 is allocated to the investors and $56,571 is allocated to the sponsor in a 70/30 split. This $132,000 fully satisfies the 12 percent return test, so the remaining capital, $891,429, drops to the next tier. It takes another $120,000 to get from 12 percent to 15 percent, so the investors get $120,000 and the sponsor gets $80,000, which takes care of the 60/40 split. After those allocations, $691,429 remains, and that drops to the next tier. The next tier is 50/50, so that amount is split equally between the investors and the sponsor.

Other Waterfall Terms

Catch-Up Provision

A "catch-up provision" is designed to make the sponsor's promote a function of the total return, instead of a percentage of the profits that exceeds a preferred return. It's somewhat of a hybrid between the two waterfalls we covered at the beginning of this chapter: a simple profit-split waterfall and a split-over-pref waterfall. Here is sample operating agreement language that includes a catch-up provision:

Cash flow shall be distributed in the following order and priority:
- *First, until the Investors have received an eight percent (8%) Annual Rate of Return on their unreturned Capital Contributions, to the Investors on a Pro Rata basis;*
- *Second, to the Manager until distributions to the Manager equal thirty percent (30%) of all distributions made under subsection (a) and (b) hereunder;*
- *Third, (i) seventy percent (70%) to the Investors on a Pro Rata basis and (ii) thirty percent (30%) to the Manager.*

At the end of the day, what the sponsor is shooting for here is to split the profits 70/30. But before they get there, the investors still have a minimum threshold of receiving the preferred return. Here is what the waterfall would look like:

	YEAR 1	YEAR 2	YEAR 3	YEAR 4	YEAR 5
Project Cash Flow	$40,000	$80,000	$600,000	$100,000	$1,620,000
100% OF REFINANCE AND SALE PROCEEDS UNTIL ALL CAPITAL RETURNED					
Starting Capital	$1,000,000	$1,000,000	$1,000,000	$500,000	$500,000
Capital Distributions	$0	$0	$(500,000)	$0	$(500,000)
Ending Capital	$1,000,000	$1,000,000	$500,000	$500,000	$0
Remaining Cash	$40,000	$80,000	$100,000	$100,000	$1,120,000

		YEAR 1	YEAR 2	YEAR 3	YEAR 4	YEAR 5
100% UNTIL REACHING 8% RETURN						
Starting Balance		$0	$40,000	$40,000	$20,000	$0
Required for 8% Pref		$80,000	$80,000	$80,000	$40,000	$40,000
Preferred Return Distribution		$(40,000)	$(80,000)	$(100,000)	$(60,000)	$(40,000)
Ending Balance		$40,000	$40,000	$20,000	$0	$0
Remaining Cash		$0	$0	$0	$40,000	$1,080,000
100% TO SPONSOR CATCH-UP PROVISION						
Investor Pref. Distribution		$40,000	$80,000	$100,000	$60,000	$40,000
Starting Balance		$0	$17,143	$51,429	$94,286	$80,000
Required for 70/30 Catch-Up		$17,143	$34,286	$42,857	$25,714	$17,143
Catch-Up Distribution		$0	$0	$0	$(40,000)	$(97,143)
Ending Balance		$17,143	$51,429	$94,286	$80,000	$0
Remaining Cash		$0	$0	$0	$0	$982,857
70/30 THEREAFTER						
Investor Share (70%)		$0	$0	$0	$0	$688,000
Sponsor Share (30%)		$0	$0	$0	$0	$94,857
Investor Net Cash Flow		$40,000	$80,000	$600,000	$60,000	$1,228,000
Sponsor Net Cash Flow		$0	$0	$0	$40,000	$392,000
CoC	10.6% (Avg)	4%	8%	10%	12%	19.2%
IRR	18.7%					
Equity Multiple	2.01					

Notice that for the first three years this waterfall functions just as in our earlier examples. But in year 4 there is $40,000 in cash that exceeds the preferred return. This entire surplus goes to the sponsor because the sponsor is due $120,000 in catch-up to achieve a true 70/30 split. In year 5, there is $1,080,000 in excess cash after the preferred return is fully satisfied. The first $97,143 goes to the sponsor to satisfy the catch-up provision, leaving $982,857 to drop to the 70/30 split tier.

The end result here is that a total of $1,440,000 in profits is distributed in this waterfall. The investors receive $1,008,000 of this total, and the sponsor receives $432,000, which is exactly 70/30.

Catch-up provisions aren't all that common, but you'll see them from time to time. Now you know what the language looks like in the operating agreement, so you can spot one if you see it. They tend to be unpopular with investors, but occasionally they can serve a purpose. I used a catch-up provision only once, for a homebuilding fund where the objective was to split profits with investors at a specific ratio. But in order to ensure that the investors would have the first claim on cash flow if the project underperformed, a preferred return was put in place with a catch-up to reverse it if performance approached our projections. It's a tool in the sponsor's toolbox, and as long as it is used fairly and investors are aware of it, fine. However, in most circumstances, especially for stabilized or value-add projects, catch-up provisions are considered rich to the sponsor.

Clawbacks

A "clawback" is a provision specifying that investors can reclaim part of the sponsor's promote in cases where a promote is paid but subsequent losses result in the sponsor being overcompensated. This might typically come up in a multiple-property fund structure where the first properties are sold for a profit and the sponsor is paid a promote, followed by subsequent sales at a loss (or a profit too small to keep up with satisfying accrued preferred return).

Either of these scenarios could result in the sponsor having been paid some promote, but at the time of the fund's liquidation there remains unpaid accrued preferred return. If that happens, a clawback provision would require the sponsor to repay some or all of the promote to the extent that the preferred return is satisfied or the sponsor has returned all promote previously paid, whichever comes first. A caveat is that the clawback is only as strong as the sponsor's ability to pay. Undercapitalized sponsors might not have the resources to repay the promote if they've already spent it.

Dual-Promote Structures

Some private offerings are funds that are investing in another offering sponsored by an operator. The upside is that by investing in just one fund you can diversify into assets operated by different sponsors and in different areas, maybe even different real estate sectors. The downside is that there is a dual-promote structure. Consider the previous examples in this chapter. The bottom of each table showed the total cash flow to investors after the sponsor's split was taken out.

Now suppose that the cash flow on that line goes into the top of another waterfall where the fund sponsor is scraping out a profit as well. That is a dual-promote structure—the operator gets a promote, and after that, the fund gets a promote. There's nothing wrong with a dual-promote structure as long as you understand what is happening and compare your options properly.

An improper comparison would be to put an operator's structure up against a fund's structure. I've heard investors say, "I chose to invest in this deal because the split was 80/20 over an 8 percent preferred return, and the other deal was a 70/30 over an 8 percent pref." But the 80/20 deal is a fund that invests in other operators, which means that investors are receiving only a portion of the investor net cash flow shown in the waterfall examples in this chapter, whereas the investors in the operator's offering receive all of the investor net cash flow. Choosing one over the other based on structure alone can result in unintended consequences if you aren't aware of what you are investing in.

This does not mean that all funds involve a dual promote. There are plenty of operators that run their own fund instead of raising capital on a deal-by-deal basis. If they are the fund and the operator, a dual-promote structure is unlikely. But if the fund sponsor is not an operator, or they are an operator that also invests their fund's money in other operators, a dual promote is nearly certain.

Other Waterfall Considerations

A few parting thoughts before we move on: Be sure that you understand how the waterfall provisions in the operating agreement work. Many sponsors are good real estate operators but struggle to understand the private equity fund structure. As a result of reading this chapter, you already know more about waterfalls than many sponsors! Don't be surprised if you find sponsors who can't thoroughly explain their waterfall or, worse, try to fake their way through it hoping you won't know the difference.

The logic and math in the waterfall calculations must match the words in the operating agreement. While at first blush this might seem obvious, they don't always jibe. To many sponsors, operating agreements and waterfalls are black boxes designed by lawyers and accountants.

However, many lawyers struggle to craft the language to conform to the sponsor's intent, and some sponsors struggle to give their counsel clear direction. Some lawyers struggle even harder to translate mathematical logic into English, and not all accountants thoroughly understand waterfalls. The result is that waterfall calculations might not match the operating agreement or the sponsor's marketing description of how the profits are to be split.

Waterfalls aren't the easiest thing to grasp for anyone in this business, that's for sure. But if you can connect the dots between the operating agreement and the logic in the waterfall using the principles detailed in this chapter, you are miles ahead of the majority of investors, and even sponsors.

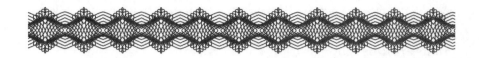

CHAPTER 17

FEES

I've often hesitated to seek the advice of a financial advisor. Although I see the value of their knowledge, I just hate the thought of paying for it. Worse, I think to myself, "Why would I want financial advice from someone who makes less money than I do?" Ultimately, both these statements are ridiculous, but they still ring true to me. I just can't help it!

It's natural to seek value. We all love buying stuff on sale or negotiating down the price of a new car with the dealer. Okay, maybe not the car dealer thing—that process is never really enjoyable. Nonetheless, we all know that the store or dealership has to make a profit in order to stay in business.

Syndication sponsors are running a business, too. If they do not make a profit, they'll go out of business. As I've been writing this book I've mostly been wearing my investor hat. For a moment I'm putting on my sponsor hat—just long enough so that you can learn more about the various fees sponsors charge and why some level of fees is appropriate. Don't worry, I'll balance my sponsor hat with my investor hat because there can be some serious gamesmanship from sponsors when it comes to fees, and you need to be aware of the nuances.

Why Fees?

Let's start with why sponsors charge any fees at all, and why they should.

Being a steward of your capital is a big responsibility, one not to be taken lightly. You would probably not be too comfortable if the person carrying this responsibility was earning less than minimum wage, or nothing at all, and stressing out over how they are going to make their next house payment.

Sponsors make their money two ways: fees and profit splits. If you recall the waterfall examples in the previous chapter, most had one thing in common: The sponsor was earning no profit split during the initial period of the investment. Depending on the property's cash flow and the structure of the waterfall, the sponsor might not earn any profit split at all until the very end, even over a ten-year (or longer) hold. Yet just like a store or a dealership, the sponsor can't stay in business if they don't turn a profit. It's unreasonable to expect sponsors to be able to wait three, five, or even ten years to receive their first paycheck. The economics just don't work. Fees address that problem.

Nonetheless, many investors are uncomfortable with the fees sponsors charge at the beginning of the investment. In the eyes of some investors, the sponsor hasn't produced a result yet, so why should they walk away from the closing table with a check? But the sponsor *has* produced a result—the opportunity to make this investment. That opportunity might not be worth much if brought forth by an inadequate sponsor, but a well-researched and well-underwritten acquisition by a strong team is a hard-fought pursuit that adds tremendous value to the passive investor.

It's quite likely that the sponsor has worked for nearly a year, without any compensation, to get to this point. They have likely put a lot of capital at risk by making earnest money deposits to escrow, good-faith deposits to lenders, and paying for inspections and staff time. They've probably spent a lot of money traveling to tour potential acquisitions that never came to fruition, and may have even lost money on inspection fees for properties they contracted to purchase but ultimately did not buy due to adverse findings during due diligence. Sponsors have data subscriptions, software, office rent, and all kinds of general overhead that must be paid in order to stay in business. My point is that getting a deal to the closing table takes considerable effort and expense, and upfront fees are designed to reimburse sponsors for those costs, and compensate them and their teams for their time. As long as the fees aren't abnormal, it's reasonable for sponsors to charge them.

Variation in Fees

In theory, the fees charged by a sponsor should reflect the underlying costs to provide their services plus a fair profit. I like to think of it this way: The fees pay the sponsors for what they do, and the promote pays them for the results they produce.

It's often said that smaller sponsors charge higher fees because they have less deal flow and it takes higher fees to cover their costs, while larger sponsors charge higher fees because they have a lot of overhead. There's a lot of truth to both halves of that statement. Maybe every sponsor's fees are perceived to be "higher," no matter how high or low they are, just because no one likes to pay fees.

Nonetheless, there is a difference in fee structure between institutional groups versus entrepreneurial smaller operators, core strategies versus value-add strategies, and triple-net single-tenant industrial portfolios versus portfolios of underperforming hotels that the sponsor intends to turn around.

Size matters! If the sponsor is to receive a fee based on a percentage of the purchase price, you wouldn't expect a small group buying a value-add property for $10 million to charge the same percentage fee as a large institutional group purchasing a $100 million stabilized core property. Just because the large group is charging 1 percent and the small group is charging 3 percent doesn't automatically make the core asset a better investment. There are many other aspects of the overall strategy and forecasted performance to consider before deciding which is right for you.

It's fair to tolerate higher-percentage fees for smaller assets, value-add properties, and turnaround plays. It's also fair to expect larger assets and core properties to carry lower-percentage fees due to the economy of scale for the sponsor and the lower degree of complexity of operating stabilized core properties.

I caution you against selecting investments based on fees alone. I'd rather pay higher fees to an established and experienced sponsor than lower fees to a first-timer. Having said that, consideration of fees has a place in selecting offerings and should play a part in your decision making. If the sponsor is charging outrageous fees, avoiding that offering probably makes sense. But if the sponsor checks every box, the real estate checks every box, the underwriting checks every box, and the returns check every box, avoiding the offering because the fees are higher than other alternatives could be a mistake, assuming that the fees are actually baked into the projected returns and aren't an afterthought.

Types of Fees

There are three points in a deal's life cycle where you are likely to encounter fees: at the beginning, during the hold, and at the end. That about covers it, right?

Notice that I've included the fee chapter in the section of the book that covers evaluating offerings. Why not in the section about evaluating sponsors? Wouldn't it be fair to ask sponsors about their fees during the sponsor due diligence phase of your research? Yes, it would, but the answer you are likely to get is "It depends on the deal." There is truth to that: Most sponsors do tailor their deal structures to fit each deal, and rightfully so. Feel free to ask about fees when interviewing sponsors, but be sure to ask again when you are presented with an offering.

One important thing to remember about fees is that they are generally charged to the deal, not to the investor. This means that if the sponsor and investors are splitting the profits 50/50, the sponsor is effectively paying half of their own fees because the fees come from the investment's cash flow—assuming that the deal turns a profit.

There are essentially two types of fees: transactional and oversight. Transactional fees are directly connected to a particular transactional event. Oversight fees are connected to general oversight of the property.

Transactional Fees

Here are the typical transactional fees you are likely to encounter as you explore various private offerings:

Acquisition. Nearly every offering will include an acquisition fee, which typically ranges between 1 and 3 percent of the purchase price of the property. In general, larger properties trend toward the lower end of the range and smaller properties trend toward the higher end. For example, you might see a 3 percent fee on a $5 million acquisition and a 1 percent fee on a $100 million acquisition. This fee helps cover the sponsor's overhead and provides compensation for their services related to locating a suitable property for the offering.

Funding. This might also be called a "capital raise fee," a "marketing fee," or an "organizational fee." Ranging between 1 to 2 percent of the amount of capital raised, this fee is to compensate for the process of raising the funds from investors. I don't see this fee charged all that often, and when I do it's usually closer to 1 percent.

Commissions. Investment shares in some offerings are sold by licensed broker-dealers, and they charge commissions on their sales. In these transactions, a managing broker-dealer charges around 1 percent of the capital raised, wholesalers and marketing expenses run between 2 and 3 percent, and the selling group members charge up to 6 percent. Broker-dealer expenses are uncommon in the entrepreneurial small-operator space, and more common in large core funds and DST offerings. Generally, these would be third-party, not sponsor, fees.

The worst part about commissions is that they are the exception to the general rule of fees being charged to the deal and not to the investor. Instead, commissions can be charged directly to the investor, essentially deducting from the investment made. For example, if you are investing $100,000 and there is a 10 percent commission, only $90,000 gets invested in the deal and the other $10,000 goes to the brokers.

Loan processing. Anyone who has obtained a home loan knows what a pain it is to borrow money. The good news is that as a passive investor in a syndicated offering, you won't have to participate in the drudgery of obtaining the financing. That's the sponsor's job, and as with most tasks the sponsor performs, they charge a fee for it. Sometimes this fee is wrapped up in the acquisition fee, and sometimes you'll find a loan processing fee listed separately. Generally, this fee is 1 percent or less of the loan amount. Sometimes this fee will apply only to a refinance of the acquisition loan, and sometimes this fee applies to both acquisition financing and subsequent refinancing. If the sponsor wraps the loan processing fee into the acquisition fee, you are more likely to see the fee listed only with a refinance. Otherwise, you might see the fee listed for both.

Loan guarantee. Repayment of a full-recourse loan must be guaranteed by a qualifying individual. This could be the sponsor, or the sponsor might bring in someone else as a key principal to act as a guarantor. Even non-recourse loans require a guarantor for specific "carve-out guarantees," and those guarantors must also have adequate qualifications that satisfy the lender. Sponsors often charge for the risk they assume as a guarantor. If they brought in an outside person to act as a guarantor, that person is likely to charge a fee.

Guarantee fees are typically 1 percent or less of the loan amount. You might also see sponsors couple the loan processing fee with the loan guarantee, calling it simply a "loan fee." Typically, this combined fee will not exceed 1 percent of the loan amount, but I have seen some sponsors charge more.

Leasing. Leasing fees are fees charged for signing new leases, mainly in retail, office, and industrial property syndications. They are uncommon in multifamily, self-storage, hotel, and mobile-home park syndications. Leasing fees for retail, office, and industrial properties are common for leasing agent commissions, and are typically third-party costs ranging up to 6 percent of the value of the entire lease. But sponsors might charge these fees too, most commonly when the sponsor is also the property manager or is also acting as a leasing agent.

Overhead. You probably won't find an "overhead fee" in an operating agreement, but you might find "overhead reimbursements." Reimbursement is customary for overhead items paid on behalf of the property, such as legal fees paid out-of-pocket by the sponsor to structure the offering.

Sponsors might charge for a few overhead items, such as technology reimbursements for investor portals, accounting systems, property management systems, and asset management systems. General overhead reimbursements for the sponsor's syndication business, such as for office rent, for example, are unusual.

Disposition. A disposition fee is charged at the time the property is sold, to compensate the sponsor for their services in facilitating the sale of the asset. Some sponsors don't charge disposition fees. While I've heard that disposition fees are often the same percentage as acquisition fees, I haven't seen that very often in practice. Disposition fees tend to be 1 to 2 percent of the sales price of the property. In my opinion, a disposition fee should be lower than an acquisition fee because disposing of a property is a lot less work than acquiring one.

Of all the various fees, the disposition fee tends to have the least impact on overall net returns because it is paid at the very end. The fee is paid from sales proceeds rather than added to the money raised to acquire the deal, as is the case with acquisition and loan fees, which further mitigates its impact on net returns. Nonetheless, disposition fees are probably among the most hated by investors because the sponsor also receives a large promote when the property sells, if things have gone according to plan. And if things haven't, the sponsor is making a fee despite subpar performance. Despite those objections, disposition fees are fairly common and probably here to stay.

Oversight Fees

Transactional fees are charged in conjunction with various transaction events, but oversight fees are charged at regular periods throughout a project or throughout an entire investment's life cycle.

Property management. Commercial real estate is operationally complex. You can't just buy it and collect rent, and even if you could, you'd still have to do the accounting. One way or another, the property needs to be managed, and property management is labor intensive and costly. Some sponsors hire third-party management companies to manage their properties, and some sponsors manage their own portfolio or have a wholly owned management company responsible for that function. Property managers typically charge a percentage of the effective gross income, and some have a minimum fee they charge in the event that the stated percentage of income falls below a certain point.

The percentage varies depending on the type of property and the size of the income stream. Single-family homes are often charged 10 percent, while a 500-unit luxury apartment complex in a high-rent area might be charged 2.5 percent. Three to 4 percent is common in the multifamily industry for properties over 75 units.

When comparing offerings from two different sponsors, take note of whether they are managing the property themselves or hiring a third-party management company. When a sponsor is also the property manager, they might show a property management fee in their operating agreement because it is being paid to a related entity (their property management entity), and it is a good practice to disclose any fees to related entities. On the other hand, if the sponsor is hiring a third-party property manager, they might not list this fee in the operating agreement because it is a third-party charge that is customary in the business. That doesn't mean the fee won't be charged, however. The bottom line is, don't choose one offering over the other just because one shows a property management fee and the other does not, unless you first examine the structure of the management. It's very likely that both will be burdened by property management fees. Whether stated in the operating agreement or not, these fees should be clearly visible on the expense forecasts. If they are not on the expense forecasts, this could signal a big problem, and you should ask the sponsor why no property management fee is shown. Even if the sponsor says that they are acting as the property manager and not charging a management fee (unlikely), there should still be a market-rate management fee baked into the NOI forecast used to calculate the resale price of the property. The next buyer is sure to have a management fee in their forecasts, and not having one in the sale assumptions artificially inflates the projected resale price.

Another consideration for sponsors that have their own property management company is to ensure that the fee charged for property management is market rate. Market rate is difficult to pinpoint because it can vary somewhat by area and will absolutely vary by the size of the property. If you examine a number of private offerings of the same asset class and of similar size, you'll be able to compare the management fees and get a feel for what is market rate. If you are looking to invest in multifamily syndications, 3 to 4 percent is typical.

Construction management. Property management is labor intensive and lasts for the entire length of the investment. Construction management is also labor intensive but usually lasts for a shorter period of time. It must be done at the same time that the property is being managed, so it is an added burden. Therefore, sponsors may charge a fee for managing larger capital improvement projects, such as exterior renovations, interior upgrades, and amenity enhancements.

They might also have to hire outside construction managers or even additional employees to accomplish such oversight. Construction management fees range from 3 to 10 percent of the cost of the capital improvements. The fee should not be charged on ordinary repairs, so if the language is unclear, be sure to ask.

Just as with property management fees, sponsors using third-party management might not show construction management fees in their operating agreement, but that doesn't mean a fee won't be charged by the management company. The fee would be stipulated in the property management agreement between the management company and the ownership entity. Make it a point to ask sponsors about undisclosed construction management fees, and be sure that they are accounted for in the renovation budget. Inexperienced sponsors might overlook a third-party management company's construction management fees until they have already completed their projections and budgets. Then when it's time to hire a property manager, they forget to ask about construction management, get hit by surprise, and don't have the budget to cover the fees.

Asset management. Chapter 4 covered the differences between asset management and property management. They are two separate functions and come with two separate fees. The asset management fee is used to pay for the asset management team, accounting group, investor reporting, office rent, and administrative staff of the sponsor. Investment offerings treat asset management fees as a simple afterthought, but this topic is complicated enough that it warrants an entire subsection in this chapter.

Asset Management Fees

Anyone who has read more than a few private offering memorandums has likely noticed that asset management fees are almost always listed simply as "1 percent." But what they usually don't say is, "1 percent of what?" What these fees are a percentage of makes a big difference not only in their cost but also in how they align, or even misalign, the sponsor's interests with the investors'. Let's discuss some of the most common methods of calculating an asset management fee, assuming a sample property with the following vital statistics.

Effective Gross Income	$2,000,000
Expense Ratio	45%
Net Operating Income	$1,100,000
Cap Rate	6%
Purchase Price	$18,300,000
Renovation & Closing Costs	$4,700,000
Total Uses of Funds	$23,000,000
Debt (75% LTV)	$13,725,000
Equity	$9,275,000

Percentage of effective gross income. This is probably the most common method for calculating asset management fees for single-asset syndications or small closed-end multi-property funds. One percent is most common. In our example, 1 percent of the $2 million EGI would yield an asset management fee of $20,000 per year.

Committed equity. In my experience, this is the second-most-common method. In our example, 1 percent of the $9,275,000 equity would be $92,750 per year—quite a difference from the $20,000 in our previous method.

Invested equity. Invested equity is different than committed equity. Using our example, let's say that the sponsor accepts *commitments* for $9,275,000 of equity but only asks the investors to contribute 75 percent of their commitment until a future time. In our example, 1 percent of the invested equity would be $69,562.50 ($9,275,000 × 0.75 = $6,956,250 × 0.01 = $69,562.50). This might come into play if the sponsor wishes to defer contributions for the capital improvements, for example. It could also come into play in a fund, where committed equity is contributed over time, and a portion of the investors' capital is returned when some properties in the fund sell while others remain held in inventory.

Net asset value. NAV is the value of the property, minus any outstanding debt on the property. In our example, the property value initially is $18,300,000 and the debt is $13,725,000, meaning the NAV is $4,575,000. One percent of the NAV would be $45,750.

Gross asset value. GAV is the value of the property. In our example, 1 percent of the $18,300,000 purchase price is $183,000 per year! Let's hope that if the sponsor of the offering you are looking at is using GAV, they are also using a much smaller percentage to calculate their asset management fee.

Debt and equity. This is the sum of the total sources of funds (the debt and the equity). In our example, that's $23,000,000, so a 1 percent asset management fee would be $230,000 per year. It may seem that this method yields the highest asset management fee, but not so fast! Over the life of the investment, asset management fees calculated as a percentage of GAV and NAV can come to exceed this method because they are tied to the value of the asset, which will likely increase over time. Read on.

Fee Method Considerations

Now that we've covered how to calculate asset management fees using various methods, let's explore other factors surrounding asset management fees, including how some of these methods impact the sponsor's motivation, and how they might align, or misalign, the sponsor's interests with that of the investors.

Percentage of effective gross income. This method increases alignment with the investors because higher income results in a higher fee.

That makes everyone happy and motivates the sponsor to perform. For a single-asset syndication, this fee works best in my opinion. For a multi-property fund, it could be problematic because it encourages the sponsor to acquire properties rapidly so as to increase the fee. And this phenomenon isn't unique to this method.

Committed versus invested equity. This might be a minor point in single-asset syndications where sponsors are delaying a small portion of capital contributions. But the distinction can be much more impactful in multi-asset funds where the sponsors accept a large amount of capital commitments up front, but call for the capital to be contributed in small chunks over time as properties are acquired. For example, they raise $100 million in commitments but they only call for $10 million to close on the first property. The difference in asset management fees as a percentage of $10 million *invested* versus $100 million *committed* is vast.

You might be inclined to think that calculating asset management fees as a percentage of invested capital is better for you than calculating on committed capital. Certainly, it's cheaper. But cheap comes at a cost. It might encourage the sponsor to hurriedly deploy capital, potentially on lesser-quality opportunities, in order to boost the fee faster. This could lead the sponsor to make hasty purchasing decisions or even miss better investment opportunities that come later.

Charging asset management fees as a percentage of committed capital is more common with non-core funds that are investing in more opportunistic and value-add strategies. The theory is that these strategies are more time-consuming, and involve higher levels of overhead and start-up costs. Core funds are more likely to charge on invested capital. These funds might have long life cycles and be ongoing investment vehicles. The fees may be lower, but that doesn't mean the returns would be higher, as core assets tend to be lower-yielding than non-core assets.

Net or gross asset value. The NAV and GAV methods calculate the asset management fee as a percentage of the value of the property. When the property is first acquired, this fee is fairly transparent and easy to calculate, but over time it becomes less clear because the property value must be continually reestablished, and the process of doing so is subjective and can be manipulated.

To reestablish the asset value for the purposes of calculating the asset management fee, a cap rate must be employed to divide into the NOI. The cap rate might be specified in the operating agreement, or it might be left up to the sponsor to use a reasonable cap rate that they can defend if questioned.

The problem with cap rates is that they can fluctuate. Even a minor fluctuation in cap rate will have significant impact on the calculated property value. For example, a decrease in market cap rates increases the value of the property, without any effort by the sponsor. This begs the question as to whether calculating the fee in this manner rewards the sponsor for market forces beyond their control. The reverse is also true: An increase in market cap rates reduces the value of the property, through no fault of the sponsor. This means that the sponsor is taking a haircut due, again, to forces beyond their control.

Equity Versus Asset Value Versus Income

It may appear that calculating the fee based on committed or invested equity is better than GAV or NAV, because either equity method wouldn't reward the sponsor for good luck (falling cap rates) nor penalize them for bad luck (increasing cap rates). However, a calculation based on equity is a static number, meaning that it doesn't reward the sponsor for skill or penalize them for poor operational performance.

Another problem (for the sponsor) with basing the fee on either committed or invested equity is in the case of high inflation. It would seem that high inflation would increase the sponsor's costs, while the management fee stays the same. Basing the fee on NAV or GAV would likely result in an increasing fee because, in theory, the value of the property or properties would be increasing in an inflationary cycle.

In the case of funds that are acquiring multiple properties, there can be nuances to the way fees are calculated that can impact returns. If the sponsor starts selling properties, basing the fee on committed capital could overcompensate the sponsor because the fee remains level even though the sponsor has less work to do with fewer properties.

On the other hand, if the sponsor refinances properties, increasing the leverage, and returns capital to the investors, basing the fee on committed capital would fairly compensate the sponsor because they would have the same amount of work to do. But in this example, if the fee were based on NAV, the sponsor's fee would be reduced because the outstanding debt rose but the property value stayed the same, causing NAV (value minus debt) to go down. This might discourage the sponsor from refinancing even though it could increase investor returns. Same goes with basing the fee on invested capital, which would go down if capital were to be returned in a refinance.

Estimates of the fair-market value of the property or properties are imprecise. Cap rates can be subjective and NOI can be manipulated by capitalizing some expenses that should have been expensed. This causes some investors to prefer that asset management fees be tied to a variable that is easier to quantify and harder to manipulate, such as effective gross income. This makes sense, especially given that investors really want to see the sponsor do everything possible to increase EGI. An increase in EGI nearly always results in an increase in NOI, which, assuming cap rates remain stable, results in an increase in property value—all of which is exactly what everyone wants to see. Calculating the fee based on income also avoids general market cap rates influencing the asset management fees.

No matter how you slice it, no method is perfect. Each one has various impacts to sponsors and investors, fair and unfair. It seems impossible to pick the perfect solution, so the best way to leave this discussion is with an awareness of the various factors.

Dual-Layer Fee Structures

You will probably see opportunities to invest in funds that acquire multiple properties. When examining these funds, it's important to determine whether the fund is acquiring properties directly or investing through joint-venture relationships with operating partners.

At first glance, a fund investing in joint ventures might appear more attractive if it has lower fees than the direct-investment fund. However, this is another example where making investment choices on fees alone could be a mistake. If the fund invests by joint-venturing with operating partners, the operating partners are charging fees just like the ones outlined throughout this chapter. On top of those fees, the fund is charging its own layer of fees, which could include every fee in this chapter or maybe just a couple of them.

In any case, you might not even notice that the operating partner is charging fees, thinking that the fees outlined in the fund's operating agreement are the only fees being charged. If the fund is acquiring property directly, that's probably the case. But in a joint venture, there are two "sponsors" that have businesses to sustain, and they both must get paid in order to survive.

The Last Word on Fees

No fee is beloved by investors, and no fee is perfect for sponsors. Some fees motivate sponsors to perform, others motivate them to acquire, and some can align and misalign interests at the same time. But fees are a necessary component of sustaining syndications and funding sponsors' businesses, so fees are here to stay. Any fees will likely vary from sponsor to sponsor, and from offering to offering from the same sponsor.

The most important thing about fees is whether they are all included in the sponsor's financial exhibits.

- Up-front fees should be listed in the sources and uses of funds table.
- Construction management fees should be included in the renovation budget.
- Property management fees should be accounted for on the income statement.
- Asset management fees should be shown on the cash flow statement.
- Fees to be paid at the sale should be included in the exit costs.

Any fees left out of any of these areas would cause the actual performance of the investment to differ from the projections. Be sure to study these statements to ensure all fees are included—you might be surprised by how often you can't find them.

SECTION V
THE INVESTING PROCESS

CHAPTER 18

MAKING YOUR INVESTMENT

Congratulations! You've finally found a sponsor that passes your due diligence, and they have brought you a well-underwritten offering that checks all your boxes. You want to invest but are unsure of the process, and the documents make you cross-eyed. This fifth and final section of the book is all about what to expect when making your investment, and what happens during and after the investment.

In industry jargon, making an investment in a private offering is called "subscribing." The first step in subscribing is to review the offering documents. By now you have probably seen the marketing materials with their beautiful color pictures of the property, description of the investment plan, and financial forecasts. You also may have reviewed all the due diligence materials. The offering documents consist of three primary documents:

- Private placement memorandum (PPM)
- Operating agreement (if LLC) or limited partnership agreement (if LP)
- Subscription agreement

Each document has a specific purpose, and you should read them all. You probably won't want to, but you should!

Private Placement Memorandum

If you've ever seen one, you are probably convinced that the PPM exists for two reasons:

1. To bore you to death.
2. To convince you that you have gone completely insane if you invest in the offering.

Don't feel bad; both are true.

The PPM is the primary disclosure document for the offering. The purpose is not to govern the terms—the operating agreement does that—but to call out important points in the operating agreement, talk about the risks of investing in the offering and real estate in general, and disclose relevant things about the sponsor's background. All these disclosures are necessary for you to make an informed investment decision.

The PPM will be broken into several sections, and the order of these sections is, to a certain extent, up to the attorney writing the PPM.

The PPM typically begins with a description of the offering and the structure of the company. This includes an introduction describing the investment and the opportunity, along with the sponsor's plans for renovating or stabilizing the property. The structure of the investment entities should be described and might include an organizational chart showing the structure of the entities.

Also included is an offering description, detailing how much money is to be raised along with other specifics. Oftentimes the waterfall, manager fees, and fees to affiliates are described here, along with the hold period and any restrictions on the transfer or withdrawal of membership interests.

Next comes a summary of the operating agreement or limited partnership agreement. It outlines select provisions of the operating agreement that are the most important for investors to understand. These may outline who the managing member is, what authority they have, and what issues require a vote of the investors. Manager compensation, fees, waterfalls, and affiliate transactions are included in the summary, along with items such as contributions, withdrawals, transfers, and dissolutions.

Sources and uses of proceeds should be outlined, showing where all the money is coming from and how it will be spent.

An entire section is dedicated to discussing the background of the sponsor and the sponsor's principals. This includes the various principals' biographies, detailing their relevant experience and disclosing their prior business history, including companies they were principals of previously. Any previous securities violations, criminal convictions, or bankruptcies should be disclosed here.

The risk factors section might be the longest in the PPM. If you've ever bought a hair dryer, you've seen the tag on the cord telling you that you can be electrocuted if you drop it in a sink full of water. That's just common sense, but if there were no warning, the manufacturer could be liable if someone dropped their hair dryer in the sink and claimed they had no idea that would be a problem. Likewise, some of the risks disclosed in this section may seem totally obvious or downright ridiculous. But they must be spelled out to protect the sponsor from you coming back later and claiming, for example, that they neglected to tell you that they depend on their tenants to pay rent, and that the tenants' inability to pay rent could reduce your distributions.

However, these investments do carry real risks, and you should be aware of them and understand them. Sometimes you'll even find risk factors unique to a particular deal or sponsor that don't sit well with you. If that happens, you should pass on that investment or, at the very least, discuss those risks with the sponsor to see if they have additional information that makes you more comfortable.

Conflicts of interest (and there are always conflicts of interest) should be disclosed. The most common conflict is that the sponsor might buy other properties in separate funds, and those properties can take time away from the management of the subject property or even compete with it. Given that most sponsors are in the business of operating real estate, it seems obvious that they are likely to acquire more than the property subject to this particular offering, but nevertheless this must be disclosed.

The PPM will likely have the operating agreement and subscription agreement attached as exhibits. If they are not exhibits, they should be delivered as separate documents so that you can examine them as well.

Some sponsors use the PPM as their primary marketing document, so you'll see marketing as well as legal language. Other sponsors use a separate marketing deck to attract investors and send the PPM only to investors who wish to proceed to the next step. In that case, you might see the marketing deck attached to the PPM as an exhibit so that its language is incorporated into the PPM.

Operating Agreement

The operating agreement is likely the most important document in a private offering because it's the governing document for the partnership. The entire relationship between the sponsor and the investors is guided by the provisions of the operating agreement. Let's walk through how the agreement is structured and discuss some things to watch for.

Any capitalized terms in the operating agreement should be defined somewhere in the agreement. Usually an entire section of the operating agreement is dedicated to defining terms used throughout the document. Some capitalized terms might not be defined in this section; instead, they will be defined within a specific provision, which means that you may have to hunt to find the definition.

Why are definitions important? Although the meaning of some terms seems obvious, they might not mean what you think. For example, you might assume that "annualized return" means the amount you would receive in a year divided by the amount invested. But it might not! In chapter 16 we talked about how annualized return can be cumulative, non-cumulative, compounding, or non-compounding. The type of annualized return will be outlined in the definition.

There is likely a section on membership, outlining various classes of members, how members are admitted, and how transfers or withdrawals are accommodated or restricted. There should also be provisions on what happens in the event of the death of an investor and how their membership interest is transferred to the heirs. Sponsors may have a right of first refusal on any units that investors want to transfer, and those rights would be spelled out in the membership section of the agreement. Pay close attention to restrictions on transferring your investment interests, because there is no secondary market for you to sell your interests. If you need to sell, you need to be aware of the restrictions on how you can do that so you aren't caught off-guard later.

Another section should address member meetings and voting. Most partnerships do not require regular meetings, but a meeting can be called by the manager. Members aren't required to attend meetings called by the manager but may wish to do so, especially if the purpose of the meeting is to hold a vote on an important issue. Some operating agreements allow members to call for a meeting if a specific percentage of members ask to do so. Given that in many cases investors don't know who the other investors are, it's unlikely that investors will ever get together and call for a meeting, so these provisions lack teeth.

You should also see an article on the rights and duties of the sponsor. Typically, sponsors have the authority to make all decisions regarding the management of the company and the property. Some operating agreements restrict certain major decision items, requiring a vote of the members. Watch for specific control rights by a third party: Sometimes sponsors enter into a joint venture in which a single large investor contributes the majority of the equity and, in exchange, demands specific control rights over major decisions. Such provisions are fairly common, but you should understand them and be sure that you can live with the terms, because another entity that you don't know will have some say in the operation of the property and the company.

The operating agreement includes a section on manager compensation detailing all fees, fees to related entities, and how profits are distributed and allocated. This section should also dictate what happens to depreciation. Some sponsors take a share of the depreciation; others allow all the depreciation to flow to the investors.

You should find a section in the agreement that outlines how long the company intends to hold property. This section might also include extension options and the right to sell earlier than the hold period if an early exit is advantageous.

The agreement should also detail how the accounting is handled, who is in charge of completing the company's tax return, and procedures for how to wind up the company. Some operating agreements have a spousal consent form that must be signed by the spouse of any married member. This consent protects the company in the event of the death of a member. The surviving spouse would be bound to the provisions of the operating agreement if the member's community property interests automatically transfer the membership interest to the surviving spouse.

Capital Calls

Watch for a provision governing capital calls. A capital call is a request, or even a mandate, by the sponsor that you contribute additional capital beyond the amount you agreed to invest. This might come into play if the company runs out of money in a down economy and needs capital to avoid foreclosure, or if a renovation goes over budget, or if the sponsor simply didn't raise an adequate amount of capital at the outset due to poor planning.

Capital call provisions range from benign to downright punitive. On the benign side of the scale, a capital call provision might say that the sponsor can ask you to contribute additional capital and you have the right to say no. If you say no, the sponsor can raise capital from new investors, which will dilute your ownership interest (meaning it will reduce your ownership percentage).

On the other extreme, some capital call provisions will penalize you if you do not fulfill a capital call. The agreement might go so far as to say that you forfeit your share of the company or forfeit your right to distributions if you do not contribute capital in response to a capital call. You should strongly consider whether investing in an offering with punitive capital call provisions is acceptable to you.

Keep in mind that punitive capital call provisions might be common in relation to planned capital calls—such as when the investment is structured so that you contribute less than your capital commitment and will be asked to contribute the rest at a future time. If you fail to fulfill your planned commitment, punitive provisions could be fair. But if these provisions relate to unplanned capital calls that go beyond your agreed investment commitment amount, you might want to think twice before investing.

Subscription Agreement

The subscription agreement is the document you sign to be admitted as a member of the company. It's an "agreement" because you are agreeing to subscribe to the terms of the operating agreement. You are also agreeing to make your investment contribution when the capital is requested, and you are making specific representations and warranties to the sponsor that you have read and understand the offering documents.

The subscription agreement includes a confidential investor questionnaire. Here you will fill in how you wish to hold title to your investment, how much you intend to invest, your name, address, Social Security or tax ID number, and payment distribution instructions. You will be asked whether or not you qualify as an accredited investor and how. You may also be asked to certify that you understand the risks of investing in the company and that you can absorb the loss of your capital if the investment fails.

By signing the subscription agreement you agree to become a member of the company, but the sponsor is not obligated to accept you as a member just yet. They can reject your subscription if they don't feel that the investment is suitable for you, or if the offering has already been filled by the time they receive your subscription agreement.

It is likely that, by signing the subscription agreement, you also represent that you understand and agree to a series of statements indicating, for example, that you have relied upon the advice of your own advisors and not the sponsor in making the investment, that the information you have provided in the investor questionnaire is true and accurate, that you have no right to cancel, and probably a dozen or two other things.

Subscribing to the Offering

You've found an offering that passes all the tests. The language of the operating agreement's waterfall provisions matches the waterfall calculations in the marketing exhibits. The fees that appear in the operating agreement are all represented in the sources and uses of funds, income statement, and cash flow statement. You can live with the transfer provisions and other terms of the operating agreement, and the PPM didn't scare you away. You are ready to invest!

The next step is to complete the investor questionnaire and sign the subscription agreement. As you prepare to do this, there are some decisions you'll need to make and some things to consider. Let's walk through them.

Minimum Investment

The subscription agreement should indicate how much the sponsor is raising for this offering and specify a minimum amount that each investor must contribute. If the minimum amount is too high for you, ask the sponsor whether they will waive the minimum. Asking to waive the minimum isn't something to be embarrassed about; it's common for investors who are investing with a sponsor for the first time to want to "test" the sponsor by making a smaller investment in the first offering, then ramp up to larger investments in subsequent offerings. Some sponsors will waive it, some won't, but the answer is always "no" unless you ask.

Common minimums are between $25,000 and $250,000, although you'll occasionally see offerings with higher or lower minimums. Lower minimums are especially common on crowdfunding websites, where investors may be more likely to point and click to invest smaller amounts.

How high to set the minimum investment is an internal decision made by each sponsor; there are no regulations requiring minimums to be any specific amount. You may notice that sponsors that have been in business for a long time tend to have higher minimums and newer sponsors have lower ones, but there's no absolute connection between minimums and experience. In my first offering, my minimum was $5,000. That amount reflected my desperation as well as the fact that my inner circle wasn't a particularly wealthy group (it was a bunch of cops, mostly). As my investor base and experience grew, I raised my minimum to $100,000. But not every sponsor follows a similar path: I've seen first-time sponsors with $100,000 minimums and highly experienced groups with $25,000 minimums.

What if the minimum investment isn't an issue for you because you are more concerned with the maximum investment? Although the offering documents don't usually specify a maximum investment, there probably is one. Regardless, the total amount to be raised in the offering could be considered a maximum investment limit. If the sponsor has already raised some of the offering, the maximum will be lower, reflecting the amount remaining to be raised. Even though the offering documents are unlikely to say so, the sponsor might also have a far lower maximum investment limit. For example, they might have a maximum of 20 percent of the offering, to avoid a lender requirement that any investor above that threshold be required to be a guarantor on the loan. Or perhaps a debt fund has a 10 percent of the total offering limit to avoid lending licensure issues whereby larger owners are required to be vetted by state regulatory authorities. There are a variety of reasons why an investment might have a maximum, so if you are considering making a very large investment, it's good to ask the sponsor about any limitations.

Holding Title

How you hold title to the investment is an important decision. Your choice can have legal and tax consequences, so you should strongly consider getting advice from your tax and legal advisors. I'm not a lawyer, so I'll avoid giving legal advice, but I will give a general overview of the various ways of holding title just so you are aware of the most common options.

The simplest way to hold title is as an individual. With this method you and you alone hold title to the investment units. If you die, your investment will likely end up in probate and pass in accordance with your will. If you are married and live in a community property state, you might have to hold title as a married person as your sole and separate property if you intend to hold title individually. Your spouse might be required to sign a spousal consent that binds them to the terms of the partnership agreement if they inherit your partnership interests.

If you are investing with another person, you could take title as tenants in common. This is similar to individual ownership but with two or more individual owners. In the event of the death of one owner, the interest of the deceased owner will not pass to the other owner; instead, it would pass according to the deceased owner's will. This method is pretty unusual for holding interests in a syndication because two joint owners could hold two separate positions as individuals. The reason people usually choose this method is to avoid minimum investment limits. Let's say the minimum is $100,000 and the sponsor is not willing to waive it. Two brothers want to invest but they only want to put in $50,000 each, so they execute one subscription as tenants in common for $100,000 and they each contribute half. The challenge with this approach is that the partnership will likely issue a single K-1 for tax reporting, and it's unlikely that two brothers file a joint tax return.

If you wish to avoid some of the problems associated with the passing of your investment in the event of your death, you might consider holding as joint tenants with right of survivorship. Under this method, if you die your interest automatically passes to the other joint tenant. If you have a trust, you can also hold title in the name of the trust. Check your trust language for exactly how to list the ownership of your trust assets. For example, instead of putting your name in the "subscriber" box on the investor questionnaire, you may have to list "The Smith Family Trust Dated January 2, 2001" as the subscriber.

If you have a corporation, partnership, or LLC, those entities can invest in private offerings; just select the correct entity type on the questionnaire. Some 401(k) plans can invest in private offerings, typically only solo 401(k)s belonging to self-employed individuals who have their own self-directed account. Plans with the typical retail 401(k) administrators won't allow you to invest your 401(k) funds in private offerings.

You can also invest in private offerings through your IRA. It must be a self-directed IRA that is held with a self-directed IRA custodian. These IRAs are different from the retail IRAs you commonly see in the mass-market financial services space, which includes banks and brokerage houses. Custodians that specialize in this type of IRA specifically allow you to invest in private offerings, among other things. To find these custodians, do an online search for "self-directed IRA custodian" and check out the various options. Fees differ from one custodian to another, and their responsiveness to your investment directives will vary. You might want to ask a few sponsors which custodians their clients use and get some feedback on which are the easiest to work with.

Investing through an IRA has some tax advantages, but it isn't a free ride. There are specific taxes that can apply to IRAs that invest in active businesses or leveraged real estate investments. This means you might pay some tax on the profits of these investments in your IRA; you should be aware of that tax so you can plan for it. I'm not a tax accountant any more than I'm a lawyer, so be sure to consult your tax advisor for advice specific to your tax situation before making an investment in a private offering through your IRA (or any other source of funds, for that matter). Some investors don't like to invest in private offerings with their IRA money because of these taxes. Other investors recognize that the returns on private offerings can be superior to more typical IRA investments despite the tax consequences. Your tolerance may vary.

If you are investing through a self-directed IRA, there are specific steps for completing the investor questionnaire and subscription agreement. The subscriber name on the subscription agreement will not be you. It will be your IRA custodian, and your custodian will have very specific instructions on how to list the name of the subscriber on the subscription agreement. Be sure to check their investing procedures so that you get it right the first time. Most custodians will require the subscriber to look something like this: "Acme IRAs, as Custodian FBO Mary Smith IRA #12345."

Your IRA custodian will have an investment packet for you to fill out, authorizing them to make the investment on your behalf. They might require the sponsor to send the offering documents to their compliance department for approval prior to allowing you to make the investment. Once the documents have been approved and you've filled out the IRA custodian's investment packet, you complete the subscription agreement as instructed and sign it as the beneficial owner of the IRA. The sponsor will then be required to send the subscription agreement to your IRA custodian for them to sign.

Other Subscription Considerations

A common concern is whether you should form your own LLC for the purposes of taking title to your syndication investment. Many people think this will provide tax advantages or additional liability protection. I think it's unnecessary, because as a passive investor in a syndication you are likely already investing as a member of an LLC or as a limited partner in a limited partnership, because the sponsor created the entity for the purpose of sponsoring the offering. This means that you already get the benefits of entity treatment without having to form your own entity.

I find it rare for people to form entities for the specific purpose of making one syndication investment, although I have seen investors form entities for the purpose of making multiple investments. Of course, investors' tax and legal situations vary widely, so you should seek competent legal and tax advice from trusted professionals familiar with your specific situation before making these important decisions.

One common scenario is for a group of friends and family members to form an LLC in order to invest in syndications. They make contributions to the LLC, and then the LLC invests in the offerings. If an offering restricts the subscribers to accredited investors only, this LLC model cannot be used to skirt the accredited investor requirement. In order for an LLC to be accredited, all the members must also be accredited unless the LLC has more than $5 million in assets and was not formed for the specific purpose of investing in the offering. See appendix A for further details about the criteria for accredited investors.

Another concern I've heard is whether you should open a separate bank account for the purpose of investing in a syndication. If your counsel advises you to do so, you should. Otherwise, I see little value to doing so.

Some people have asked whether they need an employer ID number (EIN). You will have to supply a taxpayer ID number on the investor questionnaire so that the sponsor can send you your K-1 for tax reporting purposes. If you are investing through a business entity such as an LLC or corporation, you will need an EIN, and chances are you have one already. If you are investing through your self-directed IRA or 401(k), you would use the EIN of your custodian. But if you are investing as an individual, joint tenant, or tenant in common, or through your trust, you would simply use your Social Security number, unless your trust has its own EIN, as is sometimes the case.

Completing the Questionnaire

Investor questionnaires and subscription agreements are available as paper forms, electronic PDF forms, which can be emailed and printed, or online forms, which can be filled out on a website and signed electronically. The questionnaire will require responses to the following questions, so have this information handy:

- Investment amount
- Name of the subscriber (your name, your company or trust name, or IRA custodian)
- Method of holding title
- Address, phone number, and email address
- Tax ID number (Social Security or employer ID number)
- Country of citizenship (non-US citizens can be subject to tax withholding)
- Distribution instructions (check or direct deposit)
- Bank account information (for direct deposit distributions, if desired)
- Investor suitability questions
- Accredited investor certification (usually a multiple-choice question)

After you complete the questionnaire and sign the subscription agreement, the sponsor will decide whether to admit you to the investment. If you are admitted, the sponsor will sign the subscription agreement and provide you with a copy.

Funding Your Investment

The last step will be to fund your investment. This procedure varies among sponsors and may even vary among different offerings from the same sponsor. The most common approach is to wire your funds to the sponsor as soon as possible after completing your subscription agreement. Some sponsors might instead issue a capital call—a request for investors in the offering to send money—after the subscription agreements are signed. Some offerings will call for all capital at once, which is common in single-property syndications. Multi-property fund offerings might call for capital in stages, such as a fixed percentage at fixed intervals, or specific percentages of your commitment as properties are acquired.

When the sponsor calls for your capital, they should provide you with payment instructions. Although some sponsors accept checks, that is increasingly rare. Most sponsors ask for funds via wire transfer.

If the sponsor asks for your funds via wire, be extremely careful. Wire fraud is running rampant, especially in the real estate and financial services industries. Crooks are hacking into email systems or spoofing email addresses, intercepting wire instructions, changing the account information, and forwarding them on to the intended recipient. Don't think that this won't happen to you! Once you send a wire you cannot get it back, so make absolutely certain that you are sending your wire to the correct place.

A good practice is to call the sponsor on the phone and verify the routing number, account number, and account name before sending the wire. Be sure to use a phone number that you've been using to communicate with the sponsor, or look up the number. Don't rely on a phone number shown in an email; scammers can change that number and you'll wind up talking to the scammer when confirming the wire instructions.

Once your subscription agreement has been completed and signed, the sponsor has accepted you as an investor and countersigned your subscription agreement, and you have sent your funds, you are invested in the offering!

What now? It has taken you a long time to find the right sponsor and the right offering. You've done all your due diligence, completed the paperwork, and parted with your hard-earned money. Your job is mostly done, which is why this is called passive investing. But really, this is just the beginning. Let's move on to what to expect from here.

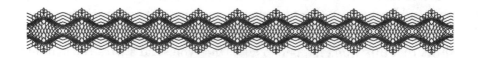

CHAPTER 19

DURING YOUR INVESTMENT

Have you ever seen one of those dating shows on television? They spend an entire season selecting the right partner and in the last episode the contestants ride off into the sunset. But then what? Did they get married, start a family, and live happily ever after? Or did they go home and immediately break up?

This is a lot like investing in a syndication: You spend a ton of time selecting a sponsor and then selecting the right offering before making your investment. You were a passive viewer of the dating show, and you are a passive investor in the syndication. But there is an important difference—you aren't in the audience this time, you are in the cast. You can't just go on and never know what happened after the last episode, or after the subscription agreement is signed.

Investor Communications

If you chose well, you hope that the deal you are in stays out of the news. If the economy and markets cooperate, you hope that you and your sponsor-partner live happily ever after. But as with any healthy relationship, communication is essential to success. Communication from the sponsor comes in many forms and at many different points in time during the investment cycle.

Closing Announcements

Often the first communication you receive after making your investment is a closing announcement. You will typically fund your investment before the sponsor closes escrow on the real estate, and some time may pass between your funding date and the closing date while final closing arrangements are being completed.

Once the property closes, the sponsor should let you know that the closing has happened and report anything significant that came up. Many times there's little to report, as these closings and takeovers tend to be more anticlimactic than you'd think. But once in a while there is some news, and it's a good practice for the sponsor to share that with you. After all, you want to celebrate the closing too!

Post-Closing Update

The early days of a new real estate investment are often a whirlwind of activity for the sponsor. Hiring new staff for the property, getting the books and records together, getting computers set up, utilities transferred, and new contracts in place are the first priorities after a takeover. Once those urgent matters are handled, the next step is to begin the renovation plan or start implementing the planned upgrades. About a month after closing is a good time to hear from the sponsor on how things are going.

For some reason, around a month into any investment investors start to get worried. Did the sponsor just take the money and flee the country? Did they buy the property, never to be heard from again? The one-month update is nice because it calms nerves. You just want to know that the plan is in motion and all is well. After that, simple periodic updates are probably just right for you to keep tabs on what's going on.

Breaking News

You want to hear from the sponsors when something happens that affects the investment, such as a fire, flood, natural disaster, or anything that is likely to have an impact on the property's performance, reputation, or cash flow. Sometimes these events can destroy an investment plan, other times they have a temporary effect, and still other times they don't have much, if any, impact.

I've heard horror stories from investors who learned about a major incident long after the fact or by catching it on the news. People appreciate knowing rather than not knowing, and they aren't usually upset with the messenger even though they might not like the message. Perhaps it's worthwhile to ask potential sponsors how they communicate breaking news—or even if they do at all.

Then there is the news of no news. One time a giant, powerful hurricane was bearing down on Florida. After it passed, we received the damage assessment—a bush had blown over, and a tree branch had fallen on the lawn and knocked over an air conditioner compressor. But if you were glued to the news, you would have expected the entire city to be wiped out. Knowing that our investors would be wondering whether the property was still standing, we immediately issued a damage, or lack thereof, report. It was greatly appreciated. Even though no news is good news, delivering the message that there is no news is even better.

Periodic Reports

Hearing from sponsors on a regular basis during the time the property is held enables you to keep tabs on how things are going, and continually resets your expectations for overall performance. If things aren't going well, you don't want to find out after the property is sold and there is no money to distribute. You should expect to be in the loop on a regular basis. You'll be in this partnership with the sponsor potentially for several years, and communication is key.

Sadly, this is an area that many sponsors struggle with. Some just forget. Others sweep updates under the rug because the investment isn't performing as expected and they don't want to admit it. Yet others excel in this area, providing regular updates to investors and really keeping them in the know. You probably won't find out how good the reporting is until after you've made your investment, because no sponsor is going to tell you they are bad at reporting when trying to convince you to invest with them. But if you know other investors of theirs, you can find out the truth ahead of time. It's worthwhile to network, and this is a great topic to discuss when talking with references.

Most syndicators report quarterly, some monthly, some irregularly. It's possible, and even likely, that reporting frequency is spelled out in the operating agreement, so you can look to the language there if you feel that the sponsor isn't fulfilling their duty. Many partnership agreements also provide for a mechanism for investors to specifically request information and financial statements, so if the sponsor isn't sending them out, you can ask for them.

You can even request financial information between typical reporting cycles if you wish, but you should use this power only as necessary. Don't call every week asking for an income statement. If the sponsors are sending reports out as required by the operating agreement and you have no reason to believe that anything sinister is going on, try to refrain from asking for additional information. Squeaky wheels do get the grease, but they also get replaced—if the sponsor is doing a good job you don't want them keeping you out of their next deal because you are a pain to deal with. However, if the sponsor is uncommunicative or not performing well, pester away! You don't want to be in their next deal anyway, if there even is a next deal.

What should you expect to see in periodic reports? What do they look like? There's no single answer to either question, as sponsors usually design their own reports and decide what the content and format will be. It's a good idea to ask for samples of reports when you are evaluating sponsors so that you have appropriate expectations.

In general, you should at least expect to see an income statement for the quarter along with a narrative of what's been going on at the property. Some sponsors go further, providing the quarter's income statement broken down by month, or even the last twelve months broken down by month. Many will provide a balance sheet and a statement of cash flows.

Some will provide a budget variance report, showing the actual income and expenses adjacent to the budget and details of any variances. This is a great practice but one that is often manipulated. It's standard procedure in the property management industry to draft an operating budget for each calendar year. These budgets tend to be created by examining the previous year's performance and making adjustments for what is expected to happen in the subsequent year. This is fine, and it is good practice in the property management industry.

What tends to happen with these annual budgets is they trend in the direction of actual performance. Let's say that this year's performance wasn't too great. Next year's budget will be based on this year's lackluster performance, so a variance report will show a comparison of how the property did against numbers that were crafted based on already-bad results.

The problem is that this tells you nothing about how the property's performance compares to the numbers you were looking at when you made your investment decision: the sponsor's projections. Now, two years into the investment, you are looking at a comparison of actual performance versus this year's budget. What you want to see is a report card comparing the original projections against the actual performance. This is the only thing that can give you a picture of how the deal is going, and tell you whether you should adjust your expectations downward or upward. Sadly, a lot of sponsors don't offer this comparison, so ask before making your investment. If the sponsor says they do offer it but later delivers actuals versus budget, call them out on it and ask them to deliver the comparison they promised.

In addition to financial statements and a performance comparison, sponsors should give you some information about what has been going on at the property, such as the status of the upgrade plan, an update on occupancy, or how things are trending toward implementing a resale plan. They should also include some discussion of challenges at the property, such as falling occupancy, resident retention issues, or escalating delinquencies, along with their action plan for solving these problems.

No matter how good the sponsor, there will always be issues, and one of the reasons you decided to invest passively is to leverage the sponsor's skill and experience with solving those problems. The sponsor shouldn't hide them from you. This is their opportunity to shine and build your confidence in them by showing you how well they handle challenges. Hopefully in a later report they can describe how successful their efforts were. If they weren't successful, they can let you know what else they are trying now.

⚠ One thing to specifically look for in your reports is the balance sheet. Look for a line item called "Accounts Receivable" or perhaps "Rent Receivable." Each month, rent comes due and is added to the "receivable" on the balance sheet. When rents are paid, the receivable account decreases. You should compare the receivable account on the balance sheet to previous balance sheets, checking to see if the amount is consistently climbing. Fluctuations are normal, but a steady climb that does not subsequently fall is a problem.

If you see this, it is likely that the sponsor is stacking up bad debt on the balance sheet and not writing it off as bad debt. What this means is that the income statement is showing more income than is actually being collected. If you look only at the income statement, you would think that the property is performing better than it is. You can ask the sponsor for a "Receivables Aging Report" if you want to investigate what is going on. An aging report will show you how much of the "receivables" are from the current month, how much of it is over thirty days late, how much is over sixty days, and how much is over ninety days. If there is a very large amount of delinquency over ninety days, that is another clue that the sponsor is stacking bad debt on the balance sheet and overstating the property's performance on the income statement.

Tax Reporting

You want to see regular financial reports and receive updates on how things are going. No one enjoys paying taxes, so one thing you don't want to see regularly is a tax report, but they are a necessary fact of life. Fortunately these come only once a year. For syndications, a tax report is your annual K-1.

What is on a K-1? Let's look at a sample.

Schedule K-1 (Form 1065)		20**18**				
Department of the Treasury Internal Revenue Service						OMB No. 1545-0123

☐ Final K-1　☐ Amended K-1

Part III Partner's Share of Current Year Income, Deductions, Credits, and Other Items

Department of the Treasury
Internal Revenue Service

For calendar year 2018, or tax year

beginning ☐ / / 2018 ending ☐ / /

Partner's Share of Income, Deductions, Credits, etc. ► See back of form and separate instructions.

Part I	Information About the Partnership
A	Partnership's employer identification number
	12-3456789
B	Partnership's name, address, city, state, and ZIP code

Marvin Gardens LLC
123 Business Park Drive
Anytown, US 12345

C	IRS Center where partnership filed return
	E-FILE
D	☐ Check if this is a publicly traded partnership (PTP)

Part II	Information About the Partner
E	Partner's identifying number
	123-45-6789
F	Partner's name, address, city, state, and ZIP code

Joe and Mary Investor
123 Main Street
Anytown, US 12345

G	☐ General partner or LLC member-manager	☒ Limited partner or other LLC member
H	☒ Domestic partner	☐ Foreign partner

I1 What type of entity is this partner? **INDIVIDUAL**

I2 If this partner is a retirement plan (IRA/SEP/Keogh/etc.), check here ☐

J Partner's share of profit, loss, and capital (see instructions):

	Beginning	Ending
Profit	1.0000000 %	1.0000000 %
Loss	1.4285714 %	1.4285788 %
Capital	1.4285714 %	1.4285788 %

K Partner's share of liabilities:

	Beginning	Ending
Nonrecourse	$ 1.246	$ 19,107
Qualified nonrecourse financing	$ 105,394	$ 105,394
Recourse	$ 0	$ 0

L Partner's capital account analysis:

Beginning capital account	$ 94,513
Capital contributed during the year	$
Current year increase (decrease)	$ -27,027
Withdrawals & distributions	$(6,550)
Ending capital account	$ 60,936

☒ Tax basis　☐ GAAP　☐ Section 704(b) book
☐ Other (explain)

M Did the partner contribute property with a built-in gain or loss?
☐ Yes　☒ No
If "Yes," attach statement (see instructions)

For IRS Use Only

Part III — Partner's Share of Current Year Income, Deductions, Credits, and Other Items

#	Description	Amount	#	Description	Amount
1	Ordinary business income (loss)	0	15	Credits	
2	Net rental real estate income (loss)	-27,050	16	Foreign transactions	
3	Other net rental income (loss)				
4	Guaranteed payments				
5	Interest income	23			
6a	Ordinary dividends				
6b	Qualified dividends				
6c	Dividend equivalents				
7	Royalties				
8	Net short-term capital gain (loss)		17	Alternative minimum tax (AMT) items	
			A		3,813
9a	Net long-term capital gain (loss)				
9b	Collectibles (28%) gain (loss)				
9c	Unrecaptured section 1250 gain		18	Tax-exempt income and nondeductible expenses	
10	Net section 1231 gain (loss)				
11	Other income (loss)				
			19	Distributions	
			A		6,550
12	Section 179 deduction		20	Other information	
13	Other deductions		A		*23
			Z		*-27,050
14	Self-employment earnings (loss)		AA		*0
A		0	AB		*268,340
			AC		*0
			AD		*0

*See attached statement for additional information.

For Paperwork Reduction Act Notice, see Instructions for Form 1065.　www.irs.gov/Form1065　Cat. No. 11394R　Schedule K-1 (Form 1065) 2018

Part I. This section provides information on the company: the employer ID number, name, and address.

Part II. This section gives information about you, the investor. Item J shows your ownership percentages. Item L shows your beginning capital account, your contributions and distributions for the year, the current year's profit and loss, and your ending capital account balance. Remember that you can get tax benefits when investing in real estate, and one of the biggest benefits is depreciation. Depreciation often results in negative income, and that is deducted from your capital account. It's not unusual for your capital account to decrease, and just because it decreases on your K-1 does not mean you've lost actual money. A decrease just reflects a tax loss or principal that has been distributed back to you.

Part III. This section shows your share of income, deductions, credits, and other items. In this example, the numbers show:

1. **Ordinary income.** This is zero because this is a rental real estate investment and didn't have any ordinary business income. Other partnerships, such as investments in businesses, or business activities that generate ordinary income, such as house flipping, would have income showing in this block.

2. **Net rental real estate income.** Because this is a real estate investment, the rental loss shows in this block. Even though the property was operationally profitable, depreciation exceeded the operating profits and resulted in a taxable loss, thus the negative number.

5. **Interest income.** Interest income appears here, separate from business income (block 1) and rental real estate income (block 2). In this sample, if you add block 2 and block 5, you get the same result as shown in part II, item L for the "Current year increase (decrease)."

19. **Distributions.** This block shows your distributions and matches what is shown in part II, item L for "Withdrawals and distributions."

20. **Other information.** This block shows any other relevant figures that your tax preparer may need to complete your tax return, and give you the benefits of various tax credits and limitations. Each line has a letter code, and page 2 of the K-1 gives you a description of each letter code. Since tax laws change frequently and the specific rules are very complex, I'll leave the discussion of this section at that.

Distributions

The primary goal when investing in a real estate private offering is to earn a return on your money. This means that everything leading up to your investment—the searching for sponsors, the due diligence, the waiting for the right offering—was worth it if you get more money back than you put in. Since receiving distributions is so important, why not dedicate a discussion to all things distribution?

Method of Payment

How you receive your distributions is up to you, but your options might be limited by the sponsor. The thought of "mailbox money" is exciting—you go to your mailbox and collect your check. It's a great way to make a living if you can, but what's even more freeing is avoiding trips to the bank altogether. Perhaps receiving your distributions by direct deposit is more your style. Forget mailbox money; this money just appears in your bank account while you are sailing around the world, or whatever it is that you like to do.

Distributions can be sent by check, direct deposited, or sent by wire transfer. Some sponsors will limit your options to one or two of these methods. Check with the sponsor to learn the available options, and make sure they work for you before you invest.

If you elect to receive your distribution by direct deposit, keep in mind that you'll need to get specific instructions from your bank. Usually all you'll need is your bank's routing number and your account number, and the instructions are often the same as for a wire transfer. But things can get more complex in some circumstances. For example, if your account is in a brokerage house, their direct deposit instructions might include specific information to route funds from the broker's account to your specific sub-account. The direct deposit instructions might also be different from the wiring instructions, so be sure to confirm with your financial institution that you are following the correct instructions for the method of payment you are choosing.

Timing

For properties that produce regular cash flow, the most common timing for distributions is on a quarterly basis, but some partnerships will distribute monthly. Good examples of investments with regular cash flow are stabilized income properties, such as apartments, self-storage facilities, and mobile-home parks.

Some partnerships will distribute whenever there are funds available, but the frequency and interval may vary. For example, there might be no distributions for the first year of a heavy value-add property with little to no cash flow in that first year. But as soon as the income increases and cash flow is available, the distributions would begin on a regular basis, such as quarterly or monthly.

Some partnerships, such as development projects that produce no income, will distribute only at the very end: When the property is completed and sold, the profit is distributed all at once. As you look through the investment projections, watch for the timing and amounts of expected cash flows so you know what to expect.

Calculating Distributions

Regardless of the timing of distributions, the amount of distributions will vary depending on how much cash is available to distribute, and there could be periods when distributions are not made if cash flow falls or unforeseen expenses pop up that need to be addressed.

Sponsors calculate the amount to distribute in a variety of ways. Generally, the first step is to evaluate the amount of cash on hand. Next, they deduct the amount of cash needed for future capital expenditures, such as completing a renovation plan or making necessary replacements. Next, needed reserves are deducted so that there is always cash on hand for emergencies. The balance of the cash is available for distribution.

The amount of the distribution is likely not equivalent to the net operating income because NOI doesn't include debt service and capital expenditure reserves, and those costs still have to be paid before distributions can be made. It's important to realize that cash flow, not income, is distributed. There is a difference. Investors frequently confuse the amount of their distribution with the amount of their income, but the two are completely unrelated.

You may recall from our earlier discussion of income statements that net operating income is operating income minus operating expenses. From NOI, debt service (principal and interest) and capital improvements are deducted to reveal cash flow.

It's possible to have income but no cash flow, such as when the principal payments on the loan suck up all the cash flow. It's also possible to have positive cash flow but no distributions, such as when the partnership needs the cash flow to save up for a new roof. It's also possible to have distributions but no income—for example, when a non-cash expense like depreciation is deducted from positive income, turning it into a loss, but the positive cash flow is distributed. It's also possible to have distributions but no cash flow, such as when the sponsor has leftover cash that they no longer need after a development project is complete, so they distribute it.

All of this goes to say that you need to forget about seeking seamless relationships between income, cash flow, and distributions. They are all related, but more like second cousins. The only time that distributions and income are equal is after the investment is all over, the property is sold, loans are paid off, depreciation is recaptured, and all remaining funds are distributed to investors and the sponsor. The total of all distributions should equal the total of all contributions and income.

Preferred Returns or Not?

Some people (investors and sponsors alike) think that a preferred return is a guaranteed payment—that the money must be paid on a schedule, like a loan payment. In reality, a preferred return, as we covered in detail in chapter 16, means that the investor is in a preferred position, in other words, they have priority on the cash flow. Until the preferred return hurdle is met, investors get 100 percent of whatever is distributed. That's all it is.

Yet, some sponsors market to investors as if the preferred return is the amount to expect to be distributed. While that might sound desirable, there are a lot of negative implications to this practice if the real estate doesn't produce enough cash flow to meet this promise. This shortage is not uncommon at all when buying an underperforming property where the business plan is to improve the property and increase the income as the improvements are made. In the first two to three years, the cash flow thrown off by the property is typically somewhat weak, such as 4, 5, or perhaps 6 percent. If the preferred return is 8 percent, there is not enough cash flow to make an 8 percent distribution in the early years.

Let's break this down with an example of how the distributions should work. Let's say that the preferred return hurdle is 8 percent, and is cumulative. In the first year, the property produces enough cash flow to distribute 4 percent. There is not enough cash flow to distribute the other 4 percent, so the unpaid balance carries over to the next year and beyond. If in year two the property throws off enough cash flow to pay the investors 8 percent, the investors get all of the distribution. If, in year three, the property throws off enough cash to pay 12 percent, the investors get all of the distribution, because the investors are owed 8 percent to meet the preferred return accrued this year, plus the 4 percent shortfall from year one. If, in year four, the property throws off 12 percent again, the investors get 8 percent to meet the preferred return accrued this year, and the remaining 4 percent drops down to the split tier(s).

Using this same example, how could a sponsor distribute 8 percent to their investors in year one? An odd and disturbing trend I'm seeing is sponsors raising additional capital and making cash flow distributions equivalent to the preferred return hurdle, regardless of the performance of the real estate. The reason I say that it's odd is it is just like saying, "Give me $100,000. I'll invest $85,000 of it in real estate, and I'll give you the remaining $15,000 back in quarterly installments over the first two to three years." As an investor, I'd say, "Uh, no thanks, I could invest $85,000 with you instead and keep my $15,000!"

Why would sponsors do this? Some might do this to mask the true performance of the investment, obscuring the actual results from unsuspecting investors that don't know any better. These investors confuse distributions with performance and think that as long as they are getting their distributions, everything is going just fine. Meanwhile, the property could be in deep trouble and the entity could eventually run out of cash.

More commonly I suspect that the reasons are less nefarious. Perhaps just a marketing strategy—a way of attracting capital because they can tell their investors that they will "make" 8 percent on their money right away. Perhaps some sponsors are doing this because they don't know how to accrue a preferred return properly, thinking that if they just distribute whatever the preferred return is, they don't have to track it.

In the case of either of these two reasons, if it's all disclosed and the investors understand exactly what is going on, no harm, no foul, I suppose. But are sponsors disclosing it? If they are, there should be a line item on the sources and uses of funds table showing exactly how much money the sponsor is raising to supplement early-year investor distributions. But I see a lot of offerings from sponsors that don't include sources and uses of funds tables at all. Investors in these offerings truly have no idea where the money is going. Not good.

What if the sponsor isn't showing any money being raised for this purpose? In that case, where is the money coming from? Maybe the sponsor is robbing Peter to pay Paul, siphoning money that was intended to be held in reserve for a rainy day or was intended to be used to renovate the property. This would compromise the business plan or even the company's solvency.

I've heard some investors say that they like to receive distributions equal to the preferred return hurdle from the beginning of the investment. That makes sense, but at what cost? At best, this practice is tying up money that isn't invested in real estate, rather, it's just held by the sponsor to give back to the investor. At worst, it could be compromising the financial integrity of the company. But even if it all works out, it comes at a price. The overall return on the investment is a function of the amount of money raised and the amount of money returned. This means that raising additional capital for the purposes of inflating early returns actually lowers the rate of return for the investment overall. More dollars in for the same profit out.

Types of Distributions

When sponsors make distributions to investors, the cash distributed can fall into two different buckets: return *of* capital and return *on* capital. Determining which can be a lot less obvious than it seems. It all depends on the waterfall rules that we covered so extensively back in chapter 16.

As you receive distributions, the amount attributable to return of versus return on capital is useful only for determining the remaining cash value of the investment for your balance sheet and computing your net worth. Some people think they need to know the difference for tax-planning purposes, but that's untrue—remember that cash flow, distributions, and income are all completely different, so even if you receive a return on your capital, you still might not owe any tax thanks to depreciation.

There are a variety of ways that capital can be returned. One is from operating cash flow in conformance with the waterfall rules. Another is from a cash-out refinance, and another, of course, is from the sale of the property.

Distribution Notices

Some sponsors issue notices along with their distributions that provide useful information. These distribution notices should show the amount of your distribution, and might show the breakdown of return of capital and return on capital. They might also show the amount of capital that remains committed to the investment, which is useful for determining your cash-on-cash return after capital is returned, such as after a cash-out refinance.

It's a good practice to review the property's income and cash flow statements to compare them to the performance that you are expecting. Remember that distributions do not represent performance, only the income and cash flow statements can represent performance. If the cash flow statements do not show that the property is throwing off enough cash to support the distributions you are receiving, the investment might be in trouble despite the fact that you are receiving distributions.

Ponzi schemes come to mind as a similar example. These are scams where the promoter is distributing more money than the underlying investments are making, using money from new investors to pay old investors. Ponzi-style scams are fortunately quite rare in the real estate syndication space, but they are out there. Comparing property-level cash flow to distributions is one way to spot this type of activity. If the cash flow statements show the property threw off $100,000 in cash flow, but the sponsor distributed $500,000 (and there was no cash-out refinance) it's probably a good idea to ask a few questions.

Tax Implications

Most of us don't like paying taxes. If that includes you, you're really going to like investing in real estate private offerings. These investments have tremendous tax advantages and, with a couple of important exceptions that I'll cover here, can include all the same tax benefits as investing in real estate directly.

Depreciation

Perhaps the most well-known tax advantage that real estate offers is depreciation. This allows you to write off a portion of the cost of the improvements located on real property each year. "Improvements" essentially means everything other than the ground itself—buildings, heating and plumbing systems, landscaping, driveways and parking lots, appliances, equipment, flooring, and so on.

Like all tax laws, the rules surrounding depreciation can be a bit complex, and they are subject to change. Fortunately for me, this book isn't about how to prepare your taxes (if you want to learn more about specific real estate tax strategies, I suggest picking up a copy of *The Book on Tax Strategies for the Savvy Real Estate Investor* by Amanda Han and Matthew MacFarland), so I'll stick to some high-level essentials here.

We know that depreciation means writing off a portion of the cost each year, but how large a portion? If the property is non-residential, such as an office building, hotel, or shopping center, the cost of the structures is written off over 39 years under the tax laws in effect at the time of this writing. Structures on residential property, such as houses and apartments, are written off over 27.5 years. Different depreciable periods apply if the sponsor makes the election out of the interest expense limitation for real property trades or businesses.

Remember, you can't depreciate the land itself, so if you bought a non-residential property for $1 million, you cannot write off $25,641 per year ($1 million divided by 39). Instead, you have to estimate how much of the $1 million price was to purchase the land and how much was for the improvements. Your tax advisor (or in the case of a passive investment in a syndicated offering, the sponsor's tax advisor) would give you guidance on how to establish this ratio. Many people use the same ratio that the property tax collector uses for their assessed value, which usually assesses the land and improvements separately, so you can calculate the ratio using the property tax bill.

Let's assume that the chosen ratio is 70 percent buildings and 30 percent land. For that same $1 million non-residential property, the depreciation deduction would be $17,949 ($700,000 divided by 39). If this property produced $15,000 of income per year, you would actually have a taxable loss of $2,949 per year despite your positive income. This makes depreciation one of the best tax shelters there is. Depreciation can offset most or even all of the income from your syndication investment, and depending on your individual tax situation and the amount of the depreciation, it might even offset some of your income from other sources.

As an investor in a private offering, you get to take your share of the depreciation deductions just as if you were a direct owner of the real estate. There can be a limited exception, however, as some sponsors allocate all of the depreciation deductions to the investors. Other sponsors take a share of the depreciation for themselves. For example, let's say that, according to the deal terms, investors and the sponsor split the profits 70/30, with 30 percent going to the sponsor as their promote. Some sponsors might allocate 30 percent of the depreciation to themselves, which leaves less depreciation for you to take than if you owned the real estate directly. Be sure to ask how depreciation is allocated so you can plan accordingly and compare offerings.

Cost Segregation
What if you could accelerate the depreciation deduction? If your tax situation is such that you can use passive losses from one investment to offset

income from other passive sources (for example, if you have taxable gain from the exit of another passive investment), taking large amounts of depreciation can provide a net benefit to you. In that case, you're in luck because a mechanism exists to speed up the amount of depreciation available to take. However, whether or not to use this mechanism is up to the sponsor, so you should ask them if they do a "cost segregation analysis" on the real estate purchased in their offerings.

Certain parts of the real estate can be depreciated faster than other parts. We all know that a stove or flooring won't last as long as a building; even the parking lot won't last as long. Because of this, the tax laws allow parking lots to be depreciated over a shorter schedule than the building, and appliances and flooring can be depreciated even faster than the parking lot. The problem is that real estate owners can't unilaterally decide how much of the cost of the property was for the parking lot and how much for appliances, plumbing, flooring, water heaters, and so on. In order to accelerate the depreciation on these non-structural items, the sponsor must employ an engineer to conduct a cost segregation analysis, which is essentially a detailed report about the property and its various components. The engineer conducts an inspection and an inventory of the property, and provides values for the various pieces that can be depreciated on various timetables. This report can then be used to form the basis of the depreciation deductions.

Cost segregation results in higher depreciation deductions, especially in the first five years following the acquisition. Since a large number of syndicated real estate investments are owned for five years or less, cost segregation is popular because it maximizes the depreciation that can be taken during the life of the investment. Despite that, not all sponsors use cost segregation, and since some passive investors can't use the excess losses due to tax law limitations, not all investors care whether it is used. Check with your tax advisor to determine whether you can utilize the losses. If you can, cost segregation might benefit you, and you should ask the sponsors of the investments you are considering whether they plan to use cost segregation.

Capital Gains

Depreciation is a great tax shelter, but capital gain is even better. Ordinary income is taxed at the highest rate of all categories of income, but income received as a result of the sale of an asset, such as real estate, is called capital gain and is taxed at a lower rate than ordinary income. This makes investments in real estate very desirable because of the lower taxes paid on the profits from the sale.

Depreciation Recapture

Real estate has great tax benefits, but there is never a free lunch. It seems that for every benefit there's something to counter all the good stuff, and depreciation is no exception. When the property is sold, you will have to "recapture" the depreciation you took. This means that you have to claim it back as income and pay taxes on it then.

However, the tax rate on depreciation recapture is lower than the tax rate on ordinary income. If you hadn't taken a depreciation deduction, you would have paid taxes at the ordinary income rate each year. But by taking the depreciation, you didn't pay the taxes each year. Instead, you'll pay them at the end, but at a lower rate.

This leaves you with two net benefits. First is the difference in taxes that you would have paid on ordinary income versus recapture. That's a direct net savings to you. Second, you are paying the tax in "tomorrow's" dollars. For example, the tax you would have paid in year 1 was instead paid in year 5, when the property was sold. Dollars five years hence are worth less, so that's an indirect savings to you.

Multi-State Tax Filings

One disadvantage of investing in syndications is that you might be required to file state tax returns (and pay state income taxes) in multiple states. If the syndication owns property in any state with a state income tax, the income associated with that property is subject to income tax in that state even if you don't live in that state. This isn't unique to syndications; it's also true if you invest in real estate directly.

If you live in a state that has an income tax, you should qualify for a credit for taxes paid to another jurisdiction that will reduce the tax you owe to your home state. If your home state tax is higher than the other state's, this dual taxation shouldn't cost you any additional money. If your home state does not have a state income tax, you will owe state tax on your investments in states that do have a state income tax. This is why investors who live in states such as Florida and Texas, which do not have a state income tax, frequently dislike investing in properties in California, which has a high state income tax.

1031 Exchanges

Another great benefit of real estate investment is the ability to defer capital gains tax and depreciation recapture if the property is exchanged for another property. Swapping one property for another is rarely done, however, because of the difficulty of executing a simultaneous swap. But the tax law recognizes this challenge and provides a mechanism for facilitating such exchanges.

Instead of the swap happening all at once, section 1031 of the Internal Revenue Code allows the outgoing property to be sold and the taxes to be deferred if a replacement property is subsequently acquired within certain time constraints. This provision of the code is so popular that the process itself is known as a "1031 exchange," after the section of the code governing the process.

A replacement property must be identified within 45 days of the sale of the outgoing property, and the purchase of the new property must be completed within 180 days of the sale of the outgoing property. If those timelines are met and all the very specific rules are followed, there will be no tax due at the time of the sale of the outgoing property. If the new property is sold, tax will be due on the sale of that property, plus taxes that would have been due when the first property was sold. Alternatively, another exchange can be performed, deferring the taxes even further.

1031 Exchanges and Syndications

Exchanges offer an enormous tax benefit. Syndications offer a great way to invest in real estate without having to do all the work associated with owning property. Unfortunately, these two are often mutually exclusive.

A 1031 exchange must be performed by the same taxpayer. This means that the owner of a property has to be the seller of the outgoing property and the buyer of the replacement property. If the owner is an LLC or a corporation, the same LLC or corporation that sells the property must buy the replacement property. If the LLC is a syndication that is funded by multiple investors, which is usually the case in private offerings, that same LLC must buy the replacement property. This means that for a 1031 exchange to work, all the investors in the syndication have to agree that the property should be sold, that they will leave their money in the syndication, and that the syndication should perform the exchange and purchase the replacement property.

In practice, that's more difficult than it sounds. Inevitably, a few investors will want to get out when the property is sold. Complicating matters further, sponsors make the majority of their money from the promote, which is typically earned upon the sale of the property. Many sponsors won't want to leave their promote in the deal for a second round, since this would lock their earnings in purgatory. This means that it's rare to receive the benefits of a 1031 exchange from a syndication investment.

It's not impossible, though. There is a rarely used process, called a "drop and swap," that allows for 1031 exchanges with syndicated investments. The investors' LLC interests are "dropped" by taking them out of the LLC and deeding the investors' direct ownership interests in the property as tenants in common. The "swap" is the 1031 exchange. In this case, the various investors, who now own small direct interests in the real estate, sell their interests in the property and then buy replacement property. The replacement property could be a single asset with all the same owners owning pieces of it, or the various investors could each buy a single property individually.

This might sound like a perfect solution, but the process is incredibly complex and not always possible. One wrong move could blow the exchange and transform it into a taxable sale, thereby defeating the whole purpose. Lenders might restrict or even prohibit the process by making such a move a violation of the loan covenants. In addition, the "swap" could be challenged by either the IRS or the state tax board as not meeting the "held for" requirements of Section 1031.

Investors often wonder whether they can 1031 their LLC interests into a replacement property. Unfortunately, the answer is no. An exchange must be performed on "like-kind" property, which means real estate for real estate. Interests in a real estate syndication aren't considered real estate; they are LLC interests, so investors can't defer the taxes on their LLC interests by exchanging them for real estate. Nor can they defer taxes by acquiring interests in another LLC: Only tangible property can be exchanged, and LLC interests aren't tangible property.

In summary, investments in a passive offering allow you to capture many of real estate's tax shelters. But you usually have to give up one—the tax-deferred exchange. Fortunately, you also give up one other thing—active real estate ownership. For many people, this trade-off is well worth it.

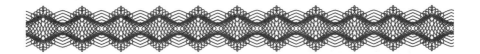

CHAPTER 20

AFTER YOUR INVESTMENT

As the saying goes, the best day of owning a boat is the day you buy it, and the second-best day is the day you sell it. The same applies to investing in real estate, especially if you own the real estate directly and have had to manage the "tenants, toilets, and trash" along the way. Owning real estate by investing in a passive syndicated offering is considerably easier, so I would hope that you aren't burned out by the time the property is sold. Maybe the sponsor of the offering is, but you shouldn't be, at least if you invested with the right sponsor.

What makes the sale so exciting is that it should bring a big payday. If you are investing solely for cash flow, maybe this doesn't excite you so much, or maybe it causes you some angst because you now have to find another investment to replace the cash flow. But if you are investing for growth, the sale of the asset is a good day. It's what this whole experience—selecting a sponsor, selecting an offering, underwriting and forecasting, all with the goal of growing your capital—has been building up to. And your payday has finally arrived!

This is a great time to reflect on your investment and take stock of how you did. You took a big leap of faith when you entrusted someone else to be a steward of your hard-earned capital. The day of sale is also a day of reckoning. Did this sponsor do what you expected? Did they handle adversity well? Did they make the right tactical and strategic decisions?

Would you invest with them again?

Before you can decide all that, you must first see two things: your money and your results. Let's walk through the process of the wind-up so you know what to expect.

Closing Distributions

Within a few days of the closing of the sale, the sponsor should send you a distribution. This distribution will typically be the majority—but not all—of what is due to you. As with most income properties, there are ongoing collections and expenses, and they don't end immediately after the sale. Knowing this, operators hold back capital to accommodate trailing expenses.

It tends to take fifteen to thirty days to close the books on monthly operations, so the first thing that has to happen is for the calendar month to close. During this time, bills are paid as usual and any remaining income is deposited. Income—such as utility reimbursements, laundry and vending income, and billboard or antenna leases—tends to arrive by mail and might not do so until after the closing. Expenses—such as closing utility bills, final payroll, advertising contracts, and myriad similar bills—arrive after the closing. It isn't unusual for expenses to continue trailing in for ninety days, and sometimes even longer.

In addition to regular expenses, most purchase and sale contracts contain a true-up clause, whereby the buyer and the seller agree to revisit income and expenses at a point in time after the sale closes and true-up items that were deposited or paid by one party but should have been attributed to the other party. A common example is property taxes: The actual amount of the tax for the calendar year might not be known until the end of the year. An assumption is made at the closing as to how much that bill will be, and the cost is prorated between the two parties. If the bill arrives and differs from the assumptions made at closing, the proration will have to be re-run and one side is going to owe the other money.

For these reasons, sponsors can't distribute all the proceeds on the day of the sale. Oftentimes they will hold back tens to hundreds of thousands of dollars, depending on the size of the property and the amount of anticipated future expenses. Let's say that after the closing the sponsor has $12.5 million in cash in the bank. Investors funded $5 million for the acquisition, so the first $5 million is allocated to the investors to return their capital. That leaves $7.5 million. The sponsor anticipates $300,000 of additional expenses, so to be safe they hold back $500,000 (which gives a $200,000 cushion) and distribute the remaining $7 million. The $7 million is run through the waterfall calculations and distributed to the investors and the sponsor in accordance with the waterfall rules in the operating agreement.

Once the sponsor is comfortable that the majority of the expenses have been paid, which is likely sixty to ninety days after the closing, they should make a second post-closing distribution. This is also unlikely to be the entire amount of the remaining capital, and I'll discuss why in a moment. In our example, $500,000 was held back. Now let's say there was $300,000 of additional expenses, leaving the company with $200,000 in cash. The sponsor might decide to distribute $125,000 now and retain the other $75,000. The $125,000 is run through the waterfall calculations and distributed to the investors and the sponsor according to the waterfall rules.

The $75,000 remaining with the sponsor is likely to be tied up in the offering for as long as a year. First, the final tax return must be completed, which will happen early in the calendar year following the closing. Some of the funds in reserve will be used to pay accounting fees for preparing the tax return as well as any taxes that are due (some states charge the entity a franchise fee, and that can get expensive after a sale).

Second, the entity will need to be shut down, which might cost a few hundred dollars in filing and legal fees. Inevitably, some random bill will show up months after closing—for example, a vendor may claim they didn't get paid on an invoice or may have just forgotten to invoice altogether—and such contingencies need to be planned for. Finally, there should be some capital left in the company in the event that a lawsuit pops up that needs to be defended.

While some of these things might sound strange, every one of them has happened to me, so I've learned to keep more in reserve after the closing than I think I'll need, and for longer than I think I'll need it. No sponsor wants to go back to their investors after the sale has closed and all the capital has been distributed, and ask them to send money back because of a trailing expense. If the sponsor of your investment distributes all the money shortly after closing, plan ahead for them to call you later asking you to return some of it. Experienced sponsors shouldn't let that happen; they will have planned ahead for contingencies, so any request for a return of capital will be due to something really unusual that no one could have anticipated.

Back to the $75,000. Once the final tax return is completed, taxes are paid, all expected expenses are paid, and enough time has passed for legal claims (twelve to eighteen months following the sale), whatever cash is left can be distributed. Just like all the distributions that preceded it, the remaining cash will be split between the investors and the sponsor in accordance with the waterfall rules in the operating agreement.

Reporting

The previous chapter discussed various reports that sponsors should be providing to you, but I saved one set of reports to discuss here. That is the closing, or wind-up, reports.

The closing reports are usually delivered at the time of the second closing distribution, that is, the one you receive about sixty to ninety days after the closing. These reports should contain the typical financial statements the sponsor has been providing during regular periodic reporting plus a few additional items.

First is an inception-to-completion financial statement. Not all sponsors provide this, but it's helpful for seeing the performance snapshot all in one place. A great way of showing this is an income statement capturing the entire period of the ownership with separate columns for each year the property was owned. Another thing you should see (and if you don't, you should ask for it) is a breakdown of the waterfall calculations. What you want is the calculation of preferred returns and performance hurdles, and a breakdown of how the cash flow was allocated to the investors as a group and to the sponsor. This should confirm that the sponsor followed the waterfall rules as set out in the operating agreement.

Then there is the granddaddy of all: the final IRR, CoC return, and equity multiple. Did the investment meet your needs and your expectations? Did the sponsor deliver on their projections? If the investment faced external adversity beyond the sponsor's control, such as an economic recession or a natural disaster, was the resulting performance acceptable once you honestly adjusted your expectations in light of the unforeseen challenge? As I often say, a good real estate operator can somehow obtain a positive outcome in the face of adversity, and a bad operator can completely screw up what should otherwise have been a great investment. Hopefully you chose your sponsor wisely, and they delivered as expected.

Now it's time to do it all again!

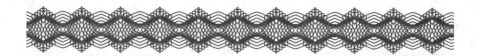

CHAPTER 21

CONCLUSION

If you need to go somewhere, chances are you'll hop in your car and drive there. But you wouldn't even think about doing that unless you first had learned the rules of the road, passed a test, and obtained a driver's license. People who ignore these requirements do so at their own peril and endanger those around them.

The same goes for passive investing in a private real estate offering. You chose wisely by picking up this book and educating yourself on how to do it the right way. You now know the importance of selecting the right sponsor, and you know how to recognize a good sponsor when you see one. You understand how to cross-check the sponsor's underwriting to ensure that the assumptions they've made are reasonable, which gives you insight as to whether the performance they are projecting is realistic. You've learned how to subscribe to an investment and what to expect from a sponsor after your investment is made.

I'll end this book with the same old saying about deals that I started with: "At the beginning, the investors have all the money and the sponsor has all the knowledge. At the end, they switch places." It doesn't have to be that way. If you invest in a deal armed with knowledge, you can come out of it with both.

One of the reasons I wrote this book is to arm you with knowledge so that you don't invest carelessly, endangering yourself and others around you. Uneducated investors fund bad sponsors. Bad sponsors give the entire industry a bad name.

I hope this book has increased your knowledge of investing in real estate private offerings, or perhaps even introduced you to an opportunity you didn't even know existed. When done properly, these investments give you the benefits of investing in real estate without all the hassles. They're the ultimate wealth-building tool, with experts who dedicate their every breath to real estate doing all the work and making the difficult decisions so you don't have to. You get to reap the rewards whether you spend your days working in the industry that *you* live and breathe, or spend your time traveling, golfing, sailing, or whatever else makes you happy.

Choose wisely, invest carefully, and most of all, enjoy the ride!

APPENDIX A

Definitions of an Accredited Investor

The following are the various definitions of an accredited investor, as defined in Rule 501 of Regulation D, current as of the date this book was written. The most current definition can be found at www.sec.gov.

Title 17: Commodity and Securities Exchanges
PART 230—GENERAL RULES AND REGULATIONS, SECURITIES ACT OF 1933

§230.501   Definitions and terms used in Regulation D.

As used in Regulation D (§230.500 *et seq.* of this chapter), the following terms shall have the meaning indicated:

(a) *Accredited investor. Accredited investor* shall mean any person who comes within any of the following categories, or who the issuer reasonably believes comes within any of the following categories, at the time of the sale of the securities to that person:

(1) Any bank as defined in section 3(a)(2) of the Act, or any savings and loan association or other institution as defined in section 3(a)(5)(A) of the Act whether acting in its individual or fiduciary capacity; any broker or dealer registered pursuant to section 15 of the Securities Exchange Act of 1934; any insurance company as defined in section 2(a)(13) of the Act; any investment company registered under the Investment Company Act of 1940 or a business development company as defined in section 2(a)(48) of that Act; any Small Business Investment Company licensed by the U.S. Small Business Administration under section 301(c) or (d) of the Small Business Investment Act of 1958; any plan established and maintained by a state, its political subdivisions, or any agency or instrumentality of a state or its political subdivisions, for the benefit of its employees, if such plan has total assets in excess of $5,000,000; any employee benefit plan within the meaning of the Employee Retirement Income Security Act of 1974 if the investment decision is made by a plan fiduciary, as defined in section 3(21) of such act, which is either a bank, savings and loan association,

insurance company, or registered investment adviser, or if the employee benefit plan has total assets in excess of $5,000,000 or, if a self-directed plan, with investment decisions made solely by persons that are accredited investors;

(2) Any private business development company as defined in section 202(a)(22) of the Investment Advisers Act of 1940;

(3) Any organization described in section 501(c)(3) of the Internal Revenue Code, corporation, Massachusetts or similar business trust, or partnership, not formed for the specific purpose of acquiring the securities offered, with total assets in excess of $5,000,000;

(4) Any director, executive officer, or general partner of the issuer of the securities being offered or sold, or any director, executive officer, or general partner of a general partner of that issuer;

(5) Any natural person whose individual net worth, or joint net worth with that person's spouse, exceeds $1,000,000.

(i) Except as provided in paragraph (a)(5)(ii) of this section, for purposes of calculating net worth under this paragraph (a)(5):

(A) The person's primary residence shall not be included as an asset;

(B) Indebtedness that is secured by the person's primary residence, up to the estimated fair market value of the primary residence at the time of the sale of securities, shall not be included as a liability (except that if the amount of such indebtedness outstanding at the time of sale of securities exceeds the amount outstanding 60 days before such time, other than as a result of the acquisition of the primary residence, the amount of such excess shall be included as a liability); and

(C) Indebtedness that is secured by the person's primary residence in excess of the estimated fair market value of the primary residence at the time of the sale of securities shall be included as a liability;

(ii) Paragraph (a)(5)(i) of this section will not apply to any calculation of a person's net worth made in connection with a purchase of securities in accordance with a right to purchase such securities, provided that:

(A) Such right was held by the person on July 20, 2010;

(B) The person qualified as an accredited investor on the basis of net worth at the time the person acquired such right; and

(C) The person held securities of the same issuer, other than such right, on July 20, 2010.

(6) Any natural person who had an individual income in excess of $200,000 in each of the two most recent years or joint income with that person's spouse in excess of $300,000 in each of those years and has a reasonable expectation of reaching the same income level in the current year;

(7) Any trust, with total assets in excess of $5,000,000, not formed for the specific purpose of acquiring the securities offered, whose purchase is directed by a sophisticated person as described in §230.506(b)(2)(ii); and

(8) Any entity in which all of the equity owners are accredited investors.

(b) *Affiliate.* An *affiliate* of, or person *affiliated* with, a specified person shall mean a person that directly, or indirectly through one or more intermediaries, controls or is controlled by, or is under common control with, the person specified.

(c) *Aggregate offering price. Aggregate offering price* shall mean the sum of all cash, services, property, notes, cancellation of debt, or other consideration to be received by an issuer for issuance of its securities. Where securities are being offered for both cash and non-cash consideration, the aggregate offering price shall be based on the price at which the securities are offered for cash. Any portion of the aggregate offering price attributable to cash received in a foreign currency shall be translated into United States currency at the currency exchange rate in effect at a reasonable time prior to or on the date of the sale of the securities. If securities are not offered for cash, the aggregate offering price shall be based on the value of the consideration as established by bona fide sales of that consideration made within a reasonable time, or, in the absence of sales, on the fair value as determined by an accepted standard. Such valuations of non-cash consideration must be reasonable at the time made.

(d) *Business combination. Business combination* shall mean any transaction of the type specified in paragraph (a) of Rule 145 under the Act (17 CFR 230.145) and any transaction involving the acquisition by one issuer, in exchange for all or a part of its own or its parent's stock, of stock of another issuer if, immediately after the acquisition, the acquiring issuer has control of the other issuer (whether or not it had control before the acquisition).

(e) *Calculation of number of purchasers.* For purposes of calculating the number of purchasers under § §230.506(b) and 230.506(b) only, the following shall apply:

(1) The following purchasers shall be excluded:

(i) Any relative, spouse or relative of the spouse of a purchaser who has the same primary residence as the purchaser;

(ii) Any trust or estate in which a purchaser and any of the persons related to him as specified in paragraph (e)(1)(i) or (e)(1)(iii) of this section collectively have more than 50 percent of the beneficial interest (excluding contingent interests);

(iii) Any corporation or other organization of which a purchaser and any of the persons related to him as specified in paragraph (e)(1)(i) or (e)(1)(ii) of this section collectively are beneficial owners of more than 50 percent of the equity securities (excluding directors' qualifying shares) or equity interests; and

(iv) Any accredited investor.

(2) A corporation, partnership or other entity shall be counted as one purchaser. If, however, that entity is organized for the specific purpose of acquiring the securities offered and is not an accredited investor under paragraph (a)(8) of this section, then each beneficial owner of equity securities or equity interests in the entity shall count as a separate purchaser for all provisions of Regulation D (§§230.501-230.508), except to the extent provided in paragraph (e)(1) of this section.

(3) A non-contributory employee benefit plan within the meaning of Title I of the Employee Retirement Income Security Act of 1974 shall be counted as one purchaser where the trustee makes all investment decisions for the plan.

Note: The issuer must satisfy all the other provisions of Regulation D for all purchasers whether or not they are included in calculating the number of purchasers. Clients of an investment adviser or customers of a broker or dealer shall be considered the "purchasers" under Regulation D regardless of the amount of discretion given to the investment adviser or broker or dealer to act on behalf of the client or customer.

(f) *Executive officer.* Executive officer shall mean the president, any vice president in charge of a principal business unit, division or function (such as sales, administration or finance), any other officer who performs a policy making function, or any other person who performs similar policy making functions for the issuer. Executive officers of subsidiaries may be deemed executive officers of the issuer if they perform such policy making functions for the issuer.

(g) *Final order.* Final order shall mean a written directive or declaratory statement issued by a federal or state agency described in §230.506(d)(1)(iii) under applicable statutory authority that provides for notice and an opportunity for hearing, which constitutes a final disposition or action by that federal or state agency.

(h) *Issuer.* The definition of the term *issuer* in section 2(a)(4) of the Act shall apply, except that in the case of a proceeding under the Federal Bankruptcy Code (11 U.S.C. 101 *et seq.*), the trustee or debtor in possession shall be considered the issuer in an offering under a plan or reorganization, if the securities are to be issued under the plan.

(i) *Purchaser representative.* Purchaser representative shall mean any person who satisfies all of the following conditions or who the issuer reasonably believes satisfies all of the following conditions:

(1) Is not an affiliate, director, officer or other employee of the issuer, or beneficial owner of 10 percent or more of any class of the equity securities or 10 percent or more of the equity interest in the issuer, except where the purchaser is:

(i) A relative of the purchaser representative by blood, marriage or adoption and not more remote than a first cousin;

(ii) A trust or estate in which the purchaser representative and any persons related to him as specified in paragraph (h)(1)(i) or (h)(1)(iii) of this section collectively have more than 50 percent of the beneficial interest (excluding contingent interest) or of which the purchaser representative serves as trustee, executor, or in any similar capacity; or

(iii) A corporation or other organization of which the purchaser representative and any persons related to him as specified in paragraph (h)(1)(i) or (h)(1)(ii) of this section collectively are the beneficial owners of more than 50 percent of the equity securities (excluding directors' qualifying shares) or equity interests;

(2) Has such knowledge and experience in financial and business matters that he is capable of evaluating, alone, or together with other purchaser representatives of the purchaser, or together with the purchaser, the merits and risks of the prospective investment;

(3) Is acknowledged by the purchaser in writing, during the course of the transaction, to be his purchaser representative in connection with evaluating the merits and risks of the prospective investment; and

(4) Discloses to the purchaser in writing a reasonable time prior to the sale of securities to that purchaser any material relationship between himself or his affiliates and the issuer or its affiliates that then exists, that is mutually understood to be contemplated, or that has existed at any time during the previous two years, and any compensation received or to be received as a result of such relationship.

Note 1 to §230.501: A person acting as a purchaser representative should consider the applicability of the registration and antifraud provisions relating to brokers and dealers under the Securities Exchange Act of 1934 (*Exchange Act*) (15 U.S.C. 78a *et seq.*, as amended) and relating to investment advisers under the Investment Advisers Act of 1940.

Note 2 to §230.501: The acknowledgment required by paragraph (h)(3) and the disclosure required by paragraph (h)(4) of this section must be made with specific reference to each prospective investment. Advance blanket acknowledgment, such as for *all securities transactions* or *all private placements*, is not sufficient.

Note 3 to §230.501: Disclosure of any material relationships between the purchaser representative or his affiliates and the issuer or its affiliates does not relieve the purchaser representative of his obligation to act in the interest of the purchaser.

360

ACKNOWLEDGMENTS

Without question, my most important acknowledgment goes to my wife, Suzi. For years she suggested that I should write a book, and for years I resisted. This also fits squarely in the "be careful what you wish for" category, as we soon discovered what a massive undertaking it is to write a book. Suzi, thank you for your patience with me while I was laser-focused on making this the best book that I could.

To my longtime securities attorney, Mark Abdou with Libertas Law Group, and my CPA from day one, Chris Paris with Moss Adams LLP—thank you for all that you've done to advance my business, and for your help with the legal and tax topics in this book.

A big thanks to everyone that played a role in making this book a reality, and for your help and opinions on the content. This book wouldn't be the same without you! Special thanks to the BiggerPockets Publishing team, Katie Miller, Kaylee Pratt, and Scott Trench. Thank you to the editorial freelance team who helped to edit this book as well: Louise Collazo, Katelin Hill, Taylor Hugo, and Wendy Dunning.

This book wouldn't have been possible without help and feedback from Brandon Turner, J Scott, Joe Fang, Chris Demetra, Hal Mooz, Steve Darby, and Mike Dymski. Thank you so much for your helpful ideas, critiques, and support. Brandon, I wouldn't have even tried to do this if it wasn't for your incredible advice that made writing a book seem almost easy! Sure, I quickly learned it isn't easy at all, but by the time I figured that out, it was too late to stop.

Huge thanks to Bob Dreher, my senior vice president in charge of investor relations. For years, you have taken such great care of the investors that have fueled our business from a small local player to a major national force. Your insight into what concerns investors the most—and what things they need to know more about—shaped this book.

To Josh Dorkin, founder of BiggerPockets: If you ignored your dream of creating the best online real estate forum in the world, this book never could have happened. Discovering it changed my life, and I will be forever grateful.

More from
BiggerPockets Publishing

The Book on Tax Strategies for the Savvy Real Estate Investor

Taxes—boring and irritating, right? Perhaps. But if you want to succeed in real estate, your tax strategy will play a huge role in how fast you grow. A great tax strategy can save you thousands of dollars a year. A bad strategy could land you in legal trouble. In Amanda Han and Matthew MacFarland's *The Book on Tax Strategies for the Savvy Real Estate Investor* you will find ways to deduct more, invest smarter, and pay far less to the IRS!

The Book on Negotiating Real Estate

When the real estate market gets hot, it's the investors who know the ins and outs of negotiating who will get the deal. J Scott, Mark Ferguson, and Carol Scott combine real-world experience and the science of negotiation in order to cover all aspects of the negotiation process and maximize your chances of reaching a profitable deal.

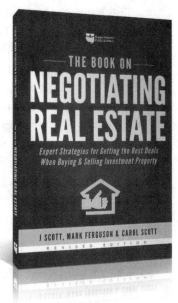

If you enjoyed this book, we hope you'll take a moment to check out some of the other great material BiggerPockets offers. BiggerPockets is the real estate investing social network, marketplace, and information hub, designed to help make you a smarter real estate investor through podcasts, books, blog posts, videos, forums, and more. Sign up today—it's free! **Visit www.BiggerPockets.com.**

The Book on Investing in Real Estate with No (and Low) Money Down

Is lack of money holding you back from real estate success? It doesn't have to! In this groundbreaking book from Brandon Turner, author of *The Book on Rental Property Investing* and others, you'll discover numerous strategies investors can use to buy real estate using other people's money. You'll learn the top strategies that savvy investors are using to buy, rent, flip, or wholesale properties at scale!

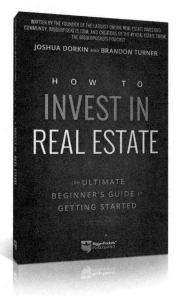

How to Invest in Real Estate

Two of the biggest names in the real estate world teamed up to create the most comprehensive manual ever written on getting started in the lucrative business of real estate investing. Joshua Dorkin and Brandon Turner give you an insider's look at the many different real estate niches and strategies so that you can find which one works best for you, your resources, and your goals.

More from
BiggerPockets Publishing

The Book on Rental Property Investing

The Book on Rental Property Investing by Brandon Turner, a real estate investor and cohost of the *BiggerPockets Podcast*, contains nearly 400 pages of in-depth advice and strategies for building wealth through rental properties. You will learn how to build an achievable plan, find incredible deals, pay for your rentals, and much more!

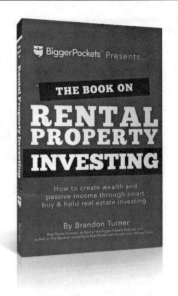

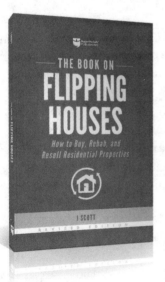

The Book on Flipping Houses, Revised Edition

Written by active real estate investor and fix-and-flipper J Scott, this book contains more than 300 pages of step-by-step training, perfect for both the complete newbie and the seasoned pro looking to build a house-flipping business. Whatever your skill level, this book will teach you everything you need to know to build a profitable business and start living the life of your dreams.

The Book on Estimating Rehab Costs, Revised Edition

Learn detailed tips, tricks, and tactics to accurately budget nearly any house-flipping project from expert fix-and-flipper J Scott. Whether you are preparing to walk through your very first rehab project or you're an experienced home flipper, this handbook will be your guide to identifying renovation projects, creating a scope of work, and staying on budget to ensure a timely profit!

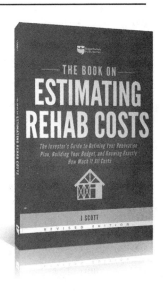

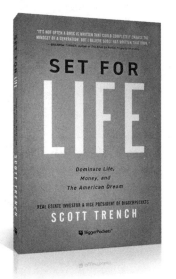

Set for Life: Dominate Life, Money, and the American Dream

Looking for a plan to achieve financial freedom in just five to ten years? *Set for Life* by Scott Trench is a detailed fiscal plan targeted at the average-income earner starting with few or no assets. It will walk you through three stages of finance, guiding you to your first $25,000 in tangible net worth, then to your first $100,000, and then to financial freedom. *Set for Life* will teach you how to build a lifestyle, career, and investment portfolio capable of supporting financial freedom to let you live the life of your dreams.

CONNECT WITH BIGGERPOCKETS

and Become Successful in Your Real Estate Business Today!

Facebook
/BiggerPockets

Instagram
@BiggerPockets

Twitter
@BiggerPockets

LinkedIn
/company/Bigger
Pockets

Website
BiggerPockets.com